Fenny Hill

Dust Hill

S. Beck inv. et del.

Excellencie's Sᴿ Thomas Fairfax: as they were drawn into
"NASBIE June the 14ᵗʰ 1645."

THE ARMY OF PARLIAMENT

THE LEFT WING: (Ireton)	THE CENTRE: (Skippon)		
Lantford hedges lin'd with Dragoons.	52 The Forlorn Hope.	58 Lt. Col. Pride's Regt.	67, 68 Col. Sheffield's Division
43 Col. Butler's Regt.	53 Majʳ Genl. Skippon's Regt.	59 Col. Hammond's Regt.	69 Sᴿ Robert Pye's Regt.
45 Col. Vermuden's Regt.	54 Sᴿ Hardress Waller's Regt.	60 Col. Rainsborough's Regt.	70 Col. Fiennes's Regt.
47 Comm. Genl. Ireton's Regt.	55 Col. Pickering's Regt.	THE RIGHT WING: (Cromwell)	71 The Associated Horse
Col. Riche's Regt.	56 Montague's Regt.	61, 62 Col. Whaley's Regt.	72 Col. Fiennes's Regt.
50 Col. Fleetwood's Regt.	57 The Generall's Regt.	63 Sᴿ Robert Pye's Regt.	73 Col. Rossiter's Regt.
The Troops of The Association	THE RESERVE	64, 65 The General's Life Guard	
		66 Col. Rossiter's Regt.	74 Lt. Col. Pride (a rear guard)
			75 The Train guarded with Firelocks

Naseby 1645

Also available from Century
By the Sword Divided John Adair

Naseby 1645

The Campaign and the Battle

PETER YOUNG

DSO, MC, MA, FSA

CENTURY PUBLISHING

LONDON

ISBN 0 7126 0489 8

British Library Cataloguing in Publication Data

Young, Peter, 1915–
    Naseby 1645: The Campaign and the Battle.
    1. Naseby (Northamptonshire), Battle of 1645
    I. Title
    942.06'2   DA415
    ISBN 0 7126 0489 8

Printed in Great Britain in 1985 by
The Short Run Press Limited, Exeter.

To

Gordon Norwood

Original Begetter of this Series

Introduction

APPENDICES:

Author's Note

Gordon Norwood, who published my books on *Edgehill* and *Marston Moor,* hoped, as indeed I did, that *Naseby* would be a companion volume. This has not come to pass, for, owing to the change in the ownership of the Roundwood Press, this volume is not illustrated in the same fashion. This I very much regret; but I do not believe it is worth while to name the individuals who are, in my opinion, responsible.

Since the text was first set by the Roundwood Press, I have made further discoveries about two of the officers who fought at Naseby. First the name of Colonel Edward Grey (1611–c. 1675) must be added to the senior commanders of the Northern Horse who were present. He came out of Pontefract Castle with Langdale after the relief of that place (1 March 1645). He had commanded a dragoon regiment at Edgehill, and was, therefore, considerably senior to Sir William Blackiston and Sir Philip Monckton. He probably commanded one of the divisions of the Northern Horse.

Second, 'Colonel Smyth', who commanded the Shrewsbury Foot at Naseby seems to have been Lieutenant-Colonel George Smyth. Captain George Smyth was serving in the Lord Lambert's Regiment of Foot in Ireland in 1642 (HMC Ormonde, I, p. 133). It seems likely that he returned from Ireland as a field officer in one of the seven foot regiments which landed in the Chester area during the winter 1643–4. He was no doubt the senior survivor of the 'Irish', who fought at Nantwich, Marston Moor and Montgomery. He evidently got away from Naseby as well, for he must be the Lieutenant-Colonel Smyth who was commanding 600 or 700 foot with Sir William Vaughan at Bridgenorth on 18 December 1645 (Symond's Diary, p. 276).

I would like, too, to acknowledge my debt to R. N. Dore, whose edition of Sir William Brereton's *Letter-Books* is eagerly awaited by all those, who are interested in the conduct of the war in Cheshire. He kindly sent me copies of lists of the 646 Royalist officers and soldiers made prisoner at Rowton Moor (24 September 1645), and of 169 taken at Whitchurch (1 November 1645). Some of these had taken part in the defence of Carlisle, and a larger contingent had served under General Charles Gerard in South Wales. Lord Byron's Regiment from the garrison of Chester was present at Whitchurch, but many had fought under Rupert and Langdale at Naseby.

Finally, I should like to acknowledge the generous financial assistance given by the Sealed Knot over the publication of this volume.

Peter Young has also written:
> THE GREAT CIVIL WAR, with the late Lt. Col. A. H. Burne, DSO, FR Hist S
> THE ENGLISH CIVIL WAR, with Richard Holmes
> CROMWELL
> OLIVER CROMWELL (International Profiles)
> EDGEHILL 1642: THE CAMPAIGN AND THE BATTLE
> MARSTON MOOR 1644: THE CAMPAIGN AND THE BATTLE
> CROPREDY BRIDGE 1644: THE CAMPAIGN AND THE BATTLE, with
>   Dr. Margaret Toynbee, Ph.D., MA., FSA., FR Hist S
> FROM HASTINGS TO CULLODEN, with Prof. John Adair, MA., B.Litt., Ph.D.,
>   FR Hist S
> STRANGERS IN OXFORD, with Dr. Margaret Toynbee
> RICHARD ATKYNS AND JOHN GWYN, with the late Norman Tucker, FR Hist S
> CAVALIER ARMY, with W. Emberton
> SIEGES OF THE CIVIL WAR, with W. Emberton
> MILITARIE INSTRUCTIONS FOR THE CAVALLRIE (ed.)
> LEADERS OF THE CIVIL WARS (ed.)
> ENGLISH CIVIL WAR ARMIES Men at Arms Series

Introduction

IT WAS IN 1935 that I first began to take an interest in the military aspects of the Civil War. In those days I was not a soldier but an undergraduate, and I suppose I knew very little of the ways in which armies operate.

At one time I used to think that service in the Second World War made it easier to understand how Cavalier and Roundhead went to work at Edgehill or Marston Moor. I am no longer altogether convinced that that is the case. It is true that any experience of Active Service gives one a certain insight into the workings of the human mind, the human heart, in the stress and strain of battle. It was quite a surprise to me when in my youth it was revealed to me that, even amongst the English, not every soldier is eager to hazard his person upon the battle-field. . . .

One of the chief difficulties we meet in studying the campaigns and battles of the Civil Wars is the sheer lack of information. I do not know of a single letter written by someone who commanded a Royalist regiment at Naseby. When we come to the days of Waterloo there are extant – thanks to the diligence of Captain William Siborne – letters written by officers of every single British regiment present. For 1645 it is not only letters that are missing. We lack the strength returns, and the casualty lists which enable us to tell with some precision what forces were available at Blenheim or at Austerlitz. This is not to say that we never come across a muster-roll or a pay warrant dating from the First Civil War, but for the year 1645 they are rare indeed for either side.

The lack of administrative papers as well as the lack of

letters, diaries and memoirs at the regimental level leaves us with many questions unresolved. Some, one hopes, may be answered as time goes by, but at the present time, as it seems to me, we cannot say with real confidence how many men fought on either side at Naseby, or how many casualties were suffered. Then again we are often told that the King's infantry were mainly Welsh, but the evidence for this popular belief seems to me to be thin indeed. Of the regiments present only two, those of Owen and Thomas appear to have been largely Welsh, and the two put together can scarcely have totalled 500 officers and men. Is it not more likely that the King's infantry was recruited when the Palatine princes were hovering about in the Severn Valley, and in Herefordshire, that Spring, waiting for their uncle to take the field?

One has come to think of the Royalist Foot as being old soldiers, but amongst the prisoners listed there were not all that many company commanders, who can be identified as serving in May 1643. Wastage amongst the rank and file must have been fairly heavy during the campaigns of 1643 and 1644. Bristol, Newbury, Cheriton, Cropredy Bridge and Lostwithiel all took their toll. We would probably be right in saying that both Astley and Skippon had men of experience as the cadres for their regiments, but that the private soldiers on both sides included hundreds of recruits. The horse on either side were, in probability, made up of men who had seen rather more service.

On the Royalist side some of the regiments had spent most of their service in garrisons: Bagot's from Lichfield, a strong regiment, is a case in point. One wonders whether a unit of this sort had the same military value as an old regiment of the marching army, like Lisle's or the Lifeguard of Foot. What again was the value of Prince Rupert's Regiment of Foot? It must have been practically annihilated at Marston Moor, but here it was again at Naseby, 500 strong and prepared to fight it out when others had thrown down their arms! How had the Prince and his colonel, John Russell, managed this administrative feat?

Even questions of armament are puzzling. In theory the infantry regiments had two musketeers to each pikeman, but a study of the surviving Royalist Ordnance Papers[1] leads one to suspect that in the King's army the proportion may have been more like one to one.

One would like also to know more about such things as the social status of the combatants, and their literacy. It is probably safe to assert that a literate soldier was unusual on either side; but an officer, who could not read or write was rare indeed — which is not to say that he did not exist. Anyway it was no good putting up Part I Orders and hoping the men would read them. The officers had to give out their orders before they dismissed their command at the end of the day's work.

In the Royalist army it was not unusual for a junior officer, an ensign of foot, or a quartermaster of horse to be of yeoman stock. The New Model was very different from Essex' Army of 1642, whose senior officers had included sixteen peers, and whose cavalry troop commanders were for the most part armigerous. Now the captains and field officers were men, who owed their commissions not to blue blood, but to hard fighting. Warriors like Christopher Bethell, Thomas Harrison, Thomas Horton and John Okey, were not made troop commanders in 1642. In the Edgehill campaign Horton and Okey had been cornet and quartermaster respectively.

In earlier books about *Edgehill* and *Marston Moor* I have touched upon some of the administrative aspects of soldiering in the First Civil War. I do not mean to repeat here what has been said previously about such things as Colours and Pay and Victuals. But if we are to understand Naseby, and, indeed, appreciate how little we know of it, something must be said of the way in which men fought their battles in those distant days.

I think it is fair to say that each army was run by rather an inadequate staff. It was not only that there was a lack of experienced staff officers — let alone ones with any actual staff training. The whole organization then, and much later, was inadequate. Imagine trying to control an army without any Command Post, or Report Centre or Observation Post! The general simply sat on his horse and tried to work out what was going on, with the aid of a perspective glass — an instrument introduced about a generation earlier. It was not easy for King Charles or Sir Thomas Fairfax to perceive what was going on. To some extent the generals gave their orders by galloping up to some brigade commander, or colonel, and telling him what to do. With Rupert or Fairfax very often it was nothing more complicated than "Follow me!" Sometimes verbal messages were sent by galloper. The generals had their Adjutant-Generals of horse of foot and their corporals of the field, who could help or hinder. Why hinder? Why not? Try passing a verbal message, by a rider on a swift horse to someone a mile away, sitting on another horse and in the midst of a complicated tactical situation. Perhaps the best example of what can happen comes from the battle of Minden (1759). Ferdinand of Brunswick, busy trying to repair the gap in his centre, sent a series of A.D.Cs. to Lord George Sackville, commanding the cavalry on his right wing. The British general was to move forward to support some infantry, whom he could not see because of a fir wood. None of the A.D.Cs. gave the same message, and Sackville, for his part had not, it seems, thought of going forward to reconnoitre. So he could think of nothing better to do than to go and ask Ferdinand what he wanted him to do. The Prince, who does not appear to have been in the right place to control events, was far from blaming himself for such blunders as the Allies had made that day, and took advantage of Sackville's 'failure' to get rid of this rather limited general, whom as it happens, he detested. He might have done well to post a few of his staff![2]

If such things could happen more than 100 years after Naseby, how much more could they come to pass when Charles I and Sir Thomas Fairfax led their little divisions against each other. Looking at Sprigge's picture map you might think that from the King's position on Dust Hill it was very easy to see the New Model laid out before him. In fact it is very unlikely that he could see Okey's Dragoons or the Train in its waggon-lager, or very much of such bodies of horse and foot as were in the second or third line.

Lord Astley, advancing with three squadrons of horse and seven weak 'battalions' of foot may – eventually – have been able to make out that he was opposed by nine larger enemy bodies, and that one of the Roundhead regiments had no Cavalier unit to oppose it. This was Sir Thomas Fairfax' own Regiment. One wonders whether the Royalist commander endeavoured to re-dress the balance by raking it with artillery, or by sending one of the squadrons of Thomas Howard's Brigade of Horse against it. These are the sort of problems which, for lack of evidence, remain unresolved.

An examination of the Estate Map of 1630, and de Gomme's map, reveals that the field of Naseby was by no means devoid of cover. There were already long fields stretching, finger-like, into Turmoore Field, and where there are fields there are hedges. This means not only that visibility would be reduced, but that a brigade of horse or foot, advancing to the assault, might well find its front broken up. Then the commander would have to call a halt in order to dress his ranks; the alternative was to stagger forward in disarray. Colonel John Okey's account, lacking in precision though it is — he was no great scholar — seems to hint that Royalist movements took place on his front and flank, which are not revealed by a study of Sir Edward Walker's 'Official History'. It may be that Major-General Eyre or one of the commanders from the King's Reserve made an advance, or a charge, which escaped the notice of other eye-witnesses.

There were those among the commanders in either army, who were quite capable of using their own initiative once battle was joined. But that, of course, was not to be expected in the opening phase of a seventeenth century battle. It may be sup-posed that an army would advance to contact in one or more columns. When it was within two or three miles of the enemy it would form from column of march into a prearranged line of battle, and march forward in proud array with colours flying in the breeze. De Gomme's plan is obviously based on the rough draft from which Prince Rupert had briefed his generals, per-haps more than a week before the battle.

Ranging the troops in line was not all that easy. Cavalry march faster than infantry, and even 6-pounder guns take time to get into position.

The signal for the attack was probably a salvo from the biggest guns. Hearing this the standard-bearers would advance; drums would beat and trumpets sound. It was no joke to keep the cavalry in line. On the Royalist right Rupert had no less than seven squadrons to keep in good order. In order to achieve this he made at least one halt. Rupert's tactics – like Frederick the Great's in the Seven Years War – were to attack at the gallop. Cromwell seems to have preferred his 'good round trot'. Either would work so long as the men kept good order, boot to boot and knee to knee.

The foot had perhaps an easier task, but even so they were probably six deep and it is never easy to march well on grass. Ceremonial drill was a complicated business at this period, but a regiment which numbered scores of recruits in its ranks could not be expected to go through all 'the postures of the pike'. No doubt experienced officers like Astley and Skippon, reduced the drill to its essentials, perhaps seven postures, and contented themselves with doing those few well. That is not to say that it was not necessary upon occasion to carry out quite complicated movements. For example, some sort of hedgehog had to be form-ed if the enemy horse bore down. A well-drilled infantry battalion of Wellington's army could form square in less than a minute. One may be permitted to doubt if the soldiers of King Charles or Sir Thomas Fairfax were capable of such alacrity. Yet one may suppose that once formed a square, whose bristling pikes shroud-ed the regiment's musketeers, was a formidable obstacle to the most gallant horse. Fortunately for the cavalry the rate of fire of the infantry was still very slow. It was not as yet possible for foot to cripple cavalry as the redcoats of Generals Kingsley and Waldegrave did the Duc de Fitz-James' squadrons at Minden.

One way and another men whose military experience be-longs to the twentieth century are worlds away from our ancest-ors of the Civil War. To a soldier of the Second World War the methods of Wellington's day are by no means so remote as to be incomprehensible, but when we go back into the days before the foot were armed with musket and bayonet, and when troopers and pikemen still wore a certain amount of armour, we seem nearer the Middle Ages than our own times. It takes a real effort of imagination to comprehend the somewhat formal tactical methods of Edgehill and Naseby. Yet in a way the very lack of staff colleges, manuals of strategy and tactics, and training instructions, led to a certain amount of originality. Men like Fairfax and Cromwell, Rupert and Langdale developed their own ideas as their own genius, and their own reading, prompted, and were capable of delivering some very unpleasant surprises to their more pedestrian contemporaries.

The result of the battle of Naseby has now been known for the last 339 years. In consequence we have begun to accept it as a foregone conclusion. I believe it was no such thing. On the contrary, as it seems to me, King Charles still had the resources necessary to destroy the New Model Army and bring the war to a successful conclusion.

It is true that we do not now possess all the information we could wish for on a number of points. How bad, for example, was the Royalist intelligence service? We suspect that it was not very good, but we simply lack any body of information such as we have for the Parliamentarian side in the papers of Sir Samuel Luke.[3]

We would like to know much more about the administration of each side. How often were the soldiers paid? How much was their pay in arrears? The Royalist garrison of Lichfield, for example, was still being paid – at least for its quarters – in the period October-November 1645. In the early months of the year the Parliamentarian garrison of Newport Pagnell suffered from a variety of wants due to the lack of money. Administrative difficulties were not a Royalist monopoly.

The Royalists – whether they saw it or not – could only win the war by wresting control of the capital from their opponents. To do this they must defeat the main Parliamentarian Army in the field. In the 1642 campaign they had marched on the capital, and, after getting rather the better of the battle of Edgehill, had occupied Oxford and made it their headquarters. Thereafter a somewhat leisurely advance had ended with a confrontation on Turnham Green, where, the London Trained Bands having swollen the Earl of Essex's Army to overwhelming numbers, the Cavaliers shirked the bloody decision of the crisis. They fell back and went into winter quarters.

In 1643 the Marquis of Newcastle had gradually cleared the North until his victory at Adwalton Moor (30 June) had made him master of all Yorkshire, save only Hull. In the West the Cavaliers had won an even more impressive series of successes, at Stratton (16 May) and Roundway Down (13 July), culminating in Prince Rupert's storming of Bristol, the second city of the Kingdom (26 July). The siege of Gloucester (10 August-5 September) had then compelled Essex to hazard his army far from his base, London, and although he had succeeded in relieving the beleaguered city he had been cut off on his way home. At Newbury (20 September) he was compelled to fight with the Cavaliers, in superior numbers, between him and London. They obligingly attacked him, when a resolute defensive was their surer game. After a hard day's fighting the King abandoned the field and a good chance — perhaps the best he ever had — of destroying the main enemy army.

The year 1644 began badly for the Royalists. The intervention of the Scots completely turned the tables on Newcastle, who had already been repulsed from Hull in the previous October. He was gradually driven back on York and there besieged.

Sir Thomas Fairfax' victory at Nantwich (25 January) and Waller's at Cheriton (29 March) were scarcely balanced by Rupert's success at Newark (21 March). But the Parliamentarians were not cooperating and when Essex and Waller found themselves before Oxford, instead of besieging the Royalist capital, they must needs go their separate ways to disaster — Waller at Cropredy Bridge (29 June) and Essex in Cornwall, where his infantry and artillery were compelled to surrender (2 September).

Rupert, after a conquering progress through Lancashire, relieved York, but then decided that he had orders to fight the Allies, whatever the odds, and was severely defeated at Marston Moor. This disaster virtually lost the North for the King. But the Scots and English allies failed to follow up their success, and so allowed it to be offset by the Royalist triumph over Essex in Cornwall.

For the Parliamentarians the campaign of 1644 ended in fiasco, and in bitter recriminations, for, having surrounded the King at Newbury, they failed to crush him (27 October) and allowed him to extricate himself that night. The quarrels that followed gave birth to the Self-Denying Ordinance and the New Model Army. In three years of war each side had dealt the other fearful wounds. Towns had been sacked, the countryside ravaged; the temper of the combatants had become ever more intolerant and unforgiving. It would be a bold man who dared assert that victory was in sight for either side. With hindsight we may say that the Parliament had the greater assets, but that was by no means clear at Christmas 1644.

THE AUTHORITIES

There are two good authorities for the story of the Naseby campaign. They are Rev. Joshua Sprigge, MA. Edin. (1618-1684), a parliamentarian divine of the most advanced independent view, and Sir Edward Walker, Kt. (1612-1677), Garter king-of-arms and secretary-at-war to King Charles I. The other authorities, even Clarendon, do little but adorn the tale with interesting points of detail. Without Sprigge and Walker we would be groping in the dark, for the lack of eyewitness accounts is most remarkable. Walker was indisputably an eyewitness, but Sprigge, though Anthony Wood[4] tells us he was a retainer of Sir Thomas Fairfax, does not appear in the list of chaplains of the New Model, and as Sir Charles Firth has pointed out,[5] 'it is difficult to say with certainty whether he actually accompanied Fairfax in the campaigns which he describes.'

Sprigge called his book: *Anglia Rediviva; Englands Recovery: being the History of the Motions, Actions, and Successes of the Army under the Immediate Conduct of His Excellency Sr. Thomas Fairfax, Kt. Captain-General of all the Parliaments Forces In England. Compiled for the Publique good.*[6] Firth writes: 'It is throughout based on the pamphlets and newspapers of the period, and contains very little information which can be regarded as embodying the author's own recollections; at the same time it is a very judicious and accurate compilation.' Firth rightly gives no credit to Clement Walker's allegation that the real author was Nathaniel Fiennes, for it seems to rest on no firmer foundation than Sprigge's justification of Fiennes' surrender of Bristol in 1643. The late Lt. Colonel A. H. Burne, DSO, was of the opinion that during the battle of Naseby Sprigge was with the baggage train. It seems unlikely that Fairfax would have employed a chaplain, but left him at home when he took the field.

Sir Edward Walker had been secretary-at-war to the Earl of Arundel in the first Scottish war (1639) and paymaster of the garrison of Carlisle (23 April 1640). He followed the King to York in 1642 and was sent to summon Hull (24 April 1642). About the end of September 1642 Charles made him secretary-at-war, and later (13 April 1644) he was sworn in as secretary-extraordinary to the privy council. He took part in the 1644 campaign and wrote a narrative called '*His Majesty's Happy Progress and Success from the 30 March to the 23 November 1644*'.[7] This work was presented to the King, who annotated it in his own hand. The '*Brief Memorials of the Unfortunate Success of His Majesty's Army and Affairs in the Year 1645*,' written at Paris in about 1647 at the request of Lord Colepeper, was intended for the use of Lord Clarendon.

*   *   *

The Diary of Richard Symonds[8] (1617-1692?), who served in King Charles I's Lifeguard of Horse for about two years, is very useful for the campaigns of 1644 and 1645, especially for the composition and movements of the Royalist Army. Being intended for his own use Symonds' work is free from any element of propaganda.

Edward Hyde, first Earl of Clarendon (1609-1674), the constitutional Royalist, in his *History of the Rebellion* leans heavily on Sir Edward Walker's 'Brief Memorials'. He was himself with Prince Charles in the West at the time of Naseby. In general he did not like soldiers, and in his writings he is not quite fair to them. Rupert and Goring both suffer at his hands. Himself innocent of military experience his strategic judgment is untrustworthy.

[1] The Royalist Ordnance Papers, 1642-1646. Ed. Ian Roy, Oxfordshire Record Society, 1963 and 1975.

[2] See *The Coward of Minden*, by Piers Mackesy.

[3] *The Letter Books of Sir Samuel Luke 1644-45*, The Bedfordshire Historical Record Society, Volume XLII, 1963. Edited by H. G. Tibbutt. *Journal of Sir Samuel Luke,* Oxfordshire Record Society (1950-53) Edited by I. G. Philips.

[4] Athenae Oxonienses, II, 726.

[5] D.N.B.

[6] London, 1647.

[7] See *Cropredy Bridge* by Margaret Toynbee and Peter Young.

[8] Camden Society, 1859.

Chapter One

THE STATE OF THE KINGDOM

"The state of the Kingdome, when His Excellencie Sir Tho. Fairfax marched forth, May 1645."

JOSHUA SPRIGGE, M.A.

IN MAY 1645 King Charles set out from Oxford upon his fourth, and last, campaign. The tide of war had turned against him in 1644, when the defeat of his nephew, Prince Rupert, at Marston Moor had lost him control of the North. But his own victories at Cropredy Bridge and Lostwithiel seemed to redress the balance, whilst the failure of his enemies to exploit their great numerical superiority at Second Newbury had left the Parliamentarians in disarray. Their quarrels had led to the Self-Denying Ordinance and the formation of the New Model Army, measures which left the Cavaliers unimpressed: the 'New Noddle' seemed to them no more formidable than the old armies of the Earl of Essex, of Sir William Waller and of the Eastern Association. In this they were profoundly mistaken.

Parliament, throughout the War, had a great asset in its control of the capital and the home counties. The Royalists depended for much of their support on the less populous and less developed regions of the country, the West and the North. North of Trent little now remained to the King, though a few fortresses still held out :-

CUMBERLAND

	Governor	Surrendered
Carlisle	*Sir Thomas Glemham, Bart.*	16 July 1645

LANCASHIRE

	Governor	Surrendered
Bolton Castle	*Colonel John Scrope*	November 1645
Lathom House	*Colonel Edward Rosethorn*	December 1645

YORKSHIRE

Pontefract Castle	*Sir John Redman*	21 July 1645
Scarborough Castle	*Sir Hugh Cholmley*	22 July 1645

Wales, save only Tenby and Pembroke, was still firmly in Royalist hands, and so was Cornwall, but control of the South West was disputed with Parliamentarian garrisons at Gloucester, Lyme, Poole, Taunton and Plymouth, the last two of which were under close siege at this time.

Oxford, with its circle of fortresses, the castles of Banbury, Faringdon and Wallingford, was not only the Royalists' capital, but their main stronghold.

In a few counties there were no Parliamentarian garrisons at all at this stage, at least none of any great importance. Cornwall, Monmouthshire, Herefordshire, Worcestershire and Oxfordshire had all been practically cleared of the rebels for the time being. But in many counties Royalist garrisons merely counterbalanced Parliamentarian fortresses. In Shropshire the Cavaliers still held Ludlow and Bridgnorth but Shrewsbury had been taken by surprise in February. The Parliament's hold on Stafford was balanced by the Royalist garrison in Lichfield Close. The Cavaliers of Nottinghamshire and Lincolnshire, who held on to Newark-on-Trent, offset the Parliamentarians of Nottingham. But there were a dozen counties around London where no Royalist banner flew, where a Parliamentarian grandee could safely make a day's journey with no more escort than his ordinary attendants. And this was the wealthiest and most populous region in the kingdom.

What numbers of men the two sides had locked up in their fortresses and garrisons, it is hard to calculate. But it seems certain that had either side decided to concentrate all those regiments and companies, which were manning the mediaeval walls of ancient cities and castles, it would have been possible to produce field armies twice the size of any seen at Newbury or Naseby. Living, as they did, off the country the generals simply did not care to loosen their control over a fertile tract of countryside, or leave a well-disposed hundred at the mercy of hostile troops of horse. One wonders what proportion of the garrison soldiers of the Civil Wars ever heard a shot fired in anger.

In the nature of things the seventeenth century soldier went into winter quarters in some garrison. In the Spring of 1645, therefore, we may imagine that King Charles and his Council of War examined the muster rolls and tried to decide what regiments to draw forth into the field. Quite a number of the old regiments which had fought at Edgehill were not going to be available simply because the fortresses in which they were garrisoned seemed too important to be abandoned :-

Colonel	Garrison
Sir Stephen Hawkins	Oxford
Thomas Blagge	Wallingford Castle
Earl of Northampton	Banbury Castle
Earl Rivers	Donnington Castle
Sir Charles Lloyd	Devizes Castle
Sir Lewis Dyve	Sherborne Castle

Others, however, could be replaced, as George Lisle's was at Faringdon by Sir Marmaduke Rawdon's from Basing House.

In the winter of 1644-1645 much of the Royalist Army seems to have been quartered west of Oxford in Berkshire and Gloucestershire, around Faringdon, Cirencester and Chipping Campden. Their quarters would be left empty when they took the field, and, in at least one case, the departing Cavaliers burnt their abandoned stronghold. This happened when Sir Henry Bard with 300 foot and 100 horse left Campden House.

The Parliamentarians meanwhile were forming their New Model Army at Windsor, building it up from what remained of the armies of Essex, Manchester and Waller, but leaving untouched the small local armies of Sir William Brereton, Edward Massey and Sydenham Poyntz.

3

The best strategy for the King was to seek out the New Model Army and destroy it, before it could settle down into a coherent force. An advance on London was the likeliest means of attaining this object. As the 1642 campaign had shown such an operation demanded a very substantial army, because the Parliamentarians could count upon their 'strategic reserve', the London Trained Bands, if the capital were threatened. It follows that a number of garrisons would have to be abandoned at about the end of April.

The Royalists had a pontoon train, but river crossings, then as now, are complicated, and since the greater part of London lay North of the Thames, a sound plan might have been to concentrate North of Oxford and advance on London *via* St. Albans. No such plan seems to have entered Charles' mind, for when on 8 May he concentrated at Stow-on-the-Wold, it was to set off upon a somewhat aimless ramble through the Midlands.

The Parliamentarians riposted rather neatly with a thrust at the Royalist capital, Oxford.

Some five weeks later King Charles I met Sir Thomas Fairfax near Naseby and fought the decisive battle of the First Civil War. By that time the Royalists may have mustered 10,000 men: the New Model Army seems to have been at least 15,000 strong. Of all the factors that decided the fate of the battle it may be that this disparity in numbers was the one which did most to settle the issue. Despite initial successes the Cavaliers were simply overwhelmed. It was not merely a question of superior tactics on the part of Fairfax and Cromwell: odds of three to two were just too much for the Cavaliers.

Four months after Naseby Sir Richard Willys, the Governor of Newark, proposed at a council of war that the King should 'putt all his garrison soldjers in a body and march after Fairfax, then about Taunton.' Newarke river[1] was fordable, and in it 4000 good foot... 'There was then Newarke, Ashby [de la Zouch], Tutbury, Lichfield, Belvoir, Werton[2] [Wiverton], Bridgnorth, Denbigh and other garrisons. Slight them all and all inland garrisons, keep your ports, as Exeter and Bristoll,[3] &c. and you will have canon and a very considerable army to fight Fairfax. Besides, Goring's army in the West was then good too. . . .'[4]

4

'The King likt it well; [John] Ashburnham embraced Sir Richard for the proposition, and so did Lord Digby like it. But they delayd, and the cowardly commissioners that lingered for compounding, they put queries. Where shall wee have winter quarters? Digby and Ashburnham were jealous Sir Richard should get too much with the King's favour. 3,000 l. was raysed by the Ingrams and the Northern gent, to give the King in his necessity, and that they might have a governor [John Belasyse] that would make good compositions for them, and this gott Sir Richard out of that government,. . . .'[5]

Sir Richard Willys' strategy was not unattractive even as late as October 1645. It would have been realistic had it been adopted immediately after Naseby and before Goring's defeat at Langport. In April 1645, when the King was preparing to take the field, it could have been decisive. At that time in order to make head against the New Model Army it behoved the King to concentrate an army of 15,000-20,000 men, and not a mere 10,000. A study of the resources at his disposal shows how this could have been done; but, at the same time we must recognize that some of the garrisons were not altogether at King Charles' command, some because they were besieged, others because they were the property of their governors. Denbigh Castle is a case in point. It had been put into a state of defence by Colonel William Salusbury and his relations, and it would not have been easy to persuade him to draw forth his garrison and join it to the field army. The same argument applies, of course, to the Earl of Derby's stronghold at Lathom House, and the Marquis of Winchester's fortress of Basing, and above all to the Marquis of Worcester's 'capital' at Raglan Castle. Even so it was for the King to dictate the overall strategy of the Royalist armies, and we may imagine that in April 1645 he spent much of his time in contemplating the shape of the coming campaign – the fourth of the war-and the resources from which he must create a field army.

"Moneys is the nerves of war", is a saying attributed to Charles, and it is obvious that possession of London was the decisive factor in the First Civil War. At a time when the country had a population of some five million, the capital already had about 500,000 inhabitants. Bristol, the second city of the kingdom had about 30,000. The financial backing of London was absolutely essential to the Roundheads. Without it they would never have won the war. The Cavaliers managed to get through three campaigns with what the Queen managed to raise in Holland, and with the normal income of those of the peerage and the landed gentry who adhered to the cause of their King. Beyond question the Cavaliers needed a short war. It was a miracle that they had got through 1644. It behoved them to win the campaign of 1645 at a blow. It was by no means a mistake to seek out and fight the New Model Army, for only its destruction could lead to the capture of London. But to challenge the Roundheads at odds of two to three was imprudent in the extreme.

One wonders how the Royalists went about planning their campaign. It seems that the council of war sat practically every other day, and that the King himself was more diligent than any of his generals in attending its sessions. A great deal of attention must have been given to the question of building up a field army for the 1645 campaign.

So far as the artillery was concerned there was no problem. Charles simply went down to Magdalen Grove and selected a dozen brass cannon from amongst the pieces of ordnance parked there.

As for the horse and foot it was a question of deciding which garrisons to abandon. It should have been obvious that a of field army of about 15,000 men was required. At Second Newbury 9,000 Cavaliers had survived the onslaught of 17,500 Roundheads. Beyond question the King now required an army of some 15,000 men, of whom at least half should be foot. With the New Model Army forming at Windsor the King's most urgent problem was to concentrate a field army to oppose it. That this must call for the evacuation of a number of garrisons, and must put others at hazard, should have been evident to Charles and his advisers. At this time the Royalists still held a number of garrisons, both great and small.

The summary that follows may be incomplete, and it is difficult to be precise as to strengths, yet it should give a fair idea of the King's remaining assets.

THE NORTH

Carlisle   *Sir Thomas Glemham*

Whitelock notes its surrender under 2 July 1645 but an eye-witness, Tullie, puts it on 25 June. When the survivors of his garrison joined the King at Cardiff at about the end of July, they numbered it seems, about 300 horse, and 100 foot, who were made the King's Lifeguard and then turned into dragoons in Brecknockshire.

LANCASHIRE

Lathom House   *Colonel Edward Rosethorn*

Surrendered on 2 December 1645, after a long siege.

YORKSHIRE

Pontefract Castle *Sir John Redman*

Surrendered on 21 July 1645. The foot, 250 strong, joined the King at Doncaster on 19 August after a brief spell in garrison at Welbeck. They had five colours, four blue and one red, and therefore probably consisted of five companies. The Pontefract garrison, which had been organized in four divisions, included a great number of officers and gentry.

Scarborough Castle   *Sir Hugh Cholmley*

The town was taken on 17 February 1645 and the castle on 22 July 1645.

All these garrisons tied up Parliamentarian forces, but their garrisons were not, of course, available to form part of 'the Oxford Army' in May 1645. Langdale with the Northern Horse, survivors of Marston Moor, had relieved Pontefract Castle by a brilliant feat of arms on 1 March 1645. They made an important part of the King's Army in the 1645 campaign, but, not unnaturally, their eyes were ever fixed on their home country.

In the North little remained to the King after Marston Moor. In the South-West the Royalists were still strong, but since the Parliamentarians still held Plymouth, Taunton and Lyme there was little enough to spare. There was in addition a peculiar command set-up.

Before Plymouth Sir Richard Grenvile (1600-1658) exercised the command. He had fought in the Low Countries in Germany and in Ireland. He had then served Parliament, until he deserted on 7 March 1644. He was a man of uncertain temper, and a heavy-handed commander, though certainly efficient. During the winter he had worked hard to recruit his forces, and by rounding up deserters and with fresh levies he had expanded his force from 300 foot and 100 horse to 5,000 foot and 1,000 horse.[6]

The titular commander in the West was the Prince of Wales, who had been appointed Generalissimo of the Royal forces in the West in January 1644-5. The Prince, who was not quite 15 years of age was accompanied by a respectable body of councillors, including the Duke of Richmond; the Earl of Berkshire, his Governor; the Earl of Southampton; Lord Capel; Lord Hopton, Lord Colepeper and Sir Edward Hyde, the Chancellor of the Exchequer.[7] In addition, as Prince of Wales and Duke of Cornwall, the Prince had his ordinary Council, which administered his lands and revenues. Not that they had much to administer. On arrival at Bristol Hyde found that the western association had failed to provide the £100 a week promised for his maintenance. '. . . only by borrowing from Hopton's private resources could the Prince obtain bread.'[8]

The strategic situation in the South West was far from brilliant. Though Cornwall was firmly in Royalist hands Plymouth, Lyme and Taunton still held out against the King, and the resources of the western Cavaliers were tied up in blockading them. In Dorset the Cavaliers held nothing but Corfe Castle[9] and the Isle of Portland.[10]

The command set-up was further complicated by the presence of Lord Goring, who held a commission, dated 21 December 1644, as Lieutenant-General of the Royal forces in Hampshire, Sussex, Surrey and Kent. He had recently failed to save Weymouth. Goring, who commanded some 3,000 Horse and 1,500 Foot, now determined to take Taunton, and ordered Sir John Berkeley, the Governor of Exeter, and Sir Richard Grenvile, to join him in this operation. It was not a bad plan for the garrison of Taunton was nearing exhaustion after a long resistance. The plan foundered because Grenvile declined to leave Plymouth. In the first place he owed no obedience to Goring, whose writ did not run in Devon. When he heard that the King approved Goring's plan, Grenvile still refused to budge because 'he had promised the commissioners of array of Devon and Cornwall that he would not advance beyond Taunton till Taunton were reduced.' Even so strict a commander as Grenvile would have had difficulty in getting his men, who were all raised in Cornwall or Devon, to march into Somerset whilst Plymouth was as yet unreduced. The idea of its garrison raiding their homes was unattractive. Eventually Grenvile yielded and marched to Cullompton (30 March), but by that time Goring had abandoned his plan, and acting upon the orders of the Prince's Council was in Dorset, bickering with Sir William Waller.

On the face of it, it would seem that the South West could have produced a field army of 10,800.

	Horse	Foot
Goring	3,000	1,500
Grenvile	1,000	5,000
Prince Charles	300	——
	4,300 +	6,500 = 10,800

In addition there were the various garrisons.

CORNWALL

	Strength	Guns	Colours	Surrendered
Pendennis Castle	886	95		17 August 1646
Colonel Sir John Arundell				
154 officers & 732 soldiers				
Dennis Fort	57	26	2	18 March 1646
Col. Sir Richard Vyvyan				
St. Mawes Castle		12	2	13 March 1646
Major Hannibal Bonython				
Fowey	PW 60	10		4 March 1646
Mount Edgecumbe		5		3 March 1646
Col. Pierce Edgecumbe				
Liskeard		3		29 February 1646
Saltash Garrison		3		28 February 1646
Launceston	K3	160		25 February 1646
Sir Thomas Bassett				

9

There was no likelihood of any of these being abandoned, and except for Pendennis Castle none of them seem to have been very strong.

	K	PW	H	Guns	Colours	Surrendered
Exeter	100	40	—	75	—	13 April 1646
Sir John Berkeley						
Dartmouth	20	800	60	106	14	19 January 1646
Sir Hugh Pollard						
Barnstaple	20	—	—	35	—	20 April 1646
Sir Allen Apsley						
Exmouth Fort	—	—	—	16	—	16 March 1646
Colonel Arundell						
Fort Salcombe	—	—	—	8	—	May 1646
Col. Sir Edm. Fortescue						
Tiverton Castle	4	200	20	4	2	20 October 1645
Sir Gilbert Talbot						
Powderham Castle	—	—	—	2	—	25 January 1646
Sir Ames Meredith, Bart.						

One would suppose that the withdrawal of Sir Gilbert Talbot's 200 men from Tiverton Castle would scarcely have prejudiced the Royalist cause.

	K	PW	H	Guns	Colours	Surrendered
Bristol	—	200	20	151	8	10 September 1645
Prince Rupert						
Bridgwater	30	1600	200	44	9	23 July 1645
Colonel Sir Hugh Wyndham						
Bath	—	140	11	6	2	20 July 1645
Colonel Sir Thomas Bridges						
Dunster Castle	20	—	—	—	6	April 1646
Colonel Francis Wyndham						
Nunney Castle	5	—	—	—	—	20 August 1645
Captain Turbervile						
Ilchester Garrison	—	—	—	—	—	8 July 1645
Colonel Robert Phelips						
Burrough Hill Fort	8	151	—	—	—	13 July 1645
Portishead Point Fort	3	—	—	6	1	28 August 1645

Whilst Taunton held out the value of Bridgwater (11 miles NE) was obvious, but 1,800 men was a lot to tie up in a place of that sort. Portishead, and Bath, with Berkeley Castle, the only remaining Royalist garrison in Gloucestershire, were necessary outposts of Bristol.

DORSET

	K	P W	H	Guns	Colours	Surrendered
Sherborne Castle	—	340	30	19	2	15 August 1645
Colonel Sir Lewis Dyve						
Corfe Castle	11	—	—	5	—	April 1646
Major Rob Laurence						
Isle of Portland						

Dyve commanded a good old foot regiment that had fought at Edgehill. His men would have been more useful with the King than locked up in Sherborne Castle, though it must be conceded that they gave a good account of themselves when they were besieged there.

Ruthless pruning of the South Western garrisons could have produced another 1,000 men for the field armies, and we are probably not far wrong in saying that 11,000 men were available in the South West in the spring of 1645. The situation was bedevilled by the Roundhead garrisons of Plymouth, Lyme and Taunton; by the animosity between Goring and Sir Richard Grenvile, and their personal ambitions. Both were determined to preserve their independence, while Goring hoped to replace Hopton as the lieutenant-general of the western army.

GLOUCESTERSHIRE

	K	P W	H	Guns	Colours	Surrendered
Berkeley Castle	40	90	—	11	—	25 September 1645
Sir Charles Lucas						

This was the only permanent Royalist garrison in Gloucestershire, and was, as we have seen, an outpost of Bristol, of which Prince Rupert, though seldom present, was Governor. Sir Charles Lucas had been Lieutenant-General of the Horse in the Marquis of Newcastle's Army, an appointment which he owed to Rupert's recommendation. Taken prisoner at Marston Moor he had been exchanged during the winter. He obviously owed the command at Berkeley to the Prince's favour. But, it was not a good appointment, for Lucas was an outstanding cavalry officer, and should certainly have been given a brigade of the field army, rather than a weak and unruly garrison.

A large body of the Royalist foot was quartered at Cirencester during the winter, 1644-1645, and a regiment at Campden House, but these forces were drawn out in May 1645 and, for the most part, fought at Naseby.

Gloucester itself was, throughout the war, one of the most important Parliamentarian garrisons, and a terrible thorn in the side of the neighbouring cavaliers. The garrisons of Bristol, Worcester and Hereford could protect their own vicinity, but they could not keep the enterprising Edward Massey within his walls.

Worcester was to spare a small contingent for the Naseby Army. It still had three regiments of foot during the siege of 1646, and they amounted to some 2,000 officers and men. Worcester had several satellite garrisons, including Hartlebury Castle and Madresfield. The most important was Evesham, where there were 560 men under Colonel Robert Legge. Evesham was not only a staging post on the way to Oxford, but it threatened the Parliamentarian line of communications between Gloucester and Warwick. Its fortifications, which, running along the line of the modern railway, sealed the loop in the River Avon, were too extensive for so small a garrison, and since the place was stormed by Massey on 26 May, we may safely assert that its garrison would have been better employed with the field army. The King drew out 150 horse and a detachment of perhaps 300 foot from Worcester itself, but as there was at this time no threat to the faithful city, it may be that he should have drawn more heavily upon this garrison.

WORCESTERSHIRE

	K	PW	H	Guns	Colours	Surrendered
Worcester				25		22 July 1646
Colonel Samuel Sandys[11]						
3 regts. F. 1 regt. H.						

	K	PW	H	Guns	Colours	Surrendered
Evesham						26 May 1645
Colonel Robert Legge						
560 FH						
Hartlebury Castle						14 May 1646
Captain William Sandys						
Madresfield						19 or 20 June 1646
Captain Edward Ashton						

HEREFORDSHIRE

The governors of Hereford, Dudley Castle and Ludlow waited upon the King at Droitwich on the night of 15 May. No doubt they discussed the question whether these garrisons could spare men for the field army. Colonel Thomas Leveson did indeed draw out 150 horse and a detachment of foot, but the other two produced nothing.

	Guns	Surrendered
Hereford		15 December 1645
Colonel Barnaby Scudamore		
Lt. Governor: Sir Nioholas Throckmorton		
Goodrich Castle		31 July 1646
Colonel Henry Lingen[12]		
Kilpeck Castle		Slighted about 27 July 1645

The strength of these garrisons is uncertain, but it would not have been unreasonable of the King to demand 150 horse and 300 foot at this time of crisis. This much, indeed more, could doubtless have been done without laying Hereford open to its active neighbour, Colonel Massey, at Gloucester.

South Wales had a few garrisons, but they had little if anything to spare beyond the garrison of Abergavenny, which was probably not very strong. The Marquis of Worcester kept his garrison in constant pay, at his own expense. It would have taken a bolder man than King Charles to demand a detachment from that private army!

	Men	K	Guns	Surrendered
Raglan Castle	300F[13]	20	23	19 August 1646
Marquis of Worcester				
Charles, Lord Somerset				
Monmouth				1645
Sir Thomas Lunsford				
Lt. Colonel Herbert Lunsford				
Abergavenny				27 July 1646[14]
Colonel James Progers				
Lt. Colonel Charles Progers				
Chepstow	300			
Sir John Winter				
Newport	50			
Colonel	*Herbert*			
Llangibby	60			
Sir Trevor Williams				

GLAMORGAN

Cardiff
  Sir Timothy Tyrell
Swansea
  Colonel Richard Donnel

BRECON

Brecon
  Colonel Turbervile Morgan
  Colonel-General Herbert Price

STAFFORDSHIRE

Staffordshire has been described as 'a key county of the Midlands, the most disputable area of all in the strategy of the war.'[15] By May 1645 it had but few Royalist garrisons.

	Surrendered
Dudley Castle	
Colonel Thomas Leveson	
Lichfield	
Colonel Richard Bagot (mw Naseby)	10 July 1646
Sir Thomas Tyldesley	
Tipton. A royalist garrison at 2 March 1644[16]	
Tutbury	
Sir Andrew Kniveton	

With Stafford and several minor garrisons in Parliamentarian hands, it was not easy for the Royalists to hold out. Nevertheless Lichfield and Dudley Castle both provided contingents at Naseby.

	Horse	Foot
Lichfield	200	300
Dudley Castle	150	?

If Staffordshire, where the Cavaliers were then so weak, could provide 350 horse and more than 300 foot, one wonders that more were not drawn out of Worcester and Hereford.

SHROPSHIRE

The loss of Shrewsbury in February 1645 had loosened the Cavaliers' hold on that county, but they still had numerous garrisons there, several of them established to serve as bases for the troops of Sir William Vaughan's Regiment of Horse, while it was in winter quarters. But the main garrison was Ludlow.

Surrendered

Ludlow Town and Castle
   Colonel Sir Michael Woodhouse
   The Prince of Wales's Regiment of foot and a regiment of horse.
Stokesay Castle   June 1645
   Captain Gerard Dannet of
   Sir Michael Woodhouse. F.
Bridgnorth Castle
   Colonel Sir Lewis Kirke
   Lt. Governor Thomas Wynne
   About 300 F and 100 H.[17]
Longford House
   Colonel John Young
Shrawardine Castle
   Captain Charles Vaughan[18]
Linshall (Lindsill Abbey) and Dawley
   Major Ratcliffe Duckenfield
   160 men
High Ercall
   Captain Nicholas Armorer
   200 men
Cawes Castle
   Colonel John Davalier or Devilliers

15

Duckenfield and Armorer belonged to Vaughan's Regiment and Davalier, a Florentine, had been a troop commander in it. Vaughan's Regiment, 400 strong, was at Naseby, but Shropshire does not seem to have provided any other troops. This is rather odd for, as we have seen, Woodhouse visited the King at Droitwich on 15 May, and in the 1643 campaign he had joined the King in time for the first battle of Newbury. It seems strange that his regiment, which was relatively strong and experienced should have been left in its quiet garrison.

In Cheshire and North Wales the Cavaliers were still strongly established. The area was important to them for it was there that the regiments sent by Ormonde from Ireland, had landed in the winter 1643-1644. North Wales was a good recruiting area, and was also noted for its cattle.

CHESHIRE

		Surrendered
Chester		3 February 1646
Lord Byron		
2000, incl. 300 Horse		
and 50 + guns		
Beeston Castle		15 November 1645
Captain	*Vallet* 56 at the surrender	
Lord Byron		
Houghton House		
Puddington		

The Parliamentarian leader in Cheshire was Sir William Brereton, an active commander. Even so the King received some support from that quarter. The cavalry regiment of Colonel Robert Werden was raised in Cheshire, and that of Colonel Robert Byron though raised in Lancashire, was probably based on Chester by this time. Each of these provided 100 men.

FLINTSHIRE

		Surrendered
Hawarden Castle		16 March 1646
Sir William Neale 120?		
Rhuddlan Castle		July 1646
Lt Colonel Gilbert Byron	200+	
Flint Castle		24 August 1646
Colonel Roger Mostyn		

16

DENBIGHSHIRE

Denbigh Castle[19]   27 October 1646
     Colonel William Salusbury
        About 500

Ruthin Castle   12 April 1646
     Colonel Mark Trevor
     Deputy-Governor, Captain   *Sword*

Chirk Castle   28 February 1646
     Lt. Colonel Sir John Watts[20]

Holt Castle   13 January 1647
     Colonel Sir Richard Lloyd

CAERNARVONSHIRE

Conway Castle
     Archbishop of York
     and/or Colonel Sir John Owen

Caernarvon Castle
     Colonel John Bodvell

ANGLESEY

Beaumaris Castle
     Lord Bulkeley

[1] The Trent.

[2] Probably Werton= Wiverton.

[3] Which had already been stormed on 10 September 1645.

[4] Though, in fact, it had been defeated at Langport on 10 July 1645.

[5] Symonds's Diary, p. 270.

[6] Coate, p. 164.

[7] Coate, p. 167.

[8] Coate, p. 168.

[9] Sprigge.

[10] Coate, p. 169.

[11] Colonel Henry Washington succeeded him and was the governor at the time of the surrender.

[12] Knighted 6 July 1645.

[13] Symonds, 25 June 1645.

[14] Burnt and the garrison drawn out.

[15] D. H. Pennington and I. A. Roots: The Committee at Stafford, 1643-1645, p. xi.

[16] Pennington and Roots, p. 62.

[17] There were still 266 F and 100 H on 20 October 1645 (Symonds, p. 248).

[18] An Irishman under Sir William Vaughan (Symonds, p. 256) Captain Vaughan was his colonel's brother.

[19] 'Denbigh Castle is governed by Mr Salisbury, repaired by him and his kinred at their owne cost.' (Symonds, p. 243).

[20] Knighted 28 Sept. 1645.

Chapter Two

THE ENGLISH SOLDIER OF 1645

THE ARMIES, THEIR officers, and the soldiers who followed them, had changed a great deal since the autumn of 1642. Men, who had not previously seen a shot fired were now veterans. Noblemen, who had commanded regiments as though by hereditary right, had vanished from the scene; some because they were tired of the struggle; some because the Parliament had had enough of them. In the Royalist armies the 'swordsmen', thanks largely to Rupert's influence, were in the ascendant. The New Model, too, was led by officers who had fought their way to the front, though few had been professional soldiers before the war. The merging of the three old Roundhead Armies into one, had completely changed the Parliamentarian officer corps, but the Royalists too had seen tremendous changes. A glance back at the hierarchy of the Edgehill armies illustrates these assertions.

	ROYALIST	
	1642	1645
Captain-General	King Charles	King Charles
Lieutenant-General	Earl of Lindsey	Prince Rupert
General of the Horse	Prince Rupert	Vacant
Sergeant-Major-General of the Foot	Sir Jacob Astley	Lord Astley
Commissary-General (later Lieutenant-General of the Horse)	Lord Wilmot	Vacant
Sergeant-Major-General of Dragoons	Sir Arthur Aston	None

Tertia Commanders	Charles Gerard	George Lisle
	John Belasyse	Sir Barnard Astley
	Richard Feilding	Sir Henry Bard
	Sir Nicholas Byron	
	Henry Wentworth	
Lt. General of the Ordnance	Sir John Heydon	Sir John Heydon

Of these senior officers, it would seem that only six were at both Edgehill and Naseby. These were:

King Charles	
Prince Rupert	
Lord Astley	
John Belasyse	Volunteer at Naseby
George Lisle	Lt. Colonel D. at Edgehill
Sir John Heydon	

Of the Edgehill hierarchy Lindsey had been mortally wounded; Wilmot had been cashiered for making unauthorized overtures for peace in 1644; Sir Arthur Aston had lost a leg in consequence of a riding accident; Charles Gerard was general of the Royalist forces in South Wales, where, though tactically successful, he was heartily detested by the local gentry. Feilding, disgraced for the surrender of Reading in 1643, was probably unemployed at this time, though he had commanded Hopton's artillery at Cheriton — and succeeded in getting his guns away. Byron and Wentworth had died in 1644.

CAVALRY

	Edgehill	*Naseby*
The Lifeguard	Lord Bernard Stuart	now Earl of Lichfield
Prince of Wales	Sir Thomas Byron	Lord Wentworth
	(- 1644)	The West
Prince Rupert	*	*
Prince Maurice	*	*
Sir John Byron	*	Chester
Lord Wilmot	*	The West
		Amyas Pollard
Lord Grandison	*	Destroyed, 1642
Earl of Carnarvon	*	The West
		Richard Neville

19

Lord Digby	*	The West
		Thomas Weston
Sir Thomas Aston Bart	*	The West
The Gentlemen Pensioners	*	Merged into the
		Lifeguard

Sir Thomas Byron had been assassinated. Grandison had been mortally wounded at Bristol, though some time after his regiment was destroyed; Carnarvon had been killed at First Newbury. Wilmot, as we have seen, had been cashiered, and Digby had given up command on being made Secretary of State. Their successors were men of somewhat lower social standing.

The King's Old Horse, with the exception of the Lifeguard, and the regiments of the Palatine princes, were not at Naseby. They were with Goring in the West.

DRAGOONS

James Usher	*	Henry Washington,
		Worcester
Sir Edward Duncomb	*	Disbanded
Edward Grey	*	Destroyed at Win-
		chester 12 December
	·	1642

The King had no dragoon regiment at Naseby.

FOOT

1642	1645	
Charles Gerard	*	Wales
Sir Lewis Dyve	*	Sherborne Castle
Sir Ralph Dutton	Sir Stephen Hawkins	Oxford
Thomas Blagge	*	Wallingford Castle
John Belasyse	Theophilus Gilby	Naseby
Sir William Pennyman	Sir Richard Page	Naseby
Richard Feilding	Lord Astley	Leicester, detachment at Naseby
Sir Thomas Lunsford	Prince Rupert	Naseby
Richard Bolle	George Lisle	Naseby
Sir Edward Fitton	Anthony Thelwall	Chester. One officer PW at Naseby
Sir Edward Stradling	John Stradling	South Wales?
Lifeguard	Earl of Lindsey	Naseby

Lord General	Earl of Forth	Woodstock?
Sir John Beaumont	John Godfrey	Destroyed at Tewkes-
	(-1644)	bury, 1644
Sir Gilbert Gerard	Ratcliffe Gerard	Naseby
Sir Thomas Salusbury	Sir Charles Lloyd	Devizes Castle
(-1643)		
Lord Molineux		Disbanded?
Earl of Northampton	Earl of Northampton	Banbury Castle
Earl Rivers	Sir John Boys	Donnington Castle
Herbert Price		Destroyed at
		Hereford, 1643

Of the regiments that had fought in the Edgehill campaign
six or eight were snugly ensconced in fortresses of greater or less
importance – an excellent arrangement from the commanding
officers' point of view, since, when the place was not actually beleaguered, he could keep his men well supplied and in good heart
by living off the surrounding district.

Of the 1645 colonels only the young Earl of Northampton
was not a soldier by trade, and he had proved himself an except-
ionally keen, and efficient officer.

The Train of Artillery had developed steadily throughout
the war. This was due to the Lt. General, Sir John Heydon. Lord
Hopton, its general, was with Prince Charles at Bristol and could
not play any part in its organization, his predecessor, Lord
Percy had been dismissed along with Wilmot in August 1644.

It is probably true to say that since 1642 the officer corps
of the Oxford Army had become more professional, and that this
was true, too, at troop and company, as well as regimental level.
Gentle birth was not in itself enough to secure a command, which
is not to say that families, important in their own counties, were
no longer represented in the army. It must be emphasized that
this tendency cannot be detected among the Northern Horse and
the men from the Newark garrison. The majority of their commanders were still, it seems, the country gentry rather than professional soldiers.

The King had given out a multitude of commissions at the
end of 1642 and in 1643. Many of the colonels had never raised
much more than a troop, and not a few, dissatisfied with the conduct of the war, had withdrawn from the struggle in 1644 : Sir

Edward Dering and Lord Chandos may be cited as examples.

In the Edgehill campaign a number of the Royalist regiments were well up to strength, but thereafter it became very difficult to get recruits, and so in early 1644 we find regiments with their full complement of officers but very few men.

Richard Symonds has preserved for us a strength return for the garrison of Reading in April 1644.[1] It includes 12 regiments. In theory they should have totalled 14,400. In fact they could muster a mere 2,231 soldiers. Even so the garrison numbered 3,147 for there were 916 officers! In this last figure, of course, they included, as was the custom in those days, the gentlemen of the arms, sergeants, corporals and drums. The smallest regiment was Sir Thomas Blackwall's, a mere handful, 86 strong. This unit had disappeared by the time of Naseby, where its colonel rode with the Northern Horse. The strongest regiment present was Pennyman's, which was to fight at Naseby as Sir Richard Page's. This, reputedly the oldest regiment of Charles' Army, mustered:

Captains	11
Lieutenants	10
Ensigns	11
Gentlemen of the Arms	11
Sergeants	23
Corporals	33
Drums	20
Soldiers	360
	479

At Naseby this unit was probably 500 strong, with a good cadre of old officers and soldiers.

At the beginning of 1644 the Royalists, who had belatedly given up their absurd practice of giving out commissions to anyone who aspired to play the part of a colonel, decided to raise 6,000 replacements by impressment. One may suppose, therefore, that those of the old regiments, which survived to make the campaign of Cropredy Bridge, Lostwithiel and Second Newbury, received recruits in the Spring. As they had a full complement of officers there would not have been any undue difficulty in absorbing and training the replacements.

The campaign of 1644 was a very successful one for the Oxford Army, which provided about two thirds of the Royalist foot that fought at Naseby. Despite arrears of pay, and deficiencies in clothing, and commissariat, we may suppose that Lord Astley's Foot were as good as any in the Kingdom, when they took the field in 1645.

*   *   *

Of the Parliamentarian Army of 1642 Philip Skippon who, though he did not actually fight at Edgehill, was listed[2] as 'Sergeant Major Generall and President of the Councell of Warr', was practically the only survivor. Essex' Army, like those of the Wars of the Roses, was led to a great extent by influential peers – men not unlike the 'over-mighty' subjects of the earlier period :-

The Earl of Essex (1591-1646)	Captain General and Colonel F.
The Earl of Bedford (1613-1700)	Lord Generall of the Horse, Colonel, H.
The Earl of Peterborough (c. 1624-1697)	General of the Ordnance, Colonel, F.
The Earl of Stamford (1599?-1673)	Colonel, F
Lord Saye and Sele (1582-1662)	Colonel, F
Lord Wharton (1613-1696)	Colonel, F
Lord Rochford (-1677)	Colonel, F
Lord St. John (1603-1642)	Colonel, F. K. Edgehill Courtesy title
Lord Brooke (1608-1643)	Colonel, F. K. Lichfield
Earl of Manchester (1602-1671)	Colonel, F.
Lord Robartes (1606-1685)	Colonel, F.
Lord Willoughby of Parham (c. 1613-1666)	Colonel, H.

There were 20 regiments of foot in Essex' Army: 10 of

them were commanded by peers. There was not a single peer in the New Model, yet of those who served under Essex only two, St. John and Brooke, had lost their lives in action.

The troop commanders of Essex' cavalry were almost all armigerous. Many of the troop commanders in the New Model were men of humbler origin, who had come to the front during the last two years. The Presbyterians, moreover, had to a great extent been ousted by the Independents. What Baxter called 'religious men', and we may be forgiven for calling fanatics, were now in the ascendant.

Few indeed of Essex' Army of 1642 figure in the 1645 campaign, and of these only one, Skippon, had been above the rank of captain.

		1645
Sergeant Major-General Philip Skippon (-1660)		Major-General of the Army

CAPTAINS

Oliver Cromwell (1599-1658)	67 Troop. H.	Lt. General of the Horse
Arthur Evelin	31 Troop. H.	Captain. Sheffeild H and A.G.
Robert Faringdon	John Hampden, F.	Lt. Colonel, Ingoldsby, F.
John Fiennes	60 Troop, H.	Colonel, H. Not New Model
Jo. Francis	Denzil Holles, F.	Lt. Colonel, Skippon, F.
Richard Ingoldsby (-1685)	John Hampden, F.	Colonel, F.
Henry Ireton (1611-1651)	58 Troop, H.	Commissary-General, H.
Walter Lloyd (-1645)	Captain, Saye and Sele, F.	Colonel, F.
Sir Robert Pye (-1701)	63 Troop, H.	Colonel, H.

CORNETS

Thomas Horton (-1649)	43 Troop, H. Sir Arthur Hesilrige	Major, Butler, H.
Edward Whalley (-1675)	60 Troop, H. John Fiennes Major, Oliver Cromwell, H., 1643	Colonel, H.

John Disbrowe	67 Troop, H.	Major, Fairfax, H.
(1608-1680)	Oliver Cromwell	
John Okey ·	6 Troop, H.	Colonel, D.
(1606-1662)	Lord Brooke	
Troopers or Gentlemen Volunteers		

TROOPERS or GENTLEMEN VOLUNTEERS

James Berry	Trooper, 1642?	Captain, Fairfax, H.
(-1655)	Capt.-Lieut. 1643	
	Oliver Cromwell	
Charles Fleetwood	Essex' Lifeguard, H.	Colonel, H.
(-1692)		
Thomas Harrison	Essex' Lifeguard, H.	Major, Fleetwood, H.
(1606-1660)		
William Packer	Trooper, 1642	Captain, Fairfax, H.
(fl.1642-1661)	Oliver Cromwell	

There were probably other Edgehill veterans at Naseby, but it is evident that, whether through battle casualties, sickness, or for political reasons, there had been a tremendous turnover of officers in the Roundhead ranks. Certainly this brought brave and talented leaders to the front, but constant changes in the officer corps cannot make for solidari·ֲ·. However, there was no actual shortage of officers ; and so the regiments of the New Model had the cadre they needed to train the pressed men brought in to reinforce its infantry regiments. It will be recalled that there were sufficient men to bring all the cavalry regiments up to strength, and this was probably the case also with Okey's Dragoons.

The main difference between the Oxford Army and the New Model, was that the latter was numerically stronger. Both were well led by experienced officers, and had plenty of old soldiers, so that there was no great difficulty in absorbing recruits. It is difficult to generalize about the battle experience of the units on either side. In the nature of things this varied. Not all the Royalist horse, for example, could claim successes such as Rupert's Regiment had enjoyed. On the Roundhead side Butler's Regiment could not look back upon as distinguished a career as Cromwell's Ironsides. This subject will be touched on again as we go along. Suffice it to say that, as in the nature of things, the regiments on either side had had their ups and down. Even an Ironside has his off days!

In organization, except for its lack of any brigade structure, the New Model had a solid advantage, in that its cavalry regiments were almost all up to strength, and its infantry consisted of big battalions. The Royalists, with regiments varying in strength from 80 to 500, had not faced up to the need for a reshuffle. During the previous winter they had contemplated the disbandment of small regiments, but this had raised a storm of protest. To take a regiment from a colonel was to rob him of his property, and to put loyal officers out of a job. This was a poor reward for three years service!

*　　*　　*

The clothing and equipment of the New Model was probably in good condition. In a letter of 6 June 1645 Sir Samuel Luke writes that a country neighbour had reported: 'Sir T. Fairfax army is the bravest that ever I saw for bodies of men, both in number, arms or other accountrements (sic), and pay for the officers.'[3] In the Royalist Army there was no longer any shortage of Arms, but many of the men wore their own clothing. The King's Lifeguard, however, was one which still had a proper issue of red caps, coats and breeches. An enterprising troop commander could sometimes get over the clothing problem. Thus *Mercurius Aulicus* recalls that on 16 November 1644 Captain John Moore of the Earl of Northampton's Regiment of Horse, raided Warwick and got back to Banbury with divers prisoners and 120 yards of red cloth 'wherewith the couragious Captaine intends to clothe his Souldiers; . . . .'[4]

Northampton's Regiment evidently did well in this respect for in a letter of 9 March 1645 Sir Samuel Luke reports that his trumpeter, coming from Banbury about the exchange of prisoners, told him that the Earl had, on the previous Thursday night brought in 60 prisoners with their horses and arms, and 80 horses laden with Gloucestershire cloth 'with which they intend to clothe their soldiers.'[5]

It is generally supposed that the New Model, at least the foot, were redcoats. This is probably correct but there were still Roundhead regiments on the establishment which wore 'uniform' of other hues. In the Spring of 1645 the garrison of Abingdon comprised three foot regiments:

Richard Browne	Greycoats
William Davies	Bluecoats
Thomas Rainsborough	Redcoats

Of these the last went into the New Model.[6]

*   *   *

The rations of the soldier of either side were uninteresting. The men were expected to support life on a diet of bread and cheese, and small beer. We need not doubt, however, that the men supplemented their rations with whatever else came their way. When pay was in arrears, which was often the case with the New Model as well as its opponents, the soldiers could not pay for what they took, even if they felt that they would like to. The burden of Free Quarters bore down heavily on the people in those parts traversed by the campaigning armies.

When pay is not punctually received, marauding is prevalent, and discipline suffers. Horror stories reached Newport Pagnell, when the Northern Horse rode to relieve Pontefract. ... 'This march of theirs was accompanied with many unheard-of cruelties. They robbed all the country people of their goods and took away their cattle. They ravished the women and bound men neck and heels together, and ravished their wives before their faces, and tied women in chairs and ravished their daughters in their sight. One woman they ravished who was within a week of her time. A gentlewoman with her daughters travelling along were ravished by them and the soldiers said frequently that the war was but now beginning. A soldier having his pocket picked by a quean, in the act of his villainy, of divers spoons and moneis and other things which he afterwards missing came to find his mate, but she being gone he took a wench which he found in the house, bound her, ripped up her clothes, laid a train of powder from her breasts downward, fired it and miserably scorched and burned her.'. . .[7]

There is no doubt an element of propaganda in this, for half the Northern Horse were officers and gentlemen, whose code would tend to discourage outrages of this sort. But the saying that the war was but now beginning somehow seems to ring true. Religious differences probably embittered the feelings of the north country Cavaliers, very many of whom were Roman Catholics. The King does not seem to have been a very stern disciplinarian, though we find a soldier being cruelly flogged for ravishing two women (24 May 1645), and another 'hangd on the tree in Wing towne, for stealing the communion plate there'. (27 August 1645).[8]

We need not think that the Cavaliers had the monopoly of indiscipline, nor ·was every Roundhead a Puritan. Sir Samuel Luke the governor of Newport Pagnell is scathing about the drunkenness prevalent in the ranks of the New Model. 'I think these New Modellers knead all their dough with ale, for I never saw so many drunk in my life in so short a time. The men I have formerly wrote to you of are extraordinarily personable, well armed and well-paid, but the officers you will hardly distinguish from common soldiers.'[9] (10 June 1645). There was considerable antipathy between Luke's men and the New Model. Luke told his father : 'you will everyday hear of new encounters.'[9] (19 May 1645).

Such then were the officers and men upon whom the fate of the Kingdom depended in the Spring and Summer of 1645.

To play his part in battle a trained soldier does not need to be a religious fanatic. If the New Model had one great advantage it was simply that it was more numerous than the Oxford Army. Three to two is long odds when it comes to hand to hand fighting.

---

[1] See Documents

[2] Peacock, p. 20.

[3] Tibbutt's Luke, p. 304.

[4] *Mercurius Aulicus*, p. 1261.

[5] Tibbutt's Luke, p. 187.
[6] BM. Rupert Correspondence.
[7] Tibbutt's Luke, pp. 204 & 205.
[8] Symonds, pp. 178 & 231.
[9] Tibbutt's Luke, p. 311 and 279. Luke was writing to his father, Sir Oliver on both occasions.

PART TWO
THE ROYALIST ARMY

Chapter Three

THE COMMANDERS

The man of blood was there
With his long essenced hair
And Astley and Sir Marmaduke
And Rupert of the Rhine.

Lord Macauley, *The Battle of Naseby*

KING CHARLES, NOW AGED 44, had acted as Captain-General of
the Royalist Army throughout the war. In 1642 he had been
without practical experience of war. But by 1645 he had been
present at Edgehill, Caversham Bridge, the siege of Gloucester,
both battles of Newbury, Cropredy Bridge and Lostwithiel. His
indifference to danger had been demonstrated on several occasions. None of his generals was more diligent in attendance at
the Council of War. He was not usually remarkable for his
powers of leadership, but in the pursuit of Essex' beaten army at
Lostwithiel he had shown vigour and ability. Three years military
experience had not removed the King's worst faults. Foremost
amongst these was that he was a poor judge of character, at once
fickle and obstinate. He was at this time very much under the
influence of Lord Digby, an indifferent amateur cavalry colonel,
who had become a disastrous Secretary of State.

Despite his defeat at Marston Moor the Prince Palatine
Rupert (1619-1682) had been made general at the end of the
1644 campaign. An intelligent and experienced professional
soldier, he had proved an excellent General of the Horse, able
to train his men as well as lead them. He had achieved remark-

able successes at Powick Bridge, Cirencester, Lichfield, Chalgrove Field, Bristol, Newark and Bolton and had shown himself as adept at laying a siege, as leading a cavalry charge. Bristol was a big operation involving two armies, but generally speaking he was at his best commanding a mixed column of 5000 to 7000 men. His reputation did not rest on the great battles, Edgehill and Newbury, but on dashing exploits like Chalgrove and Newark. His defeat at Marston Moor, when he had offered battle to a superior army, in the mistaken belief that he had no alternative, had probably eroded his self-confidence, though not his matchless valour. Rupert was certainly the most versatile of the Civil War generals. Unfortunately he was of a somewhat rough and proud nature, and at the age of 25 he had not yet learned to suffer fools gladly. He had a great following amongst the soldiers – the swordsmen – but was gravely mistrusted by many of Charles' courtiers. His own morale was gradually being worn down by the intrigues of Digby and John Ashburnham. A wiser monarch than King Charles I might have made Lord Hopton his general, and left his nephew to lead his cavalry.

Lord Astley (1579-1652) had been Sergeant-Major-General of the Foot from the beginning of the war. He was a little taciturn, silver-haired veteran of the Dutch Service, who thoroughly understood his profession, and had the added advantage that he got on well with Prince Rupert. If the old Royalist foot regiments had become formidable, we may attribute it to the skill and discipline of honest old Astley who had commanded them at Edgehill, Gloucester, Newbury, Cropredy Bridge and Lostwithiel.

COMMANDERS OF HORSE

Prince Maurice (1620-1652) was also with the Army, but without any particular command. He was sound rather than brilliant, but had defeated Waller at Ripple Field (13 April 1643) and played a valiant part in the important victory at Roundway Down (13 July 1643). He was perfectly capable of commanding a body of horse, such as that which formed the Royalist right wing at Naseby. Had he been given that command

31

Rupert could have got on with his proper job of commanding the whole army.

Sir Marmaduke Langdale (1598?-1661), who was Major-General of the Northern Horse, was a dour Yorkshire Roman Catholic. He defeated the Scots cavalry at Corbridge, Northumberland (19 February 1644). At Marston Moor his command had formed the extreme left of Goring's wing, whose first charges had routed most of Sir Thomas Fairfax' horse. After the battle he had rallied survivors from many regiments and, despite setbacks at Ormskirk (21 August) and Malpas (26 August) had brought them south to join the King.

Early in 1645, Langdale had been given permission to attempt the relief of Pontefract Castle. He defeated Colonel Edward Rossiter at Melton Mowbray (25 February) and raised the siege of Pontefract on 1 March. This Sir Charles Firth described as 'his most brilliant piece of soldiership during the war'. After this famous exploit Langdale rejoined the King's 'Oxford Army'.

Langdale's devotion to the Royalist cause is said to have cost him £160,000, and though created a peer at Bruges in 1658, he was too poor to attend the coronation of King Charles II. Clarendon, who had disagreed with him describes him as 'a hard man to please, and of a very weak understanding, yet proud, and much in love with his own judgment.' Be that as it may Slingsby, who admired him, tells us that he was very secret in his military operations, never telling his men where they were going until about a quarter of an hour before the move. His own son, it is said, was so frightened of him that when the old man was dying he dared not tell him that his time was come! Such was the formidable commander of the Northern Horse.

The other brigade was commanded by Sir William Blakiston, of Newton, Durham, who had been knighted at Oxford on 12 April 1643. He had doubtless served throughout the war, but his early services do not seem to have been recorded. He commanded two regiments of horse in Goring's success at Haleford[1] (8 June 1644), and a brigade at Marston Moor, where he broke right through the foot in the Allied centre. On 30 September 1644 he was reported to have been severely wounded in the thigh in an attack on a house near Monmouth.[2] He was then commanding a brigade. He had recovered in time to sign the petition of the Northern Horse (Feb. 1645), and doubtless commanded his brigade at Melton Mowbray (25 Feb.) and the relief of Pontefract Castle (1 March). He certainly did at Leicester (May) and Naseby. He survived the rout at Rowton Moor to distinguish himself by his outstanding bravery in Digby's defeat at Sherburn-in-Elmet (15 Oct. 1645).[3] His record, if more shadowy than one could wish, seems to reveal a brave and efficient commander.

James Compton, third Earl of Northampton (1622-1661) commanded a brigade of horse. At 23 he was a veteran of Edgehill, Hopton Heath, Middleton Cheney, and Cropredy Bridge, where he had particularly distinguished himself by repulsing Waller's attack on the rear of the Royalist Army. He had fought in the Cornish campaign and had relieved Banbury Castle, which his brother, Sir William Compton, had successfully defended (26 March 1644). An otherwise successful career had been marred by the rough handling his brigade received from Cromwell at Islip on 25 April 1645.

Colonel Thomas Howard (1619-1706), second son of the Earl of Berkshire, a captain in 1641, who now commanded a brigade of horse, had been commissioned to raise a regiment soon after Edgehill. He had probably commanded a brigade at Cheriton.[4] He seems to have recruited in Wiltshire for the most part. At the rendezvous at Aldbourne Chase on 10 April 1644 he had nine troops, and his regiment, 300 strong, was one of the strongest in the army. This argues that he had proved himself an efficient commanding officer. He sat for Wallingford in the Long Parliament, and succeeded his brother Charles, becoming Third Earl of Berkshire in 1679.

COMMANDERS OF TERTIAS OF FOOT

Colonel Sir Barnard Astley (d.-1645), was the second son of Lord Astley, whose major he had been in 1640. He had commanded the Marquis of Hertford's Regiment at the storming of Bristol (1643) and had he not fallen ill Lord Hopton would have made him Sergeant-Major-General of his foot. He had commanded a tertia of foot in the Cornish campaign of 1644, and had particularly distinguished himself at Second Newbury.

Sir Henry Bard (c.1615-1660) was a soldier and diplomatist. He was educated at Eton College and King's College, Cambridge, where he took his master's degree and became a fellow. He had travelled in France, Italy, Turkey, Palestine and Egypt, and knew several languages. Anthony Wood describes him as 'a compact body of vanity and ambition, yet proper, modest, comely,' which sounds rather contradictory.

Bard led a regiment of foot at the battle of Cheriton 'with more youthful courage than soldier-like discretion,'[5] and some attribute the defeat to his bad tactics. He was severely wounded, lost an arm, and was taken prisoner. Released in May 1644 he was created a baronet on 8 October 1644 and governor of Camden House, Gloucestershire. There were several Royalist colonels whose claims to command a brigade were better than his. We need only mention Thomas Blagge (1613-1660) who had commanded the first tertia in the successful 1644 campaign. However, Bard was a friend and protégé of Prince Rupert. Even so he seems to have done well at Leicester, and the defeat at Naseby cannot be attributed to any failure on his part.

Colonel George Lisle (-1648) was one of the best infantry officers in the Royalist armies. He had learned his trade in the Netherlands and had distinguished himself at First Newbury, at Cheriton and in the Cornish campaign. At Second Newbury his tertia, though greatly outnumbered, repulsed Manchester's Army. 'We profess', wrote *Mercurius Aulicus* 'we want language to express his carriage, for he did all things with so much courage, cheerfulness, and present dispatch, as had special influence on every common soldier, taking particular care of all except himself.' During the winter of 1644-1645 he was governor of Faringdon Castle.

*　　*　　*

Sir Edward Walker (1612-1677). In both armies the Secretary-at-war was a staff officer of the first importance, though it would be difficult to equate his rôle precisely with that of any

34

particular department of a modern General staff. Judging from Sir Edward Walker's surviving papers he performed some of the duties of the Military Secretary and of the Adjutant-General's Department.

Walker was the second son of Edward Walker of Nether Stowey, Somerset. His mother was Barbara, daughter of Edward Salkeld of Corby Castle, Cumberland. His younger brother, Philip, was colonel of a regiment of foot. Edward entered the service of Thomas Howard, Earl of Arundel (1585-1646), in 1633, and accompanied him on his visit to the emperor in 1636. It was thanks to Arundel's influence that he found his way into the College of Arms where he met with rapid advancement: Blanch Lion pursuivant-at-arms extraordinary (1635); Rouge Croix pursuivant (1637); Chester Herald (1638).

When in 1639 the austere Arundel commanded the royal army against the Scots in the first Bishops' War, he made Walker his secretary-at-war an appointment in which, as he himself assures us, 'I served him and the public with the best of my faculties.'[6]

Walker was with the King throughout the First Civil War. He was one of the heralds sent to demand the surrender of Hull (24 April 1642), and to proclaim Sir John Hotham a traitor should he refuse. In September the King made Walker his secretary-at-war. To this later was added the post of secretary-extraordinary to the privy council. After his victory at Cropredy Bridge the King sent Walker, in his heraldic capacity, to offer his gracious pardon to Waller's defeated army, and, before Essex' disaster in Cornwall he played a similar rôle. In 1644 Walker was created Norroy King-of-Arms, and upon the death Sir Henry Saint-George (1581-1644), he was appointed Garter King-of-Arms. He was knighted on 2 February 1645.

Besides being a diligent staff officer and a learned herald, Walker was a historian of repute. His *Historical Discourses* contain what amounts to the Official History of the King's campaigns of 1644 and 1645.

During the years of exile Walker found plenty to grumble at for his office of Garter was not very profitable. He exasperated Sir Edward Nicholas (1593-1669) and Sir Edward Hyde[7]

(1609-1674). In 1653 the former wrote: 'Sir Edward Walker is a very importunate, ambitious, and foolish man, that studies nothing but his own ends, and every day hath a project for his particular good; and if you do him one kindness and fail him in another, you will lose him as much or more than if you had never done anything for him.'[8] To this Hyde wittily replied: "Why should you wonder that a herald, who is naturally made up of embroidery, should adorn all his own services and make them as important as he can? I would you saw some letters he hath heretofore writ to me in discontent, by which a stranger would guess he had merited as much as any general could do, and was not enough rewarded."[9]

When in 1656 King Charles II assembled a small army for the Spanish service in the Netherlands, Walker was once more secretary-at-war.

At the Restoration it fell to Walker to arrange the ceremonies at the coronation. His latter years were embittered by disputes with Clarenceux, Norroy and Chester. It may be that he was of a somewhat quarrelsome disposition: certainly he was one to stick up for his rights. Nevertheless he was an accurate historian, and a competent staff officer.

He died at Shakespeare's house, New Place, Stratford-on-Avon, which he had purchased in 1675.

1 Between Hale and Runcorn.
2 CSPD p. 18.
3 Clarendon MS., 25.
4 Adair, p. 102.
5 Colonel Walter Slingsby.
6 Historical Discourses, pp. 217 & 263.
7 The future Earl of Clarendon.
8 Nicholas Papers, ii, 11.
9 Calendar of Clarendon Papers, ii, 222, 346.

Chapter Four

THE ROYALIST HORSE

KING CHARLES LEFT Oxford on 7 May and, moving via Wood-stock and Stow-on-the-Wold, reached Evesham on the 9th. He had concentrated 11,000 men, 6,300 horse and 5,300 foot, but this formidable force was not to stay together long. That very afternoon General Goring, with 3,000 horse, marched into the West. That Goring was a bold and successful cavalry commander cannot be denied, but he was not the man to be entrusted with an independent command, nor was it prudent to entrust him with so large a body of the old horse. With the New Model about to take the field the King would have done better to retain at least 5,000 cavalry with his main army. Although Royalist intelligence was rather indifferent, the King must have known that the New Model had well over 5,000 horse. In fact it had over 7,000. Even had the West been devoid of mounted troops. which was not the case, Goring should have been able to cover the siege of Taunton with 1,300 men.

To make up for the loss of Goring's men, Charles drew contingents from his various garrisons and by the end of May he had 5,620 horse at his command. But on 4 June Sir Richard Willys and 400 of the Newark Horse returned to their garrison. And so at Naseby the King had about 5,590. Beyond question he could have found work for some of the regiments he had so unwisely entrusted to General Goring.

The organization of the Royalist cavalry left something to be desired, because although the body of the horse was divided into four brigades, a number of units were left independent.

Two Southern Brigades	Strength	
Earl of Northampton	950	1830
Colonel Thomas Howard	880	

Two Northern Brigades
Sir Marmaduke Langdale ⎱ 1500
Sir William Blackiston ⎰

The Newark Horse
Major-General Anthony Eyre ⎱ 800
Colonel Ned. Villiers ⎰

The King's Lifeguard
Earl of Lichfield (formerly Lord Bernard Stuart)　　　500

Prince Rupert's Regiment
Major Sir Thomas Dallison　　　400

Colonel Sir Horatio Cary's Regiment　　　200

Prince Rupert's Lifeguard
Sir Richard Crane　　　140

Prince Maurice's Lifeguard
Lord Molineux　　　120

Sir George Boncle's Regiment　　　100?

　　　—————
　　　5590
　　　—————

PRINCE RUPERT'S LIFEGUARD

The Lifeguard was originally part of Prince Rupert's Regiment, but was made independent during the first winter of the war. Its commander from the outset was Richard Crane, who had served with the Prince on the continent. He was knighted for Powick Bridge. He fell at Bristol in 1645, and was probably succeeded by Colonel Thomas Daniel.

At Leicester in May 1645 the troop numbered 140 and so it was stronger than many a regiment. A normal troop would only have four commissioned officers, but the Lifeguard, not surprisingly, seems to have had more. In *A List of [Indigent] Officers, 1663*, we find a number listed under Sir Richard Crane :-

⎰ Major Edward Williams	
⎱ Cornet Thomas Williams	I. O. Brecon
⎧ Captain Richard Fox	
⎪ Lieutenant Thomas Cayney	I. O. Stafford
⎨ Major Richard Fox	
⎩ Q.M. Edward Robinson	I. O. Salop.
⎰ Captain Will. Rumball	
⎱ Q.M. Anthony Exton	I. O. Hereford
Q.M. Roger Burton	I. O. Salop.

Under Prince Rupert we find :-

Q.M. Will. Montgomery "Quart. to the Life Guard.

It is not impossible that the Lifeguard absorbed the remnants of other units as the war went on. It rather looks as if it may have been organized in small bodies the size of the troops in an ordinary regiment.

The Lifeguard was the Prince's usual escort, and so its history is his own war record. Needless to say it saw as much fighting as any unit on either side, and was a formidable body of men.

It was disbanded at Oxford on 25 April 1646.

PRINCE MAURICE'S LIFEGUARD

Symonds, writing in May 1645, describes this as 'One troope consisting of above 100 gentlemen, &c., and reformados, commanded by the Lord Molineux.'[1] It was 120 strong.

This troop was probably raised in 1642, and as late as 10 April 1644 was part of the Prince's regiment of horse. At that time its captain-lieutenant was Hugh Williams, a professional soldier.[2] At the beginning of the war Lord Molineux had raised a regiment of foot, but he also had a regiment of horse. The majority of his indigent officers came from Lancashire. Presumably Molineux' units were no longer in existence at the time of Naseby.

The officers of Maurice's Lifeguard included Captains Thomas Gerard and Sir Stephen Tempest, Lieutenant Baxter and Quartermaster Simpson, all of whom were taken at Naseby, and some of whom may have been reformado officers.

Amongst the indigent officers under Prince Maurice, we

39

find 'L & W. Watts, John Quart. to the Life Guard,' but there is no evidence that he was at Naseby.

Symonds tells us that on 13 August: 'The Scotts beate up Prince Maurice's troops of Reformadoes, commanded by Lord Molineux at their quarters at Bewdley; tooke them almost all.'[3] However that may be, the troop, 'partly commanded by Lord Molineux, and partly by Sir Thomas Sandys,' escorted the Prince on his march from Bridgnorth to Worcester.[4] On 1 November part of Prince Maurice's Lifeguard seconded the Arcall Horse[5] in charging their pursuers after Denbigh fight.[6] This is the last we hear of them, but they were probably not disbanded until April 1646.

PRINCE RUPERT'S REGIMENT

The Regiment was probably the best in any of the Royalist Armies. Not only was it among the strongest, but it was by far the most experienced. It was with the Prince in all his many triumphs, as well as the disasters of Marston Moor and Naseby.

Its original officers included at least five who were soldiers by trade: Lt. Colonel Daniel O'Neill; Major Will. Legge; Lieutenants Clement Martin and Richard Grace; and John Richardson, who had been a quartermaster in 1641.

By 23 December there were six troops, excluding the Lifeguard, which was shortly to be made independent. The strength was then 365 men and 430 horses. The troop commanders, all older than their colonel, were then:

> Lt. Colonel Daniel O'Neill (c.1612-1664)
> Major Will. Legge (c.1607-1670)
> Sir Lewis Dyve (1599-1669)
> Sir Thomas Dallison (1591-1645)
> Lord Dillon (c.1615-1672)
> Sir William Pennyman (1607-1643)

By 8 January 1643 there was a seventh troop, under Captain John Villiers, a brother of Lord Grandison. *Mercurius Aulicus* relates how he lost his way on a night march near Cirencester and was captured by Roundhead scouts.

By 2 February 1643 a Captain Curson had brought a troop to the Regiment: he does not seem to have lasted long. He was probably a casualty of First Newbury. By June Captain Thomas Gardiner had raised a troop, and Clement Martin, now a captain, led a troop at Chalgrove Field (18 June 1643).

Although the Regiment was in the thick of many a fight its original troop commanders seem to have been lucky. Pennyman had died in his bed, but the others were still alive when on 19 March 1644 Prince Rupert relieved Newark. On that occasion the Regiment had ten troops divided into five squadrons.

Troop Commanders[7]	Probable Squadron Commanders
Lt. Colonel Daniel O'Neill	Major Legge
Absent	
Major Will Legge	
Captain Thomas Gardiner	Captain Gardiner
Captain John Richardson	
Sir Francis Cobbe. Absent?	Captain Martin
Captain Clement Martin	
Lord Grandison	Sir Thomas Dallison
Sir Thomas Dallison	
Sir Lewis Dyve. Absent	Lord Dillon
Lord Dillon	

Sir Lewis Dyve was governor of Abingdon. Sir Francis Cobbe, who came from Otringham near Hull, was probably at York, for he was governor of Clifford's Tower during the siege of the following summer. In the absence of O'Neill, Legge commanded the regiment. Whether he commanded a squadron as well is perhaps a little doubtful.

At Marston Moor the Regiment was 500 strong. There the unfortunate Lord Grandison, formerly Captain John Villiers, suffered no less than ten wounds.

Later in the year we find Captain Richard Grace commanding a troop. It may be that he had succeeded Lord Dillon. He had a long military career ahead of him. He was killed as a colonel when, in 1691, Ginkel surprised Athlone.

Before Leicester in May 1645 the Regiment, eight squadrons, was still 400 strong. Legge was now governor of Oxford, and Sir Thomas Dallison was commanding the regiment.

The Regiment had recently lost not only Legge's troop, but also those of Gardiner, Grace and Warner (Dyve) which were with him at Oxford. This left:

Troop Commanders:

Lt. Colonel Dan O'Neale
Sir Thomas Dallison   C.O. MW Naseby
Lord Grandison   W Marston Moor, but in the
                                  siege of Bristol (September 1645)

Captain Clement Martin
Sir Francis Cobbe   Probably at Skipton Castle
Lieutenant George Blakeston of Hayton,   PW II Bristol
     Yorkshire
Captain John Richardson

Dallison fell at Naseby, and thereafter Grandison evidently commanded the regiment, whilst Charles Hart, the tragic actor, took over Dallison's troop.

A List of [Indigent] Officers, 1663 names a number of officers of the Regiment of whom the majority will have been at Naseby.

Southamp.	Cornet Edmond Hooke		Sir Thomas Dallison, Bart.
	or		
York	Cornet Jeremy Bower		
L & W	Cornet John Hubert		Lord Grandison
Salop	QM Roger Armstrong		
York	Lieutenant George Blakeston		Sir Francis Cobbe
Suffolk	QM Thomas Thwaytes		
L & W	Captain Clement Martin		Clement Martin
Wilts	QM Rob Thacham		
Durham	Lueitenant Bryan Richardson		Captain John Richardson
Wilts	QM Rob Jackson		

Two of the new troops may have been commanded by:—

     Capt. Hugh Davis, I. O. York
     Capt.   Smith or
     Capt. Will. Bowes

Sir Thomas Gardiner, knighted for Newark, was slain in a skirmish near Aylesbury at the end of July. His brother Henry, who presumably succeeded him was killed in the successful raid on Thame (7 September 1645).

John Richardson was killed in a sally from Oxford on 3 June 1646. Clement Martin survived the Restoration, and was one of the band of Gentlemen Pensioners, as was Lord Grandison.

The Hertfordshire County Records preserve the name of

one of Rupert's troopers. Robert Keene was in Col. Richard Grace's troop 'from the very beginning of the wars of England till the royal party were quite extinct.'[8]

The Regiment was disbanded at Oxford on 25 April 1646.

THE QUEEN'S REGIMENT OF HORSE

The Regiment was raised in Lancashire in 1643. The first commanding officer was the Queen's favourite, Lord Jermyn (c.1604-1684). There were a number of Frenchmen in the Regiment.

Late in 1643 the major, John Cansfield was knighted for leading a desperate charge across Olney bridge, when he was wounded.

The Regiment fought at Cheriton (29 March 1644), where Colonel Walter Slingsby was unimpressed by its performance. 'Lord John Steward (seeing our foote like to be opprest with freshe horse) sends downe the Queenes Regiment of horse, which were most Frenche, who descended the hill into this ground with seeming resolution, but retreated after an unhandsome charge.'[9] Lord Hopton thought better of them. At the end of the day he rallied 300 horse to cover the retreat of the army. 'The greater part of that little number of horse that stayed with hime [Hopton] were of the Queene's Regiment, where Monsr. de Plurie [Raoul ffleury] theire cheife Commander doing his duty like a very worthey person in the head of them had his legg shott off to the anckle with a great shott, whereof he shortly after dyed. . . .'[10]

Symonds (October 1644) made some notes on the Regiment from which it appears, as one would expect, that it had seven troops. By May 1645 Cansfield was the commanding officer and the strength of the Regiment had dwindled to 150[11], of whom perhaps 28 will have been commissioned officers.

It is not easy to say who the troop commanders now were, but this list is perhaps not far wrong :

(Lt.?) Colonel Sir John Cansfield
Major Lawrence Clifton K. Shelford House
Captain George Markham?

Captain Charles Charbo. French	Lieutenant at 27 Nov. 1643.
	Captain *vice* Sir Thomas Smith.
	K. Shelford House
Captain Gautier? French	Captain *vice* Raoul ffleury?
Captain John Clifton	Captain *vice* ?
	PW Shelford House
Captain Thomas Brockholles	I. O. Middlesex
or	
Captain Simon Norton	Northants

The Regiment did not distinguish itself at Naseby. Afterwards Cansfield went to Oxford to command the horse of that garrison, where he did very well.

The Regiment was massacred when, in November 1645, Shelford House was stormed by Colonel-General Sydenham Poyntz; at least two of the troop commanders being slain after a stout resistance.

PRINCE MAURICE'S REGIMENT OF HORSE

Prince Maurice's Regiment was raised in 1642, and fought at Edgehill.

According to Captain Richard Atkyns, a troop commander in 1643, it was one of the most active regiments, and usually placed in the 'out-quarters'. It fought at Little Dean and Ripple Field; at Caversham Bridge, Chewton Mendip, Lansdown and Roundway Down. After the capture of Bristol it was left there to recruit and Hopton tells us that its strength doubled to 400.[12]

The Regiment was at the Aldbourne Chase rendezvous on 10 April 1644. It was then 300 strong, organized in seven troops, and with seven red cornets.

1. Prince Maurice
   Capt. Lieut. Hugh Williams
2. Lt. Colonel Guy Molesworth
3. Major Robert Legge
4. Captain Wolley Lee (-1644)
5. Captain William Sheldon
6. Captain James Elliot
7. Captain John Freake

Not all these fought with the Regiment at Naseby.

Prince Maurice's Troop, probably the strongest, must have been his Lifeguard, which as we have seen formed a 'division' with Prince Rupert's Lifeguard.

Robert Legge, though still described as its major in May 1645[13], had become a colonel and, very briefly, governor of Evesham, which fell to Colonel Edward Massey on 25 May 1645. Robert Legge, Captain William Sheldon of Broadway, Worcestershire, and the latter's cornet, George Guise of Sandhurst, Gloucestershire, were among the officers taken. Thus the Regiment lost two troops: perhaps about 65 officers and men. Captain Wolley Lee had died in December 1644, and who took over his troop is not known.

Thus Maurice's Regiment, 150 strong before Leicester, seems to have had four troops in June 1645. Lt. Colonel Guy Molesworth, wounded at Naseby, was the commanding officer, an appointment he had enjoyed throughout the war. He was a professional soldier and had been captain-lieutenant of the Earl of Northumberland's Regiment of Foot in 1640.

It may be that James Elliot and John Freake were still among the troop Commanders. There will have been about sixteen officers in all and they probably included all or some of the following:

		Troop Commander
Cornet John Turner	L & W	Molesworth[14]
Lieutenant Richard Elliot.	L & W	Elliot
Lieutenant Will Horton.	Gloucestershire	Freake
Cornet Will Mason	Warwickshire	

Molesworth recovered from his Naseby wound and with the remnants of the Regiment, perhaps about 100, was still campaigning, under Lord Gerard, as late as 14 January 1646.[15] The Regiment may have been disbanded in April, at the same time as Prince Rupert's forces.

EARL OF NORTHAMPTON'S REGIMENT

At Edgehill Spencer Compton, second Earl of Northampton (1601-1643), a veteran of Breda and Lemgo, had led a troop of 100 gentlemen, which formed part of the Prince of Wales's Regiment. On 25 November 1642 he was commissioned to raise a regiment of horse. When he was killed at Hopton Heath he was succeeded by his son, and lieutenant-colonel, Lord Compton (1622-1681). James, the third earl, though very young to exercise command, was an excellent cavalry officer. As a colonel he routed the Roundheads at Middleton Cheney (6 May 1643), and as a brigadier he particularly distinguished himself at Cropredy Bridge. More recently, however, he had suffered a sharp reverse, when Cromwell routed his brigade at Islip.

Both at the Aldbourne Chase rendezvous (10 April 1644) and before Leicester (May 1645) the Regiment numbered 250. On each occasion, we may be sure there was in addition a troop or two at Banbury, the base from which the Northamptons operated.

When in August 1644 the King dismissed Lord Wilmot 44 of the officers of the Old Horse petitioned to know the reason. These included:

Northampton	Colonel
Charles Compton	Lt. Colonel
Philip Honeywood	Major
Gyles Slany	Captain
Henry Brown (-1644)	Captain-Lieutenant.
	K. Relief of Banbury Castle.[16]
Will Whitney	Lieutenant. Colborne's Troop.
	I. O. Essex PW Rowton Heath
Francis Rainsford	Cornet PW Rowton Heath

At Naseby the Regiment probably had at least seven troops present though one or two of them may have been at Banbury.

Troop Commanders
Earl of Northampton	
Lt. Colonel Charles Compton	Colonel 21 January 1646
Major Philip Honeywood	Pass to go abroad, 13 December 1645
Captain Sir William Farmer	Compounded December 1645
Captain George Rawleigh	
Captain Flamock Colborne	{ PW, Rowton Heath
	{ Major, 21 January 1646
Captain Gyles Slany	

46

Captain, later major, Flamock Colborne was severely wounded at Althorpe on 18 March 1645, but his troop may have been at Naseby under Lieutenant Will. Whitney, who appears in the list of indigent officers as an officer under Major Colborne. Colborne was promoted major on 21 January 1646.

Another troop commander, who was active during most of the war was Captain Matthew Clarke of Oxhill, Warwickshire. He was captured at Compton House in June 1644, but did not spend the rest of the war in captivity, for he was made Lt. Colonel (21 January 1646) and was in arms under Sir Thomas Glemham at Oxford in 1646.[17]

Junior officers present may have included:

		Troop Commander
Quartermaster Daniel Blackford	I. O. Warwick	Matthew Clarke
Quartermaster William Wisdom	I. O. Northam	Giles Slaney

SIR WILLIAM VAUGHAN AND HIS REGIMENT OF HORSE

"Why didst Thou suffer that Castle [Chirk] which was the seat of holiness to be possessed with profaneness and Popery? O curse with a heavy curse the Great Devil of Shrawardine, what doth torment Thy children and let all the righteous and holy say Amen."
Prayer of a Puritan Lady,
Mercurius Aulicus, 1 February 1645[18]

D. Llenfer Thomas, writing in The Dictionary of National Biography, opined that Sir William Vaughan (k. 1649) probably belonged to one of the Shropshire or Herefordshire families of that name, but the indigent officers listed under him include Lieutenant Morgan Vaughan from Radnor, who may have been one of his family. He may be the William Vaughan who was admitted to Shrewsbury School in 1596, in which case he must have been born somewhere about 1585.

Vaughan figures as a captain in the list of officers who served in 'forraine parts', and, at some time before 27 July 1639, elected to serve King Charles in the Bishops' War.[19] He may well have been the Captain Vaughan who served in Lord Cromwell's Regiment of Foot raised for Mansfeld's Expedition in 1624.[20] If so he was fairly senior by 1641, when we find him commanding the sixth troop in the Earl of Carnarvon's Regiment of Horse.[21] His officers then were:

> Lieutenant Thomas Crofts
> Cornet Richard Tailer
> QM James Vaughan, who was one of his brothers

This troop was one of those sent to Ireland to take part in the suppression of the rebellion of October 1641.

Vaughan commanded Sir Richard Grenvile's cavalry at the battle of Rathconnell (7 February 1643), and was chosen to carry the news of the victory to Dublin. For this service he was knighted by the Marquis of Ormonde. After the signing of the cessation (15 September) Ormonde was able to send reinforcements to the Chester area. In all these amounted to about 5,700 foot (seven regiments) and 300 horse under Sir William Vaughan, who now became a colonel. (See Appendix A on page 64).

A list of 'Troopes in Leinster' dated 1643 includes four troops to be sent for England :-

> Sir William Vaughan
> Captain John Dauelier [Devilliers]
> Captain Thomas Crofts
> Captain John Bomer

Each troop was to consist of :—

Captain	1
Lieutenant	1
Cornet	1
Quartermaster	1
Corporals	3
Other officers	4[22]
Troopers	40 mounted
Troopers	10 unmounted[23]
	61 Total 244

Another document is entitled 'A lyst of horsemen ready to goe for England'. They were drawn from the troops of Captain Povey ; Sir Thomas Armstrong ; Lord Leicester, and Sir Adam Loftus, which were to be, or had already been, reduced. They included :-

Lieutenant	Bernard
Cornet	Cullin
Quartermaster	Lyneker[24]
Corporals	4
Troopers	84

91

The troopers included :-

John Bambricke,
Arthur Bambricke,
Richard Bambricke,
Phelim Dempsie,
William Whitinge,
John Fitzgerald,
Richard Doson,
George Taylor,
William Mandvill,

who were described as 'Sir Adam Loftus his reduced men'.[25]
The Bambricke s, Dempsie and Fitzgerald sound like native
Irish.

It seems that Vaughan may have had as many as 335 officers
and men when he sailed for England.

Ormonde had great difficulty in fitting out these troops.
On 5 February 1644 he wrote to Sir Edward Nicholas from
Dublin : 'The truth is, I have had much ado (at so low an ebb in
present is this revenue) to provide for their passage, and furnish
them for their service in that measure they are ; being enforced
to take up of some merchants here, upon my own engagement,
a provision of great saddles and arms for the horse. . . .'[26]

Vaughan, like all the commanders who came over from
Ireland, must have been very much concerned with the problem
of keeping his regiment up to strength. To achieve this it was
necessary to keep his men paid, clothed and housed. Vaughan
solved his problem by putting his troops into little garrisons all
over Shropshire, and living off the country. He became known
as 'the Devil of Shrawardine', being appointed governor of the
castle there on 28 September 1644. He was able to raise fresh
troops locally, and companies of foot to guard his bases. He was

joined by a troop of horse under Captain George Hosier, son of Richard Hosier of Cruckton, Salop, whose commission seems to have been of earlier date than those of some of the captains from Ireland. The regiment had six troops when it came over. The troop commanders then were :-

{ Colonel Sir William Vaughan		
{ Capt.-Lieut. Beverley Usher		
Lt. Colonel Henry Slaughter of Keighley, Yorkshire	}	Captains in Ireland Both promoted before Marston Moor
Major Radcliffe Duckenfield of Duckenfield, Cheshire	}	
1. Captain Thomas Crofts, son of Sir Christopher Crofts		K. Longford, 25 March 1644
2. Captain John Devilliers		A Florentine
3. Captain John Bomer		Cornet in 1641[27]

Vaughan began his career in England with two minor successes. He and Colonel Robert Ellice, who commanded a regiment of foot, laid siege to Apley Castle, Shropshire, and compelled the garrison to surrender (24 March 1644).[28]

Ellice and Vaughan followed this up next day by routing Colonel Thomas Mytton near Longford. Mytton is said to have lost 245 casualties out of a force of 410 horse and foot. The Cavaliers lost very few besides Captain Crofts (25 March 1644). Nicholas Armorer, who had been Crofts' lieutenant in Ireland took over his troop. Little victories of this sort will have put money in the mens' pockets ; improved the armament of the regiment; given them some useful horses, and raised morale generally.

Vaughan's Regiment was with Prince Rupert in his 'Yorke Marche', and no doubt saw the storming of Bolton (28 May 1644) and the siege of Liverpool (7-12 June). At Marston Moor the regiment, perhaps 500 strong, was in the front line of the right wing under Lord Byron.

Vaughan was at Byron's attempt to recapture Montgomery Castle (18 September 1644), which resulted in disaster. Arthur Trevor in a letter to Ormonde wrote : 'Sir William Vaughan was the occasion of fighting the enemy in that place ; but as my Lord

Byron tells me, contributed not much to the action.'[29] Byron was not the one to confess to his own tactical blunders.

Vaughan's next enterprise was more successful. On 24 October he surprised Sir John Price at Welshpool, taking many prisoners.

Vaughan was now made 'General of Shropshire', and quartered his regiment in these garrisons :-

Shrawadine Castle	Commander: (Deputy Governor?): Dr Charles Vaughan, a parson and brother to Sir William.
Dawley House	Major Radcliffe Duckenfield
Lilleshall Abbey	Captain Henry Bostock, under Duckenfield
Caus Castle	Captain John Devilliers
Leigh Hall	Captain David Lloyd, under Devilliers
High Ercall	Captain Nicholas Armorer

Symonds, in October 1645 records that Davalier, as he calls him, 'tooke his troope to Ludlowe, and is now colonel'.[30] As the regiment still had seven troops at that time it is evident that Vaughan had raised another, though we do not know precisely when. This he gave to his brother, James, who had been his quartermaster in 1641.

On 27 November Sir William and his men robbed the Dolgellau drapers of '£140 in money besides commodities'[31]. No doubt this raid was typical of the activities that won him his nickname, and enabled him to pay and clothe his men. In consequence the regiment emerged from its winter quarters stronger than ever. At Leicester at the end of May it could muster 400 – the same number as Prince Rupert's which had long been the strongest in the Royalist Army. On his way to join the King he had beaten up some Shropshire horse near Wenlock (early May).

All seven troops, with about 28 officers, were probably present at Naseby. Five officers and one reformado were captured.

Lt. Colonel Henry Slaughter		
Captain George Hosier		Acting major
Lieutenant	Armstrong	
Cornet	Edmonds	
Quartermaster	Nurse	
Lieutenant	Billingley (sic)	Reformado[32]

51

Vaughan, who charged right through Ireton's wing, also figures in the list of prisoners, but by mistake. It was Colonel Henry Vaughan (1587?-1659?) who was taken[33]. We find Sir William commanding a brigade on 7 July.[34]

John Massy of Boughton, Cheshire, was killed at Naseby, serving as a trooper.[35]

Hosier, as we have seen, was a Shropshire man. As he was acting major Duckenfield must have been absent, presumably because his garrison, Dawley House, was beleaguered. Hosier must have brought a formed troop into Vaughan's regiment soon after he landed. That would account for his being senior to the other captains.

Despite the disaster at Naseby and the surrender (24 June) of Shrawardine Castle, Sir William was as active as ever. On 4 July he beat up the rebels at Bancroft Castle, taking 50 men and 86 horses. One of his garrisons, Caus Castle, fell on 23 June, but two days later the Colonel relieved High Ercall in gallant style. The Parliamentarian losses were put at 100 killed, and 350 prisoners, including Lt. Colonel William Reinking. Towards the end of August Vaughan pillaged and burnt Bishop's Castle. On 24 September the Regiment was in the defeat at Rowton Heath, but none of its officers can be identified in the list of prisoners.

In October 1645 the regiment still seems to have had seven troops under :-

{Colonel Sir William Vaughan
{Capt.-Lieut. Beverley Usher
Major Radcliffe Duckenfield
Captain John Bomer
Captain Nicholas Armorer
Captain James Vaughan
Captain   Dixie, *vice* Henry Slaughter, PW
Captain [Bartholomew] Brookes, *vice* Hosier, PW?

Duckenfield had abandoned Dawley House on 23 August 1645, and marched to join Armorer at High Ercall.

Dixie had risen from corporal to be cornet to Sir Thomas Lucas, who had stayed in Ireland, and then to be lieutenant to Slaughter. Slaughter never returned to the regiment after Naseby because he had the bad taste to change sides, engaging to serve

Parliament under Colonel John Booth.[36] He was still alive in 1663.[37]

Brookes was doubtless Bartholomew Brookes, who had been QM to Captain Henry Percy in one of His Majesty's Troops of Horse in 1641.[38]

Vaughan, now General of the Horse in Wales, Shropshire, Worcestershire, Staffordshire and Herefordshire, though defeated by Mytton at Denbigh on 1 November, managed to slip a supply of brimstone into Chester. He then retreated to Llanrwst, where he halted for five days to rest his men and horses, before marching via Newtown to Knighton. There on 13 November his party dispersed, Devilliers going to Ludlow and Vaughan himself to Leominster.

We next hear of Vaughan at Pembridge on 23 November, when, according to Webb, the Herefordshire historian, two of his regiments (troops?) were beaten up. However that may be, early in December he was ordered once more to attempt the relief of Chester. He managed to concentrate 500 horse and 600 foot, with whom he marched to Ludlow only to be refused admittance by the governor, Colonel Sir Michael Woodhouse.

Vaughan now heard that the Parliamentarians had occupied Wrockwardine with the intention of straitening High Ercall. Sir William fell upon them, and though he failed to take the church, burnt the village. High Ercall was relieved once more.

In January 1646 Lord Astley and Sir Charles Lucas came to Bridgnorth, where Vaughan, who had concentrated his forces at High Ercall, now joined them. The idea was to relieve Chester, but for some reason nothing came of it. Astley fell back to Worcester and Vaughan returned to the Welsh Marches. In February we find him raiding Clun, Presteign, and Leintwardine.

At the end of the month his regiment plundered Richard Jones of Trewern in the parish of Gladestry, Radnorshire, to the value of £400 or £500, including all his writings, and the very rings from his wife's fingers.[39]

Early in March Vaughan rejoined Lord Astley and was with him in his last fight at Stow-on-the-Wold (21 March 1646). Sir William narrowly escaped, but not without some wounds. An unidentified Captain John Bonner who is listed among the prisoners, may have been Vaughan's captain, John Bomer.

Armorer held out at High Ercall until 28 March 1646. His garrison, 212 strong, which on the testimony of its enemies were 'all good plucked, brave fighting men' was permitted to march to Worcester.[40] Most of them disbanded, but on 29 May 1646 Armorer had a company of 5 officers and 36 men in Colonel Henry Washington's Regiment of Foot and his troop, now only 17 strong, was one of five of varying size which made up the 224 horse of that garrison.[41]

Vaughan made his way to the Hague. In November 1648 Rupert gave him command of a ship, in which it seems he went to Ireland, and became major-general of the horse to Ormonde. He led a countercharge when Colonel Michael Jones surprised the Royalists at Rathmines, and died bravely at the head of his men, who, after his fall, could not be rallied.

Vaughan was a 'character'. Surprised by Sir Thomas Mytton while at prayer in Shrawardine Church, he bluffed the enemy into letting him go into the castle to order the garrison to surrender (13 October 1644). Needless to say, once inside, he did not emerge again. . . .

When on 17 May he met King Charles at Newport, Shropshire, he was travelling with his coach and six horses, his wife and other women, all with their portmanteaux furnished for a long march. No doubt his soldiers looked after themselves pretty well too – at the expense of the good people of Shropshire – and that is why his regiment managed to keep up its strength. Some helped Vaughan willingly enough. George Crosse of Ford, Shropshire, was accused of pressing men to serve against Parliament, supplying Shrawardine Castle with beer from Shrewsbury; plundering iron from the ironworks of Sir Thomas Middleton and General Mytton, and selling it for their own benefit. John Waring set out his son, John, in arms against Parliament.[42]

Rowland Morris of Montford, Salop. was in favour with Sir William's brother, Charles, and feasted him when he was governor of Shrawardine, as well as Captain Johnson, the captain of the dragoons. When the Parliamentarians approached he took refuge in the castle, and gave the Royalists intelligence. His son, Sylvanus, was one of the trained band, and his other sons were in arms at Wem.[43] It was men like these that helped Sir William to man and supply his garrisons.

Despite Marston Moor and Montgomery Castle Vaughan's regiment before Leicester was 400 strong. And he must have had nearly as many, horse, foot and dragoons holding his Shropshire strongholds.

On 21 June 1643 Colonel Sir William Savile wrote to his major, Thomas Beaumont, who was governor of Sheffield Castle : 'bee sure yow want not any mony nether for your selfe nor your frends, soe long as any Roundhead hath either fingers or toas left, within tenn myles of the Castle.'[44] This no doubt was the spirit in which the Devil of Shrawardine went to work. But at least it must be conceded that no Cavalier colonel was more successful in keeping his regiment up to strength.

OFFICERS UNDER SIR WILLIAM VAUGHAN

HORSE

Captain Thomas Fox	I. O. Montgom.
Lieut. Morgan Vaughan	I. O. Radnor
Captain Edward Jones	I. O. Salop
Cornet Thomas Wright	I. O. Durham
Captain George Hosier	I. O. Salop
Captain Dixy	
Lieut. William Sugar	I. O. Salop
Lt. Colonel Slater [Henry Slaughter]	
Lieut. Thomas Moon	I. O. L & W
Cornet William Ling	I. O. L & W
Cornet John Cotton	I. O. York
Cornet Thomas Sherwood	I. O. Somerset
Captain [John] Bomer	
Quartermaster Huntingdon Crosman	I. O. L & W
Quartermaster Alex. Shelton	I. O. L & W
Quartermaster John Newton	I. O. Chester
Captain Radcliffe Duckenfield	
Quartermaster Thomas Aston	I. O. Lancaster

FOOT

Captain Nicholas Armorer	
Lieut. Thomas Lingen	I. O. Salop
Ensign Fran. Thornes	I. O. Salop

The Cheshire Quarter Sessions Records preserve the names of two troopers of Vaughan's Regiment. One was Richard Wright of Roshterne who served under Colonel Henry Slater (sic) at Marston Moor and Ormskirk[45] (19 August 1644). The other was John Massy of Boughton whose widow, Bridget, a very poor woman, petitioned for relief after the Restoration. Massy had served as a trooper under Colonel Robert Werden and 'afterwards under Coll. Vaughan at the fight at Naseby where he was slaine.' He had bought horses and arms upon his credit and the persons to whom he was engaged did 'daily threaten to sue' the petitioner.[46]

SIR GEORGE BONCLE'S REGIMENT

This regiment was formed in 1643 by Sir Arthur Aston, who became governor of Oxford about August 1643. The regiment fought at the capture of Bristol and the first battle of Newbury. In October 1643 it was 200 strong.

Symonds saw the regiment at the Aldbourne Chase rendezvous (10 April 1644) and noted four standards, which were black with silver crosses engrailed.

The plain black cornet would be the colonel's. There were 120 men present at Aldbourne, but the regiment had probably left two troops on duty at Oxford.

A document of 26 September 1644 names the 'Officers of the Gouernours Regem". at Oxford :-

Lt, Colonel[George] Bunckle, (1616-1645), of Greenwich, but his father, John, was a Scot who came to England with James VI and I.
Major [Sebastian] Bunckle (1621-   ). Brother of Sir George.
Captain [Thomas] Stanton [Staunton]. Of Harringer or Staunton, Suffolk. Compounded on Faringdon Articles.
Captain [Michael]Trollop, (-1651), RC.
Captain [Edward] Armerye,[47] Ensign, 1640. II Foot. Probably from Kerry.

It is evident that the regiment comprised six troops, including Sir Arthur Aston's. Lt. Colonel Boncle led part of the Horse when Sir Henry Gage relieved Basing House (9-13 September 1644).

Aston, who had lost a leg due to a riding accident, resigned the governorship of Oxford in December 1644. Boncle, who had been his lieutenant-governor, was replaced though, by way of consolation he was knighted (30 January 1645). He had been created D.C.L. on 1 May 1644.

Neither de Gomme, Walker nor Symonds mentions the presence of Boncle's Regiment at Naseby, but it must have been present for Boncle himself was taken. It is more likely to have been in Northampton's than Howard's Brigade.

Boncle, who was according to Lloyd,[48] an 'Ingenious Gentleman and a good commander,' died in prison at Lambeth (13 August 1645). Lloyd attributes this to 'hard usage', but it seems there was 'a great mortality' at Lambeth that autumn.[49]

* * *

It is probably true to say that the units on the Royalist right were the pick of their horse, including, as they did, those with the best fighting records; well led and for the most part fairly well up to strength.

COLONEL THOMAS HOWARD'S BRIGADE

This Thomas Howard was the second son of Thomas 1st Earl of Berkshire. A captain in 1641 in the regiment of the general of the horse, Viscount Conway, he probably fought at Edgehill. He was commissioned to raise a regiment of 500 horse on 31 December 1642.[50] He raised many of his soldiers in Wiltshire, and seems to have operated largely in that county. He was with Prince Maurice at Lansdown (5 June 1643).

Howard does not seem to have been a brigadier for long. He commanded a brigade before Leicester and at Naseby and probably at Cheriton in 1644.

Symonds gives the composition of the brigade as it was at the end of May 1645.[51]

		Cornets
Samuel Sandys, Governor of Worcester	150	—
Thomas Howard	80	—
Thomas Leveson, Governor of Dudley Castle	150	3[52]
Richard Bagot, Governor of Lichfield	200	3[53]
Sir Robert Byron	100	—
Sir Henry Bard, under		
[George] Barker	100	—
Robert Werden, formerly John Marrow's	100	—
	880	

They were a mixed bag, for three at least having spent most of their time in garrisons, though maybe adept at raiding, can have been but little accustomed to manoeuvre with a large formation. However, this may not have been all that important for the brigade, employed to support Astley's foot, was organized in three more or less separate 'divisions'. One of these will have comprised three regiments, and the other two will have had two. The regiments were really the equivalent of troops, or perhaps squadrons.

Colonel Thomas Howard's Regiment was 300 strong on 10 April 1644,[54] and it is not to be supposed that it had lost 220 men in the interim. There is evidence that several troops were in Wiltshire at the time of the battle of Naseby. It is likely that one of Howard's field officers was with his other troops in Wiltshire.

The organization of the three 'divisions' was probably :

Colonel	Lt. Colonel	Major	Strength
Thomas Howard (1619-1706)	William Chamberleyne	Edward Nott	80
[Sir Robert Byron] PW	William Walton. K. (-1645)	John Lowick	100
[Robert Werden] PW (1622-1690)	Geoffrey Shakerley (1618-1696)	Cornelius Dewit	100
			280
Richard Bagot (1618-1645)	Harvey Bagot[55]	Will (Crab) Warner	200
Sir Henry Bard (c.1604-c.1660)	George Barker, Lincolnshire		100
			300
Thomas Leveson (-1652)	[Walter Gifford] PW February 1645	Christopher Heveningham	150
Samuel Sandys	Windsor Hickman	Thomas Wylde	150
			300

The military value of this brigade is hard to assess. Shakerley greatly distinguished himself at Rowton Heath. *Mercurius Aulicus* mentions several successful raids by Captain Christopher Heveningham. Symonds describes Bagot as the 'stout governor' of Lichfield. His major 'Crab' Warner was noted for his sour temper, which may only be evidence that he was a strict disciplinarian.

Sir Marmaduke Langdale commanded 1500 Northern Horse with the Royalist Army before Leicester at the end of May. They were then organized in two brigades under Langdale himself and Sir William Blackiston. The majority had shared in the fatal defeat at Marston Moor, but more recently had seen success at Melton Mowbray (25 February 1645) and at the relief of Pontefract Castle (1 March). A high proportion of the Northern officers were Roman Catholics.

On 5 February 37 of their officers had signed the 'Northern Horse Petition to goe Northward'.[56] They hoped that by invading the North they could raise fresh forces, and relieve the garrisons that still stood out for the King. Their native counties 'as valuable and considerable, as we conceive, as any other parts of your Majesties dominions,' lay 'enthralled under the pressures and insolencies of the enemy. . . .'

The feelings of the commanders of the Northern Horse are clearly expressed in this passage from their petition :

'And seeing that many of our soldiers are already wasted, and do daily moulder away, and that the main of our present strength consists of officers, gentlemen of quality, and their attendants, unmeet for these duties which are expected and required ; and that the loss of any of them is not small, but involves in it such multitudes as may, by their power and respect, be raised if they once approach their own habitations.' Under all the circumstances one can sympathize with their desire to show their colours in their home country, but although their victory at Pontefract enabled the castle to hold out until 21 July 1645 it brought them no great accession of strength. The recruits they got were sufficient to make up for their casualties : little more. Despite his success Langdale, instead of going on to attempt the relief of Scarborough or other fortresses rejoined Rupert near Chester.

Of the 37 signatories of the Northern Horse Petition the majority can be identified. Fortunately it was in those days customary to sign one's name legibly, and, with one exception, the names can be read without difficulty. Langdale himself,

feeling no doubt that he should refrain from any attempt to bring
pressure to bear on his sovereign, did not sign, nor did a number
of field officers, who were certainly present. The signatories seem
to have included :-

Colonels	14[57]
Lieutenant-Colonels	11
Majors	7
Captains	4
Captain-Lieutenant	1
	37

Four of the signatories cannot be assigned to any regiment.
At least 18 regiments are represented by one or more officers :-

1. Colonel Sir William Blackiston
   Lt. Colonel John Thornton
   Major Raphe Brandlinge?
2. Colonel George Wray
   Lt. Colonel Raiph Myllot
   Major Gilbert Markeham? or
   Major Raph Hodshon
3. Colonel John Forcer
   Lt. Colonel John Sayer
4. Colonel Sir Francis Anderson
   Lt. Colonel George Tonge
5. Colonel Sir William Mason
   Lt. Colonel Jo Gallard
6. Colonel Francis Hungate
   Major Adam Bland
7. Colonel Sir Phillip Monckton [Ex-Sir William Savile?]
   Captain Olevir ffletewood
8. [Colonel Francis Carnaby]
   Lt. Colonel Raynald Carnaby
   Capt.-Lieut. Raulfe Carnabye
9. Colonel Henry ffetherstonhaugh
10. Colonel Sir Francis Middleton
11. Colonel Sir Gamaliel Dudley
12. Colonel John Smyth
13. Colonel John Shallcross
14. Colonel ffrancis Melham
15. [Colonel Sir Marmaduke Langdale]
    Lt. Colonel Sir Robert Hildiard

16. [Colonel Edward Grey]
    Major Peregrine Palmer
17. [Late Colonel Thomas Howard]
    Major Willam Reueley
18. [Colonel Rowland Eyre]
    Captain Howard Brocke

To these we must certainly add the regiment of Colonel Sir John Gerlington, who was to fall in the operation the petition recommends. In addition the correspondence of Sir Samuel Luke, the Parliamentarian Scoutmaster-General, has something to say about the Northern Horse. On 25 February Colonel Lydcot, after a brush with them, wrote: 'The party were at least 1,500. Some of our scouts took two of them from whom I got intelligence that they are all Northern men. They were quartered all this Winter near Salisbury, their officer in chief is Sir M. Langdale. The following colonels were under him, Col. [John] Errington, Col. Forcer, Col. Mason, Col. Baxton [Blackiston], Col. Carnaby's brigade consisting of 3 or 4 colonels more.'[58]

Next day Luke passed on this news to the Earl of Essex. 'Those forces which went from Banbury towards Newark prove to be the broken forces belonging to the Earl of Newcastle which have wintered near Salisbury and are belonging to Sir M. Langdale's brigade under these colonels, Wayne, Errington, Farrer [Forcer], Mason, Baxton [Blackiston], with Carnaby's brigade consisting of three or four colonels more, which are to recruit themselves in the North and to relieve those places in danger by our forces.'[59] The information in this letter is clearly taken from Lydcot's of the previous day, so it is not clear why Luke should have added Wayne to the list of colonels. There was no such officer. Perhaps he meant Sir John Mayney, but none of the regiments the latter commanded in 1644 seem to have been with the King in 1645.[60] We should certainly add John Errington to the list of colonels.

It is not possible to say with any certainty how Langdale's score of regiments were brigaded. It is not altogether unlikely that Langdale, who came from the East Riding, had a brigade of Yorkshiremen, with the handful from Lancashire and Derbyshire for good measure. Blackiston, who was from Northumberland, may well have commanded the men of Northumberland and Durham.

We may safely assign Sir Phillip Monckton to Langdale's Brigade, for he commanded it at Rowton Heath (24 September). Indeed it seems likely that the two 'divisions', into which Langdale's Brigade was formed at Naseby, were led by Monckton, and Sir Gamaliel Dudley, who had been Sergeant-Major-General of Dragoons in Newcastle's Army in 1643, and had commanded a brigade of horse at Corbridge (19 February 1644).

It is no more than an hypothesis, but, if there is anything in it, a possible organization could have been :-

LANGDALE

Colonels
Sir Marmaduke Langdale
Sir William Mason
Francis Hungate
Sir Phillip Monckton
Henry ffetherstonhaugh
Sir Francis Middleton
Sir Gamaliel Dudley
John Shallcross
Francis Melham
Rowland Eyre
Ex Sir John Gerlington

BLACKISTON

Sir William Blackiston
George Wray
John Forcer
John Errington
Francis Carnaby
Sir Francis Anderson
Ex-Thomas Howard?[61]
William Smyth
Edward Grey

As we have seen, Luke, writing on 25 February, described Carnaby as a brigadier, and he was certainly a senior colonel. He had been one before Adwalton Moor (30 June 1643), where he was wounded. George Wray, a colonel by September 1642, was perhaps the senior colonel of those that came from Northumberland and Durham. He and Carnaby seem the likeliest candidates for the command of 'divisions'. Carnaby was probably second-in-command to Blackiston, whose wound near Monmouth in September 1644, would have called for a colonel taking temporary command of the brigade.

With not less than 20 regiments combining to make a strength of 1,500 it is clear that few of the regiments amounted to more than a strong troop. Forcer's, formerly Sir Robert Clavering's, which had missed Marston Moor, was probably much stronger than the average.

The four bodies in which the Northern Horse were formed at Naseby must each have comprised the remnants of four or five regiments. According to Sprigge's map each 'division' consisted of two squadrons and few of these can have comprised a single regiment. We may suppose that Sir Robert Hildiard, Lt. Colonel John Thornton and Major Thomas Craithorne led squadrons, but most of the squadron commanders will have been colonels.

In theory a Royalist regiment had seven troops, each with four officers. In practice, however, the number of troops varied, and so we dare not assert that Langdale had 560 officers among his 1,500 followers at Naseby, for casualties would not necessarily have been replaced. On the other hand there were now quite a number of infantry officers serving as troopers. The front rank of the brigades of Langdale and Blackiston, drawn up three deep, probably consisted entirely of officers and gentlemen.

Several of the officers, who were with the Northern Horse in February, became casualties before the battle of Naseby was fought :-

Colonel Sir John Gerlington	K. Melton Mowbray	25 February
Captain Gascoigne	K. Melton Mowbray	
Colonel John Shallcross	PW Pontefract?	
Captain Will Redmaine	K. Pontefract, 21 March	
Colonel John Forcer	PW Evesham, 25 May	
Lt. Colonel John Sayer	SW Nr. Naseby, 13 June	
Forcer's Regiment		

Among the infantry officers who now rode with the Northern Horse were :

Colonel Sir Thomas Blackwall
Colonel Henry Chaytor (1617-1664)
Colonel Sir Timothy ffetherstonhaugh
Colonel Sir Richard Hutton (-1645)
Lt. Colonel Richard Atkinson of Whixley. Sir Henry Slingsby. F.
Lt. Colonel Michael Pemberton (1615-1652)
Ensign John Hett. I.O. Durham

The last two named had belonged to the regiment of Cuthbert
Conyers, who was slain at Malpas (26 August 1644).

To sum up there were two brigades of Northern Horse
under Langdale and Blackiston, and the former commanded the
left wing as well as his own brigade. The brigades were each
divided into two bodies or 'divisions', each about 375 strong, and
each comprising the remnants of four or five regiments. Three
of the 'division' commanders were almost certainly Sir Gamaliel
Dudley, Sir Phillip Monckton, and Francis Carnaby. The fourth
may well have been George Wray. It is emphasized that these
conclusions are to a certain extent hypothetical.

How good – or how bad – were the Northern Horse?
Clearly it would have been simpler to handle them had they been
remodelled into a single brigade of, say, five regiments. It is not
easy, for lack of evidence, to tell which were the best regiments,
and which were not so good. Certainly it was not the Northern
Horse that lost Marston Moor : all had done brilliantly at Pontefract. All we can say is that there were some very resolute and
distinguished officers among them. These included the two
brigadiers, Langdale and Blackiston ; Sir Gamaliel Dudley ; Sir
Phillip Monckton, Sir Francis Monckton, Sir William Mason,
Sir Robert Hildiard, and Francis and Raynald Carnaby. No
doubt, could they speak, these officers could tell us which of their
friends and followers bore the heat of the day. The Northern
Horse were a hard-bitten crew, nearly as dour as their leader,
Langdale. They lacked only the troopers to follow them.

SIR HORATIO CAREW'S REGIMENT

In 1642 Sir Horatio Carew of Crockham, Somerset, was
major to Sir William Waller in the Parliamentarian Army, and
commanded the 14th Troop of Horse in Essex' Army.[61] He was

probably with Waller at Edgehill, and he was certainly with him at Chichester in the following December.

In the following June Carew changed sides, and on 29 September his regiment, 100 strong, was assigned to Hopton's Army.[63] He is said to have received a dangerous wound at Cheriton.[64] However that may be he was commanding a brigade at the rendezvous at Aldbourne Chase on 10 April 1644. This formation had been commanded formerly by Lord John Stuart, who had fallen at Cheriton. The first regiment of this brigade is described by Symonds as 'S^r. Horato Carys wch was ye Ld. John's Reg'.[65] No doubt, however, the remnants of Carew's own troops were absorbed in the same unit.

For some reason both regiment and brigade passed to the Earl of Cleveland, who commanded them until he was taken at Second Newbury. The explanation is probably that Carew's Cheriton wound disabled him for active service during the summer of 1644. The regiment was 200 strong in September 1644,[66] precisely the same strength that it had at Leicester in May 1645.

Carew survived Naseby and was commanding a brigade of horse which went to Oxford when Rupert surrendered Bristol in September 1645.[67]

On 10 April 1644 the troop commanders of Carew's Regiment were :-

1. Colonel Sir Horatio Cary
2. Lt. Colonel John Fleetwood
3. Major Agmondisham Pickhay
4. Captain   Bennet (-1645). Killed near Oxford 30 May 1644.[68]
5. Captain   Clarke
6. Captain   Barber.

Which, if any, of these troop commanders were at Naseby, is not known.

Coll. Sir Horatio Cary (L & W) appears in *A List of [Indigent] Officers, 1663* under Prince Rupert. He was in the Second Civil War.

THE KING'S LIFEGUARD

The King's Lifeguard, which consisted of two troops and mustered 130 at the siege of Leicester, was classed as a regiment;

indeed on the day of battle it was apparently the largest in the whole army, with 500 horsemen in its ranks. That is not to say that it was the most effective, for gallants and courtiers, who were prepared to hazard their persons with it in action, were not the sort of men, who would deign to exercise with the Regiment, and learn to ride, knee to knee, in rank and file.

For the first three years of the war the commander of the Regiment was Bernard Stuart, Earl of Lichfield (1623-1645), who had been commissioned Captain-General of all His Majesty's Horse Guards at Boconnoc on 20 August 1644. The major of the Regiment was Sir Edward Brett, the captain of the Queen's Lifeguard, who had been knighted in the field for his gallantry during the pursuit of Essex' Army from Lostwithiel to Castle Dore (31 August 1644). The other officers included :-

King's Troop
Capt.-Lieut. Sir Troilus Turbervile, RC. Killed 'at His Majesties going from Newark to Oxford'. 1645[69]
Cornet: (Sir) John Walpole, knighted 31 July 1645.
Quartermaster Thomas Sheldon, PW, Rowton Heath. I.O. Warwick under 'Earl of Lichfield'.
Queen's Troop
Captain Sir Edward Brett
Lieutenant
Cornet:
Quartermaster John Deale. I.O. L & W

By 23 September the organization of the Regiment seems to have changed. It was now about 200 strong and had four troops :-

The King's
The Queen's, Sir Edward Brett, Major of the Regiment.
Earl of Lichfield's, Lt. Colonel [James] Gourden, a Scot.
Sir Henry Stradling's[70]

Richard Symonds, who was himself one of the Lifeguard, tells us that Lichfield's troop were 'most Scotts officers', and that Stradling's came from Carlisle, which surrendered on 25 July, with Sir Thomas Glemham. Stradling was not long in the Regiment for he was taken at Rowton Heath (24 September). Rowton Heath was, indeed, a bad day for the Lifeguard. Lichfield was slain, his quartermaster, Sheldon, taken along with about 20

66

gentlemen of the King's own troop.[71] Captain St. Michael, who wore the Queen's scarf, was another prisoner. No doubt he was a Frenchman (St. Michel), as were a number of her officers. He had been in the Queen's Regiment of Foot,[72] but perhaps by this time he was a reformado. He may even have acted as Lieutenant to Sir Edward Brett.

The Lt. Colonel Gordon, who was taken at Sherburn-in-Elmet (15 October 1645) was probably the commander of Lichfield's troop.

Individuals who served in the regiment included :-

Sir Peter Browne, Oxfordshire.	Knighted 2 November 1644. MW & PW Naseby. RC.
Sir Edward Cooper.	Gentleman Pensioner. Knighted 20 December 1645.
Gosnal [Rob. Gosnold]	Stradling's troop[73]
Edward Heath[74]	K.B. 23 April 1661 ⎰Sons of Sir Robert
John Heath[80] of Brasted, Kent.	Knighted 27 May ⎱Heath of Cottesmore
	1644 Rutland.
Minor (Mynors)[73]	
Sir Henry Wroth[73] & [75]	Gentleman Pensioner. Knighted at Hereford, 6 September 1645. Of Durance, Middlesex. Compounded on Oxford Articles.
Sir Rob Wynde[76]	Gentleman of the Privy Chamber. Of Terrington, Norfolk. Compounded on Oxford Articles.

Gosnal, Mynors, Symonds and Wroth distinguished themselves in the action at Huntingdon on 24 August 1645.

Richard Symonds, who seved in the Regiment throughout the campaigns of 1644 and 1645, is useful for its movements, but tells us all too little about its personnel.

The standard of the King's Troop was gules, with a lion passant, crowned or with DIEU ET MON DROIT for motto.

THE NEWARK HORSE

There were about 1900 or 2000 horse and dragoons in the garrison of Newark. A Parliamentarian, Richard Halter, reporting on 17 August 1645[77] credits the Newarkers with 1500 horse and 500 dragoons. When in October the new governor, Lord Belasyse, remodelled the garrison, he kept 800 under Major-General Anthony Eyre and a troop of 100 gentlemen volunteers under Colonel Marmaduke Darcy.[78] He sent away 1000, 'being the worst', to Lichfield. The implication is obvious. For one reason or another about half the Newark Horse did not pass muster. Perhaps they were ill-armed or ill-mounted; perhaps their training and discipline did not come up to standard. It would be strange if some at least of the 800 Newark Horse, led by Eyre and Colonel Edward Villiers at Naseby, were not among those dismissed by Belasyse. At least a dozen regiments were in the garrison of Newark at one time or another :-

Colonels

Maurice Baud (-1645)
Sir Peregrine Bertie
Sir Charles Dallison
Sr Robert Dallison
Ralph Eure
Sergeant-Major-General Anthony Eyre
John Frescheville
John Heron
Late Richard Neville (-1644). Ex-Sir John Henderson.
Charles Leeke (-1645)
Late Sir William Pelham (-1644)
Roger Molyneux
Edward Villiers (1620-1689)
Sir Richard Willys (1614-1690)

Presumably Willys took his men with him when he returned to Newark, but all the others may have been represented. The casualties included :

⎰Sergeant Major General Eyre	W	
⎱Lt. Colonel Ralph Pudsey	K	
Colonel Maurice Baud	K	
Major Thomas Eyre	MW	Colonel Roger Molyneux
Major Charles Wilson	K	Sir Peregrine Bertie's Regiment

In addition a Captain King was taken, but one cannot be sure whether he belonged to Sir Robert Dallison or Sir Peregrine Bertie's Regiment.

It seems likely that Eyre's force at Naseby consisted of 800 horse drawn from a dozen regiments, none of which was anything like up to strength. It may be that some of these horse compared

68

but ill with Cromwell's 'Ironsides' or Rupert's Lifeguard, but there were gallant men among them: Anthony Eyre, Villiers, Lt. Colonels William Rolleston (Ralph Eure's Regiment), and Charles Wheler to name but a few.

Field Officers of the Newark Horse

Colonel	*Lt. Colonel*	*Major*
Anthony Eyre, W. (1612-1672)	Ralph Pudsey, K. (-1645)	
Edward Villiers (1620-1689)		
Maurice Baud K. (c.1606-1645)		
Sir Peregrine Bertie	Sir Charles Bolle Skipwith	Charles Wilson, K.
Sir Charles Dallison		John (?) Chappel
Sir Robert Dallison	Valentine Brown or Vavill	Thomas Heron
Ralph Eure	William Rolleston	Mansford
John Frescheville (1606-1682)	Sir Henry Hunloke	Jack Jammot
John Heron		
Charles Leeke (-1645)		
Roger Molyneux	William Whitchcot	Thomas Eyre, MW (-1645)
Late Richard **Neville** (**-1644)**		Trevor ?
Late Sir William **Pelham** (-1644)	William Booth	Scrop e
[Sir Richard Willys (1614-1690)	William Willys (1615-1676)	Sir Richard Hatton]

APPENDIX A

TROOPS SENT FROM DUBLIN BY ORMONDE

The first contingent, 2500 foot, embarked on 11 November, sailed on the 16th, and landed at Mostyn, Flintshire, on the 18th. It consisted of three regiments of foot under:

Sir Michael Erneley,
Sir Fulk Hunckes,
Richard Gibson.

The second contingent, 1500 foot, landed at Neston, Wirral, on 6 December 1643. It consisted of the regiments of:

Sir Robert Byron,
Henry Warren.

All five of these regiments suffered severely at the battle of Nantwich on 25 January 1644.

The third contingent consisted of 1800 foot and 300 horse. The foot were the greencoat regiments of:

Robert Broughton,
Henry Tillier.

The horse were Sir William Vaughan's Regiment.

They sailed from Dublin on 3 February 1644 and landed at Neston on the 7th.

APPENDIX B

LETTERS OF CAPT. JOHN DEVILLIERS AS GOVERNOR OF LEIGH HALL

1. 'October, 1644. To the Constable of Stockton. You are required to send me on Friday morning, at six of the clock, four men with hand barrows, and pitchforks, on payne 2s. for every man that refuseth to come.
Dated at Lee, this present Wednesday.' – John Devilliers.

2. Received of John Phillips, of Stockton, the sum of 27s. in part payment of the last month's contribution. – J.D. October 1644.

3. 'These are in his Majestie's name to will and command you to bring into my Garrison of Lee Hall, on Monday next, for the wicke's provision beginning ye 22nd of November, being Friday, as agreed by ye Gentlemen of ye County, as is mentioned in this warrant; viz :- one quarter of beef, one side of mutton, three strikes of oates, two of rye, fourteen pounds of cheese, seven pounds of butter, one cuple of pultry, and in money 5s. which if you refuse you may expect my coming to fetch it, for which this shall be my warrant this 19th of November. – J. Devilliers.

4. To the Petty Constable of Walcott and Stockton. 'In regard that I was fully resolved to send unto the severall townes within the whole divisions to fech in my whole contributions both for this month and the remaynder that was behinde

70

for last month, upon further consideration and ye request of ye High Constable and other gentlemen of the Countrey, I will forbeare, and give you tyme till Thursday next, to bringe itt in : otherwise I will forbeare no longer, and if any mischeife befall you by my soldiers in going forth, you must blame yourselves for itt, and stand ye perill. Given under my hand ye 26th of November. John Devilliers. – You the said Constables of Walcott and Stockton, to returne ye names of ye refusers, and ye somme.

5. 'I doe require Mr Harris to bring in on Wednesday, from Harris's house,

	£	s.	d.
October	3	7	0
November	1	15	0
December	4	15	0
January	4	15	0
February	2	5	0
March	2	5	0

'If you bringe not this money to-morrow morning, and ye provisions in arreare, I assure you I will not stay longer.

John Devilliers

LETTERS FROM LEIGH HALL WRITTEN BY DAVID LLOYD, GOVERNOR UNDER DEVILLIERS, THEN GOVERNOR OF CAUS CASTLE

'To the Constable of Stockton, This is to certifie you that I returned a warrant from the hand of ye Right Worthy *Captain* Devilliers, Governor of Lee Hall, whereby I am to certifie you, that if you come not in between this and Monday next, to bringe in your accounts, and do bringe in your arrears, if not, he threatens to burne all ye bookes, and to make you all pay anew, and so I remaine your loving friend,

David Lloyd. Lee Hall,
23rd January 1645

To the Constable of Stockton. This is to let you knowe that I have received a warrant from the Worshipful Captain John Devilliers, whereby you are required to impress one teame, and five workmen out of ye township. and then to send them to Lee Hall, this day, being this instant, yesterday being ye 3rd of March, and then to labour as directed ; this faile not at your perill, and bringe meate for ye same, and spades, and pickaxes.
Your loving friend.
David Lloyd.

To the petty Constables of Stocken (Stockton), Walcott, and Chyrbury, and to every one of them. These are in his Majesty's name strictly to will and requir of you, and every of whom these may concerne (by virtue of his Majestie's warrant to me directed) to all men within your liberty from the age of sixteen to threescore, to be all ready with what armes you can gett to attend me upon the next summons; furthermore you are to give warning to all ye inhabitants of your several Constable's weeke that they bringe noe money or provisions into any of the rebell's Garrisons. And upon any approach to them made, you are to give present notice thereof to his Majestie's next adjoyneinge Garrisons, as also you and every one of you with your forces are to ayde and assiste any of the partyes that shall oppose any partye, or partye reseting them. and whereas I am informed by the Governors of his Majestie's Garrisons here in the County of Sallop, that upon the goinge with any of his Majestie's partyes, you doe suddenly rise in arms, and ring bells and the like — these are certifie you, that if henceforth you offende in the like nature that such towne or townes soe doeinge shall be burnte and sett on fire. All which our pro-clammation, you and every one of you are to take special notice att your perills.

Given under my hand at the Garrison of Cause Castle, 29th Maye, 1645. John Devilliers.[79]

APPENDIX C

SIGNATORIES OF THE NORTHERN HORSE PETITION, 5 FEBRUARY 1645

LEFT COLUMN

Sir Ty. ffetherstonhaugh,[80]	RC. Of Kirkoswald, Cumberland. Colonel. F.
Robt. P. [illegible]	Lt. Colonel?
Sir Robert Hildiard (1611-1684)	Of Beverley. Lt. Colonel to Langdale
John forcer	RC. Of Kelloe and Harbour House, Durham. Colonel *vice* Sir Robert Clavering (-1644). RC. Considered by Langdale to be very reliable
He: ffetherstonhaugh[80]	(-1651) Of Kirkoswald. Colonel *vice* Sir Richard Dacre (-1644).
John Sayer	RC. Lt. Colonel to Forcer
Will Brooke	Lt. Colonel?

John Thornton (-1674)	RC. Of Wilton Castle. Lt. Colonel to Blackiston of Felling, Northumberland
Raphe Brandlinge	Major to Blackiston?
Raiph Myllot	RC. of Whitehall and Mayland, Durham, Northumberland. Lt. Colonel to George Wray.
Sir ffrancis Middleton	Lancashire
Adam Bland	RC. Of South Cave, Yorkshire. Major to Francis Hungate. Married Sir John Gerlington's widow.
Tim: Calverley (1605-)	Of Eriholme, Yorkshire. In Newark at the surrender. Captain.

CENTRE COLUMN

Sir Gam: Dudley	SMG. D. Colonel. HD.
Sir Francis Anderson (1614-1679)	Of Newcastle. Colonel. Considered by Langdale to be very reliable (1656).
ffra: Hungate (-1645)	RC. Of Saxton and Nunburnholme, Yorkshire. Colonel *vice* Sir Walter Vavasour, c.3 May 1644
John Smyth	RC. Eshe, Durham. Colonel
Phill: Monckton (1622-1679)	Of Cavil, Yorkshire. Colonel (*vice* Sir William Saville, 1644?)
Willm. Reueley (1621-1645)	RC. Major. Late Thomas Howard.
George Tonge (1617-)	Of Denton, Durham. Lt. Colonel to Anderson.
Gilbert Markeham (-1645)	Captain or Major. Possibly in George Wray's regiment.
Jo: Gallard (-1651)	Lt. Colonel to Sir William Mason.
Willm Tompkins	Lt. Colonel?
J[oseph] Naylor	Of Fanshaw, Leeds. Major.
Ho[ward]: Brocke[81]	Of Brough, Derbyshire. I.O Captain. Rowland Eyre's Regiment.

RIGHT COLUMN

Sir W[illiam] Mason[82]	Colonel Knighted 28 March 1645, presumably for the relief of Pontefract.
Sir Will. Blackiston (c.1621-1692)	Of Archdeacon Newton. Colonel and brigade commander.
Jo: Shallcross	Of Shallcross, Derbyshire. Colonel and High Sheriff of Derbyshire.
Oleuir ffletewood	Captain. Late Sir William Saville. Later under Monckton?

73

Geo Wray	Fourth son of Sir Nicholas Wray of Yarm. RC. Lemington, Northumberland.	
ffrancis Melham (-1660)	RC. Of Elslack, Yorkshire.	
Raph: hodshon [alias Hudson] (-1645)	Related to the Myllots. Major, possibly to George Wray.	
Henry Sotheby	Of Thoralby, Yorkshire. Lt. Colonel? Withdrew from the King's Army, Nov. 1645.	
Raynald Carnaby (1620-1657)	Lt. Colonel to Francis Carnaby. Considered by Langdale to be most reliable (1656).	
Peregrine Palmer (1605-1684)	Of Stogursey, Somerset. MP for Bridgwater, 1669. Major to Edward Grey, who was himself in Pontefract Castle.	
Will Redmaine (-1645)	Of Thornton-in-Lonsdale. Eldest son of Sir John Redman.	
Raulfe Carnabye (-1662)	RC. Halton, Northumberland. Capt.-Lieut. to Francis Carnaby.	

APPENDIX D

FIELD OFFICERS OF THE NORTHERN HORSE, 1645

Colonels	Lt. Colonels	Majors
Sir Marmaduke Langdale	Sir Robert Hildiard	Michael Constable
Sir William Mason	Jo: Gallard	
Francis Hungate	John Vavasour	Adam Bland
⎰Sir Phillip Monckton	Matthew Wentworth	John Beversham
⎱Ex-Sir William Saville	(1622-)	
Henry ffetherstonhaugh	Francis Carre?	
Sir Francis Middleton		
Sir Gamaliel Dudley	William Thompson?	Richard Sherborne (-1649)
John Shallcross		
Francis Melham		
Rowland Eyre[83]		
Sir John Gerlington	William Middleton	[John Watson]
Sir William Blackiston	John Thornton	Raphe Brandlinge?
George Wray	Raiph Myllot	⎰ (Raph hodshon [Hudson]? ⎱ or (Gilbert Markeham?
John Forcer	John Sayer	Thomas Craithorne
John Errington		
Francis Carnaby[84]	Raynald Carnaby	Thomas Carnaby
Sir Francis Anderson	George Tonge	Samuel Davison (1616-1671)

[Ex-Thomas Howard]		William Reueley
John Smyth		
[Edward Grey]	Fran. Carre	Peregrine Palmer
Sir Richard Tempest?	Sir Fran. Liddell?	

1 Diary, p. 181.
2 Symonds. Harleian MSS. 986.
3 Diary, p. 223.
4 Diary, p. 245.
5 Captain Nicholas Armorer's Troop of Sir William Vaughan's Regiment.
6 Symond's Diary, p. 258.
7 Rushworth, III, II, 308.
8 Vol. I, p. 153.
9 Bellum Civile, p. 102.
10 Bellum Civile, p. 83.
11 Diary, pp. 146 and 181.
12 Bellum Civile, pp. 60 and 61.
13 Symonds, p. 181.
14 *A List of [Indigent] Officers, 1663, ff.* 93 and 95.
15 Symonds, p. 277.
16 *Mercurius Aulicus*, p. 1222.
17 C.A.M. 1435.
18 p. 1364.
19 NLW Chirk, F. 7442.
20 Rushworth, Part I, pp. 153-4.
21 Cottesloe MS.
22 Presumably 2 Trumpeters and a Farrier, but what was the fourth? A saddler perhaps.
23 HMC Ormonde, I, p. 146
24 From Captain Povey's Troop. Collins, an Irishman and a plunderer, cornet to Captain James Vaughan, was killed at Myddle, Salop (Shrops. Arch. Soc. II Series, Vol. 7, p. 137, quoting Richard Gough's "Antiquities and Memoirs of the parish of Myddle.") There was a QM Thomas Lynaker in the Marquis of Winchester's Foot *(A List of [Indigent] Officers,* 1663, coln. 146.)
25 HMC Ormonde, I, p. 147.
26 HMC Ormonde, New Series, I, 72.
27 He had been Cornet to Captain Thomas Pinchbeck in Lt. General Sir John Conyers' Regt; and in Ireland to Captain George Villiers (Cottesloe MS, and Symonds' Diary, p. 255).
28 The Articles are No. CCIV of The Ottley Papers.
29 Carte's Collection of Original Letters, I, p. 64.
30 Symonds, p. 255.
31 Parry's Royal Visits and Progresses, p. 356.

32 Probably one of the Shropshire Billingsleys.

33 Peacock, pp. 98 & 100. Also D.N.B.

34 Worcester. Prince Maurice to Prince Rupert.

35 Cheshire QSR.

36 After his capture at Naseby he was taken to London, and afterwards sent on parole to Halton Castle, Cheshire. He compounded for his delinquency and was fined £130 on 10 March 1646 (CCC 1121).

37 Cheshire QSR.

38 Cottesloe MS.

39 Rev. J. Webb. Civil War in Herefordshire, Volume II, p. 265.

40 John Vicars: Burning Bush Not Consumed. 1646.

41 Diary of Henry Townsend. II, 112 and 113.

42 CCC 879.

43 CCC 1816.

44 Beaumont Papers, p. 74.

45 Hilary 1662. Chester 13 January 1662/3. Nos. 133 and 143.

46 Epiphany 1661/2. No. 143.

47 Mrs Aston Stackhouse: Garrisons of Shropshire.

48 The Papers of Captain Henry Stevens, Oxfordshire Record Society, 1962. Edited by Margaret Toynbee, p. 32.

49 *Memoirs* (1668), p. 689.

50 Lysons *Environs of London: Surrey*, p. 273.

51 B. M. Harl. 6852, f. 1.

52 Diary, p. 182.

53 On 15 May Symonds noted these three cornets of Colonel Leveson's, belonging to Dudley Castle:
'Sable, an ostrich or, holding in its mouth a sword proper, and standing on a scroll with the motto HOC NUTRIOR.
Vert, with a charge somewhat like a sun in splendour.
A scroll with the letters SA – SA. (Diary, p. 168).
Sa, Sa meaning *Kill, Kill!* was the warcry of the Imperialists in the Thirty Years War.

54 Blue cornets without any badge, motto or distinction. (Symonds Diary, p. 172).

55 Howard's cornet was green (Symonds. Harleian MSS, 986, f. 85).

56 He was lieutenant-colonel of both his younger brother's regiments, horse and foot. He had probably been left in command at Lichfield.

57 The present writer was permitted to copy this document on 19 July 1963. Warburton's transcription of the signatures is far from accurate.

58 One, Sir Timothy ffetherstonhaugh, was a colonel of foot.

59 Tibbutt, p. 462.

60 Tibbutt, p. 165.

61 cf. The Diary of Sir Henry Slingsby, p. 123.

62 Howard fell at Adwalton Moor, and we do not know who was his successor.

63 Their signatures, written in a copybook schoolboy hand, are practically identical.

64 Brocke was the only one of the 37 signatories to claim as an indigent officer, which is perhaps an indication that they were men of property.

65 His name is written level with Anderson's.

66 There is no evidence that he was present in person.

67 This regiment had been 200 strong at Marston Moor.

68 Peacock, p. 48 and 50.

69 B.M. Harl. MS. 6804, f. 224./171.

70 John Adair. *Cheriton 1644: The Campaign and the Battle*, p. 192.

71 Harl. 986, f. 86.

72 Symonds' Diary, p. 102.

73 C.S.P.D., 1645, p. 142.

74 Symonds' Diary, p. 7.

75 *Mercurius Rusticus.*

76 Symonds, p. 242.

77 Symonds, p. 243.

78 Lieutenant John Livermore (L & W) is listed under him in *A List of [Indigent] Officers* (113).

79 Symonds, 231.

80 CCC 1471.

81 CCC 1567.

82 CCC 1475.

83 H.M.C. Portland, I, 253.

84 Moone, 390.

Chapter Five

THE ROYALIST REGIMENTS OF FOOT

SIR BERNARD ASTLEY'S TERTIA

DUKE OF YORK. Redcoats

THE REGIMENT WHICH had the young Duke of York, the future James II (1633-1701), for its colonel, had come over from Ireland, landing no doubt at Bristol. Symonds notes that it 'lay at Marlborough a full Regiment' at the time of the rendezvous at Aldbourne Chase (10 April 1644), and notes two of its colours. Its commanding officer was Lt. Colonel Sir William St. Leger, who fell at II Newbury (27 October 1644), and who was succeeded by Theodore Kirton.

The establishment of a regiment was 1200, but the biggest regiment of the 12 garrisoned in Reading in April 1644, was Sir James Pennyman's with 479 officers and men, so by that period of the war 500 or 600 would have passed for a full regiment. There is no evidence that the Regiment suffered heavily between April 1644 and June 1645, though it must have suffered some casualties in Cornwall and at Newbury. It was still strong enough to form a body on its own at Naseby.

The officers taken were:

Captain	Fitzmorris, [Acting major]
Captain	Widnam
Captain	Hill
Captain	Dier
Capt. Lieut.	Hawksworth [The Duke of York's Company]
Lieut.	Rosley or Rossey
Lieut.	Carles, or Carlys (Carlos?)

Lieut.	Ryley
Ensign	Bennet or Bunch
Ensign	Rosley
Ensign	Young or Goring
Ensign	Bradshaw

Lt. Colonel Theodore Kirton was in the defence of Bristol in September, so he evidently escaped. The regiment had at least seven companies, for Sprigge notes the capture of the Duke of York's standard, and six of his colours. It is, of course, quite possible that the companies averaged 70. It seems more likely that there were eight or 10 companies, and that at least another dozen officers were present, whose fate is unknown.

The Indigent Officers' list is not particularly helpful for this regiment. Under Sir William St. Leger it lists Lieutenant Richard Mountayn of Captain Hill's company. Hill, as we have seen, was taken at Naseby.

Under the Duke of York we find

Major Rich. Woodward	L & W
Capt. James Roche	L & W
Capt.-Lieut. Edm. Gayton	Oxon
Ens. Hen. Crook	L & W. Maj. Kirton's company
Ens. Geo. Sewell	L & W Cap. Peaker's company

It is unlikely that Woodward, Gayton or Crook was at Naseby. One of the lists of PW states that Capt. Fitzmorris was acting major. There was only one captain-lieutenant and that was Hawksworth. Had Crook still been in the regiment he would have described Kirton as lieutenant-colonel. It is quite likely that Captains Roche and Peaker, and Ensign George Sewell were at Naseby. It is not impossible that Peaker died there, but this is mere speculation.

SIR EDWARD HOPTON. Redcoats

The regiment was raised by Allen Apsley (1616-1683),[1] most of whose officers came from the West Country. Apsley himself was a captain in February 1643 in Sir John Byron's Regiment of Horse, before being commissioned to raise a regiment of Foot. At some time after the Cornish campaign, but before December 1644 the Regiment passed to Edward Hopton, because Apsley had been sent to the West Country, where he became Governor of Barnstable.

Hopton, knighted (4 June), for his gallantry at the storming of Leicester, was wounded at Naseby. It may be that W. Woodhouse, who was taken prisoner was his lieutenant-colonel,[2] but his regiment as a whole does not figure in the lists. It is as unlikely that all his officers were killed, as that they all escaped. The lists are simply deficient.

SIR RICHARD PAGE'S REGIMENT

This was the oldest regiment in the Royalist Army. It was raised in Yorkshire by Sir William Pennyman (1607-1643) in 1642, and on his death (22 August 1643), passed to his cousin Sir James Pennyman (1608-1679). On 27 November 1644 Sir James Pennyman told Richard Symonds the names of the company commanders, who were :-

> Colonel Sir James Pennyman[3]
> Lt. Colonel George Symms[3] Major in 1642, Marske, Yorkshire.
> Major Will. Wyvell, Yorkshire[3] (Captain in 1642) d. 1643
> 1. Captain Richard Page 'now Leift:Colonel, Nov. 1644'
> 2. Captain Francis Lawson, Lincoln.
> 3. Captain William Bridges, 'a scrivener in Chancery Lane, Knighted at Leicester.'
> 4. Captain Francis Bateson, Yorkshire
> 5. Captain John Jackson, Yorkshire.
> 6. Captain Anthony Norton, Yorkshire.
> 7. Captain George Etherington, Yorkshire.
> 8. Captain Robert Carington, Yorkshire.

The three field officers seem to have left in the winter of 1644-1645 and Page, Lawson and Bridges ruled in their stead. Page and Bridges were both knighted for their part in the storming of Leicester.

This Yorkshire regiment was clearly a good one, for in 1642 it was one of the four that made up the garrison of Oxford, which was evidently chosen from among those that had fought best at Edgehill. With 479 officers and men it was the strongest regiment in the garrison of Reading in April 1644, and, despite casualties in the campaign that followed, it was still strong at Naseby. It may be that it had absorbed some smaller regiment and so kept up its strength.

At Aldbourne Chase on 10 April 1644 Symonds noted that the regiment had ten colours, nine of which were green, and one silver. The latter, no doubt, belonged to a company from some other regiment ,which had been amalgamated with Pennyman's.

De Gomme's plan shows the regiment forming one of the nine bodies of foot, on its own, and as no less than 20 of its officers are listed as prisoners we may conclude that it was still some 500 strong. There were still at least nine companies :-

Colonel Sir Richard Page	PW
Lt. Colonel Francis Lawson	MW and PW
Major Sir William Bridges	PW
Captain Francis Bateson	PW
Captain Anthony Norton	PW
Captain George Etherington	PW
Captain Robert Carrington	PW
Captain John Simpson	PW
Captain Pearson	PW

The other officers taken were :-

Lieutenants	Allan Sartan, L & W
	John Eggleston, Durham[4]
	Pilkington
	Bates
	Roundtree
	Flexney or Floynee[5]
	Ballard
	Roberts
Ensigns	Etherington
	Andr. Lengo. York. Capt. Anth. Northon's company
	Scot.

BARD'S TERTIA

SIR HENRY BARD'S REGIMENT. Greycoats

The Regiment was one of two formed in 1643 from commanded men from the Yorkshire regiments of Newcastle's Army, who had escorted a convoy of ammunition to Oxford. The first colonel was Thomas Pinchbeck, who was buried at Oxford on 28 January 1644. He had been mortally wounded at I Newbury. The regiment fought at Cheriton and Symonds who saw it on

10 April 1644 drew 5 of its colours, and noted that it had marched out of Oxford 176 strong on 7 April (Harleian MS. 986). It may be that this figure did not include officers. Bard's and Percy's regiments marched with the Train of Artillery. Presumably their musketeers were armed with firelocks.

In the 1644 campaign the regiment served in Colonel Thomas Blagge's tertia.

The regiment was apparently stronger in May 1645 than it had been in April 1644. It spent the winter 1644/1645 at Campden House in Gloucestershire, and Symonds tells us that when it marched away with the field army it was 300 strong.

At least four of its colours were among the trophies taken at Naseby. The prisoners included:

Captain	Lesley
Captain	Devolet
Capt. Lieut. John Lawson,	I. O. Northum
Lieut.	Fowler
Lieut.	Twifield
Lieut.	Windsor
Ensign	Dobyson
Ensign	Fairbrother

One would suppose that there were several other officers, including two or three ensigns to carry the colours that were taken, and a field officer to command the regiment in Bard's absence. It is probable that several of the officers were killed, and it is not impossible that one or two got away.

THE QUEEN'S LIFEGUARD. Redcoats

This Regiment, probably of 10 companies, was raised in 1643, and came south with the Queen. Its field officers were Colonel Lord Jermyn, Lt. Colonel Richard Gerard, and Major Rhys Thomas[6] (c.1602-1645). It formed part of the garrison of Oxford for many months, and detachments took part in the relief of Basing House and other exploits.

Though Thomas was promoted colonel, Richard Gerard was still serving in 1646, from which it would seem that the original regiment had been divided so as to form the cadre of two units. It is not unlikely that Thomas, who is thought to have

been the fifth son of Sir William Thomas of Aber, Caervarvon-
shire, had built up his new unit in Wales.

Sprigge[7] tells us that four of the Queen's colours were taken
at Naseby, from which we may suppose that at least four companies, each about 50 strong, were present. Colonel Thomas is
thought to have served abroad before the Civil War, and so his
selection to command a new regiment is understandable. Sprigge
has a story of his cruelty when trying to enlist some of the prisoners taken at Leicester.[8] He was killed at Naseby, and his
brother, Lt. Colonel Thomas, was taken. Who the other company commanders were is uncertain, for the Regiment is not in
the lists of prisoners. However, two captains appear under 'Rice
Thomas' in *A List of [Indigent] Officers*.[9] They are Edward Barry
and James Edwards, both from Glamorgan. Captain St. Michel
taken at Rowton Heath, had also belonged to this Regiment.

John Hughes, W and PW at Naseby says he was under
Colonel Rhys Thomas, Major Wynne of Llanvair near Ruthin
and Lt. Humphrey Gethin when he received his wound.[10]

A tentative list of company commanders then would be :-

Colonel Rhys Thomas	K (1602-1645)	
Lt. Colonel Thomas	PW	
Major Wynne of Llanvair, Denbighshire		
Captain St. Michell,	PW Rowton Heath[11]	
Captain Edward Berry, Glamorgan		
Captain James Edwards, Glamorgan		

COLONEL RADCLIFFE GERARD'S REGIMENT

This regiment had been part of the garrison of Worcester.
Raised by Sir Gilbert Gerard in Lancashire in 1642, the regiment
fought at Edgehill. In May 1643 it had nine companies. Its
colours were probably blue, as the arms of Gerard were 'Azure,
a lion rampart ermine, crowned or'. . . .

Sir Gilbert Gerard became Governor of Worcester where he
died, being succeeded (c. 27 Jan. 1645) by his lieutenant-colonel
and twin, Radcliffe. The latter had three sons, Radcliffe, John and
Gilbert, all of whom, we are told, served in the regiment.

The whole regiment was not at Naseby. At least three of

its captains had been taken at Evesham when it fell on 25 May 1645; and a detachment under Captain Edward Asheton, was in garrison at Madresfield; which he surrendered basely in 1646. It seems that Worcester provided a contingent, perhaps no more than 100 strong, to reinforce the marching army.

1. Colonel Radcliffe Gerard, of Barton, Lancashire
2. Lt. Colonel Richard Bishop   PW Naseby
3. Major Gilbert Houghton   Major 27 Jan 1645, (d. 1661)
4. Capt. William Booth   PW Naseby
5. Capt.   Gerard[12]   PW Evesham
6. Capt.   Young[13]   PW Evesham
7. Capt. William Stanley   PW Evesham. I.O. Middlesex
8. Capt. Edward Asheton   Governor of Madresfield
9. Capt. Hugh Floyd   I.O. Carmarthen (Radcliffe Gerard)

It is highly improbable that more than five companies were at Naseby, those of the three field officers, Captain Booth and, perhaps, Captain Floyd.

The officers taken were but four in number :-

Major Bishop. Really Lt. Colonel w.e.f. 27 Jan. 1645
Captain Booth
Ensign Bland, or Blancy [Blaney?]
Ensign Perrin

Richard Bishop regained his liberty in time to take part in the defence of Worcester in 1646.

After the disasters at Evesham and Naseby there can have been little left of Gerard's Regiment, though he himself survived to be taken prisoner along with Lord Astley on 21 March 1646 at Stow-on-the-Wold — the last battle of the First Civil War.

SIR WILLIAM RUSSELL'S REGIMENT

This regiment belonged to the garrison of Worcester. It was raised by Sir William Russell of Strensham, who had been the first Royalist governor of that city. Its lieutenant-colonel, Davies, was killed at Naseby, which may be taken to argue the presence of a small contingent marching no doubt, with the men of Colonel Radcliffe Gerard's Regiment.

84

On 29 May 1646 at the beginning of the siege of Worcester the regiment still had seven companies, and numbered 319 officers and men. One Goffe or Gough, who had succeeded Davies had 6 officers and 42 men in his company.[14]

Except for the death of its lieutenant-colonel there is no evidence that Russell's Regiment played any part at Naseby.

SIR JOHN OWEN'S REGIMENT

John Owen (1600-1666) was commissioned in September 1642 and raised his regiment in North Wales. At Culham Camp on 23 May 1643 it had eight companies. It was at the storming of Bristol, where Owen was severely wounded; the siege of Gloucester and both battles of Newbury, as well as taking part in the Cornish campaign of 1644. Symonds preserved a 'State' of the garrison of Reading for April 1644[15] which shows that by that time there were only four companies in the regiment. It follows that the officers of the remaining four had returned to North Wales to act as the cadre for a new regiment, which Owen was to form there.

Owen, who was knighted at Oxford on 17 December 1644, returned to North Wales, was promoted major-general, and appointed governor of Conway. His original regiment was taken over by Lt. Colonel Roger Burges, an excellent officer, who after defying Cromwell at Faringdon Castle, had the misfortune to be taken at Naseby. He reappears later in the defence of the Channel Islands.

The regiment does not figure in the lists of prisoners, but de Gomme shows it united with Colonel Radcliffe Gerard. It was probably 200-250 strong and organized in four or five companies. There is evidence[16] that the company commanders were :-

Lt. Colonel Roger Burges
Major Hugh Hookes, of Conway
Captain John Brynkir of Brynkir,   Captain *vice* his brother William,
                                     K. I Newbury
Captain Richard Thomas,
Captain Rowland Vaughan   (c. 1590-1667)

Vaughan, who came from Caer Gai, Merioneth, was a celebrated Welsh scholar, poet and translator. He had been High

Sheriff in 1643 and a Commissioner of Array, and is said to have fought at Naseby.[17] He was afterwards to translate *Eikon Basilike* into Welsh, dedicating it:

'To his honourable Colonel, Sir John Owen, knight, and eternal joy is the wish of his unworthy soldier. R.V.'

The names of a few of the soldiers, who served in the regiment at Naseby have been preserved amongst the Caernarvonshire and Denbighshire Quarter Sessions Records:

		Company
John Griffith ap Hugh	W & PW	
Robert Owen	W	Hugh Hookes
Thomas ap Richard Owen	PW	Capt. Hugh Hookes
John Williams		Major Hugh Hookes
		and
	W & PW	Capt. Richard Thomas
Edward Ellis		Capt. John Brynkir

Hugh ap Edwards of Llanasaph, co. Flint, served for four years in Owen's Regiment, was wounded at Leicester, taken at Naseby, carried to Lambeth House and banished. He afterwards became a sea soldier under Sir Edward Broughton.

RICHARD BAGOT'S REGIMENT

When on 21 April 1643, Prince Rupert captured Lichfield he made Richard Bagot (1618-1645) its governor. He belonged to an important local family,[18] had fought at Edgehill as a captain in Colonel Richard Bolle's Regiment of Foot, and was known for his courage. Bagot immediately began to raise regiments both of horse and foot.

Richard Symonds names some of its officers :-

{Colonel Richard Bagot, third son of Sir Harvey
{Capt. Lieut. Ralph Swift
Lt. Colonel Harvey Bagot, second son of Sir Harvey
Major   Cooper [1643]
Major Roger Harsenett 1644
1 Capt. [Anth.] Dyott. Barrister. Eldest son of Sir Richard
2 Capt. [Will] Baderley (sic)
3 Capt. [Thomas] Glasier. Chorister at Lichfield [Cathedral]

It appears that at first the regiment only had six companies.

In a later marginal note Symonds adds that in January 1644[5], it was 400 strong, which would mean an average of about 65 to a company.

On 17 May Colonel Bagot joined the King's Army with 300 Foot and 200 Horse; a valuable reinforcement, which left Lichfield with 200 foot, at most, and 100 horse. Symonds tells us that Bagot's foot colours were 'Azure, a mullet or, on a canton a cross.'

By 11 October 1645 there were eight companies though the eighth consisted only of two officers and six other ranks. These were, it seems, the cadre of a company of citizens who did guard duty in the garrison, but were not on the pay-roll. In June the regiment had for active service seven companies: 21 officers. Of these four were at Naseby, where eight officers and one reformado were taken. They were:

> Capt. Anthony Dyott
> Capt. Thomas Glasier
> Lieut. Alexander Ward
> Lieut.   Baggeley
> Lieut.   Cowper, Reformado
> Ensign   Sharpe
> Ensign Rob. Blencarne [Blenkhorne. Dyott's company.]
> Ensign   Emmins
> Ensign   Thomas

Four of its colours may be identified amongst the trophies. Lt. Colonel Harvey Bagot, being no doubt well-mounted, was not among the prisoners.

After the battle Harvey Bagot set to work to rebuild his dead brother's regiment. He himself became colonel, but Major Harsnett was not promoted lieutenant-colonel. Dyott and Glasier were not replaced, presumably because Bagot hoped to exchange them. Three of the Naseby captives were back with the regiment by 11 October. They were Lieutenant Baggeley (Bagaly); Ensign Rob Blenkhorne and Ensign Emmins. Perhaps they were exchanged. More likely they were young, active and enterprising and managed to elude their escort before they got to London. By 11 October Blenkhorne was a lieutenant.

At that time the officers were:

Colonel Harvey Bagot		
Major Roger Harsnett (d. 1693)		
Captain Anthony Dyott		PW
Captain Will Baduleye		
Captain Thomas Glasier		PW
Captain Ralph Swift		
Captain	Benskin	
Captain Zachariah Turnpenny		Citizens' Company
[Captain-]Lieutenant Francis Collier		Later captain
Lieutenant Timothy Startin		In prison at Nantwich.
		Later Capt.-Lieut.
Lieutenant Mich. Est (or East)		
Lieutenant	Bagaly (Baggeley) [20]	
Lieutenant John Stow		
Lieutenant	Burden	
Lieutenant	Robinson	Turnpenny's company
Lieutenant Rob Blenkhorne[20]		Dyott's company
Ensign Rich. Walmsley		
Ensign	Emans[20]	
Ensign	Butler	
Ensign [Francis] Fisher		Brother of Sir Clement
		Fisher of Packington,
		Warwickshire
Ensign	Sharpe	PW
Ensign	Thomas	PW
Ensign	Pyott	In prison at Nantwich
Ensign	Stanford	Newly joined

Although Bagot had not replaced Dyott or Glasier, Lieutenant Ward was evidently not, for some reason, expected to return: his place had been filled. Perhaps he had been badly wounded.

Stanford had probably been commissioned very recently for whilst the other officers received a fortnight's pay on 11 October, he was only paid for one week. Perhaps he had only just reached military age. Francis Fisher, too, was very young, for he was under age in 1642.

The accounts of Lichfield Garrison for October 1645 still exist.[21] They show that at that time two of the officers were prisoners at Nantwich:

Lieut. Timothy Startin	
Ensign	Pyott

By order of Lord Aston and the other commissioners Startin's wife, Anne, was given £7.00 towards their relief. Where and when they were taken does not appear, but as they were incarcerated at Nantwich they had probably fallen into the hands of Sir William Brereton's men.

When on 11 October the regiment was paid the companies varied greatly in strength.

	DM	S	D	C	S	Pages	TOTAL
Colonel Bagot	1	2	1	3	52	5	64
Major Harsnett	—	2	2	3	69	5	81
Capt. Dyott	—	2	2	2	64	1	71
Capt. Baduleye	—	2	1	2	31	3	39
Capt. Glasier	—	2	1	2	31	2	38
Capt. Swift	—	2	1	3	77	4	87
Capt. Benskin	—	4	1	3	73	4	85
Capt. Turnpenny	—	1	1	—	—	4	6

471[22]

The strength, including officers, was now 489, which means that, despite Naseby casualties – perhaps as many as 300 – the Regiment was apparently stronger that it had been in January 1645, when it will be recalled, Symonds made it 400. Few Royalist regiments can have been growing at this stage of the war, but the reason must be that the garrison of Lichfield was still being paid. Under the circumstances it would not be strange if diehard Cavaliers from other regiments or garrisons listed under Harvey Bagot.

Most of the officers were Staffordshire men: the Bagots, Dyott, Glasier, Turnpenny, Startin, East, Blenkhorne, Walmsley and Pyott to name but a few. Ensign Stanford sprang from a family which had branches in Staffordshire and Warwickshire. Ensign Fisher was certainly Francis, younger brother of Sir Clement Fisher, 2nd Bart.[23] of Packington Magna, Warwickshire, who was related to the Bagots by marriage and who compounded on Lichfield Articles.[24]

Beyond question, this was a Staffordshire Regiment, and some of the officers came from families of some importance: Bagot, Dyott, Fisher and Stanford. There was musical talent too! Michael Est (1580?-1680?), a very elderly subaltern, was a composer and had long ago been made choir-master (c.1618) at Lichfield Cathedral. Glasier and Turnpenny were also members of St. Chad's choir.

Under 'Sir Richard Bagott' and Harvey Bagott *A List of [Indigent] Officers, 1663* names sixteen officers of the regiment of whom 12* claimed as indigent:

L & W	Captain Will. Bodeley*	Richard Bagott
	Captain Hugh Henne	" "
Stafford	Lieut. Mich. East*	" "
	Capt. Anth. Dyott	" "
Stafford	Lieut. Rob Blenkhorne*	" "
	Capt. Zach. Turnpenny	" "
Stafford	Ens. Zach. Bakewell*	" "
	Captain Fran. Collier	Harvey Bagott
Salop	Ens. Ralph Buckeridge*	" "
Stafford	Capt. Lieut. Timothy Startin*	" "
Stafford	Lieut. Rich. Walmsly*	Richard Bagott
L & W	Lieut. Tho. Wadeson*	Harvey Bagott
Stafford	Ens. Walter Petty*	Richard Bagott
York	Ens. Jam. Byrd*	Harvey Bagott
Stafford	Q. Joh. Bilks*	Harvey Bagott
Stafford	Q. Tho. Horsman*	" "

COLONEL THOMAS LEVESON

This was the garrison of Dudley Castle, which seems to have contributed, not only a regiment of horse, but a handful of foot to the Naseby army. Under Colonel Lewsey (sic) three officers are listed. Of these one was the commander of the colonel's company, Captain-Lieutenant Parker. The other two were lieutenants Johnson and Cole. This was clearly a very small contingent.

LISLE'S TERTIA

COLONEL GEORGE LISLE

This regiment was raised by Lord Paget in Staffordshire in 1642. It had been in all the major operations of the 'Oxford Army'. It had eight companies in May 1643. Its first commander, Colonel Richard Bolle, (b. 1590) was killed in Alton Church on 13 December 1643.

For some reason Bolle was not succeeded by his lieutenant-colonel, Edward Littleton, though he had distinguished himself by his bravery at Bristol in July. George Lisle was brought in from outside.

In April 1644, the regiment had seven silver (white) colours, and was still 270 strong. At the time of Naseby there were still seven company commanders :-

Colonel George Lisle	W
Lt. Colonel Edward Littleton	MW & PW
Major Fowler	PW Captain at 23 May 1643
Captain Rob. Skerrow	PW I.O. L & W[25]
Captain Humphrey Whitgrave	PW I.O. Essex
Captain Rugely Littleton	PW I.O. Stafford
Captain Thomas Pocklington	PW I.O. L & W[26]

Lisle though wounded escaped to Leicester. One of the colours taken may possibly have been that of Lt. Colonel Littleton's company.

As to the numbers of the regiment one may suppose that it was still rather more than 200 strong. With nine officers taken prisoner it may possibly have been as strong as Bagot's or Bard's, that is to say about 300.

The subalterns captured were but three in number :

Lieutenant Carter	
Ensign Turpin	
Ensign James Littleton	I.O. Stafford [27]

The regiment seems to have been in the thick of the fighting and many of their comrades must have been amongst the slain.

CAREER OF MAJOR ROBERT SKERROW

			Colonel
	1640	Ensign	Sir Thomas Lunsford
11 December	1640	Discharged as a papist	
	1642	Ensign. Captain (Thomas) Throckmorton	Richard Bolle
23 October		Battle of Edgehill	
30 October		Lieutenant to Throckmorton	
April	1643	Defence of Reading	
23 May		Culham Camp. 4 Captain	
26 July		Storming of Bristol	
Aug.-Sept.		Siege of Gloucester	

20 September		I Newbury	
	1644	Captain	George Lisle
13 May		Mentioned in a warrant of Colonel John Penruddock	
29 June		Cropredy Bridge	
Aug.-Sept.		The Cornish campaign	
27 October		II Newbury	
14 June	1645	1 Captain. PW Naseby	George Lisle
	1648	Major	William Ayliffe
28 August		PW Colchester Prisoner in Windsor Castle	
	1663	Indigent Officer. L & W.	William Ayliffe

LATE COLONEL WILLIAM ST. GEORGE

Colonel St. George had been killed at the storming of Leicester on 29 May, and at Naseby his regiment may have been commanded by his major, Whitmore, who was taken. Little is known of the unit or its previous history. St. George may have been related to John St. George of Hatley St. George, Cambridge, who compounded for delinquency in arms (11 March 1647) being fined £625.

St. George was at Gainsborough in 1643 and, as there is no reference to his regiment ever serving in the Oxford Army it seems not unlikely that he had come with Sir Richard Willys from Newark.

The regiment must have had at least five companies, which argues a strength of not less than 150 officers and men. The officers taken were :-

> Major [Thomas?] Whitmore
> ⎰Captain Owen
> ⎱Lieut. David Jones. Hereford
> Captain Thomas Lorrayne. Northum.
> Captain Nicholas Lorrayne. Northum.
> Captain   Herne [Heron?]
> Lieut.   Nassey
> Lieut.   Jones
> Lieut.   Jones
> Ensign   Fenn

A Major Thomas Whitmore was killed in a sortie from Newark in 1646, when the garrison attacked the Scots at Muskham.[28] It seems not impossible that he was the same man that commanded St. George's Regiment at Naseby. Quartermaster Matthew Cartwright, I.O. York, appears in *A List of [Indigent] Officers 1663*,[29] but if he was at Naseby, he got away from the baggage train before the Ironsides arrived there.

COLONEL THEOPHILUS GILBY

This regiment was raised by John Belasyse in Nottingham-shire and Yorkshire in 1642. It fought at Edgehill and in the defence of Reading, and on 23 May 1643 at Culham Camp it had 10 companies. The regiment fought in all the major oper-ations of the 'Oxford Army'.

When, in the second winter of the war, Belasyse was com-manded northwards to assist the Marquis of Newcastle, the regiment was given to Lt. Colonel Theophilus Gilby of Everton, Nottinghamshire.

Its presence at Naseby is recorded by Belasyse's secretary,[30] Joshua Moone, and Richard Symonds tell us that it was in Lisle's tertia.

The three senior officers were all taken at Naseby :-

> Colonel Theophilus Gilby
> Lt. Colonel Francis Godfrey
> Major John Beverley. Of Great Smeaton, Yorkshire[30]

The last named had been a captain in May 1643, which shows that there had been a considerable number of casualties of one sort and another. But it would be odd indeed if the regiment now had only three companies, and those all commanded by field officers. However that may be there is no general list of prisoners belonging to this regiment.

A List of [Indigent] Officers[31] supplies the names of nine of Gilby's officers, but with the exception of the major, their pres-ence at Naseby cannot be proved, but that of Captain Francis and Lieutenant Rythe is very probable.

Lt. Colonel Sir Bartholomew Pell	L & W
Major John Beverly (sic)	—
Lieut. Charles Askew	York
Capt. Will. Marsh	Sussex

Capt. Martin Frobisher	Lincoln	
Lieut. Stephen Forster	York	
Capt. Matthew Francis	—	
Lieut. James Rythe	L & W	St. Martins-in-the-Fields. Son-in-law of Francis. Laid down his arms upon the surrender of Bristol[32]
Ensign Will. Kay	York	

Sir Bartholomew Pell had been made governor of Langford House, near Salisbury, Wiltshire, and so had left the regiment before Naseby. He surrendered to Cromwell on 18 October 1645, on rather indifferent terms, at the first summons.[33] He had perhaps been given his company as part of his garrison.

But if the regiment no longer had ten companies it would be very strange if it had sunk to three or even – including Captain Francis' company – four. Indeed it seems likely that Gilby's was the strongest regiment in the body which it formed with Lisle's and St. George's Regiments.

At Reading in 1644 Gilby's Regiment was 375 strong, and still had 10 companies. At this time Lisle had only 270 officers and men.

Gilby was not long in captivity for on 27 October 1645 he was knighted at Newark.

CAREER OF LT. COLONEL FRANCIS GODFREY

			Colonel
	c.1613	Born of a Norfolk Roman Catholic family	
Before	1639	Ensign in foreign parts	
	1640	Ensign. Captain John Waldgrave	Sir Thomas Glemham
11 December	1640	Discharged as a papist	
	1642	Captain?	John Belasyse
23 October		Edgehill	
April	1643	Defence of Reading	
23 May		Culham Camp. 1st Captain	
26 July		Storming of Bristol	
Aug.-Sept.		Siege of Gloucester	
20 September		I Newbury	

94

Winter	1643/4	Major *vice* Sir Barholomew Pell, on Belasyse leaving the regiment	Theophilus Gilby
29 June	1644	Cropredy Bridge Cornish campaign	
8 August		Signs letter to the Earl of Essex	
27 October		II Newbury Lt. Colonel *vice* Sir Bartholomew Pell	
14 June		PW Naseby	
	1658	His son Charles Godfrey (1658-1715) born. He became MP for Malmesbury	
	1688	Died	

His son, Charles Godfrey (1658-1715), married Arabella Churchill (1648-1730) sister of the great Duke of Marlborough (1650-1722), and Mistress of King James II. Brigadier-General Francis Godfrey (-1712), who fought at Oudenarde in command of the regiment, which became the 16th Foot, therefore, had two Cavalier grandfathers, the other being Sir Winston Churchill (1620-1688) who had been a captain in the Marquis of Hertford's Regiment of Horse.

THE SHREWSBURY FOOT

This unit, commanded by Colonel Smith, whoever he may have been, was made up of the survivors of regiments sent over by Ormonde from Ireland in the winter of 1643-1644. They had suffered severely at Nantwich, Marston Moor and Montgomery Castle. Smith was probably only a lieutenant-colonel.

Officers from five 'Irish' regiments were taken at Naseby :-

		Officers PW	*Approx. strength*
Colonel Robert Broughton.	Greencoats	9	200
Colonel Henry Tillier	"	8	200
Colonel Sir Fulk Hunks		3	
Colonel Henry Warren	Redcoats	2	100
Colonel Richard Gibson		1	
		23	500

95

Broughton's and Tillier's having missed Nantwich, were much stronger than the others.

Except for Colonel Smith the only field officer certainly known to have been present was Major Daniel Moore of Warren's Regiment, who was among the officers taken prisoner, but it is possible that Major Denn, who was taken, was captain Nicholas Deane, who came over from Ireland in Richard Gibson's Regiment.

When Rupert's Foot joined the King at Stow-on-the-Wold, on 8 May it was 1000 strong. The Prince's Regiment was 500 strong, and these Shrewsbury Foot made up the other 500. It is not unlikely that they, like Rupert's Bluecoats, were organized into 10 companies each approximately 50 strong.

If this is so the company commanders may have included:

		Regiment
Major Daniel Moore	⎫	Warren's
Captain Robert Berkeley	⎬	
Captain Hill	⎫	Broughton's
Captain [Hugh?] Polden	⎬	
Captain Church	⎫	Tillier's
Captain Dykes	⎬	
Captain John Cressy?[34]	⎭	
Major Nicholas Denn?		Gibson's

THE RESERVE

THE LIFEGUARD OF FOOT. Redcoats

The Regiment was raised in 1642 by Lord Willoughby d'Eresby, who had been a captain in the Dutch Army. He recruited his men from Lincolnshire, Derbyshire and Cheshire, and at least seven of his officers had seen previous service.

Lt. Colonel Sir William Vavasour,
Major William Leighton,
Captain Thomas Mynne,
Captain Thomas Leigh,
Lieutenant Edward Mackworth
Lieutenant John Cranfield,
Ensign Charles Fox

The regiment suffered severely at Edgehill, where Lord Willoughby and Vavasour were taken prisoner and Leighton was wounded.

In the following winter the Cheshire captains seem to have returned home, no doubt because of the threat to their homeland posed by Sir William Brereton. But the Regiment was now in garrison at Oxford and the University provided at least three officers: Captain Rob Levinz, a Fellow of Lincoln College; Peter Mews (1619-1706), St. Johns, and Rob Chamberlain (1619-   ) of Pembroke.

The regiment fought in all the main engagements of the 'Oxford Army' with the exception of the storming of Bristol.

On 9 May the regiment, according to Symonds, was 200 strong; Walker, however, says that at Naseby it numbered 300. The latter is the more probable figure for it formed a body on its own, and it still had 8 or 9 companies. The officers present included :-

Colonel	Montague Bertie, Earl of Lindsey[35] (1608-1666)	W
Capt.-Lieut.	Waller	PW
Lt. Colonel	William Leighton. DCL	
Major	Robert Markham	
Captain	Rob. Levinz DCL, MA (1615-1650)	PW
Ensign	Peter Mowshall. Warwick	PW
Captain	Charles Fox, MA	PW
Ensign	William Berkenhead. L & W	PW
Captain	Peyne Fisher. Sr., MA	PW
Captain	John Beeton, MA. I. O. Berks.	PW
Captain	Nicholas Bertie, MA (1621-1671)	PW
Captain	Rob. Johnson, MA?	—
Lieut.	Peter Mews, MA (1619-1706)	PW
Lieut.	Brown or Browne	PW
Lieut.	Humphrey Legh (fl. 1600-1670)	SW
Ensign	Porter	PW
Ensign	Ingoldsby	PW
Ensign	Wildhali	PW

It is not certain whether Lindsay or Leighton commanded the regiment at Naseby, Symonds seems to imply that the Earl was with the King's immediate entourage. Leighton and Markham got away : presumably they went into action on horseback.

Lieutenant Legh was left for dead, but somehow got away. He was Serjeant-at-Arms attending the Great Seal, and went to York in 1642. He was in all the battles where the King was present and served until the surrender of Oxford. He was alive in 1671 when he asserted that he had held his office for more than 50 years under nine Lord Chamberlains and Lord Keepers.[36]

Peter Mews, who was wounded nearly 30 times in the war, lived to become Bishop of Wells and of Winchester. He was to be in battle again, forty years after Naseby at Sedgemoor, where, at a critical moment, he moved some royalist guns with his own carriage horses, when their drivers had taken to flight. For this King James II rewarded him with a medal.

Charles Fox had been an ensign in Sir William Vavasour's Regiment in 1640. It may be supposed, therefore, that he was lieutenant of his former colonel's company in 1642, and that he succeeded to its command w.e.f. 14 June 1643 when Vavasour left the Regiment.

Payne Fisher was father of Cromwell's poet laureate, 'Paganis Piscator', (b.1616) who, as a major, led 300 of Sir Patricius Curwen's Regiment of Foot at Marston Moor, and being captured, changed sides.

Captain Nicholas Bertie, son of Sir Peregrine Bertie, KB., was first cousin to his colonel. Their grandfather was the 'brave Lord Willoughby'[37] of the ballad, who had so distinguished himself in Queen Elizabeth's wars in the Low Countries.

Rob Levinz' wife was a daughter of Sir Peregrine Bertie. He came to a bad end. Commissioned to raise troops in England, at the time of Charles II's Scottish expedition he was discovered, arrested, court-martialled as a spy. He was offered his life if he would betray his accomplices. This he refused to do. He acknowledged his own part in the plot, but protested the justice of his cause. He was hanged over against the Exchange on 18 July 1650. He was, according to Lloyd,[38] a man of prudence and integrity

It seems not unlikely that Ensign Porter was Philip, third son of Endymion (1587-1649), MP for Droitwich in the Long Parliament, and confidant of King Charles. Philip (born 1628) was imprisoned in 1654 for his part in a plot against the Protector, 'Otherwise', writes C. H. Firth, 'he is only heard of as a swashbuckler of the worst type.'[39]

William Leighton was knighted at Hereford in September 1645, and was there when it fell. Walker gives him the character of a vigilant and faithful commander. In 1648 he took part in the defence of Colchester. In 1654 he seems to have been serving the King abroad, and in 1656 and 1657 he was in the Swedish service. Leighton was in the Tower from May 1658 to February 1659, because of his part in a Royalist plot. His name appears in the *List of [Indigent Officers,]* published in 1663, but he was fortunate enough to be given a command soon after. On 17 March 1664 he was commissioned as captain in the King's Regiment of Foot [Guards][40] under Colonel John Russell, *vice* Colonel Henry Washington, deceased. This regiment was, in a sense, the successor of the Lifeguard in which he had served from 1642-1645, so it was an appropriate appointment. He did not enjoy this command for long as he retired on 18 October 1665; perhaps he was in poor health.[41]

There is a short history of this regiment in *Strangers in Oxford*.

PRINCE RUPERT'S REGIMENT. Bluecoats

With 500 men Rupert's was probably the strongest Royalist regiment present at Naseby. It was raised in Somerset in 1642 by Colonel Sir Thomas Lunsford with a cadre of officers and men, who had served under him in the Scots War of 1640-1641.

Sir Thomas was taken at Edgehill and succeeded by his brother Henry, who fell at the storming of Bristol. Rupert then took the regiment under his wing, giving the actual command to Lt. Colonel John Russell.

The Regiment fought at Bolton, the siege of Liverpool and Marston Moor, but after the vicissitudes of the 1644 campaign must have recruited well, probably in and around Bristol, during the following winter.

The regiment wore blue coats and had black and white colours of an unusual pattern. In 1645 Russell was still lieutenant-colonel and Major Mitchell was his second-in-command. There is no list of officer prisoners, but we know that Lieutenants

George Gery of Bushmead, Bedfordshire,[42] and Fisher, and Sergeant William Stoakes of Shepton Mallet were all taken. Stoakes' petition is printed in *Edgehill, 1642*. He had served throughout the war.

7 September	1642	Fight at Babylon Hill, near Yeovil
23 October		Battle of Edgehill
12 November		Brentford Fight
April	1643	Defence of Reading
26 July		Storming of Bristol
August-September		Siege of Gloucester. Promoted sergeant.
27 May	1644	Taking of Bolton
7-11 June		Siege of Liverpool
2 July		Battle of Marston Moor. 'many dangerous hurts'.
14 June	1645	Battle of Naseby. PW

Five of the colours taken at Naseby clearly belonged to Rupert's Regiment.[43]

No less than 25 of Rupert's officers besides two of Sir Thomas Lunsford's appear in the 1663 lists,[44] but in most cases it is difficult to say whther they belonged to the Bluecoats or to Prince Rupert's Firelocks, or at what period they were serving.

Rupert's Regiment seems to have been badly cut up at Naseby, as well as at Marston Moor.

COLONEL SIR THOMAS LUNSFORD

	Lieutenant	*Ensign*
Capt. [Valentine] Pine		John Hill, Denbigh

PRINCE RUPERT

Prince Rupert	Capt.-Lieut. Nich. Barker, L & W	
	Capt.-Lieut. Rich. Joyner, Kent	
Lt.-Col. [John] Russell	George Gery L & W[45]	
Major Æneas Lyne, L & W	James Hinane L & W	Mortaugh O'Donoghue
	Owen Carty L & W	
Capt. [Valentine] Pyne		William Pyne, Somerset

Capt. Gerard White, L & W
Capt. Tho. Nicholls, L & W
Capt. Rich. Basket, Wilts.
Capt. John Tilden, Monm.

Capt.	Gardiner	Roger Hillary, Dorset	Tho. Osborne, Salop
Capt.	Nelson	Matthew Howell, L & W	
Capt.	Baxter		Tho. Woogan, Worcest.
Capt.	Walwyn		Rich. Walwyn, Hereford
		John Sparrey, Worcest.	
			William Coningsby, L & W

It is, of course, possible that a number of these officers belonged to Prince Rupert's Firelocks.

Major Mitchell was with the Bluecoats, and so Æneas Lyne, whose officers were evidently all Irishmen, must belong to some other period, or possibly to the Firelocks, whose major, Bunnington, a gentleman pensioner, fell at the storming of Leicester. There is no evidence that the firelocks were at Naseby, but they were with Rupert when he marched out of Bristol. They were redcoats.

SIR MATTHEW APPLEYARD'S REGIMENT. Yellowcoats

The history of this regiment was similar to that of Sir John Paulet. Under Colonel Sir Charles Vavasour, Bart., it came over from Cork to Bristol in October 1643, and was sent by Hopton to take part in the siege of Wardour Castle. Here it mutinied, but Hopton, acting swiftly and suddenly, surrounded it in its quarters and strung up some of the ringleaders.

Vavasour died and was buried at Oxford on 1 March 1644. He was succeeded by Matthew Appleyard (c.1606 or 1607-1676), who distinguished himself at Cheriton and elsewhere, and was knighted at Leicester on 2 June 1645. Appleyard was not at Naseby, for he had been made Governor of Leicester. It is likely that most of his regiment was there with him, but four captains and four lieutenants were taken at Naseby. It seems likely that these officers led one of the bodies of commanded musketeers. They were :-

Captain John Tirwhytt, L & W
Captain George Masters
Captain   Sanderson
Captain   Hubbard[46]
Lieut.   Middleton
Lieut. James Thomson, L & W.   Lieut to Major [Giles] Palmer.
Lieut.   Lewen
Lieut.   Baker

Major Giles Palmer (1615-1665) of Compton, Warwickshire had estates there and at Charingworth and Quinton,
Gloucestershire.[47] He came of a very ancient Warwickshire
family, being the eighth son of John Palmer of Compton Scorfen,
by his wife, Eleanor Rouse. On 19 September 1650 he begged
leave to compound on the Articles of Oxford, alleging that he
had aided Parliament in Ireland for two years after the surrender
of Oxford and received no pay. He was nevertheless fined at $\frac{1}{5}$,
£1,236. 13s. 4d. The Latin scholars among you will enjoy
working out his Monumental Inscription in Ilmington Church.

EGIDIVS PALMER DE COMPTON ARMIG:
FILIVS 8^{vus} JOHANNIS PALMER ET ELEO-
NORAE ROVSE, OBIIT 16 DIE 8^{bris} ANNO
1665. ANNO AETATIS 50°. IN CVIVS ME-
MORIAM MAESTISSIMA VXOR ELIZABE-
THA FILIA HENRICI JONES DE CHA-
STETON IN COM. OXON. ARMIG. HOC
VLTIMVM AMORIS MONVMENTVM PO-
SVIT
Reliquit Superstises Johannem unicum filium,
tres filias, viz. Elizabeth am, Anne m, & Mariama
POSTQV AM HIC MILITIAM COMPLEVIS-
SET (IN REBELLES SCOTOS VEXILLARIVS
ANNO 1638. In REBELLES HYBERNOS
DVX ANNO 1642. IN REBELLES ANGLOS
DVX MAJOR ANNO 1645) PER GRADVS
MILITARES SVMMVM IN PATRIA HONO-
REM OBTINVIT.

Major Giles Palmer was probably at Leicester during the
battle of Naseby. In 1640 he had been the junior ensign *vexill-
arius*, aged 25, in Sir Charles Vavasour's Regiment, in which
Matthew Appleyard was Major.[48]

The regiment was raised by Colonel Richard Feilding in 1642, and fought at Edgehill. Feilding was cashiered for the surrender of Reading and his regiment was given to Sir Jacob Astley. In May 1643 it had eight companies.

In 1643 and 1644 the regiment campaigned with the main Royalist Army. At Aldbourne Chase (10 April 1644) it formed a body with Stradling's Regiment. Symonds noted five colours on this occasion – the colonel's, lieutenant-colonel's, first and second captains of Astley's and Colonel John Stradling's, which were argent. Astley's captains bore white cinquefoils on a blue field. In April 1644, Astley's was in the garrison of Reading, and numbered about 200, in seven or eight companies.

At Naseby only seven officers were taken : five captains (one Baskerfield, being a reformado), and two ensigns.

But it seems likely that by this time the ranks of the regiment were but thin, and Baskerfield may not have been the only reformado present.

The regiment is not shown in de Gomme's plan, from which it may be deduced that it was only represented by a body of commanded musketeers, and that the main body, presumably under its lieutenant-colonel, Thomas Conyngsby, was at Leicester. Conyngsby is *not* listed among those taken at Naseby, and he was with Rupert in the defence of Bristol in September 1645. It seems unlikely that he was at Naseby. The officers taken were :

Captain Isaac Walley	}	Both captains by 23 May 1643
Captain Jackson	}	
Captain Raphe Wright		Distinguished himself at Bristol 1643, as a lieutenant.
Captain	Fowler	
Captain	Baskervile, Reformado[49]	
Ensign	Ridley	
Ensign	Rowland	

Bennet, Corporal of the field, is also in the list, but he was no doubt an A.D.C. or galloper on Lord Astley's staff.

SIR BARNARD ASTLEY'S REGIMENT

The regiment was raised by the Marquis of Hertford in

1643. Barnard Astley (c.1610-1645) had then been its lieutenant-colonel. It had five green colours at the Aldbourne Chase rendezvous (10 April 1644). In the 1644 campaign it served in the third tertia, which was commanded by its colonel.

This regiment is not shown by de Gomme and may therefore have been part of the garrison of Leicester. The nine officers taken at Naseby may have been with the commanded musketeers supporting Rupert or Langdale. They were :-

Captain	Hoare,
Captain	Fisher,
Lieut.	Weller,
Lieut.	Simons,
Lieut.	Smith,
Lieut.	Harden,
Ensign	Chester
Ensign	Holmes
Ensign	Simmons or Symons

SIR JOHN PAULET'S REGIMENT. Yellowcoats

In October 1643 this regiment and Sir Charles Vavasour's sailed from Cork to Bristol, and marched to join Lord Hopton, who tells us that the two amounted to no more than 400 to 500 'bold, hardy men, excellently well-officer'd, verie mutenous'. . . . In a petition after the Restoration one of its veterans, Samuel Holton, a Wiltshire fel-maker, describes the unit as 'the oldest regiment of Irish yellowcoats.' It fought at Cheriton and was probably in Sir Barnard Astley's tertia throughout the 1644 campaign.

Hopton soon made Sir John Paulet 'his major Generall of foote' and who commanded the regiment thereafter is not quite clear. One Braket (Brocket?) was lieutenant-colonel in 1642, but whether he came to England with the regiment cannot be said. The major was John Pinchbeck, and he was with it at Cirencester on 23 December 1644.

Of eleven officers taken at Naseby only one was a captain. It may be supposed that several others were killed, but it seems more likely that the regiment was only represented by a party of musketeers, and it may be that some of the subalterns were reformadoes. The officers taken were :-

Captain	Mason
Lieut.	Birket or Birkwhit
Lieut.	Wynn
Lieut.	Hickman or Kirkman
Lieut.	Bradford
Lieut. John Barling. I.O. L & W to Cap. [William] Neve.	
Ensign	Yate
Ensign	Glascock
Ensign	Hutchins
Ensign	Price or Rise [Rice?]
Ensign	Cooke

Sir John Paulet (1615-1665) 'an old souldier' was, Sprigge[50] tells us, in Winchester at the surrender, 8 October 1645.

COLONEL WILLIAM MURREY

Murrey was with the Army in Cornwall in August 1644 and with Rupert at Bristol in September 1645, but the history of his regiment is obscure. There are indications, however, that it was the one which had belonged to Lord Percy, the General of the Artillery, who was dismissed in August 1644. This regiment, like Bard's, had been formed in 1643 from commanded men who escorted a convoy of ammunition from Yorkshire to Oxford.

At Naseby only five officers are listed as prisoners, and one of these was a reformado. Major Whitford was the only company commander taken, from which one may conclude that the regiment was a mere handful, possibly forming a body with Bard's, but more probably guarding the train. The five officer prisoners were :

Major	William Whitford (——c. 1652). A Scot.
Lieut.	Sneyles or Surles
Lieut.	Griffiths
Ensign	Higham
Ensign	Cecil, reformado

Lord Percy's officers included :

Major Henry Crompton[51] Lieut. Tho. Theobald (Suffolk)
Capt. David Whitford (L & W) Brother of Major William
Whitford?
Capt. Andrew Forrester. Lieut. John Steley (L & W)[52]

When the Roundhead clerk wrote down *Sneyles*, or *Surle*, one supposes that he should have written *Steley*.

We are, therefore, inclined to cast Murrey's as 'firelocks to guard the train'. The point is not of great importance for the regiment can hardly have been strong enough to influence the fate of the day.

Colonel Sir Henry Vaughan (1587?-1660) was taken prisoner at Naseby. He had been major-general under his nephew, Richard Vaughan, Earl of Carbery in Carmarthen, Cardigan, and Pembroke, but there is no evidence that he had a regiment at Naseby. He was brought before the House of Commons on 18 June and spent the next few years in the Tower and the Fleet. He was 'a right true blue', active and irreconcilable Royalist.[53]

He is sometimes confused with his son Colonel Sir Henry Vaughan the younger (1613-1676), who no doubt was the officer defeated by Cromwell at Bampton-in-the-Bush, Oxfordshire, on 27 April 1645. It may be doubted whether his regiment had survived that ordeal. The presence of his father cannot be taken as evidence that any part of it was at Naseby.

Captain Peter Leigh, who was taken at Naseby belonged to Anthony Thelwall's Regiment,[54] but it is not likely that a detachment was present for Thelwall was commanding 800 men at Chester. The regiment had been in Lisle's Tertia in 1644, and it may be that Leigh was still serving under that commander.

FIELD OFFICERS OF THE ROYALIST FOOT AT NASEBY

Colonels	Lt. Colonels	Majors	
[Duke of York]	Theodore Kirton	Captain	Fitz-morris (acting), PW
Sir Edward Hopton, W	W... Woodhouse. PW		
Sir Richard Page, PW	Francis Lawson, MW & PW	Sir William Bridges, PW	
[Sir Henry Bard]			
Rhys Thomas, K.	Thomas, PW	Wynne	
[Sir John Owen]	Roger Burges, PW	Hugh Hookes, PW	
Radcliffe Gerrard	Richard Bishop, PW	Gilbert Houghton, 27 January 1645	

George Lisle, W	Edward Littleton, MW & PW	Fowler, PW
[Late William St. George]		Thomas (?) Whitmore, PW
Theophilus Gilby, PW	Francis Godfrey, PW	John Beverley, PW

THE SHREWSBURY FOOT: (Lt.) Colonel   Smith

[Robert Broughton]		
[Henry Tillier]		
[Sir Fulk Hunks]		
[Henry Warren]		Daniel Moore, PW
[Richard Gibson]		Nicholas (?) Deane, PW
[Richard Bagot]	Harvey Bagot	[Roger Harsnett]
[Thomas Leveson]	John Beaumont	Simon Heveningham
[Sir William Russell]	Davies, K.	[Edmund Goffe]
Lifeguard of Foot	Sir William Leighton	Robert Markham
Earl of Lindsey		
[Prince Rupert]	John Russell	Dominic Mitchell
William Murrey		William Whitford

Those in square brackets were not with their regiments in person, though Rupert, Bard and Bagot were in the battle. It cannot be said whether the field officers of Bagot's and Leveson's regiments were present.

The regiments of Sir Matthew Appleyard, Sir Barnard Astley, Lord Astley and Sir John Paulet are not included as their main bodies were probably at Leicester.

WHEREABOUTS OF EDGEHILL REGIMENTS AT THE TIME OF NASEBY

Colonel/Regiment	Colonel in 1645	Location
Charles Gerard	Lord Gerard	South Wales
Sir Lewis Dyve	Sir Lewis Dyve	Sherborne Castle
Sir Ralph Dutton	Sir Stephen Hawkins	Oxford
Thomas Blagge	Thomas Blagge	Wallingford Castle
John Belasyse	Theophilus Gilby	Naseby
Richard Feilding	Lord Astley	Leicester, Detachment at Naseby
Sir Thomas Lunsford	Prince Rupert	Naseby
Richard Bolle	George Lisle	Naseby
Sir Edward Fitton	Anthony Thelwall	Chester
Sir Edward Stradling	John Stradling	South Wales?
The Lifeguard of Foot	The Lifeguard of Foot	Naseby
Lord General	Patrick Ruthven, Lord Forth	Woodstock?

Sir John Beaumont, later	John Godfrey (K. 1644)	Destroyed at Tewkesbury in 1644
Sir Gilbert Gerard	Ratcliffe Gerard	Naseby, Detachment at Madresfield.
Sir Thomas Salusbury	Sir Charles Lloyd	Devizes Castle
Lord Molineux		Probably disbanded
2nd Earl of Northampton	3rd Earl of Northampton	Banbury Castle
Earl Rivers	Sir John Boys	Donnington Castle

1 Knighted in 1646. Shaw, II, 221.
2 BM. Add. MS 18981.
3 Their promotions would have been with effect from 22 August 1643, the date of Sir William Pennyman's death.
4 He listed himself under Captain Mallory, but Sir William Mallory was buried at Oxford on 22 July 1643, and we are not told which company he was in thereafter. *A List of [Indigent] Officers*, 1663 (f.104).
5 What the Roundhead scribes thought this officer's name was is a mystery.
6 Roy, II, 281. On 28 August 1643 Thomas signed for spades, pickaxes and hoes for work on the fortifications at Oxford.
7 p. 40.
8 p. 51.
9 f. 128.
10 Caernarvonshire Quarter Sessions Records.
11 He had been in the Queen's Lifeguard in November 1643. (Roy, p. 307).
12 It is uncertain whether this is John Gerard or Radcliffe Junior.
13 There were two Youngs in the regiment. Gabriel, I.O. Surrey; and William, both listed under Sir Gilbert Gerard (f.54).
14 Diary of Henry Townshend, II, 99.
15 BM. Harleian MS. 986.
16 Norman Tucker. Royalist Officers of North Wales, 1642-1660, p. 32.
17 Tucker, p. 62.
18 Richard Bagot was third son of Sir Harvey Bagot, Bart., of Blithfield, Staffordshire (c.1591-1660), who was created baronet on 30 May 1627.
19 Harl. 986.
20 Taken at Naseby, but rejoined.
21 Lichfield Joint Record Office. Public Library, Lichfield.
22 It will be noticed that there was a slight shortage of corporals and drummers, but not of sergeants. This no doubt means that it was not easy to select new corporals after the heavy losses at Naseby. It is never easy to train drummers — at least not quickly.
23 Succeeded 1647= Jane Lane.
24 CCC 1793.
25 Listed as major under William Ayliffe under whom he served in 1648.

26 Listed under Richard Bolles (sic). *A List of [Indigent] Officers 1643*.

27 Listed under Richard Bolles (sic).

28 *Mercurius Rusticus*, 1647.

29 f.114.

30 C.C.C. 1077.

31 f.55.

32 C.C.C. 1715.

33 Sprigge, pp. 145/6.

34 PW at Nantwich, and again at Shrewsbury but present at Oxford in 1646.

35 Lord Willoughby had succeeded to the title on the death of his father, the Lord General, who was mortally wounded at Edgehill.

36 CSPD.

37 Peregrine Bertie, Lord Willoughby de Eresby (1555-1601).

38 Memoirs, 1668, p. 560.

39 D.N.B.

40 Now the Grenadier Guards.

41 *Strangers in Oxford*, p. 140.

42 I.O. L. & W. He belonged to Lt. Colonel Russell's Company. *A List of [Indigent] Officers*, f.112.

43 A brief history of *Prince Rupert's Bluecoats* by Lawson C. Nagel, was privately printed in 1973.

44 *A List of [Indigent] Officers*, f.112.

45 But really from Bushmead, Beds. (CCC 1558).

46 Hubbart in one list, and Huband in the other.

47 CCC p. 1853.

48 Peacock, pp. 82 and 83.

49 Given in one list as Basberfield, and in the other as Bakerfield.

50 Sprigge, 132.

51 Garrison Major at Oxford.

52 *A List of [Indigent] Officers*, f. 105 under Lord Henry Percy.

53 D.N.B.

54 I.O. Chester. *A List of [Indigent] Officers*, f.128.

Chapter Six

THE ORDNANCE

THE ROYALISTS TOOK the field with 12 brass cannon and two mortars. The guns were :-

Demi-cannon	2
Demi-culverin	2
Sakers	8

From surviving ordnance papers[1] it is possible to deduce the detailed breakdown of this train.

In the first place this number of guns required a numerous personnel. The following list is only approximate.[2]

Controller of the Trayne	1	[Captain Henry Younger?]
Controller's Clerke	1	
Gentlemen of the Ordnance	6	
Clerke of the Stores	1	
Quarter Master	1	
Chirurgeon	1	
Chirurgeon's mate	1	
Conductors for the Municon, ... artillery and draught horses	12	
Gunners	34	
Matrosses [Assistant gunners]	64	
Pioneers	20	
Carpenters	3	
Wheelwrights	2	
Smiths	3	
Collarmaker	1	
Coopers	2	
Carters	33	

It seems that the crews required for the various guns were :-

	Gunners	Matrosses
Demi-cannon	3	6
Demi-culverin	2	4
Saker	2	4
Mortar	2	6[3]

The ammunition required would be iron roundshot, and cases of tin or wood filled with musket balls (caseshot). The scale of ammunition was usually 40 or 50 roundshot and 10 caseshot per gun; a total of 600-720 rounds of both kinds. It is not improbable that ammunition expended at Leicester had been replaced from captured stores. The mortars probably had 30 shells per piece.[4]

The Trayne had a considerable transport problem. It had to move :-

    a) 12 brass guns mounted upon field carriages,
    b) 2 mortars,
    c) Ammunition,
    d) Municon for the Trayne,
    e) Utensils incidental to the Trayne,
    f) Iron and iron work,
    g) Materials,
    h) Municon for the foot
    j) The Pontoon train,
    k) The Controller's Waggon
    l) The Chirurgeon's instruments and stores.

a)   The guns had 'ffore Carriages'[5] to which the horses were harnessed. The method of traction was primitive. The horses, instead of being harnessed in pairs, wandered along tandem, wasting much of their energy. The pieces themselves were long and awkward, and in consequence they needed more horses than guns of the same calibre would have required at the time of the Napoleonic Wars.

	Calibre	Weight of shot	Weight of cannon	Length of cannon	Horses
Demi-cannon	6-in.	27-30 lbs.	6000 lbs.	12 feet	17[6]
Demi-culverin	4½-in.	9-10 lbs	3600 lbs.	10 feet	10?
Saker	3½-in.	5-6 lbs	2500 lbs.	9½ feet	5

b)   The mortar pieces and their platforms were carried in 4 carts each requiring 5 horses.[7]

c) *Ammunition.* The ammunition was carried in 'Tumbrells' and carts, each drawn by 5 horses. Each tumbril was capable of carrying a load of 1110 lbs. or more.[8] It would seem, therefore, that the ammunition for the brass cannon required 7 tumbrils, each requiring 5 horses. The mortar shells required 2 carts, each drawn by 5 horses.

d) *'Municon for the Trayne'*

Powder	10 barrels	⎫	1 Waggon.
Match	1 cwt.	⎭	5 Horses[8]

e) *'Vtensills incident to the Trayne'*

Gynne furnished	1		
'Municon Tents'	2		
Mitch [Wedge]	1		
Budge Barrells[9]	6		
Grease	1 cwt.		
Soap	1 cwt.		3 Carts
Tanned hides	10		15 Horses.
Horse harness for the Thill	2 pair		
for the Trace	2 pair		
'Spare Extrees for Ordnance'	5[10]		

f) *'Iron and Iron worke'*

'Nayles of all sorts	3000		
Lynch Pynns	30		
Washers	30		
Clowtes	50		1 Cart
Clowte Nayles	400		5 Horses
Horse shooes	500		
Horse shooe Nayles	4000		

g) *'Materialls'*

'Shovells	30		
Spades	15		
Pickaxes	15		1 Cart
Hedging Bills	20		5 Horses
Hatchets	12		
Axes'	8		

h) *'Municon for the foot'*

i) Powder	50 cwt.	2 Waggons	10 Horses
ii) Match	50 cst.	2 Waggons	10 Horses
iii) Musket Shot	50 cet.	2 Carts	10 Horses[11]

j) *The Pontoon Train.*
The ordnance papers give no indication of the number of vehicles required for 'the Bridge of Boates newly made for the use of his Ma^{ts} L.Traine.'[12] However, it would be strange if there were less than a dozen boats, in, say, 4 waggons, each needing 5 horses.

k) *The Controllers Waggon.*
The commanding officer had to keep records, and, no doubt, was glad to have a vehicle for his own kit. Another 5 horse cart, no doubt.

l) *The Chyrurgeon's Cart.*
The surgeon must have had some means of transporting the instruments of his horrid trade, and there is little evidence of the use of pack-horses. No doubt the Quarter-master would also get hold of a cart if he could!

It is not easy to estimate the strength of the Trayne in men, horses and vehicles, but it was certainly an elaborate organization. Perhaps this will serve as an estimate :-

Officers and men[13]

Personnel	186
Vehicles	33
Horses	249

Of course, some of the more senior officers must have had riding horses and grooms or pages to look after them. No doubt there was the usual little flock of wives, doxies, and camp followers, to cook, nurse, launder and groom.

On 26 April 1645 two branding irons were provided by Michael Bastion, Master Smith, to mark His Majesty's horses : one with a 'Caterne Wheele & flowerdeluce' the other with a 'fflowerdeluce' only.

One is left with the thought that this elaborate Trayne, though useful as an Ordnance Field Park, and invaluable for a siege, gave rather little in the way of fire support when it came to operations in the field.

A great deal of money was spent on the train of artillery, and its value at a siege cannot be doubted. It played a more or less effective part in certain battles of the Civil Wars – for example Braddock Down (19 January 1643), where the Royalists gained a surprise by suddenly unmasking two small guns, and Langport (10 July 1645), where the cannon of the New Model quickly silenced Goring's few guns.

Owing to the old-fashioned and inefficient way in which the horses were harnessed the guns could not be manoeuvred with any great speed. The rate of fire was certainly slow. Taking into account the elaborate gun-drill of the day it seems unlikely that it can have exceeded one round every two minutes. The scale of ammunition was only 50 rounds per gun. It follows that even if they shot off every round – which is highly improbable – the Royalists were only going to get off 600 rounds. Whilst some would plough into good targets such as a stand of pikes, many would miss their mark. With all these limiting factors it seems unlikely that the artillery played any great part in the struggle.

[1] The Royalist Ordnance Papers, 1642-1646. Edited for the *Oxfordshire Record Society*, by Dr Ian Roy, MA. Ph.D. 1964 and 1975.

[2] But compare the list of 'Officers and Mynisters' of 17 June 1644. (Roy, 354).

[3] Roy, pp. 156, 157, 233, 251.

[4] Roy, p. 270.

[5] Roy, p. 105.

[6] Roy, p. 255.

[7] Roy, p. 270.

[8] Roy, p. 353.

[9] A small powder barrel, with an easily fitted leather top, for use near the cannon when in action.

[10] Roy, p. 353.

[11] Gunpowder measures:-   100 lbs = 1 cwt.

                        24 cwt = 1 last or ton.

It seems, therefore, that these 5 horse vehicles could each manage one ton.

[12] 28 April 1645. Roy, p. 146.

[13] The Conductors and Gunners seem to have been the Warrant Officers and Senior NCOs. The Gentlemen of the Ordnance might be considered as junior officers.

PART III

INTRODUCTION TO PART VII

THE NEW MODEL ARMY

. . . a company of poor ignorant men . . .
Oliver Cromwell

THE NEW MODEL ARMY came into being by an Ordinance of
11 February 1645.

The establishment was :-

General Officers[1]
11 Regiments of Horse
1 Regiment of Dragoons
12 Regiments of Foot
Train of Artillery.

The Regiments were to be :-

Horse	6 Troops	600
Dragoons	10 Companies	1,000
Foot	10 Companies	1,200

They were to be drawn from :-

HORSE

THE EARL OF ESSEX' ARMY

Colonels	Troops
Sir Philip Stapleton	8
Sir William Balfour	6
Hans Behre	5 }
John Dalbier	4 }
James Sheffeild	6
Sir Robert Pye	3
	32

ARMY OF THE EASTERN ASSOCIATION

Colonels	Troops
Earl of Manchester	11
Lt. General Oliver Cromwell	14
QMG Vermuyden	5
Charles Fleetwood	6
Sir John Norwich	3
	39

SIR WILLIAM WALLER'S ARMY

Sir William Waller	9
Sir Arthur Hesilrige	8
Jonas Vandruske	6
Edward Cooke	4*
Sir Michael Livesey	5
Richard Norton	5
George Thompson	6?
John Fitz-James	—*
	43+

Two of Essex' regiments, those of Behre and Dalbier, were sent to reinforce Massey at Gloucester. Those of Cooke and Fitz-James seem to have been sent into the West. Fifteen regiments comprising some 101 troops, were reduced into the 11 regiments and 66 troops of the New Model. Each regiment in the new army was to consist of 600 men, and so the three old armies had to find 264 commissioned officers and 6,336 'other ranks' a total of 6,600 horse. The 101 troops of the old armies should have had something like 404 commissioned officers, 140 more than would be required in the New Model. It follows that even if not every one of the old troops had its full complement of officers, a great number of officers were going to be redundant. It was a splendid opportunity for Cromwell and the Independents to rid themselves of Presbyterians and Scots – and they did not lose it.

*These two seem to have been sent to the West, and probably did not contribute to the New Model.

In July 1644 the four cavalry regiments which were to join the New Model from Essex' Army had something like 92 commissioned officers and 1,842 'other ranks'.[2] The Army of the Eastern Association was even stronger in horse 'No compulsion was required to fill the ranks of the cavalry regiments.'[3]

DRAGOONS

The New Model was to have one regiment of dragoons, 1,000 strong and consisting of 10 companies.

In July 1644 there was only one company of dragoons in Essex' Army.[4] Waller, however, had his own regiment of at least six companies, and in the Army of the Eastern Association there seem to have been two or three regiments[5] with not less than 16 companies. There can have been little difficulty in raising the men required for Colonel John Okey's Regiment, which like the cavalry regiments must have been complete from the first.

THE FOOT

THE EARL OF ESSEX' ARMY*

Colonels	Companies
Earl of Essex	10
Philip Skippon	
Edward Aldrich	10
Lord Robartes	10
Richard Fortescue	
Richard Ingoldsby	10
Henry Barclay	
William Davies	

* It was evident that the regiments of Essex' Army, when they were raised in 1642, had an establishment of 10 companies.

THE ARMY OF THE EASTERN ASSOCIATION

Colonels	Companies
The Earl of Manchester	18
Sir Thomas Hogan	8
Sir Michael Hobart	8
Francis Russell	10
Edward Montagu	10
Major-General Lawrence Crauford	10
John Pickering	10?

Sir William Waller	6
Sir Arthur Hesilrige	4
Samuel Jones	10?
Sergeant-Major-General James Holborne	5
Ralph Weldon	9

It may be that this list is not quite complete, but not less than 20 regiments, comprising perhaps 188 companies were reduced to form 12 regiments (120 companies), which it was intended should total 14,400 foot.

The New Model required 360 officers of foot, but, as there may have been as many as 564 available, this was no problem, and in fact 'divers inferiour officers . . . listed themselves as common souldiers :' . . .[6]

In March 1645 the three old armies could muster no more than 7,174 foot.[7] Of these 3,048 belonged to Essex' Army and 3,578 to Manchester's. Waller's regiments, it seems were but thin. The Parliamentarians were compelled to resort to impressment in order to try and raise nearly 7,000 new foot. It was not easy and we may be sure that none of the regiments were up to strength by the time of Naseby. Even so they were a great deal stronger than any in the King's armies.

The organization of the New Model Army could have been improved by organizing the regiments of horse and foot into brigades and tertias. As it was Skippon had to deal direct with eight regimental commanders; and Ireton and Cromwell, the commanders of the two wings of horse, had to deal with six or eight subordinates respectively. The transmission of orders cannot have been easy.

[1] Including staff officers.
[2] Symonds' Diary, p. 73.
[3] Firth And Davies, I, xviii.
[4] Captain Jeconiah Abercromy had 9 officers and 65 dragoons in July 1644 (Symonds' Diary, p. 73)
[5] Under Charles Thomas Ayloffe and Valentine Walton, and Lt. Colonel John Lilburne.
[6] Letter of Francis Allein and John Dethick, Treasurers at War, to the Hon. William Lenthall, Speaker of the House of Commons. Reading, 6 April, 1645. (Firth and Davies, II, 426.)
[7] Ibid. I, xviii.

Chapter Seven

THE COMMANDERS

GENERAL SIR THOMAS FAIRFAX (1612-1671)

SIR THOMAS WAS the son of Ferdinando, second Baron Fairfax of Cameron (1584-1648), who commanded the Parliamentary forces in Yorkshire. The father was no great soldier, but the son was a brave and resolute officer with real powers of leadership. He had learned his trade in the Low Countries under Sir Horace Vere, whose daughter, Anne, was to become his wife (1637). He was at the siege of Bois-le-Duc (1629).

Fairfax commanded a troop of 160 Yorkshire dragoons in the first Scotch War, and was knighted by King Charles in 1640. In 1641 Fairfax was one of the troop commanders in Lt. General Sir John Conyers' Regiment of Horse.[1] Despite these services he was from the outset of the civil war a prominent supporter of the Parliament, and second in command to his father in Yorkshire. Sir Thomas disintguished himself in the fighting in those parts, though he was not so uniformly successful as his Short Memorial might lead one to believe. His recapture of Leeds (23 January 1643) was counterbalanced by a severe defeat at the hands of General Goring on Seacroft Moor (4 April 1643). Nothing daunted Fairfax struck back, storming Wakefield though outnumbered by two to one, and taking Goring prisoner (21 May 1643). This he regarded, not unreasonably, as 'more a miracle' than a victory. The next round went to the Royalists, who completely defeated the Fairfaxes at Adwalton Moor (30 June). In the retreat that followed Sir Thomas was severely wounded.

The tide turned and on 11 October Fairfax took part in Manchester's victory at Winceby. The latter wrote 'Sir Thomas Fairfax is a person that exceeds any expressions as a commendation of his resolution and valour'. His own spirit is shown by his remark when he saw the Cavaliers drawn up in battle array "Come let us fall on, I never prospered better than when I fought against the enemy three or four to one. . . ."

On 25 January 1644 Fairfax inflicted a severe defeat on Lord Byron, and relieved Nantwich. On 10 April he captured Lord Belasyse at Selby, destroying much of his force.

At Marston Moor Goring routed the Allied right wing where Fairfax commanded, and, bleeding from a slashed cheek, he only escaped by a strategem. A more serious wound followed when a musket ball smashed his shoulder at the siege of Helmsley Castle in August. He recovered slowly, but in time for the House of Commons to vote, by 101 votes to 69, that he should be given command of the New Model Army (21 January 1645).

The Royalist, Secretary Nicholas, writing to Rupert of Fairfax' defeat on Seacroft Moor, had described him as 'the man most beloved and relied upon by the rebels in the north'. He believed in offensive action, and his personal courage was of the highest order. Whitelocke, describing him in 1646, wrote : 'The general was a person of as meek and humble carriage as ever I saw in great employment, and but of few words in discourse or council. . . . But I have observed him at councils of war, that he hath said little, but hath ordered things expressly contrary to the judgment of all his council ; and in action in the field I have seen him so highly transported, that scarce any one durst speak a word to him, and he would seem more like a man distracted and furious, than of his ordinary mildness, and so far different temper.'[2] He was, according to Aubrey, a lover of learning.

Fairfax, who was rather above the average height, was so dark as to be nicknamed 'Black Tom'. He did not enjoy very good health, suffering from arthritis, rheumatism and the stone.

OLIVER CROMWELL (1599-1658)

At the last moment the Member for Cambridge, who strictly speaking should have retired from the Army under the Self-

Denying Ordinance, was given command of the cavalry of the New Model. Parliament really had no choice, for the commander of Essex' Horse, Sir William Balfour, who had greatly distinguished himself at Edgehill, Cheriton and in Cornwall, was a Scot and Scots were not employed in the New Model.

Captain Cromwell had taken the field in 1642, innocent of any previous military knowledge, and though he had no opportunity to distinguish himself in the Edgehill campaign, had been quick to discern the shortcomings of Essex' cavalry, telling Hampden that the Roundhead troopers were "most of them old decayed servingmen and tapsters" while the Royalist troopers were "gentlemen's sons, younger sons and persons of quality". Cromwell had proved a pioneer of personnel selection, content with "a russet-coated captain that knows what he fights for, and loves what he knows," to officer his freeholders and freeholders' sons, who, as Bulstrode Whitelocke puts it, 'upon a matter of conscience engaged in this quarrel.' Cromwell was a disciplinarian. If his men swore they were fined; if drunk they were set in the stocks, 'or worse' – whatever that means. If one called his comrade "Roundhead" he was cashiered! Two deserters were whipped in the market-place at Huntingdon and 'turned off as renagadoes'.[3]

Cromwell had a little victory near Grantham on 13 May 1643, but it was the battle of Gainsborough (29 July) that first showed his flair for cavalry tactics. In a fierce action he routed the enterprising young Royalist general, Charles Cavendish (1620-1643), who was slain, and then finding himself in presence of Newcastle's whole army, skilfully withdrew by alternate squadrons, a manoeuvre which seems to have been quite beyond the capacity of most of the cavalry engaged in the First Civil War. Cromwell's part in the great victory at Marston Moor is too well-known to require description here.

His famous double regiment formed two of the regiments of the New Model, those of Fairfax and Whalley.

SERGEANT-MAJOR-GENERAL PHILIP SKIPPON (c.1600-1660)

Philip Skippon was an officer of outstanding merit. Born in Norfolk in about 1600 he had served under Sir Horace Vere in the Palatinate, before entering the Dutch service. 'From a common soldier', according to Clarendon, he 'had raised himself to the degree of a captain and to the reputation of a good soldier'. He took part in both sieges of Breda (1625 and 1637), being wounded at the former, and was at the sieges of Bois-le-Duc and Maastricht (1632). Returning to England he was admitted to the Honourable Artillery Company (23 October 1639). In January 1642 the House of Commons, alarmed by King Charles' attempt to arrest the five members, applied to the City for a guard whereupon the Common Council made Skippon sergeant-major-general, gave him command of the City Trained Bands, and ordered him to raise a guard for the defence of Parliament (12 January 1642). He was made a Freeman of the City, an honour of which he was to prove himself well worthy – 'When the Assault was intended to the City.'

On 12 November he marched out to Turnham Green at the head of the London Trained Bands, reinforcing the Army of the Earl of Essex, which the Cavaliers had worsted at Edgehill.

Skippon well knew how to steady his raw troops. "Come, my boys, my brave boys, let us pray heartily and fight heartily. I will run the same fortunes and hazards with you",. . . Thus he spoke to every company, and, as Whitelocke tells us : 'the soldiers seemed to be more taken with it than with a set formal oration.'4 Well they might be.

The Earl of Essex, appreciating Skippon's support, made him Sergeant-Major-General of his army, an appointment to which the Common Council acquiesced with reluctance. (17 November 1642).

Skippon took part in the siege of Reading, and the relief of Gloucester. At First Newbury he commanded the left wing of the Roundhead Foot and greatly distinguished himself (1643).

When Essex abandoned his army at Fowey he left Skippon to make what terms he could. Skippon exhorted his officers to try and fight their way out as Sir William Balfour and the horse had done, but his Council of War were not for it. He was obliged to surrender guns, arms and baggage. In this trying time his patience, wisdom and courage deeply impressed his officers.

Skippon had his revenge at Second Newbury when with 'the

poor handful of my lord general's old foot' he stormed the Royalist redoubt by Speen Village and recaptured six of the guns lost in Cornwall.[5]

Skippon's next appointment was Sergeant-Major-General of the Foot in the New Model. He did invaluable work in reducing the old regiments, and settling the officers and men into their new regiments. It was largely due to his reputation, his administrative skill and his powers of leadership, that this awkward operation passed off in a good spirit.

Skippon was a worthy rival to his great opponent, Lord Astley.

COMMISSARY-GENERAL HENRY IRETON (1611-1651)

The son of German Ireton of Attenborough near Nottingham, Henry Ireton had the benefit of an excellent education for he became a gentleman-commoner of Trinity College, Oxford in 1626 and took the degree of B.A. (1629). Wood says 'he had the character in that house of a stubborn and saucy fellow towards the seniors and therefore his company was not at all wanting'. It may be noted, *en passant*, that except for Ireton and Edmund Ludlow, the Trinity men, who took a prominent part in the Civil Wars, were Cavaliers.[6] He entered the Middle Temple (1629) but was not called to the bar.

Ireton was living on his Nottinghamshire estates when the Civil War broke out, and, as Mrs Hutchinson puts it, 'having had an education in the strictest way of godliness, and being a grave and solid person, a man of good learning, great understanding, and other abilities, to which was joined a willing and zealous heart in the cause and his country, he was the chief promoter of the parliament's interest in the county.'[7] The House of Commons chose him to be captain of the troop of horse to be raised by the town of Nottingham[8] (30 June 1642). Ireton gathered a troop 'of those godly people which the cavaliers drove out,' and joined the Earl of Essex. After Edgehill he was sent back to Nottinghamshire 'for the present service of his country, till it was put into a posture of defence . . . and was major of the horse regiment.'[9] This was under Colonel Francis Thornhagh. Ireton took part in Cromwell's victory at Gainsborough (28

July 1643) and thereafter 'began an inseparable league' with him.[10] Cromwell made Ireton his deputy-governor in the Isle of Ely, which he fortified and where he allowed the sectaries such freedom that the presbyterians called it 'a mere Amsterdam'.[11] Ireton served with the Army of the Eastern Association in 1644, and was appointed quartermaster-general. After Second Newbury he joined Cromwell in his attack on the Earl of Manchester.

It was originally intended that Ireton's New Model Regiment should be under Sir Michael Livesey, who, not without reason, was deprived of his command for disobedience, cowardice and incompetence. On the eve of Naseby Ireton beat up the Royalist quarters and took many prisoners. He was appointed Commissary-General of the Horse, and was, therefore, second-in-command to Cromwell. It is difficult to discern anything in his military career to warrant such promotion, but he was undoubtedly a clever man and *persona grata* with the Lieutenant-General of the Horse.

COLONEL CHARLES FLEETWOOD (c. 1620-1692)

The third son of Sir Miles Fleetwood of Aldwinkle, Northamptonshire (d. 1641), who was receiver of the court of wards. The eldest son, Sir William Fleetwood (1603-1674) was a Royalist, and the second, George (1605-1667) spent nearly 40 years in the Swedish service, becoming a general and a baron.

Charles entered Gray's Inn (30 November 1638) and was one of those young gentlemen of the Inns of Court who in 1642 enlisted in Essex' Lifeguard. In 1642, though but a gentleman volunteer, he was employed by Essex to take a letter, containing overtures of peace to the Earl of Dorset. He rose quickly to the rank of captain and was wounded at First Newbury. In May 1644 Parliament rewarded his services with the receivership of the court of wards, which had been forfeited by his Royalist brother. By this time he was colonel of a regiment of six troops in the Army of the Eastern Association. It was full of fanatical independents. 'Looke on Col. Fleetwood's regiment, with his Major Harreson,' wrote a presbyterian, 'what a cluster of preaching officers and troopers ther is.'[12] Thomas Harrison, like his colonel had been in Essex' Lifeguard at the outbreak of the war.

He must have distinguished himself at Marston Moor, for he was selected to carry the news to Parliament.[13] From October 1644 to April 1645 Fleetwood's rôle was the defence of Lincolnshire. It was then merged into the New Model, two of the troop commanders, Major Thomas Harrison and Captain Selby remaining with the regiment. At Naseby Fleetwood was the senior officer in the second line of Ireton's wing. Had the New Model possessed a brigade organization, we may suppose that Fleetwood would have been one of the brigadiers.

LT. GENERAL THOMAS HAMMOND (-c.1652)

The Lt General of the Ordnance is frequently confused with his nephew, Colonel Robert Hammond (1621-1654), who commanded one of the New Model regiments of foot.

In August 1642 he was the commander of 40 Troop in the horse belonging to the Army of the Earl of Essex.[14] He does not appear to have been in the 1640 Army.

His military career is shrouded in obscurity. He was one of the unlawful tribunal that tried King Charles I, and, though he did not sign the death warrant, attended regularly. Though he was dead before 1652 he was one of twenty regicides excepted from the Act of Indemnity (1660): his estate was therefore forfeit.

THOMAS RAINBOROW (-1648)

Thomas Rainborow[15] was a son of a distinguished sea-captain, William Rainborow (d.1642), and was himself bred to the sea. One of his sisters married John Winthrop (1588-1649), Governor of Massachusetts, and another married his fourth son Colonel Stephen Winthrop (1619-1658).

In 1643 Rainborow was in command of *Swallow* (34), and took a ship carrying reinforcements to the King. As captain of *Lion* he landed 100 men to help Lord Fairfax' defence of Hull and, leading a column of 500 musketeers, was captured in the great sally which terminated the siege (11 October 1643). From this time he is described as a colonel, and his later service was all on land. He raised a regiment of foot for the Army of the Eastern

Association. Three of his original officers, Lt. Colonel Israel Stoughton, Major Nehemiah Bourne and Captain John Leverett, were citizens of Massachusetts.

Rainborow was not at Marston Moor but he took Crowland in December 1644, but his regiment in the New Model was made up from other regiments from Manchester's Army. With this he took Gaunt House near Oxford on 1 June 1645.

At Naseby Rainborow was in Skippon's second line, or reserve, but it cannot be said whether he was in command of it. It is likely for he was senior to Colonel Robert Hammond and Lt. Colonel Thomas Pride, who commanded the other two regiments in the reserve.

Rainborow seems to have been a brave and determined officer, who used his initiative, and was capable of exercising independent command.

EDWARD WHALLEY (-c.1675)

Whalley was a kinsman of Oliver Cromwell, and had been his major, then his lieutenant-colonel in the Army of the Eastern Association. He was the second son of Richard Whalley of Kirkton and Screveton, Nottinghamshire, by his second wife, Frances Cromwell, Oliver's aunt. Whalley was apparently a woollendraper before the war, and in 1642 was probably cornet to Captain James Fiennes' troop. When Cromwell began to raise his regiment he became major, and greatly distinguished himself by the handsome retreat he made after Cromwell's victory at Gainsborough. He fought at Marston Moor as lieutenant-colonel, and when Cromwell's double regiment was split to make two in the New Model, one of them naturally went to Whalley. He commanded the front line of Cromwell's wing at Naseby.

CAPTAIN RICHARD DEANE (1610-1653)

Little is known of Deane's early years, save that he was born at Temple Guiting in Gloucestershire. He was related to Sir Richard Deane, Lord Mayor of London, 1628-1629, and it is thought that, with a fair wind from that quarter, he embarked upon a mercantile career and made several trading voyages in which he acquired a practical knowledge of seamanship. It is thought that he also served in a ship of war, probably as a gunner. Deane may have been at Edgehill and at First Newbury: he was certainly with Essex in Cornwall in 1644, and the Earl thought him 'an honest, judicious, and stout man.' He was one of the twenty officers who made up Skippon's Council of War when the Parliamentarian Army surrendered at Lostwithiel, of whom only seven held commissions in the New Model Army.

HUGH PETERS, MA (1598-1660)

Hugh Peters,[16] the independent Puritan divine was a Cornishman. Sent up to Cambridge at the age of fourteen he was a member of Trinity College. About 1624 he married Elizabeth, widow of Edmund Read of Wickford, whose daughter, Elizabeth, was the wife of John Winthrop the younger (1606-1676), the future governor of Connecticut.

Peters was ordained by Bishop Mortaigne of London, and appointed lecturer at St. Sepulchre's. About 1629 he decided, perhaps because he would not accept episcopal government, to settle in Holland. There it is thought he was chaplain to Sir Edward Harwood, the colonel of one of the English regiments in the Dutch Service, who fell at the siege of Maestricht in 1632. About that time Peters became minister of the English Church at Rotterdam. Sir William Brereton (1604-1661), the Parliamentarian commander in Cheshire during the First Civil War, visiting Rotterdam in 1634, found Peters 'a right zealous and worthy man', evidently admiring the independent principles of the pastor and his flock.

Meanwhile Archbishop Laud was endeavouring to make the British churches in Holland conform to the doctrine and ceremonies of the Anglican Church, and Peters decided to depart for New England. Not without difficulty he evaded an attempt by the English government to arrest him and reached Boston in 1635. He was admitted a freeman of Massachusetts and established as a minister of the church at Salem. Thanks to his Winthrop connections, he was from the outset prominent in the affairs of the colony. Under his strict ministry his community grew and prospered, for he was both active and public spirited.

The troubled state of England in 1641 decreased the trade of the colony and dried up the stream of emigration. Peters and two other agents were sent to England to represent the difficulties and seek support. They had some success, but Peters became involved in the struggle between King and Parliament. He was for a few months a chaplain to the forces in Ireland. He preached against Archbishop Laud, and is said to have proposed that he be punished with transportation to New England. He went on a mission to Holland in order to raise money for Parliament and to explain the justice of its cause.

In May 1644 Peters had a taste of amphibious warfare, accompanying Warwick in his relief of Lyme. The Earl employed him to bring the needs of the forces in the West to their masters in Parliament. As a chaplain in the New Model he performed a similar service for Fairfax. His eloquence was deployed whenever a storming party was to 'go over the top', and Sprigge and Vicars testify to the inspiration he gave to the pious soldiery before Bridgwater, Bristol and Dartmouth.

JOHN RUSHWORTH, MA (c.1612-1690)

John Rushworth, the lawyer and historian, was not the least distinguished member of the General Staff of the New Model Army. He came from Northumberland. Wood tells us that he was educated at Oxford, but his name does not appear in the matriculation lists. On 13 April 1638 he was appointed solicitor to the town of Berwick-on-Tweed with a none too princely salary of £4 per annum. The Wiltshire Quarter Sessions Records for 1660 preserve the names of several badly maimed soldiers whose annual pension was the same. . . . He was admitted to Lincoln's Inn in 1641, but, more interested in history than the law, he soon began to collect information about the eleven years of King Charles' personal rule.

'I did personally attend', he writes, 'and observe all occurrences of moment during that interval in the Star Chamber, Court of Honour, and Exchequer Chamber, when all the Judges of England met there upon extraordinary cases; at the Council-table when great cases were heard before the king and council. And when matters were agitated at a greater distance, I was there also, and went on purpose out of a curiosity to see and observe the passages of the camp at Berwick, at the fight at Newburn, at the treaty at Ripon, and at the meeting of the Long Parliament, and present every day at the trial of the Earl of Strafford.' Whatever one may think of the Cause he served, one can only applaud the way he went to work. His diligence, and his skill in shorthand, were rewarded when, at the request of Henry Elsing, the clerk of the House of Commons, he was appointed clerk-assistant (25 April 1640). He was often employed as a messenger between Parliament and its committees at York, Oxford and elsewhere (1641-1643).

Rushworth was with Fairfax throughout the offensive of the New Model Army, and again in 1648, and became an influential political personage. Not only did he write narratives of Fairfax' operations, for Speaker Lenthall, but he kept Lord Fairfax informed of his son's military and political proceedings, until, according to Denzil Holles, the signature 'John Rushworth, secretary,' was 'now far above John Brown or Henry Elsing,' the clerks of the two Houses of Parliament.

At Naseby Rushworth was with the baggage train.

GENERAL OFFICERS

General Sir Thomas Fairfax (1612-1671). Commissioned 17 Feb. 1645.

Secretary to the General and Council of War.	John Rushworth, Esq., MA. (c.1612-1690)
Clerks to the Secretary	Mr Thomas Wragge
	Mr William Clarke
Chirurgion to the General's own person.	Master Winter

FOOT

Major General Philip Skippon (c.1600-1660). Commissioned 17 Feb. 1645.

Quartermaster-General (1)	Spencer
	then
(2)	Gravesnor
Assistant to the Q.M.G.	Master Robert Wolsey (W Naseby)
Adjutant-General	Lt. Colonel James Gray (-1647)
[Provost] Marshal-General	Captain Wykes

HORSE

Lt. General Oliver Cromwell (1599-1658). Commissioned June 1645.

Commissary-General	Henry Ireton (1611-1651)
Quartermaster-General	Richard Fincher
Adjutants General	Captain Christopher Fleming
	Captain Arthur Evelyn
Commissary-General of the Horse Provisions	(1) Captain Cooke (-1645). K. Naseby.
	then
	(2) Commissary Jones.
[Provost] Marshal General	Captain Richard Lawrence *Approved by The Commons, 28 March 1645.*
Markmaster General	Mr Francis Child.

ORDNANCE

Lt. General Thomas Hammond (-c.1652)	
Comptroller	Captain Richard Deane (1610-1653)
Chaplain to the Train	Master Hugh Peters MA (1598-1660)
Engineer-General	Peter Manteau van Dalem
Engineer Extraordinary	Captain Hooper
Chief Engineer	Eval Tercene
Engineers	Master Lyon
	and
	Mr Tomlinson.
Master Gunner of the Field	Master Francis Furin
Paymaster to the Train ·	Master Matthew Martin
Commissary of Ammunition	Master Phips
Commissary of the Draught Horses	Mr Thomas Robinson
Firelocks	Capt.-Lieut. Desborow
	Capt.-Lieut. Brent
Pioneers	Captain Cheese

'THE TREASURERS AT WARRE'

Sir John Wollaston
Thomas Adams, Esq.
John Warner, Esq.   } Aldermen
Thomas Andrewes, Esq.
George Wytham, Esq.
Francis Allein, Esq.

Abraham Chamberlain, Esq.
John Dethick, Esq.
Captain John Blackwell, 'Deputy-Treasurer at Warres'

MUSTERS

Commissary-General	Stane
Deputies to the	⎧ Mr James Standish
Commissary-General	⎩ Mr Richard Gerard

SCOUTMASTER GENERAL

Scoutmaster General   Major Leonard Watson

JUDGE ADVOCATE

John Mills, Esq.
Master   Boles

VICTUALS

Commissary General	(1) Commissary	Orpin
	then	
	(2) Commissary	Cowling

WAGGON-MASTER GENERAL

Master   Richardson

[MEDICAL]

Physicians to the Army	Doctor	Payne
	and	
	Doctor	Strawhill
	then	
	Doctor	French
	vice Strawhill	
Apothecary to the Army	Master	Webb

MESSENGERS TO THE ARMY

Mr Richard Chadwell
Mr Constantine Heath

COMMISSIONERS OF PARLIAMENT RESIDING IN THE ARMY

Colonel   Pindar
Harcourt Leighton
Colonel Thomas Herbert
Captain   Potter, K. Naseby, then
Captain Vincent Potter

[1] Sir Jacob Astley's Muster Roll.

[2] Memorials, ed. 1853, ii, 20.

[3] Young, p. 40.

[4] Memorials, i, 190, ed. 1853.

[5] Rushworth, v. 723.

[6] They included the Earls of Cleveland and Craven, Sir Thomas Glemham, Sir Philip Musgrave and Sir Edward Fitton.

[7] Memoirs of Colonel Hutchinson, ed. 1885, i, 168.

[8] 58 Troop. Peacock. The Army Lists of the Roundheads and Cavaliers, p. 55.

[9] Hutchinson, I, 199.

[10] Hutchinson, I, 234.

[11] Camden Soc. 1875, pp. 39, 73.

[12] Manchester's Quarrel with Cromwell, p. 72.

[13] Firth and Davies, p. 91.

[14] Peacock, p. 53.

[15] Alias Rainborowe and Rainsborough.

[16] He actually signed himself 'Peter'.

Chapter Eight

THE NEW MODEL HORSE

THERE WERE 11 REGIMENTS of horse in the New Model, of which 10 were present at Naseby. In addition two regiments which did not belong to the New Model were in the battle. The absent New Model regiment was that of Colonel Richard Graves, which was with the force sent to relieve Taunton.

NEW MODEL HORSE AT NASEBY

RIGHT WING

LIEUTENANT-GENERAL OLIVER CROMWELL (1599-1659)

Colonel	Major
Sir Thomas Fairfax' Lifeguard	
and Regiment	John Disbrowe
Sir Robert Pye	Matthew Tomlinson
Absent. PW at Leicester	(1617-1681)
Edward Whalley	Christopher Bethell
(-1675)	(-1645)
Edward Rossiter	Philip Twistleton
Thomas Sheffeild	Richard Fincher

LEFT WING

COMMISSARY-GENERAL HENRY IRETON (1611-1651)

Henry Ireton	George Sedascue
(1611-1651)	
Cornelius Vermuyden	Robert Huntingdon C.O.
Retired.	
John Butler	Thomas Horton
Charles Fleetwood	Thomas Harrison
Nathaniel Rich	John Alford

The two non-New Model regiments present at Naseby were :

John Fiennes	Right Wing
The Associated Horse.	A squadron on each wing.

The strength of a New Model cavalry regiment was supposed to be 600, and the three old armies of Essex, Manchester and Waller had sufficient cavalry to bring them up to strength without resorting to impressment.[1] Strength returns of Fairfax' Army have not come down to us, but 7000 is a moderate computation of the strength of his horse at Naseby. They outnumbered the Royalist cavalry by about 1500 men.

THE LIFEGUARD

The origin of this unit was the Lifeguard raised for the Earl of Essex in 1642. This had been recruited amongst the young gentlemen of the Inns of Court, among them several of the field officers of the New Model. Colonel Charles Fleetwood and his major, Thomas Harrison; Colonel Nathaniel Rich, and Majors Matthew Tomlinson and Philip Twistleton had all served in Essex' Lifeguard. The unit distinguished itself at Edgehill and First Newbury, but after some initial success was routed by the King's Lifeguard at Second Newbury.[2]

On 14 April 1645 the Committee of the Army was ordered to consider 'how the troop of gentlemen which were of the lifeguard to the Earl of Essex may be taken on in the New Model', and on the 25th it was ordered that it should be one of the six troops in Fairfax' Regiment. The gentlemen were to have three shillings a day more than the ordinary troopers.

Captain Charles D'Oyley, from Graves' Regiment, was given command of the Lifeguard, and proved a valiant commander. Before the war he had been a student at Oxford University. Unfortunately for him he backed the loser in the quarrel between army and Parliament, 1647, and was dismissed.[3] The Lifeguard itself was disbanded in 1648, the Levellers asserting that the reason for this was a sinister one: 'Upon pretence of easing the charge of the commonwealth, the life-guard must be disbanded, because consisting of discerning men, faithfull to their country and former promises, and many others of like principles were pickt out of every regiment; the designe being by weeding the choisest and best resolved men, to make the army wholy mercinary, slavish, and the executioners of a few mens lusts and lawlesse pleasures.'[4]

THE REGIMENT OF SIR THOMAS FAIRFAX

The succession of colonels in this Regiment was:

Sir Thomas Fairfax	18 March 1645
Oliver Cromwell	June 1650
Richard Cromwell	w.e.f. 3 September 1658
William Packer	July 1659
Sir Arthur Hesilrige	c. 12 January 1660
Lord Fauconberg	April 1660
The Duke of York	June or July 1660.

The regiment was formed from Cromwell's famous regiment of Ironsides. This had grown until it had 14 troops, six of which now made up Fairfax' Regiment. The troop commanders were:

1.	Sir Thomas Fairfax	Colonel 18 March	1645[5]
	Capt. Lieut. John Gladman	Capt. Lieut. Aug.	1644
		Captain	1648
		Major	1659
2.	Major John Disbrowe	QM	1642
		Captain	1643
		Major by April	1644
		Governor of Yarmouth	1648
		Colonel	1649
		Lt. General	1659
3.	Captain Adam Lawrence	Captain by 13 Oct.	1643
		K. Colchester	1648
4.	Captain John Browne	Captain c. Mar.	1644
		Major w.e.f. 15 Sept.	1648
		Left	1652
5.	Captain William Packer	Trooper	1642
		Lieutenant	
		Captain w.e.f. 2 July	1644
		Major	1652
		Colonel	1659

6.	Captain James Berry	Trooper	1642
		Capt. Lieut.	1643
		Captain Aug.	1644
		Major to Twistleton	
		14 June	1647
		Colonel	1651

The commanding officer was the 'grim gyant Desborough', who had been Cromwell's quartermaster in 1642, and afterwards his major. Before the war he was an attorney and a farmer. In 1636 he married Cromwell's sister, Jane. 'Desborough's patriotism was tempered by a strict regard for his own interests'.[6] Nevertheless he was a good soldier, and particularly distinguished himself at Langport (10 July 1645).

Captain Lawrence was a friend of Richard Baxter, and was orthodox in his religious views. He was killed at the siege of Colchester in 1648.

When Oliver Cromwell, junior, died of small-pox at Newport Pagnell in about March 1644, his troop was given to Browne.

Captain Walton, mortally wounded at Marston Moor, was succeeded by his Anabaptist lieutenant, William Packer, who commanded the regiment at Dunbar and Worcester and became its major in 1652. As Packer had served under Cromwell, when he was a captain[7] we may suppose that he was one of the original members of 67 Troop in Essex' Army.

James Berry, succeeded a Leveller, William(?) Ayres or Eyres, when he left the regiment in the Summer of 1644. Berry, who before the war had been a clerk in an ironworks had probably been with Cromwell from the outset, for in 1643 he was made his captain-lieutenant. He proved an officer of extraordinary valour.[8] It was he that slew Lt. General Charles Cavendish, 'with a thrust under his short ribs' in the fight at Gainsborough (29 July 1643). Berry stayed with the regiment until 1647, when he became major to Colonel Philip Twistleton.

The original troop commanders had included one of Cromwell's sons; his brother-in-law, Disbrowe; and a nephew, Walton, who was son of Colonel Valentine Walton (d.1661), the governor of Lynn, and Cromwell's sister, Margaret. It is likely that most of these troop commanders, and some of the other officers, had been in Cromwell's original troop which rode in the Lord General's Regiment in 1642. Disbrowe certainly had, and so it seems had Packer, Berry and Eyres.[9] Lawrence and Browne, who were senior to Packer, may be supposed to have been with Cromwell from the first.

In 1650 the troop commanders were:

{Colonel Oliver Cromwell,
{Capt. Lieut
Major John Browne, *vice* Disbrowe
Captain William Packer,
Captain John Gladman, *vice* Lawrence,
Captain William Disher *vice* Berry,
Captain Christopher Covell *vice* Browne.

The last two proved unsatisfactory. Covell was cashiered in October 1650 for denying the humanity of Christ. Disher, who, amongst other things, had cheated his troopers of their pay, resigned in order to avoid a court martial (1651).

There were some odd characters in the regiment at one time and another. These included Cornet George Joyce, who seized the King at Holdenby House (3 June 1647); Cornet Edmund Rolph, who was accused of plotting to kill the captive King at Carisbrooke Castle in 1648. Lieutenant, afterwards Colonel, Richard Rumball (c.1622-1685), who died on the scaffold for his complicity in the Rye House Plot, and Edward Sexby (d.1658), agitator and conspirator, who died in the Tower for plotting the assassination of the Protector. They were a difficult bunch, and in 1658, the troop commanders proving disaffected, their old colonel sacked the lot. They had become discontented because the gradual increase of the Protector's authority seemed to threaten both their civil liberties and their liberty of conscience. Packer refused to own Cromwell's second chamber as a House of Lords. The troop commanders purged at this time were:

Major William Packer,
Captain John Gladman,
Captain William Malin (or Malyn), cornet to Berry at Naseby,
Captain William Barrington
Captain Anthony Spinage
Capt. Lieut. John Hunter.

Packer had in effect been the commanding officer for years. He drew a colonel's pay (£666. 13. 4 p.a.); he had been deputy to Fleetwood, when the latter was major-general in Berkshire, Buckinghamshire and Oxfordshire – a lucrative appointment. He and some of his brother officers had bought the royal manor of Theobalds and lived there in some state. He was a J.P. and a Member of Parliament. When Oliver died he opposed the recognition of Richard Cromwell as Protector without first limiting his powers by law. He told the House how his old C.O. had sacked him.

'I thought it [the second chamber] was not a 'Lords' House, but another House. But for my undertaking to judge this, I was sent for, accused of perjury, and outed of a place of 600 l. per annum. I would not give it up. He told me I was not apt: I, that had served him fourteen years, ever since he was a captain of a troop of horse [1642,] till he came to this power; and had commanded a regiment seven years: without any trial or appeal, with the breath of his nostrils I was outed; and lost not only my place, but a dear friend to boot. Five captains under my command, all of integrity, courage, and valour, were outed with me, because they could not comply; they could not say that was a House of Lords.'[10] It must be painful to admirerers of the· Protector to contemplate his removing his old Ironsides in this arbitrary fashion. Officers whose commissions are signed by a King of England enjoy a rather greater security of tenure.

The wheel goes round and in 1659 Packer was made colonel of his old regiment, with Gladman as major. Barrington and Hunter were also restored. The other two troops went to Robert Hall and John Spencer, an officer who had distinguished himself by a desperate charge in the 1648 campaign.

In 1659 Packer backed Lambert, and when, in October, the Army was purged once more, only Spencer retained his troop. Sir Arthur Hesilrige now became colonel, and Major Browne, who had left the Regiment in 1652, came back in place of Gladman. In the crisis of 1660 he managed to keep the regiment together.

In April 1660 Monck had given the Regiment a sixth colonel: Lord Fauconberg, who though he had married Cromwell's daughter, Mary, was now as eager as any to bring about a restoration. When King Charles landed the Regiment was given to the Duke of York. It was one of the last to be disbanded, perhaps as late as February 1661.

Packer and Gladman were arrested in 1661, the former spending many months in the Gate House without trial. Gladman was imprisoned again in 1664, charged with planning to raise 400 men in Staffordshire at a time when a rising in the north was intended. When Colonel Rumbold's Rye House Plot was unmasked in 1683, Gladman was one of the first to be arrested.

As a fighting unit the Regiment proved its worth on the fields of Naseby, Langport, Dunbar and Worcester, but the man who commanded this band of religious and republican ranters and fanatics had no light task! It is almost a relief when we read that in the purge of 1659 three of the subalterns were dismissed for ordinary human failings. Cornet Richard Hobson was 'old and scandalous'; Cornet Thomas Mason played at table on the Lord's Day; Quarter-master Thomas Kitterd (or Riddard) — besides speaking words against the Parliament and the Council of State, kept a woman and gave her £3 a month — not a bad income in those days.

* * *

SIR ROBERT PYE'S REGIMENT

Succession of colonels:

Sir Robert Pye
Matthew Tomlinson
George Monck

Sprigge[11] lists these six troop commanders:

Colonel Sir Robert Pye	Captain 63 Troop, 1642.
(-1701)	Colonel, Essex' Army.
	W. Cirencester, 15 April 1643.
	Colonel, NM, 18 March 1645.
	Left the Army June 1647.
Major Matthew Tomlinson	Gentleman volunteer, 1642.
	Essex Lifeguard.
	Captain at Abingdon.
	Major, NM, 18 March 1645.

	Colonel June 1647 -
	Knighted by Henry Cromwell, 24 Nov. 1657.
Captain Ralph Margery	Captain, Cromwell H, Eastern Association.
	Captain, N.M., 18 March 1645.
	Left late 1653.
Captain Ralph Knight	Captain, N.M., 18 March 1645.
	Major June 1647
	Colonel Dec. 1659
Captain Sam Berry	Captain 1645
	Left the Regiment 1647?
	Served with distinction in the West Indies.
Captain Thomas Rawlins	Captain 1645
	Still serving, late 1648
	To Ireland. Major H.
	Drowned at sea, Aug. 1659

Other officers, who were probably:

Lieutenant Allen	Barry's Troop, by 10 Nov. 1645[12]
Lieutenant William Cove	By 30 Dec. 1645[12]
Cornet Paul Bunting	Cornet in Butler's Regt. by 5 April 1645. Cornet in Barry's Troop by 18 March 1647[12] and still serving June 1647.[13]
Cornet William Rand	Cornet by 31 Oct. 1645[14]
Cornet Nathaniel Waterhouse	Pye's Troop by 3 April 1645[12]
Quartermaster Thomas Walker	Tomlinson's Troop by 27 Dec. 1645.[12]
Quartermaster Benjamin Pott	By 10 Feb. 1646[12]
Surgeon Crosse	By 17 Aug. 1647[15]

Sir Robert Pye had taken Taunton Castle in 1644, and so had missed Essex' disaster in Cornwall. His regiment had only three troops,[16] and so his New Model unit was drawn from several sources.

Tomlinson and Rawlins were Yorkshiremen, and the former was from the Inns of Court. Margery was not a gentleman by birth. Cromwell defended him in a well-known letter to the Suffolk Commissioners (29 August 1643) . . . 'I had rather have a plain russet-coated captain that knows what he fights for, and loves what he knows, than that which you call a gentleman and is nothing else. I honour a gentleman that is so indeed.'

Rawlins it is thought was the 'most honest man' whose appointment Cromwell asked of Fairfax on 4 June 1645.[17] Little is known of the origin of Pye's officers. They do not seem to have come with him from the army of the Earl of Essex.

Symonds presrrved a note of musters taken at Tiverton in 1644 from which it appears that the regiment had only three troops, and numbered no more than 240 officers and men. The captains, Adrian Scrope and Pyle, did not go with Pye into the New Model. It is evident that well over half of the new Regiment came from outside. Margery's was no doubt as good a troop as any of the others of Cromwell's Ironsides, but the rest seem to have been rather a job lot.

Pye played a leading part in the defence of Leicester, where he was taken (31 May). Though released on parole (4 June) and soon after exchanged for Colonel Henry Tillier,[18] he almost certainly missed Naseby.

Pye took part in the siege of Bristol, and commanded at the siege of Faringdom Castle, which surrendered on 24 June 1646.

In 1647 part of the Regiment was detailed to guard the King at Holdenby House. The men sided with the rest of the army against the proposals for disbanding. Pye and his own troop supported the Parliament, and were considered renegades. Quartered at Deptford the troop was attacked and four were killed by their former comrades.

Parliament thanked Pye for his fidelity (5 June 1647), but even so he was compelled to go abroad. Tomlinson was promoted in his place. The Regiment was sent to Scotland to reinforce Cromwell after Dunbar (1650). It fought at Worcester in 1651.

In December 1654 Monck unmasked the movement, known as Overton's Plot, to seize him and persuade the army in Scotland to declare against Cromwell. Lieutenant Christopher Keymer of Tomlinson's was arrested. A far more dangerous conspirator was Miles Sindercombe (d. 1657), who had enlisted as a private soldier in Tomlinson's own troop, with the object of propagating Leveller principles. He had been a quartermaster in Reynolds' Regiment and had been one of the leaders of the

Burford Mutiny (May 1649), but he had managed to get away. Monck discharged him as 'a busy and suspicious person,' and was very mortified when he found that he had let one of the chief conspirators slip through his fingers. During the next two years Sindercombe, supported by Edward Sexby, plotted the murder of Oliver Cromwell, until he was severely wounded and arrested after an attempt to set fire to the chapel at Whitehall with an incendiary machine. He was condemned to death for high treason, but avoided being hanged, drawn and quartered: his sister smuggled him some poison and he died in the Tower. A few weeks later Sexby published his 'Killing no Murder' in which he asserted that Colonel John Barkstead, the governor of the Tower had put Sindercombe out of the way. 'Had he lived...' wrote Sexby, 'his name had been registered with Brutus and Cato, and he had had his statutes as well as they.'

Monck himself now became colonel instead of Tomlinson, and was quick to punish sedition. Lieutenant Lee of Major Knight's Troop was ordered to take evidence about Trooper Nicholas Popplewell, 'his being a Quaker, and what expressions he hath used tending thereto, or to persuade others to the same.' Captain Robert Glynn was compelled to resign for being 'the cheefe cause of makeing this regiment soe disaffected to the government as it has bin'. . .[19]

At the end of 1659 Monck reorganized his cavalry, which comprised only three regiments and one of dragoons, with the object of having officers he could trust in the key appointments. Thus Major Knight became colonel of Thomas Saunders' Regiment.

The Regiment took part in Monck's famous march from Coldstream to London, which began on 1 January 1660. His own regiment, 'and he in the head of them gallantly mounted', led the procession into the capital (3 February), every man with a carbine by his side, as well as his sword and a case of pistols. The Regiment was quartered in the Mews, the site of Trafalgar Square, and in the Strand. It gave Monck no trouble at this period, and was with him at Blackheath to welcome King Charles II (28 May 1660). It was disbanded about the end of the year. Parliament sent Sir Robert Pye to the Tower (25 January

1660), for presenting an address from the county of Berkshire, in which the readmission of secluded members was demanded. He was released when those members did actually reenter the House (21 February 1660). He represented Berkshire in the Convention Parliament and lived to join William of Orange in his march on London (1688). He died in 1701.

Colonel Matthew Tomlinson (1617-1681), though named as one of Charles I's judges did not sit in the court. He was excepted from the order for their arrest and suffered no penalty, beyond the loss of Ampthill Park which he had acquired during the Commonwealth. He gave evidence against Colonel Francis Hacker, and took the opportunity to put his own actions in a good light. This was ill-done for Hacker had not been one of the King's judges, and though he commanded his escort, had treated Charles respectfully.

The services of this Regiment were by no means as remarkable as those of some of the other regiments of the New Model. It went through a bad patch, politically, at the time of Overton's Plot, but under the command of the astute and vigilant Monck it became a reliable instrument, and played a worthy part in bringing about the Restoration.

COLONEL EDWARD WHALLEY'S REGIMENT

Succession of colonels:

Edward Whalley	1645
Robert Swallow	
Thomas Saunders	
Lord Falkland	

The original troop commanders were :-

Colonel Edward Whalley (-1675)	Captain by 25 April 1643. Distinguished himself at Gainsborough, 27 July 1643. Major by 27 July 1643. Lt. Colonel, Cromwell H. Eastern Association, 18 March 1645. W Dunbar, 3 Sept. 1650. Commissary-General Oct. 1650. Major-General 1654-1658. Died in exile in America.

Major Christopher Bethell (-1645)	Captain by April 1644. Major 18 March 1645. MW Bristol 10 Sept. 1645. Died Oct. 1645.
Captain Robert Swallow	Captain by Dec. 1643. Major c. Nov. 1645.
Captain John Grove	Captain by Jan. 1644. Major. Hacker H. c.1652. Living in Holland, 1666.
Captain Henry Cannon	Captain, New Model. Deputy-Governor, Dover Castle July 1650.
Captain William Evanson	Trooper, Cromwell's Troop 1642. Lieutenant, Whalley's Troop. Captain, New Model. Distinguished himself at Mussel- burgh, 30 July 1650. Still serving March 1655. Retired. Returned, 1659.

*　　*　　*

John Pitchford	Lieutenant to Bethell by April 1644. Captain vice Bethell by 5 Dec. 1645. Retired, 1647.

This regiment, like Fairfax' was entirely formed out of Cromwell's famous double regiment in the Army of the Eastern Association. One would expect such a corps to be one of the crack regiments of the New Model, and indeed it did very well both at Naseby and at Langport.

Its commander, Edward Whalley, was Cromwell's cousin. All the troop commanders with the possible exception of Cannon had served under Cromwell in Manchester's Army, and several, no doubt, had been with him in 1642. Baxter names Evanson among those religious men that Cromwell took special care to get into his troop.

At Bristol' Major Bethell's were the first horse that entered the line, who did behave himself gallantly, and was shot in the thigh, had one or two shot more, and had his horse shot under him.' Hugh Peters said of him that 'he lived without pride, and died full of faith'. He was one of those rare leaders who expose themselves on every occasion. He had been taken by Goring's horse at Radcot Bridge – 'engaging too far' – (May 1645); he had again been slightly wounded at Langport, where he led the attack with admirable gallantry.

Though Bethell was a valiant officer his troop was, according to Baxter, full of violent sectaries. Captain Evanson had told Baxter that the Regiment was 'the most religious, most valiant, most successful of all the army, but in as much danger as any one whatsoever,' and in June 1645 Whalley who 'was orthodox in religion, but engaged by kindred and interest to Cromwell', invited him to become his chaplain. Baxter found the man very recalcitrant to sound doctrine.[20]

In the quarrels of 1647 Whalley and his officers took the part of their men. Whalley told Skippon and the Parliamentary commissioners : "I find that both my officers and souldiers are not transported or carryed away by passion. Reason sways them ; and truly reason is so prevalent with them, in these humble desires that they make in the way of grievances to Parliament, as I am confident they will deny themselves in every thing, if there may be as reasonable a reason given why they may not goe on."[21]

Fairfax selected Whalley's Regiment to guard the King, and it did that duty from June to November 1647. When on 11 November Charles escaped he left a letter in which he acknowledged that he had been 'civilly used' by Whalley and Major Huntingdon. The soldiers too had behaved themselves.

The Regiment took no part in the mutiny of the Levellers at Ware (13 November 1647).

In the Second Civil War the Regiment fought at Maidstone (June 1648), and was sent to pursue Goring when the Kentish Cavaliers retreated towards Essex.

'We marched close in the rear of him,' Whalley reported, 'but he doth so overpower us with foot, that we cannot engage in this close country but with great disadvantage, to the hazard of the brigade.'[22]

The Regiment took part in the siege of Colchester and

Whalley was one of those who witnessed the shooting of Sir Charles Lucas and Sir George Lisle.

About this time the men complained that they had served for the last five months without pay.

Whalley sat in the tribunal which tried King Charles and was one of those who signed the death-warrant.

The beginning of the Republic was marked by a mutiny, when on 24 April 1649, Robert Lockyer and 30 of Captain John Savage's men seized the standard of their troop and barricading themselves in the Bull Inn in Bishopsgate Street, refused a lawful order to march into Essex and demanded an advance of pay. Whalley suppressed them with a heavy hand. Six were sentenced to death, and five to ride the wooden horse for an hour, and be discharged from the army. At Cromwell's request five of those condemned to death were pardoned after expressing their penitence. The ringleader, Lockyer, was shot in St. Paul's Churchyard (27 April). His speech to the firing squad is an interesting illustration of the Leveller's outlook : "Fellow souldiers, I am here brought to suffer in behalfe of the people of England, and for your priviledges and liberties, and such as in conscience you ought to own and stand to : But I perceive you are appointed by your officers to murther me, and I did not thinke that you had had such heathenish and barbarous principles in you as to obey your officers in murthering of me, when I stand up for nothing but what is for your good."[23] The Levellers, sporting sea-green and black colours, gave Trooper Lockyer what amounted to a state funeral. During the following week the revolt of the Levellers broke out, but Whalley's Regiment took no part in it. Instead of sea green and black they wore blue ribbands in their hats : the colours of Sir Thomas Fairfax. But if Whalley had a good grip on his Regiment, an old corporal of Bethell's Troop, William Thompson, was among the ringleaders of this dangerous movement. He had been cashiered in 1647 for a drunken affray. He questioned the justice of his sentence, and hung about the quarters of the regiment stirring up sedition. Thereafter he formed an armed gang, whose activities made them no better than highwaymen. On 6 May 1649 he published his manifesto

'Englands Standard Advanced in Oxfordshire, or, A Declaration from Mr Wil. Thompson, and the Oppressed People of This Nation, Now under this Conduct in the Said County.'

Colonel John Reynolds, with three troops of horse, fell on Thompson near Banbury (10 May), and routed him, with ease. Thompson himself escaped, but was surprised near Wellingborough (20 May). He shot a cornet and a trooper, receiving two shots himself. He scorned to take quarter and a corporal shot him with Colonel Reynolds' carbine, which, we are told was 'charged with seven bullets'. So another of those strange Ironside soldiers met his end.

The Regiment was with Cromwell in Scotland and did well at Musselburgh (30 July 1650). Whalley was wounded at Dunbar and had his horse killed under him. He was made Commissary-General in October 1650, an appointment he held at Worcester in 1651.

In 1653 Captain Edmund Chillenden left the Regiment. He was in trouble thanks to his peculiar theological views, indeed he may have been a Fifth Monarchy Man. Cromwell did not cashier him, and Chillenden was duly grateful: 'Your Excellency being just and full of pity, you were not minded to make me a public example, but to put me off that I might not be utterly ruined (30 November 1653). In 1655 he was in trouble again for lending his chapel in St. Paul's to one John Biddle, who preached against the divinity of Christ. However, Chillenden protested that he never did anything against Cromwell or his government, and the Protector evidently believed him for no proceedings were taken against this curious zealot.

Whalley, being Cromwell's cousin, was one of his most loyal supporters, and his Regiment – unlike the other made up from his old Ironsides – played no part in the opposition to the Protector's arbitrary power. Whalley was one of the major-generals (1654-1658) and a member of Cromwell's House of Lords (December 1657). In April 1659 he adhered to Richard Cromwell, but most of his men marched to join Fleetwood and Disbrowe, . . . 'which he seeing, opened his breast, and desired them to shoot him.'[24] The Regiment was given to its old major, Robert Swallow. Another of its original troop commanders,

William Evanson, now reappeared. Swallow fought under
Lambert during Sir George Booth's insurrection and sided with
him in his quarrel with Parliament (October 1659). Parliament
dismissed him and most of his officers (10 February 1660)
giving command to Colonel Thomas Saunders. He did not last
long and in June was compelled to hand over to Lord Falkland,
who had little to do but preside over its disbandment, which took
place before the year was out.

Whalley, being a regicide, fled overseas, and died in New
England (c.1675). Captain John Grove, another old officer, went
to live in Holland.

One would suppose that the composition of this Regiment
was much the same as that of Sir Thomas Fairfax, for both came
out of Cromwell's Ironsides. If this one gave the Protector's
government comparatively little trouble we may attribute it
to Colonel Whalley's influence. He was evidently a good tactician, and a firm and loyal commanding officer.

COLONEL EDWARD ROSSITER'S REGIMENT

Succession of colonels :

Edward Rossiter	21 Jan. 1645
	Confirmed 18 March 1645.
Philip Twistleton	4 August 1647
John Clobery (d.1687)	1659
Troop commanders 1645;	
Colonel Edward Rossiter	Major, Lincolnshire H.
(c.1617-1669)	Siege of Newark, 1644.
	Colonel, Lincolnshire, H.
—	Colonel, N.M. 21 Jan. 1645.
	Defeated at Melton Mowbray
	25 Feb. 1645.
	Dismissed, August 1647.
	Victor at Willoughby Field,
	5 July 1648.
Major Philip Twistleton	18 March 1645.
Captain Anthony Markham	1645
	Left soon after 3 June 1647.
Captain John Nelthorpe	18 March 1645.
	Still serving 1649.

Captain Original Peart	18 March 1645.
	Still serving 1649.
Captain Henry Markham	Captain 1645.
	Still serving 1649.

Rossiter, who was from Somerby, Lincs., commanded a Lincolnshire Regiment, which no doubt came more or less complete into the New Model. A strong Presbyterian he supported Parliament in the quarrel with the Army and was dismissed. Anthony Markham left at about the same time, and was replaced by Captain Owen Cambridge, who had been a major of foot in the garrison of Leicester. He was to be major of Twistleton's from c.1651 to 1659.

Fairfax gave the command to Philip Twistleton, and brought in the valiant James Berry from his own Regiment as major (14 June 1647).

The Regiment fought at Preston (17 August 1648) and Berry, who took the news to the Commons, was given £200. Twistleton's served both at Dunbar (1650) and Worcester (1651).

The Regiment was in Scotland from about 1652 to October 1654, when Cromwell ordered them back to England. 'I could very ill spare them', wrote Monck, and, ironically enough, they found so little to do at home that they disappear from view until in August 1658 they were sent back to Scotland, and caused Monck a lot of trouble. When, on 19 October 1659, he declared for the restoration of the Parliament most of the troop commanders, including both Twistleton and Cambridge were absent. One captain, Thomas Deane, adhered to Monck, but unfortunately he was a pretty useless officer, and when he was sent to secure Carlisle, most of his men deserted him.

Monck lost no time in disarming the recalcitrant troops. According to his chaplain: 'Most of Twistleton's regiment refused the service, but being quartered in such convenient places they were dismounted, and red coats put upon their horses'.[25] Of course, any foot soldier who could stay on a horse was delighted to get the far better rate of pay enjoyed by the trooper of those days. Monck's difficulty was to find officers. Soon lieutenants and cornets found themselves commanding troops.

149

Monck gave the command to his kinsman, another Devonian, John Clobery; and the majority to Jeremiah Smith (d.1675), a versatile captain in his own regiment, who, from being a shipowner at Hull, had commanded a man-o'-war under Monck in 1653, and had been Adjutant-General of the army in Scotland (1655).

Colonel Clobery had a Royalist brother-in-law, one John Otway, who had managed to bring him round to his own views. These two contrived to put Monck's intentions in a good light to Sir Edward Hyde, King Charles' chief minister, and so had some influence in bringing about the Restoration.

Poor Twistleton was in a quandary. He was not a supporter of Fleetwood and Lambert, nor did he throw in his lot with Hacker, Saunders and their other opponents. 'Col. Twistleton . . . hath disserted the army, but is ingaged not to meddle on either side.'[26] Such a man had no hope of being employed by Monck, and in fact in the crisis of 1660 his successor, Clobery, proved a valuable ally. On 7 June 1660, King Charles II honoured Monck by supping with him at the Cockpit, and Clobery by conferring a knighthood upon him. He 'had deserved so well in his constant adhering to his Excellency, and prudent management of affairs for the happy restoring of his Majesty to his people.' More to the point he got a pension of £600 a year. The Regiment was disbanded in Lincolnshire at the end of October 1660.

Clobery was to serve again in Monmouth's rebellion (1685). When his militiamen from Hampshire and Wiltshire proved disaffected he served at Sedgemoor as a volunteer. His effigy may be seen in Winchester Cathedral.

Twistleton, along with Colonel Swallow, was sent to the Tower on 20 November 1662, but was set free on 5 December, having given security for £1,000 and taken the oath of allegiance.

Rossiter played a minor part in bringing about the Restoration, but does not figure in History thereafter.

This old Lincolnshire regiment does not seem to have been particularly *difficile*. Indeed it was one which Monck, with his extraordinary powers of organization was able to forge into a trustworthy weapon, when in 1660 he began to show his hand. It may be that the private soldiers from Lincolnshire were not as politically minded, or as fanatical in questions of religion, as the men of East Anglia.

COLONEL JOHN FIENNES' REGIMENT

Colonel John Fiennes (c.1614-1696)
Major *Vacant*
Captain John White[27]
Captain John Hunt[27]
Captain Thomas Brews[27]
Captain
Captain   28

This was not a New Model Regiment and its history is rather obscure. It may have been raised in North Oxfordshire.[29] Fiennes, the third surviving son of the first Viscount Saye and Sele ("Old Subtlety") had raised a troop (60)[30] in 1642, and became a colonel in the summer of 1643. He was at Bristol when his brother, Nathaniel, surrendered the city in July 1643. In 1644 he besieged Banbury Castle from 27 August until 25 October, when his force was routed by the Earl of Northampton. This defeat was considered discreditable even by some Parliamentarians. On 10 November Sir Oliver Luke wrote: 'There was a report made by recommendation of the Committee to our House in behalf of Col. Fiennes for money for his soldiers and provision of arms and presently it was laid hold on and a reply of what great sums they had in that family already, and desired before more was granted there might be an examination of the carriage of the business at Banbury, for they heard that they of Banbury had 300 horse and 400 foot more than the enemy.'[31]

In November 1644 the CBK ordered 200 pair of pistols, and 200 backs, breasts, and pots for the arming of the Regiment. Evidently these were to make up for losses sustained in the defeat at Banbury.[32] In December it was one of three regiments at Abingdon, and the three together did not make above 300 horse.[33] The Governor, Major-General Richard Browne reported: 'Great want of money to encourage the soldiers, who have none even to shoe their horses'.[34]

151

In April 1645 Fiennes served for a time with Cromwell, who thought well of him: 'His diligence is great, and this I must testify, that I find no man more ready to all services than himself ... I find him a gentleman of that fidelity to you and so conscientious that he would all his troop were as religious and civil as any, and makes it a great part of his care to get them so.'[35]

On 24 June the Committee of Both Kingdoms commended the Regiment for its good service, particularly at Naseby. It was its opinion that it should be continued in service. It was to receive £1000 at once and a settled course was to be taken for it's future pay.[36] On 5 July the C.B.K. ordered: '13. To write to Sir Thos. Fairfax, that, in regard Col. Fiennes lost many horse of his regiment in the last battle [Naseby], that he be furnished with some of those to be raised within the enemy's quarters. ...'[37]

Fiennes' Regiment escorted the Royalist prisoners to London after Naseby. He was selected MP for Morpeth (1645), and thereafter seems to have soldiered no more. On 13 August 1645 CBK made the following order: '10. That it be reported to the House of Commons, that in regard there is no money nor employment for Col. John Fiennes' regiment he may have leave to dismiss the soldiers with their horses.'[38] No doubt the Regiment was disbanded in the autumn of 1645.

It may be doubted whether Fiennes' regiment was as formidable as some of those of the New Model, notably those of Fairfax and Whalley. Still – quite apart from the rout at Banbury – it is evident that Fiennes had had considerable administrative difficulties, due to arrears of pay,[39] and shortage of arms and armour, and even of horseshoes.

Fiennes was summoned to Cromwell's House of Lords (1657), but after the Restoration the Royalists left him in peace, and he suffered no penalty for his activities during the Great Rebellion. He married a lady many years younger than himself, Susannah Hobbs (1657-1715), who lies buried at Broughton, which is still the seat of the Fiennes family.

It would seem from Sir Samuel Luke's correspondence that there were those in the Regiment, who were no better than horse-thieves: 'Col. Fiennes' horse are the horse drivers – you may see how the country suffers.'[40]

succession of colonels :

Thomas Sheffeild	After 12 April, but before 14 June, 1645. Retired June 1647.
Thomas Harrison (1606-1660)	By 23 June 1647. Dismissed 22 Dec. 1653.
Stephen Winthrop (1619-1658)	1654.
Edward Montagu (1625-1672)	16 Sept. 1658.
Matthew Alured	6 Aug. 1659.
Edward Montagu (1625-1672)	20 April 1660

troop commanders :

Colonel Thomas Sheffeild	Captain, James Sheffeild, H. Essex' Army. In 1644.
Major Richard Fincher	Captain Major 1645. Quartermaster-General H. 1645. Retired, June 1647.
Captain Robert Robotham	Captain, James Sheffeild, H. Essex' Army. Captain, N.M. 18 March 1645. Retired, June 1647.
Captain William Rainsborow (Rainborow)	Major by 5 July 1647. Dismissed 1649.
Captain Gabriel Martin	Captain Balfour, H. Essex' Army. Captain N.M. 18 March 1645. Retired June 1647.
Captain Arthur Evelyn	Captain, 51 Troop 1642[41] Served under Major-General Richard Browne, Governor of Abingdon. Captain, N.M. 18 March, 1645. Governor of Wallingford Castle 24 July 1646. Still Troop commander 26 April 1647. Adjutant-General, H. 1645-(?) 1648

Thomas Sheffeild was one of the 20 children of Edmund, first Earl of Mulgrave. It was originally intended that his eldest brother, James, who had commanded a regiment under Essex, should command the New Model Regiment, with Thomas as major, but for some reason this did not come to pass. Colonel Thomas Sheffeild and Captain Robert Robotham both commanded troops in James Sheffeild's Regiment in 1644,[42] while Captain William Rainsborow came from Sir William Balfour's Regiment, which also belonged to Essex' Army.

In 1644 there were six regiments of horse in Essex' Army:

Colonel	Troops	Strength Summer 1644
Sir Philip Stapleton	8	725
Sir William Balfour	6	494
Hans Behre	5	425
John Dalbier	4	310
James Sheffeild	6	475
Sir Robert Pye	3[42]	240
	32	2669

Behre's and Dalbier's were sent to reinforce the garrison of Gloucester. The rest were 'reduced and settled'[43] into the New Model Regiments of:

Colonel Richard Graves   Not at Naseby
Colonel Sir Robert Pye
Colonel Thomas Sheffeild

As the four reduced regiments had 1934 officers and men in mid-1644, they would, despite casualties suffered in Cornwall and at II Newbury, be able to find 1800 officers and men for the three new regiments without much recruiting.

We may be sure that the men of Sheffeild's Regiment came from Essex' Army, but from two or more different regiments. Thus, quite apart from the fact that Essex' cavalry had a less impressive fighting record than those of the Eastern Association, the regiments of Graves, Pye and Sheffeild must at first have lacked the solidity of regiments formed entirely from Cromwell's Ironsides.

Major Fincher, 'a stout man and a good soldier',[44] distinguished himself in the cavalry action at St. Columb, Cornwall (7 March 1646).

Sheffeild took the side of Parliament when in 1647 it attempted to disband the army. Captain Evelyn's men made their views abundantly clear: 'Before any man of us list our names for Ireland, wee desire satisfaccion for our arreares here in England. . . . Though wee are perswaded that the kingdome stands in neede of helpe, yett wee conceive that wee are nott soe to help them as wholly to deprive our selves of our just rights and liberties.'[45] According to a contemporary newsletter Sheffeild's Regiment 'continue their red collours, and say they are England's collours, and that they will not goe for Ireland.'[46] Presumably the red colours were not their standards, but some kind of cockade or favour.

Major Thomas Harrison from Fleetwood's Regiment replaced Sheffeild. He was the arch-type of Roundhead cavalryman; gallant in action, yet ruthless; soldierly in his bearing, cheerful and eloquent. He was also a firm believer in the Kingdom of the Saints and the Fifth Monarchy. In 1642 he had served in Essex' Lifeguard and thereafter he had been Fleetwood's major at Marston Moor, Naseby and Langport. His military reputation stood very high – and justly so. The troop commaders were now :—

Colonel Thomas Harrison
Major William Rainborow
Captain John Peck
Captain   Whitehead
Captain Henry Cromwell (1628-1674)
Captain Stephen Winthrop (1619-1658)

Rainborow was brother of Colonel Thomas Rainborow. Henry Cromwell, Oliver's second surviving son, was to become Lord Deputy of Ireland. Winthrop, fourth son of John Winthrop (1588-1649), the first Governor of Massachusetts, was married to Rainborow's sister, Judith.

Harrison's Regiment appeared – uninvited – at a rendezvous at Corkbush Field, near Ware (15 November 1647), with the paper known as *The Agreement of the People* stuck in their hats, and the words *England's Freedom, and Soldiers Rights* writ large on the outside.

'I perceived,' wrote Fairfax, 'the men were merely cozened and abused with fair pretences of those men which acted in the London councils.' The men submitted to their general, cheerfully enough, throwing away the political manifesto.

Harrison's Regiment checked the Scots advanced guard in the fight at Appleby on 17 July 1648. The Colonel himself boldly laid his hand upon an enemy standard, and received three sore wounds for his pains. Thus he missed the battle of Preston.

In December Harrison commanded the escort that took Charles from Hurst Castle to Windsor, and the King was very pleased with his troop, who were well horsed and armed. Harrison himself was 'gallantly mounted and armed; a velvet montier [montero] was on his head, a new buff-coat upon his back, and a crimson silk scarf about his waste richly fringed.' Charles, who had heard that the army meant to murder him, and that Harrison was to be its instrument, discounted the story, saying 'he look'd like a soldier, and that his aspect was good, . . . and that having some judgment in faces, if he had observ'd him so well before, he should not have harbour'd that ill opinion of him.'[47] Nonetheless Harrison sat in the tribunal that tried the King, and he signed the death-warrant.

In May 1649 the men of Peck's and Winthrop's troops joined in the rising of the Levellers, and were well cudgelled for their pains. It was probably thanks to Harrison that the other four troops remained obedient.

In 1649 Cromwell dismissed Major Rainborow, whose blasphemous views were thought to be bad for discipline. His cornet, Wentworth Day, who also left the army, became prominent as a Fifth Monarchy man. He was arrested in 1655 for preaching a sermon at All Hallows, in which he denounced Cromwell as a perjurer and apostate. Nothing daunted he committed a similar offence in 1658. It cost him £500 and a year in prison.

Henry Cromwell left in 1649 to be a colonel in Ireland. His troop went with him as a cadre for his new regiment.

In 1650 Harrison was made commander-in-chief of the forces in the south of England, during the absence of Fairfax and Cromwell, with the rank of major-general. He fought at Worcester (1651). Elected a member of the Council of State, Harrison was the leader of those officers who wanted to dissolve the Long Parliament, and in the disorderly scene which eventually brought this about he went up to the Speaker saying: "Sir, seeing things are brought to this pass it is not requisite for you to stay there".... To this William Lenthall (1591-1662) replied that he would not come down unless he was pulled out.

"Sir," said Harrison, "I will lend you my hand," whereupon Lenthall put his hand into Harrison's and came down without any pulling. That, at least is Harrison's version of what took place, and whatever else he was, he was an honest man.

For the next few months Harrison was the leader of the dominant party in the assembly known as the Barebones Parliament, but his political pre-eminence was shortlived. He declined to recognize the Protectorate; his commission was taken from him (22 December 1653), and he spent some months in prison at Portsmouth, and Carisbrooke or in the Tower. He was suspected of supporting the plot of the Fifth Monarchy men or Anabaptists.

Harrison took no part in the political crises that followed the death of Oliver, for wounds and imprisonment had undermined his health.

Stephen Winthrop was eventually made colonel in place of Harrison. He had long been suffering from 'zeatica' (sic) 'My much lying in wet feilds vppon the grownd hath brought it vppon me, as it hath vppon many others.' Poor fellow! He longed to return to America but the Regiment was posted to Scotland where, Winthrop wrote, the 'eyre is two moist for me, & breeds rumes & coughes'. They carried him off in the Spring of 1658, and Richard Cromwell appointed Edward Montagu, who had commanded a regiment of foot at Naseby, in his place.

About this time a troop commander, named Benjamin Oakeshott, was appointed. He was probably a Naseby veteran :-

QM to Winthrop's Troop	c.1647
Cornet	by 1655
Capt.-Lieut.	in 1656
Captain *vice* Winthrop	1658-1659

Montagu was in the Baltic (March-September 1658), with the fleet sent to mediate between Sweden and Denmark. He returned to find that Richard Cromwell had fallen, and that he himself had been dismissed from his commands by land and sea. The Regiment was given to Matthew Alured, who had commanded the Parliament's guard.

In the crisis of 1660 Alured supported Monck, and did good service by persuading Overton peaceably to surrender the government of Hull.

Two troops of the Regiment joined Lambert when he escaped from the Tower and set up his standard at Daventry. But, confronted by former comrades under Ingoldsby, they would not fight.

Monck reappointed Montagu (20 April 1660) but seven months later the Regiment was disbanded.

Thomas Harrison, the Regiment's second C.O. was the first of the regicides to be executed after the Restoration. As he was drawn to the place of execution upon a hurdle a spectator called out "Where is your good old cause now?" To which the old Roundhead replied with a cheerful smile, clapping his hand on his breast and saying: "Here it is, and I am going to seal it with my blood."

Samuel Pepys, who had seen the King beheaded, saw Harrison die on 13 October 1670, and said he looked "as cheerful as any man could in that condition."

Incredible though it may seem Pepys was actually on the strength of Harrison's old regiment at this time ! The idea of that aspiring civil servant soldiering alongside the veterans of Naseby has a certain piquancy. It was not quite like that, however. The explanation is that he was the colonel's secretary, and appeared on the books as a trooper. This disreputable fiddle brought in £23. 14. 9, which Samuel gratefully described as 'a great blessing'. . .

COMMISSARY-GENERAL HENRY IRETON'S REGIMENT

Succession of colonels :

Succession of colonels:

| Sir Michael Livesey | 18 March 1645-3 May 1645 |

Henry Ireton (1611-1651)	w.e.f. 3 May 1645
	Died in Ireland 25 November 1651.
Charles Fleetwood (-1692)	July 1652
Thomas Cooper (-1659)	Died 21 Dec. 1659
Henry Markham (-)	18 Jan. 1660.

Troop commanders 1645

1. Colonel Henry Ireton
   Capt.-Lieut. John Degennis

   Captain 1642.
   Captain, Cromwell, H.
   QMG
   Colonel
   Commissary-General, NM, 14 June 1645

2. Major George Sedascue

   Major. Livesey.
   Major, NM 18 March 1645.
   Left the Regiment in 1647.
   Adjutant-General, H. Oct. 1648.

3. Captain William Guilliam
   (-1645)

   Capt. Hesilrige, H. 29 Aug. 1643[48]
   Captain Waller, H. 7 Feb. 1644.
   Captain NM by 5 April 1645.
   K. Bristol, 1 Sept. 1645.

4. Captain Robert Gibbons

   Captain, Livesey H.
   Captain, NM 18 March. 1645.
   Major *vice* Sedascue by 12 July 1647.
   Governor of Rye, 1648.

5. Captain John Hoskins
   (-1645)

   Captain, Livesey H.
   Captain, NM, 18 March, 1645.
   K. Naseby.

6. Captain John Bury (or Barry)

   18 March 1645.
   Retired some time after 6 March 1646

Troop commanders promoted after Naseby :-

| Captain William Cecil | Captain *vice* Hoskins w.e.f. 14 June 1645. Still serving in 1648. |
| Captain Henry Pretty | Captain *vice* Guilliams w.e.f. 1 Sept. 1645. Left the Regiment 1649. |

Captain Anthony Morgan (c.1621-1668)	Of Rynyzwen, Carmarthen, educated at Magdalen Hall, Oxford. Royalist. Changed sides 1645. Captain *vice* Bury after 6 March 1646. M.D. Oxon. Major *vice* Gibbons, 1649.
Captain Robert Kirkby	Troop commander *vice* Sedascue by 12 July 1647. Left the Regiment, 1649.
Capt.-Lieut. John Degennis	Lieutenant to Ireton's Troop, 58. 1642. Capt.-Lieut. 1645. Died in Ireland.

Major Sedascue and two of the captains, Gibbon and Hoskins, had served in Sir Michael Livesey's Regiment in Sir William Waller's Army, while Guilliam came from Waller's own regiment. The colonel had a bad reputation for disobedience and even cowardice. On 3 May 1645 he was ordered to be sent to London in custody for disobeying Fairfax, and was deprived of his command.[49] His regiment was given to Henry Ireton, who had been Quarter-master-General in the Army of the Eastern Association.

The Regiment was largely raised in Kent, and had fought at Cheriton.

Captain Guilliam, who fell at Bristol is described as 'a valiant, faithful, and religious man'.[50]

On 15 June 1646 Ireton married Cromwell's eldest daughter, Bridget.

Ireton's Regiment was in the forefront of the struggle with Parliament over disbanding. The nub of the matter was 'That we are put upon the business of Ireland or else disbanding, before the real freedom of the people of England be established, according to the end wherefore this Parliament was called, and the army raised for the preservation and defence of the same.'[51] In the autumn the Regiment, along with those of Cromwell, Fleetwood, Rich and Whalley, chose new agitators and put forward their own constitution: 'The Agreement of the People'. Even so the men were not mutinous.

In 1648 the Regiment was with Fairfax at Maidstone. Three troops under Captain Cecil were in the fight before Colchester (13 June), and two under Major Gibbon were with the force that defeated the Earl of Holland's army at Kingston (6 July), afterwards proceeding to Colchester. It was due to Ireton's influence that Sir Charles Lucas and Sir George Lisle were shot after the surrender. Able with tongue and pen he was now Cromwell's chief adviser as well as his son-in-law. It was he that arranged for Cornet Joyce to seize the King. 'Pride's Purge', too, was really his work. He sat in the unlawful tribunal that tried the King, and he signed the death warrant.

The Regiment's pay was by this time well in arrears, and the men had not even been paid the gratuity promised on the taking of Colchester. Labouring also under purely political grievances, they were now following the Levellers' line. In the spring of 1649 John Lilburne was denouncing Ireton as a tyrant and a renegade who had not only opposed the establishment of the absolute democracy for which they yearned, but had insisted on maintaining discipline. Chosen by lot to serve in Ireland the Regiment, for the most part, joined in the mutiny of the Levellers. Much good it did them. Cromwell fell upon them at Burford on the night of 14 May 1649, taking about 340 and scattering the rest. The troops of Major Gibbon and Captain Morgan kept out of this business but 35 of Ireton's Troop, and 33 of Pretty's signed 'the humble petition of the sad and heavy-hearted prisoners remaining in the church of Burford.' The troopers were pardoned, but only, presumably, because they now agreed to go to Ireland.

Upon the death of Ireton (26 November 1651) Charles Fleetwood succeeded him both as commander-in-chief in Ireland and colonel (July 1652).

At this period the former Royalist, Major Morgan, was a great man, trusted by the Cromwell family. Educated at Oxford he was an eloquent orator, and a valued correspondent of Henry Cromwell's. Indeed he ultimately lost his commission thanks to his connection with the latter.

Fleetwood, who had regiments both of horse and foot in England, gave up command of his regiment in Ireland in July

1659. Colonel Thomas Cooper left a regiment of foot to take over. He was, it seems, a good officer, but he did not last long. He died suddenly 'in his chair' on 21 December 1659. On 18 January Parliament appointed Colonel Henry Markham, who was also made one of the commissioners for the management of affairs in Ireland. Thereafter the Regiment disappears from view.

Edward Warren, who had been major to Cooper was executed on 15 July 1663 for conspiring with other former Cromwellian officers to overthrow the new government. Anthony Morgan did much better. He had been knighted by one of the Cromwells, and on 19 November 1660 he was knighted all over again by Charles II. He was one of the original members of the Royal Society and Pepys who met him on 5 March 1668 thought him 'a very wise man'. He was certainly wise enough to recognize the winning side when he saw it.

THE REGIMENT OF COLONEL B. VERMUYDEN

Succession of colonels:

Succession of colonels:	
B. Vermuyden	Colonel Eastern Association NM 18 March 1645. Resigned 8 June 1645.
Oliver Cromwell (1599-1658)	June 1645.
John Disbrowe (1608-1680)	Sept. 1649.
Valentine Walton (-1661)	12 January 1660
Charles Howard	25 February 1660

Troop commanders:

1.	B. Vermuyden Capt.Lieut. Joseph Wallington	
2.	Major Robert Huntington	Captain, Vermuyden, E. Assoc. 18 March 1645. Resigned June 1648.
3.	Captain John Jenkins (or Jenkyn)	Captain NM 18 March 1645. Served until 1660.
4.	Captain Henry Middleton	Captain NM 18 March 1645. Court-martialled Oct. 1647.
5.	Captain John Reynolds	Captain, NM, 18 March 1645. Colonel Volunteer Regiment, H. 1648.

6.	Captain	Bush (	-1645)	Captain NM 18 March 1645. K. Naseby.

	*	*		*
Captain John Blackwell				Capt. *vice* Bush. Also a Deputy Treasurer at war. Left c. June 1648.
QM Richard Cadwell				Jenkin's Troop by 29 May 1645.

The troops of Vermuyden, Huntington and Jenkins came from the former's regiment in the Army of the Eastern Association, and it seems likely that the majority of the officers and men came from that source.

Vermuyden, 'in regard of some special occasions which . . . he had to draw him beyond seas' laid down his commission and received his discharge (8 June). On this Fairfax and other officers wrote to the House of Lords, pointing out the imperative need for a general officer to command the horse. Cromwell was appointed lieutenant-general and given the vacant regiment.

In the quarrel of 1647 the Regiment was one of the first to oppose disbanding. Major Huntington resigned in June 1648, choosing, as he said, to quit his command after serving Parliament 'for these five years past,' rather than 'by hopes of gain, with a troubled mind, continue an abettor, or assistant, of such as give affronts to the Parliament and Kingdom, by abusing their power and authority to carry-on their particular designs.' However true the major's views may have been they were ill-timed, for they came at a moment when Cromwell was on the march to meet the Duke of Hamilton and the Engagers.

John Blackmore, 'a godly man and a good souldier,' now became major (14 June 1648).[52]

The Regiment took part in Cromwell's Welsh campaign and in the battle of Preston.

Although some of the troopers held extreme religious and political views, so far from supporting the revolt of the Levellers, the Regiment expressed its abhorrence of it, and denounced a false rumour that it had designed 'to have seized upon the person of the Lieut.-General.'[53]

When he went to Ireland Cromwell handed over his Regiment to his brother-in-law, John Disbrowe, under whom it fought at Worcester (3 September 1651). In 1655 it helped to put down Colonel John Penruddock's rising.

When Oliver died Disbrowe was one of those who planned to make Fleetwood commander-in-chief, independent of Richard Cromwell. The 'grim Gyant' threatened his nephew, saying 'that if he would dissolve his parliament, the officers would take care of him; but that if he refused so to do, they would do it without him, and leave him to shift for himself.'[54] The Rump was restored, and Disbrowe was elected one of the council of state (13 May 1659).

In the events that followed Disbrowe supported Lambert against Monck, but his Regiment did not support him, resolving to stand for the restored Long Parliament (24 December 1659). Disbrowe's submission followed (29 December) but he lost his commission when commissioners were appointed to weed out the disaffected. Valentine Walton was made colonel in his stead. Monck, however, did not trust Walton who was closely allied to the Cromwell family, and he gave the colonelcy to Charles Howard (25 February 1660). The Regiment was disbanded in October 1660.

After the Restoration Disbrowe spent seven years in the Tower, but was released in 1667 and spent his last years in peace.

COLONEL JOHN BUTLER'S REGIMENT

Succession of Colonels :

John Middleton	Lt. General, H. Waller's Army.
	Colonel, NM, 18 March 1645, but did not serve.
John Butler	Captain, Hesilrige, H.
	Major, Hesilrige, H.
	Colonel, NM by 20 May 1645.[55]
	Retired June 1647.
Thomas Horton	Major, NM 18 March 1645.
	Colonel by 23 June 1647.
	Died in Ireland, Oct. 1649.
Jerome Sankey	Capt.-Lieut. to Brereton, H. 1645.
(-c.1687)	Major, 1646.
	Colonel w.e.f. Oct. 1649.

Troop commanders:

Colonel John Butler
Major Thomas Horton

Captain Edward Foley	Captain, Hesilrige, H. Waller's Army. Fought at Cropredy Bridge. Captain, NM 18 March 1645. Left before 22 March 1647.
Captain Samuel Gardiner	Captain, Hesilrige, H. Waller's Army. Fought at Cropredy Bridge. Captain, NM 18 March 1645. Retired, 1649.
Captain Thomas Pennyfather	Captain, Hesilrige, H. Waller's Army. Captain, NM 18 March 1645. Major *vice* Bethell, 1649. Died in Ireland.
Captain Walter Perry (-1645 or 1646)	Captain, Hesilrige, H. At Cropredy Bridge. Captain, NM, 18 March 1645. Died between 6 Nov. 1645 and 23 Jan. 1646.[56]

✽ ✽ ✽

Captain Walter Bethell	Captain, Cromwell, H, Eastern Association. Captain *vice* Perry by 23 Jan. 1646. Major *vice* Horton c.June 1647.[57] Retired, 1649.

✽ ✽ ✽

Other officers:

Benjamin Burgess	Lieut. Foley's Troop by 6 Nov. 1645.[58] Captain *vice* Foley by 22 March 1647. SW Pembroke, 1648.
Joseph Molyneux	Capt.-Lieut. w.e.f. 10 July 1645. *vice* Capt.-Lieut. (name unknown) K.[59] W. Carmarthen, April 1648.

Thomas Ellis	Cornet, Foley's Troop by 6 Nov. 1645.
	Lieut. *vice* Burgess.
	Still serving 28 Nov. 1648.
	Wrote a good account of Cropredy Bridge.[60]
Eli Green	Lieut. Molyneux' Troop, 1647.
	Captain by 1649.
Paul Bunting	Cornet by 5 April 1645.
	In Pye's Regt. by 20 Jan. 1646.[61]
John Phelps	Cornet, Gardiner's Troop, Hesilrige H.
	Cornet, Gardiner's Troop, NM.
	Still serving as cornet in Oct. 1647.[62]
Cleare	Surgeon, by Aug. 1647.[63]

Butler's Regiment represented Sir Arthur Hesilrige's famous 'Lobsters', from Waller's Army. They had met with disaster at Roundway Down and triumph at Cheriton; had done good service at Lansdown and had come pretty well out of Waller's repulse at Cropredy Bridge. This was probably the most formidable regiment of Waller's Army, but at Naseby, with the advantage of numbers, it proved no match for the Lifeguards of the Palatine Princes. Both its field officers were wounded, and in their absence Quarter-master-General Richard Fincher commanded it at the blockade of Berkeley Castle. Butler recovered in time for the siege of Bristol, and wrote a letter to Waller in which he vindicated Rupert's conduct in surrendering. He found the Prince 'much inclyn'd to a happy peace.' He signed himself 'your corpulent servant for ever'.[64]

Butler defeated Major-General William Webb and Lord Hopton's cavalry, near Stratton on 25 February 1646. During the summer the Regiment took part in the siege of Oxford.

In the quarrel over disbanding Butler took the side of Parliament, and in June Fairfax gave the command to Horton. Thomas Horton who had been Sir Arthur Hesilrige's falconer before the war, had been his cornet in 1642.

In the second Civil War Horton played an important part in the campaign in South Wales, and decisively defeated the

Royalists at St. Fagans (8 May 1648) where Major Bethell and Lieutenant John Godfrey distinguished themselves. Horton later defeated Sir Henry Lingen near Presteigne (July).

Serving in Wales the Regiment played but little part in the events leading up to the trial of the King. It was out of range of Leveller propaganda.

Chosen by lot to serve in Ireland, half the Regiment disbanded rather than go there. Major Bethell, and Captains Gardiner and Burgess were among those who declined to go. Horton himself swiftly succumbed to 'the country-disease.' 'He was,' wrote Cromwell, 'a person of good integrity and courage. His former services, especially that of the last summer, I hope will be had in remembrance.'[65] The major, Thomas Pennyfather, also died in Ireland.

The next colonel was Jerome Sankey, a Shropshire man, who at Cambridge had shown himself to be 'more given to manly exercises than logic or philosophy, . . . a boisterous fellow at cudgelling and football playing, and indeed more fit in all respects to be a rude soldier than a scholar or a man of polite parts.'[66] Sir William Brereton, no mean judge, described him as 'A very valiant man and commands my own troop.' (January 1645). In 1646 Brereton made Sankey his major.[67] In 1648 the parliamentary visitors made him a fellow of All Souls, and only a year later he was sub-warden! The University – no doubt on the principle of 'Set a Thief to catch a Thief – appointed this boisterous cudgeller its junior proctor. It fell to his lot to present Fairfax and Cromwell for honorary doctorates, and a dozen colonels for the degree of M.A. (19 May 1649). This was called 'the Fairfaxian creation'.

Sankey proved an active commanding officer, but though he scored several successes over the Irish, his reputation is stained by various acts of cruelty. Henry Cromwell, though he knighted him (17 November 1658), did not trust him. However, his Regiment, which remained part of the standing army in Ireland, was kept up to full strength.

In 1659 Sankey, as the senior colonel, was sent to England with 500 horse and 1000 foot to assist in the suppression of the Royalist rising. Too late to assist in Lambert's victory over Sir

George Booth, they took part in the siege of Chirk Castle. Instead of returning to Ireland, Sankey seduced the Irish Brigade from its duty, and threw in his lot with Lambert. He was employed to negotiate with Monck, but that astute general trusted neither Sankey nor those that sent him, and merely used the negotiations to gain time. When Lambert's Army broke up, Monck gave the command of the Irish Brigade to Colonel Daniel Redman.

Sankey, who was not a regicide, suffered no punishment at the Restoration, and even contrived to hang on to some of the lands he had acquired in Ireland. His major, Elias Green, managed to do the same in Tipperary.

The date of disbandment of the Regiment does not appear to be recorded.

COLONEL CHARLES FLEETWOOD'S REGIMENT

Succession of Colonels :

Charles Fleetwood (c.1620-1692)	Gentleman volunteer, Essex' Lifeguard, 1642. Captain, H, 1643. W. I Newbury. Colonel, H, Eastern Association 1644. Colonel, NM 18 March 1645. Lieutenant-General, H, 1650. Commander-in-Chief in Ireland. 8 July 1652 – September 1655.
Sir Anthony Ashley Cooper (1621-1683) Later (1672) 1st Earl of Shaftesbury	Royalist Colonel, H, 1643 – Jan. 1644. Changed sides. Colonel 11 Jan. 1660.

Troop commanders 1645 :

Colonel Charles Fleetwood (c.1620-1692) Major Thomas Harrison (1606-1660)	Major, Fleetwood, H, 1645. Major NM, 18 March 1645. Colonel *vice* Sheffeild (qv) June 1647.

168

Captain William Coleman	Captain, NM, 18 March 1645. Major *vice* Harrison, c. June 1647. Left 1647.
Captain Thomas Selby (-1645)	Captain, Fleetwood, H, Eastern Association. Captain, NM, 18 March 1645. K. Naseby.
Captain Richard Zanchy (or Sankey)	Captain, NM 1645. Left, Oct. 1651.
Captain Thomas Howard	Captain, NM, 1645. Left 1647.
Captain James Laughton (Leighton?) (-1647)	Captain *vice* Selby, w.e.f. 14 June 1645. Died between 16 July and 4 Sept. 1647.[68]
Griffith Lloyd	Lieutenant by 21 March 1647. Troop commander *vice* Harrison after 11 June 1647. Captain by Oct. 1647. SW Dunbar. Served until 1660. Fairfax called him a 'faithfull man'.[69]
Gilman Taylor (-1650 or 1651)	Lieutenant, Howard's Troop by 9 June 1645. Captain *vice* Howard, 1647. Killed in Scotland.
Stephen White	Lieutenant by 27 April 1647. Captain *vice* James Laughton c. Sept. 1647. Left 1651.
Joseph Blissett	Capt.-Lieut. by 22 July 1646. Captain *vice* Coleman Oct. 1649.
Samuel Boalley	Cornet, Margery's Troop, Cromwell, H, Eastern Association. Cornet, Laughton's Troop by 30 March 1646.[70]

Charles Fleetwood was the third son of Sir Miles Fleetwood of Aldwinkle, Northamptonshire. In 1644 he commanded a regiment of six troops in the Army of the Eastern Association. When the New Model was formed Fleetwood's Regiment joined it more or less complete. There were a few changes amongst the officers, but on the whole Fleetwood's was, as Sir Charles Firth pointed out, 'more homogeneous in origin and character than most of the regiments'. Like Cromwell's Ironsides it was full of fanatical Independents.

'Looke on Col. Flettwoods regiment with his Major Harreson, what a cluster of preaching offecers and troopers ther is.' But Harrison, as we have seen, was a brave and efficient officer. He had been singled out to carry the Marston Moor despatch to Parliament, which was the seventeenth century way of bringing a deserving officer to notice. King Charles usually knighted the man who brought him the news of a victory. Harrison led one of the storming parties at Basing House (14 October 1645), where he is alleged to have killed a Royalist, Major Robinson, in cold blood. 'Accursèd be he that doth the Lord's Work negligently', he is said to have remarked.

In 1647 the Regiment would neither go to Ireland, nor accept the terms for disbanding. But though it was one of the eight regiments which led Army opposition to Parliament, it 'was not much infected by the Levellers' doctrines,' (Firth) and behaved well throughout 1648 and 1649.

Five troops under Major Coleman were in the fight before Colchester (13 June 1648), while Captain Sankey with a detachment captured the fort on Mersea Island (15 June), cutting the Cavaliers' communications with the sea.

Coleman left the Regiment in 1649 and was succeeded by Hezekiah Haynes, who had been a captain of foot in 1642, and after Preston was one of those to whom the Duke of Hamilton surrendered (25 August 1648). Haynes served with the Regiment for ten years, and as Cromwell made Fleetwood lieutenant-general of the horse for his Scottish campaign (1650) Haynes was for all practical purposes the regimental commander.

The Regiment fought at Dunbar and Worcester.

In 1655 Cromwell made Haynes major-general for Norfolk, Suffolk, Essex and Cambridge. The Regiment spent two years in Scotland 1655-1657. Its troop commanders were now:

Lt. General Charles Fleetwood
Major Hezekiah Haynes
Captain Griffith Lloyd

Captain Joseph Blissett
Captain Thomas Izard (or Izod)   Major, 1660.
Captain Thomas Else

In the crisis of 1659 Haynes supported Fleetwood and
Lambert. Lloyd was unhappy: 'wee live in a very unsettled,
distracted ayre', he wrote. Oliver Cromwell had thought him a
person of integrity and Lambert employed him to negotiate with
Monck. But by the end of December Fleetwood, realizing that
the game was up, had withdrawn the guards from the Parliament
House, permitting the members to return to their duties. On
11 January the seven commissioners in whom they vested the
command of the Army gave Fleetwood's Regiment to one of
their number: Sir Anthony Ashley Cooper, who had once been
a Royalist colonel. Izard now became major, but the other captains appointed had not previously served with the Regiment.

Under Major Izard the Regiment spent its last months in
the West Country, doing useful work 'in aid of the Civil Power',
and suppressing a dangerous insurrection of the apprentices and
others at Bristol. Izard was replaced in June by a Presbyterian
Royalist, Major Robert Harley, who left almost at once to serve
under his brother, Sir Edward, at Dunkirk. When in November
the Regiment was disbanded at Salisbury the major was an old
Cavalier, 'a gallant commander', named Colonel Brown.[71]

At the Restoration Fleetwood suffered no worse penalty
than perpetual incapacitation from holding any office of trust.
His Regiment had as good a fighting record as any in the New
Model, even the two formed from the Ironsides, and although
there were fanatics in its ranks, was one of the best behaved. The
credit for this must go to its officers, notably Fleetwood himself,
Harrison, Lloyd, Haynes and Izard.

COLONEL NATHANIEL RICH'S REGIMENT

Succession of Colonels:

Algernon Sidney   Colonel, Manchester, H.
(1622-1683)   Approved as Colonel, N.M.
                         18 March. Commissioned 2 April,
                         1645.[72]
                         Governor of Chichester, 9 May 1645.

Nathaniel Rich (c.1620-1701)	Gentleman Volunteer, Essex' Lifeguard, 1643. Captain, Manchester, H. 1643. Lt. Colonel, Manchester, H. 1644. Colonel, NM, between 21 April and 14 June 1645. Deprived of his command 1654.
Charles Howard	Governor of Carlisle. Colonel *vice* Rich, Jan. 1655. O.C. Lifeguard, H. Sept. 1655.
Richard Ingoldsby (-1685)	Colonel F. 1645. Colonel *vice* Howard, Sept. 1655. Deprived of command 28 April 1659.
John Okey (1606-1662)	Colonel, D. 1645. Colonel, 28 April 1659.
Nathaniel Rich	Colonel, 9 July 1659.
Richard Ingoldsby	Colonel 26 February 1660.

Troop commanders:

Colonel Nathaniel Rich	
Major John Alford	Major, Manchester H. Eastern Association. Major, N.M., 18 March 1645. Retired c. 14 June 1647.
Captain Jonas Nevill	Captain, Manchester, H. Eastern Association. Major, N.M., 18 March 1645. Left June 1647.
Captain Thomas Ireton	Captain, Manchester, H., Eastern Association. Captain, N.M., 18 March 1645. SW Bristol, 1645. QMG *vice* Fincher, c.June 1647. Governor of Landguard Fort, and left Regt. 1648.
Captain Edward Dendy	Captain, Manchester, H., Eatern Association. Captain, N.M. 18 March 1645. S till serving 17 Oct. 1645. Left by 17 Jan. 1646.
Captain Bough	Captain, N.M., 18 March 1645. Gone by April 1646.

*   *   *

Captain Azariah Husbands	Captain Pickering, F. Eastern Association and N.M. 1644 and 1645.
	Capt. *vice* Dendy by 17 Jan. 1646.
	Major *vice* Alford after 14 June 1647. 1647-1654.
Captain Francis Hawys (Hawes)	Capt. *vice* Bough by 26 April 1646.
	Still serving, 16 Nov. 1648.

*   *   *

Other officers :

John Merriman	Lieut. by 27 April 1647. ·
	Capt. *vice* Nevill by 12 June 1647.
	W. London riot, 8 April 1648.
	Still serving 1654
Henry Barton	Capt. *vice* Alford after 12 June 1647.
	Left c. June 1649.
Edward Lisle	Capt.-Lieut. at 26 April 1647.[73]
	Captain
	Left c. 1 Oct. 1656.
William Weare	Capt.-Lieut. by 27 April 1647.
Ralph Hooker	Lieut. Nevill's Troop by 15 April 1645. Still serving 22 June 1647. Gone by 1 July 1647.
Roger Hopkins	Lieut. Alford's Troop by 15 April 1645.[74]
George Watson	Lieut. Ireton's Troop, 27 Jan. 1646.[74]
Francis Rawson	Cornet, Alford's Troop by 26 April 1647.[73]
	Captain by Dec. 1654.
Richard Blunt	QM Alford's Troop by 25 April 1646.[74]

Nathaniel Rich was the son of Robert Rich of Stondon, Essex. Admitted to Gray's Inn (13 August 1639), he was one of the young gentlemen who formed Essex' Lifeguard in 1642. His Regiment in the New Model was formed from the Earl of Manchester's double regiment belonging to the Army of the Eastern Association. Its ranks, no doubt, were full of men, who though foiled at Second Newbury, had won the great victory of Marston Moor.

Major Alford led the Forlorn Hope at the storming of Bristol, where Captain Ireton had his arm broken by a brace of bullets, a wound which tortured him for months.

Rich scored a success when with 1000 horse and dragoons he was sent to attack 600 Royalist horse at St. Columb, Cornwall. Their commander, Major-General Pert, led 'a good home-charge',[75] but was wounded and taken with 100 prisoners more (7 March 1646).

The Regiment was to the fore in the quarrel of 1647, its agitators, John Breman and Nicholas Lockyer voicing its complaints with verbose rhetoric.

The Regiment was one of two involved in a great riot in London on 9 April 1648, in which Captain Merriman and another officer were hurt.

Major Husbands distinguished himself in the suppression of the rising in Kent (May 1648). After taking part in Fairfax' hard-won victory at Maidstone, he went on with only 100 horse and some foot to relieve Dover, and recapture Deal, Walmer and Sandown Castles, foiling an attempt to relieve the last named. Parliament, impressed by the skill with which he had managed his business voted him £150 to buy horses.

Two troops took a part in routing the Earl of Holland and his followers at Kingston (7 July).

It fell to Captain Merriman to remove King Charles to Hurst Castle (30 November 1648). For the next two years the Regiment was quartered in London and the neighbouring counties. In December 1650 Rich was sent to suppress a Royalist insurrection in Norfolk, which was swiftly put down by three of his troops and some local forces.

Rich won Major-General Harrison's praise for his skilful handling of the rearguard near Warrington when, in August 1651, King Charles II and the Scots were advancing on Worcester.

The next few years passed quietly for Rich and his regiment. But when, in December 1654, some Fifth Monarchy Men were imprisoned for preaching and acting against the government, Harrison and Rich were the leaders of those who demanded that 'the prisoners of the Lord might be set at liberty'. They told

Cromwell's Council that his government was anti-Christian and Babylonish. Rich also endeavoured to hinder the raising of taxes and was arrested. He was in trouble again in 1656, and was imprisoned in Windsor Castle. He was an obstinate man, and refused to promise to live peaceable, largely because he felt that Cromwell had no right to demand it.

Meanwhile the Regiment had been sent to Scotland, where it had some minor successes including the defeat of Colonel Edward Wogan, who had fought at Naseby as a captain in Okey's Dragoons.

Rich's Regiment was deeply involved in Overton's Plot, and, in consequence, five officers were court-martialled and cashiered (February 1655). They were:

Lieutenant John Breman	Captain John Merriman's
Cornet John Toomes	Troop.
Lieutenant Francis Rawson	Captain Thomas Babington's
Quartermaster John Waltridge	Troop
Quartermaster William Barford	Colonel Rich's Troop

By this time Cromwell had selected a new colonel to replace the contrary and somewhat muddle-headed Rich. He was Charles Howard, the governor of Carlisle. However, he did not stay long for in September he went back to his former command : Cromwell's Lifeguard. The Protector now gave the Regiment to his kinsman Colonel John Ingoldsby, who had commanded a company in Hampden's regiment in 1642, and a regiment of foot in the New Model. An opposition news-sheet of the time described him as 'a gentleman of courage and valour, but not very famous for any great exploits, unless for beating the honest inn-keeper of Alisbury'. He was a regicide for, though he had not attended the sittings of the tribunal which tried King Charles I, he had signed the death warrant.

When the Regiment returned to England Cornet Sumpner brought charges against the major, Thomas Babington, who, he alleged browbeat the honest men of the Regiment and countenanced drunkards, liars, swearers and haters of goodness.

Richard Cromwell, who was now Protector, took this mighty ill:

. . .'You article against your major because he is for me?

You are a company of mutineers, you deserve a hundred of you to be hanged; and I will hang you, and strip you as a man would strip an eele; you talk of preaching and praying men, they are the men who go about to undermine me. And clapping his hand upon Colonel Ingoldsby's shoulder, said, Go thy way, Dick Ingoldsby, thou canst neither preach nor pray, but I will believe thee before I will believe twenty of them, and says he to the cornet, You never owned my father; you have lost your commission, and shall never ride more in the army, &c. and a great deal more to the purpose.'[76]

Ludlow tells us that these words were soon published in the City and the Army to the great prejudice of the Protector (c. March 1659).

In the crisis that followed the greater part of the Regiment followed Fleetwood and on 28 April Ingoldsby was replaced by Colonel John Okey, who had commanded the dragoons at Naseby. But the Committee of Nomination drew up a new list of officers (25 June) which the restored Long Parliament voted on 9 July:-

Colonel Nathaniel Rich	Dismissed, 1654.
Capt.-Lieut. John Toomes	Cashiered as a cornet, 1655.
Major John Merriman	From retirement.
Captain John Barker	
Captain Charles Duckett	
Captain John Barrington	
Captain John Breman	Cashiered as a lieutenant 1655.

Thomas Sumner (or Sumpner), the cornet who had accused Major Barrington, reappeared as a lieutenant. Another cornet, John Gregory, had been cashiered as a quartermaster in 1655. How little these arrangements pleased Ingoldsby and his displaced officer you may well imagine!

"Just now', wrote John Mordaunt to the King on 16 June, 'we received great assurance of Colonel Ingoldsby, and of several of the cast-out officers.'[77] Three, implicated in Sir George Booth's rising, were arrested, but Ingoldsby and Major Babington managed to vanish.

Rich and his officers were trusted neither by Lambert nor Fleetwood nor by Monck. In December they were sent to reduce

Portsmouth, whose garrison had admitted Sir Arthur Hesilrige and declared for the restoration of the Long Parliament. Major Breman persuaded five troops to change sides, and when they joined the garrison, Rich went with them (20 December 1659). When they returned to London at the end of the month, Rich ˜eceived the thanks of Parliament (29 December), and the Regiment was voted a month's pay (3 January). They were then sent to quarter at Ipswich, Colchester, Norwich (2 troops), Bury St. Edmunds and Yarmouth. The news that Monck had readmitted the excluded members of the Long Parliament caused much unrest, and even mutiny in the troop at Ipswich. R ich held ˄ general rendezvous near Bury on 25 February, 'where many ˜eproachful expressions were vented against Monck.'[78] It was rumoured that the sectaries in Norfolk and Suffolk were arming.

Monck lost no time in scotching this trouble, sending Ingoldsby to replace Rich once more (26 February). Rich hoped for support from the foot quartered at Colchester, but his own Regiment was not solidly behind him, and he gave up his commission quietly on 1 March 1660. Another purge of the officers followed, and Thomas Babington became major once more.

When Lambert escaped by night from the Tower (10/11 April), and began to collect men in Northamptonshire, Monck sent Ingoldsby against him. The Regiment, dispersed in Norfolk and Suffolk, concentrated at Cambridge on Friday 20 April, and marched the 50 miles to Northampton by the Saturday evening : a very creditable performance. Reinforced by two companies of foot and a troop of horse, the Regiment met Lambert's men near Daventry on Easter Sunday, and found that his followers had little heart for a fight.

Lambert himself was 'mounted on a barb which might have hastned him in his flight', but 'Providence had so ordered it, that he was on ploughed land, where his horse could prove of little advantage to him. Colonel Lambert was taken by Colonel Ingoldsbys own hands'.[79]

Disbanded at Northampton on 5 December Ingoldsby's Regiment was one of the last to go.

'See how the Fates their gifts allot'. Ingoldsby, regicide though he was, reaped the reward of his services, though, as the

Earl of Northampton told the King: "Your pardon and forgiveness of his former errors was all he aimed at."[80] On 12 May he declared in Parliament that, when the death warrant was signed, 'Cromwell held his hand, and forced him to subscribe the sentence'. This Mrs Hutchinson tells us was 'a false tale',[81] and certainly his name was written firmly enough. So far from suffering any of the penalties endured by the other regicides, Ingoldsby was created a Knight of the Bath at the coronation of King Charles II (20 April 1661), and so his sins were washed away. He survived until 1685, having represented Aylesbury in all four Parliaments of Charles II's reign. He was buried in Hartwell Church, Buckinghamshire, on 16 September 1685.

Nathaniel Rich spent a spell in the Fleet at the time of Venner's rising, and later was imprisoned at Portsmouth. In 1663 he married, secondly, Elizabeth Kerr, daughter of the Earl of Ancram. His friends – or hers – were able to obtain his liberty. He retired to his estate in Essex and lived there peacefully for the next 35 years or so.

Major Breman, frequently arrested for supposed complicity in various risings, including that of Lambert (1660) and the Rye House Plot (1683), was MP for Chichester when the Whigs were at the height of their power (1679-1681). He lived to see the Revolution of 1688, and in July 1689 was major of a volunteer regiment of horse composed of 400 London citizens, which had King William for its colonel.

THE ASSOCIATED HORSE

Sprigge's picture map shows two bodies labelled The Associated Horse, one on each wing. One might suppose, therefore, that they were the equivalent of a regiment, with an establishment of 600 officers and men.

When the horse of the Earl of Manchester's Army was absorbed into the New Model Army a certain amount of cavalry was left under the direct control of the East Anglian county committees, but who their commanders were is not at present known. It seems likely that these troops were of rather lower military value than the regiments of Whalley, Vermuyden and Fleetwood.

1 Firth and Davies, p. xviii.
2 Firth and Davies, p. 45.
3 See Edgehill, 1642, pp. 157-8 for further details of his career.
4 Firth and Davies, pp. 49-50 quoting John Lilburne: *The Second Part of Englands New-Chaines Discovered* (1649) p. 8.
5 The troop commanders chosen for this New Model Regiment had new commissions dated 18 March 1645.
6 Gordon Goodwin in D.N.B.
7 D.N.B.
8 Reliquiae Baxterianae, p. 57.
9 Reliquiae Baxterianae, 1696 p. 98.
10 Firth and Davies, I, 74.
11 p. 330.
12 WO. 55/1646.
13 Thoresby, 140.
14 WO. 55/1647.
15 Thoresby, 160.
16 Symonds, p. 73.
17 Carlyle. Letter XXVIII.
18 Tillier had been major-general of the foot to Rupert who evidently valued his services. He was afterwards with the Prince at Bristol, and in the defence of Oxford.
19 Firth and Davies, pp. 134-135.
20 Reliquiae Baxterianae, p. 51.
21 Firth and Davies, I, p. 215.
22 Firth and Davies, p. 217.
23 The Army's Martyr: or A Faithful Relation of the Barbarous and Illegal Proceedings of the Court-Martiall at White-hall upon Mr Robert Lockier (1649).
24 Ludlow, II, 69.
25 Gumble, p. 142.
26 Contemporary newsletter.
27 On 12 June 1645 these three made a statement to the Speaker of the House of Commons, concerning the character and questionable behaviour of Purbeck Temple, late major of Colonel John Fiennes' Regiment. Tibbutt's Luke p. 621.
28 The Regiment had seven troops. Tibbutt's Luke, p. 58. Sir Samuel to Sir Oliver Luke, 5 Nov. 1644.
29 CSPD. 1644/5, p. 175.
30 Peacock, p. 55.
31 Tibbutt's Luke, p. 389.
32 CSPD, 1644/5, pp. 100 and 118. 6 & 13 Nov. He had still not received the pistols by 1 May 1645 (p. 447).
33 CSPD, 1644/5, p. 195. Browne to the C.B.K. The other two were those of Lt. Col. Francis Martin, the deputy-governor, and of Colonel Heriott Washbourne.

34 CSPD, 1644/5, p. 204. Browne to C.B.K., 30 Dec. 1644.
35 To the Committee of Both Kingdoms. Carlyle, *Cromwell*, Appendix No. 7.
36 CSPD, 1644/5, p. 609.
37 CSPD, 1645, p.6.
38 CSPD 1644/5, p. 62.
39 cf. Letter of Colonel John Fiennes to Sir Samuel Luke. 5 Nov. 1644. Tibbutt's Luke, p. 379.
40 Tibbutt's Luke, p. 76. Sir Samuel Luke to Sir Oliver Luke, 12 Nov. 1644.
41 Peacock, p. 51.
42 Symonds, p. 73.
43 Skippon, 14 April 1645, quoted in John Vicars' *Burning Bush*, 1646, p. 133.
44 Sprigge, p. 60.
45 Firth and Davies, p. 178 quoting Clarke Papers, I, p. 17.
46 Firth and Davies, p. 178, quoting Clarke Papers, I. p. 25.
47 Sir Thomas Herbert, *Memoirs* (1813), pp. 139-42.
48 But failed to raise his troop.
49 CSPD, p. 453.
50 Firth and Davies, p. 116.
51 Firth and Davies, p. 118.
52 Firth and Davies, p. 202.
53 Firth and Davies, p. 204, quoting *Cromwelliana*.
54 Ludlow, II, 69.
55 WO. 55/1646.
56 WO. 55/1646.
57 Clarke Papers, I, p. 151.
58 WO. 55/1645.
59 See Rushworth, VI, p. 56.
60 Toynbee and Young, *Cropredy Bridge*, p. 128 *et seq.*
61 WO. 55/460.
62 Clarke Papers, I, p. 437.
63 Thoresby, p. 159.
64 *Nicholas Papers*, ed. G. F. Warner, I, p. 65.
65 Carlyle, Letter CXII.
66 Anthony Wood, *Fasti Oxonienses*, ed. Philip Bliss, part 2, p. 119.
67 Canon R. H. Morris: *The Siege of Chester*, pp. 71-2.
68 Clarke Papers, I, p. 176.
69 Clarke Papers, I, p. 129.
70 WO. 55/1646.
71 Firth and Davies, p.101
72 Fairfax Correspondence, III, pp. 213-214.
73 Rushworth, VI, p. 465.
74 WO. 55/1646.
75 Sprigge, 208.
76 Firth and Davies, p. 153.

77 Firth and Davies, p. 155.

78 Firth and Davies, p. 157.

79 Mercurius Politicus, p. 269.

80 Carte, *Original Letters*, II, p. 333.

81 Memoirs of the Life of Colonel Hutchinson, p. 323.

Chapter Nine

THE NEW MODEL FOOT

ONLY EIGHT OF the 12 regiments of foot took part in the battle of Naseby. They were those of :-

> Sir Thomas Fairfax,
> Edward Montagu,
> John Pickering,
> Sir Hardress Waller,
> Philip Skippon,
> Thomas Rainborow,
> Robert Hammond,
> Edward Harley.

Fairfax and Skippon, being generals, their regiments were commanded by Lt. Colonels Thomas Jackson and Jo. Frances respectively. Sir Hardress Waller appears to have been absent, and so was Harley who had been severely wounded in the shoulder on 1 August 1644. Their regiments, too, were commanded by their lieutenant-colonels : Ralph Cottesworth and Thomas Pride.

Had the regiments been up to strength the New Model should have had 9,600 Foot in the line of battle on 14 June 1645. But the three old armies of Essex, Manchester and Waller had produced no more than 7,174 foot, when they were reduced into the New Model. Skippon needed some 7,000 men to bring his regiments up to strength. It may be that he had raised half that number by the following June. It seems likely, therefore, that the Foot numbered about 6,500 at Naseby, about a third of them being new recruits.

Manchester's Army produced 3,578 foot for the New

Model. Except for its repulse at Second Newbury, it had had a successful career, notably the great victory at Marston Moor. The same cannot be said of the armies of Essex, which provided 3,048 foot, and Waller's, which had no more than 548 available. It is true that the Earl had scored a good success by his relief of Gloucester and his victory at First Newbury. But 1644 had been a year of disaster. The surrender at Lostwithiel can scarcely be said to have been offset by the storming of Speen village at Second Newbury.

Waller, having lost his first army at Roundway Down, had won an important victory at Cheriton with his second. This, however, had achieved little or nothing since its defeat at Cropredy Bridge.

One might perhaps expect a better performance from the troops drawn from Manchester's Army, than from those of Essex or Waller, but we should not make too much of this factor. Given good officers an infantry regiment is a resilient organization, which can build on its triumphs, and shake off its disasters.

FAIRFAX

Succession of Colonels:

Sir Thomas Fairfax (1612-1671)	
[1]Oliver Cromwell (1599-1658)	1650
[1]William Goffe (-c.1679)	
Oliver Cromwell	1655-1658
William Goffe	Cashiered. 1659
[1]Edmund Ludlow (c.1617-1692)	1659
Herbert Morley (1616-1667)	9 July 1659
2nd Earl of Peterborough (1624-1697)	August 1660

The Lords passed the list of company commanders on 18 March 1645.[2] Many of the men probably came from the Army, if not the regiment of the Earl of Essex. Captain Foulke Muskett had been a lieutenant in Essex' Regiment in 1642. At least four company commanders, Manesty, Boyce, Gooday and Johnston came from the Earl of Manchester's Regiment in the Army of the Eastern Association and doubtless brought their companies with them.

The Regiment fought at Bridgwater, Bristol, Torrington and the siege of Wallingford Castle, and did good service.

During the military revolution of 1647 the Regiment was as mutinous as any.

In the Second Civil War the Regiment fought well at Preston (17 August). Its commanding officer, Lt. Colonel William Cowell, seems to have been mortally wounded. Cromwell thought him an 'honest worthy man'. At Naseby he had been major to Harley's Regiment.[3]

Major Francis White, amongst other officers, argued that the court which tried King Charles had no legitimate authority to judge him – which was perfectly true. He thought it was just that the sword should take away the King's power and restore it to the people: 'its originall fountain next under God'. It was just to dethrone the King and to keep him a prisoner of war, but not to behead him. 'I do not,' wrote White, 'understand any essentiall good can acrew to the people, by the taking of his life. For it is not so much the person that can hurt us, as the power that is made up in the Kingly office by this corrupt constitution.' These views appealed to the Levellers, but not to Fairfax and Cromwell, and instead of White being promoted in Cowell's place, Goffe was brought in from Pride's Regiment. Goffe was to be one of the regicides. He and White were both promoted for their services at Dunbar, and the latter presented the captured colours to Parliament, delivered a narrative of the campaign and was given £300.

The Regiment fought at Worcester, and in the Dutch War acted as marines. Its last colonel, appointed by Monck, was a Royalist, the Earl of Peterborough.

The Regiment was disbanded at Reading on 15 November 1660. It had a good fighting record, but was not very steady under the stress of political events.

MONTAGU

Succession of Colonels:

Edward Montagu (1625-1672),	resigned at the end of 1645.
	1st Earl of Sandwich, and K.G.
	1660. Killed in the battle of Solebay.

John Lambert (1619-1683), Major-General. Died in prison in Guernsey.
Sir William Constable, Bart. (c.1575-1655). December 1647-14 June 1655.
John Biscoe   December 1655-1 February 1660
(1) George Fleetwood (1622-).   25 February 1660. Regicide. Condemned to death at the Restoration, but not executed. Probably died in America sometime after 1664.
Sir Henry Cholmley   4 June-8 October 1660.

On 20 August 1643 Montagu was commissioned to raise a regiment of 1,000 men in Cambridge and the Isle of Ely. The regiment, one of those that fought at Marston Moor, came into the New Model with the exception of two companies which had mutinied over their pay (February 1645) and a few officers. On 6 May we find an order of the Committee of Both Kingdoms to the Committee of Cambridge, Huntingdon and Hertfordshire, to hasten their recruits from St. Albans to Colonel Montagu's Regiment.[4]

The Regiment was at the capture of Bridgwater and Bristol, and with Cromwell at Devizes, Winchester and Basing. Under its new colonel, John Lambert, it took part in the storming of Dartmouth.

In the quarrel between Parliament and Army (1647), the Regiment was solidly with its comrades. During the years that followed it was on garrison duty at Bristol, Gloucester and Wallingford though seven companies were sent to Scotland to help in the suppression of Glencairn's rising (April 1654). One company was in garrison at Dunkirk in July 1658. Four served under Lambert during Sir George Booth's insurrection.

In its last days Monck put the Regiment under Sir Henry Cholmley (4 June 1660), with two resolute cavalier colonels, Sir Matthew Appleyard and Sir Jordan Crosland, amongst his company commanders. They did not enjoy their new commands for long for the Regiment was disbanded on 8 October 1660. Cholmley and Appleyard do not appear to have served in Charles II's Army, but in 1661 Sir Jordan Crosland was Governor and Captain of Scarborough Castle. In 1666 he commanded a regiment of the Yorkshire Trained Bands.

Succession of Colonels :

John Pickering (-1645). Colonel, F, in 1644. Marston Moor.
[1]John Hewson (-1662). Colonel, *vice* Pickering.
John Streeter (-1670). Colonel, 12 January 1660.
Lord Bellasis (1614-1689).

Pickering's Regiment from the Army of the Eastern Association was incorporated in the New Model Army, and men from Colonel Thomas Ayloffe's Regiment, which was reduced, were brought in to bring it up to strength. Eight of the ten company commanders selected had been with the Regiment in 1644.

Part of the Regiment took part in Cromwell's unsuccessful assault on Farringdon Castle, in which Captain Jenkins and his lieutenant lost their lives.[5]

Lt. Colonel Hewson led the Forlorn Hope at the storming of Bridgwater. The Regiment did well at Bristol, and served under Cromwell at Devizes, Lacock House, Winchester and Basing House.

Pickering, 'a little man, but of a great courage' (Sprigge), died of a fever, 'the new disease', at the blockade of Exeter (November, 1645). In 1647 Hewson, his successor, was one of the leaders of the Army's opposition to disbanding or volunteering for Ireland, and the Regiment was solidly behind him. Even so its conduct was exemplary.

The Regiment bore the brunt of the fierce street-fighting at Maidstone (1 June 1648). 'I cannot but take notice', wrote Fairfax, 'of the valour and resolution of Colonel Hewson, whose regiment had the hardest task (Major Carter . . . being hurt, and Captain Price, a deserving and faithful officer slain.)[6] The Regiment took part in suppressing the rising in Kent, a work in which both Hewson and his lieutenant-colonel, Daniel Axtell, distinguished themselves, the latter showing himself, in Colonel Nathaniel Rich's opinion, 'extraordinary active and diligent.'

Hewson was one of the King's judges and attended the trial with great regularity. He signed the death warrant. Axtell, commanded the guard in Westminster Hall on the day when sentence was pronoucned. At the Restoration he was alleged to have ordered his men to fire on a lady, who interrupted President Bradshaw's speech, and incited them to shout *Justice* and *Execution*. The Regiment was chosen by lot to serve in Ireland (20 April 1649) and seems to have made no trouble about it. It took part in the storming of Drogheda and the massacre that followed.

In 1659 the Regiment, under Lt. Colonel John Duckenfield, who distinguished himself, played an important part in the suppression of Sir George Booth's rising. On 5 December, a day of hard frost, it was one of the two regiments sent into the City to enforce the Committee of Safety's prohibition of the circulation of petitions for a free Parliament. They were greeted with brickbats, stones, rubbish, turnips and tiles, 'and when Colonel Hewson came in at the head of his regiment they shouted all along "A cobbler, A cobbler!"'[7]

John Streeter, who had been quartermaster-general of the foot in Ireland, had attacked Cromwell for expelling the Long Parliament, and had found himself in the Gatehouse (September 1653). He was given the Regiment on 12 January 1660, but although he enjoyed Monck's confidence, in July his command was given to a Cavalier, who had fought at Naseby. This was John, Lord Bellasis, 'who by his wounds and imprisonment hath sufficiently testified his honour and loyalty to his Majesty'.[8] Colonel Anthony Gilby, another diehard Royalist became its lieutenant-colonel, and Streeter was reduced to the rank of major!

The Regiment was disbanded on 5 October 1660, but four companies were kept to garrison Hull. In 1661 there were in fact six companies there, and Bellasis, who was Governor, and Anthony Gilby, both had companies. The posting must have suited Gilby, for he was still at Hull as Deputy-Governor in 1680.[9] Fourteen of the 18 officers of the 1661 garrison were old Cavaliers or their relations – but we may suppose that the majority of the soldiers were cobbler Hewson's veterans, who had served for 15 years or more in one of the best regiments of Cromwell's Army.

SIR HARDRESS WALLER

Succession of Colonels:

[1]Sir Hardress Waller (c.1604-1666). Knighted, 6 July 1629.
Governor of Cork, 1644.
Regicide. Died in prison.

John Clerke

Waller, who had probably seen service in Holland or Germany, commanded a regiment in Munster during the rebellion. He was given the regiment intended for Sir William Waller's major-general, James Holborne. The latter, being a Scot, refused to serve in the New Model. The cadre of the new unit no doubt came from Waller's Army.

The Regiment fought at Bridgwater, Bristol, Devizes, Lacock House, Winchester and Basing House, where Sir Hardress, 'performing his duty with honour and diligence' (Sprigge) was wounded during the storming. It was afterwards engaged at the siege of Exeter, which Waller conducted for a time. He was afterwards at the siege of Oxford.

Sir Hardress was prominent in the quarrel between Parliament and Army, but his Regiment remained orderly.

In May 1648 Waller was engaged in suppressing a rising of the Cornish 'malignants'.

In 1648 Waller played an active part in Pride's Purge. He was one of the King's judges, attended the High Court regularly and signed the death warrant. In December 1649 he landed with five of his companies and some recruits at Kinsale. He became major-general of the foot and was at the sieges of Carlow and Limerick.

The Regiment saw no further fighting. It seems to have split and to have provided the cadres of two regiments, one in England and one in Ireland. Colonel John Clerke, who sat in all the Parliaments of the Protectorate and of Richard Cromwell, seems to have married Colonel Isaac Ewer's widow. He was a relative of John Thurloe's and a friend of John Disbrowe's. Such an one could not prosper in the circumstances of 1660, and on 13 January he was ordered by the Council of State to quit London.

SKIPPON

Succession of Colonels:

Philip Skippon (c.1600-1660).	
William Sydenham	13 February 1649
Alban Coxe (-1665)	c.June 1649
Richard Ashfield (-1677)	By July 1651

Skippon's Regiment was raised in the City of London. Its captains were commissioned on or about 19 November 1642, and from then on it served in all the main operations of Essex' Army. On 8 April 1645 the Regiment was joined at Reading by the two weak regiments of Sir Thomas Hogan and Sir Miles Hobart from Manchester's Army, and 'the two regiments were reduced into Major[-General] Skippon's. . . .'[10]

The Regiment served at the sieges of Bridgwater, Bristol, Berkeley Castle, Exeter, Oxford and Raglan Castle.

In the Second Civil War the Regiment recaptured Tyne-. mouth Castle, whose governor, Colonel Henry Lilburne, had declared for the King. It was one of those that occupied London in the following December.

In November 1649 five companies were sent to Guernsey, and in the following March the colonel, now Alban Coxe, got a severe reprimand for being absent without leave! A detachment took part in the capture of Jersey (March 1652), but the main body went to Scotland with Cromwell in 1650, and formed part of the garrison of Edinburgh (October). Later it was at the siege of Stirling and the storming of Dundee, seeing a good deal of hard duty, perhaps because of the absence of Colonel Ashfield in London, who, at that distance, was unable to look after its interests.

Ashfield, who had been prominent in military politics was one of the officers cashiered by Parliament, along with Lambert (12 October 1659). The Regiment, which evidently supported Lambert, was dispersed by Monck, and is not heard of after January 1660.

RAINBOROW

Succession of Colonels:

Thomas Rainborow (-1648)
Richard Deane (1610-1653). w.e.f. 26 September 1647-25 February 1649.
Oliver Cromwell (1599-1658), 1649.
Henry Cromwell (1624-1674), 1655.
Edmund Ludlow (c.1617-1692), 1659.

Rainborow, captain of the *Lion*, landed 180 of his crew to help in the defence of Hull, and leading a column of 500 musketeers in the great sortie of 11 October 1643, was taken prisoner. In his account of the fight Fairfax describes him as a colonel. His New Model regiment comprised companies from three regiments of Manchester's Army: Ayloffe's, Francis Russell's and Major-General Lawrence Crawford's.

Rainborow's Regiment took the field on 8 May 1645. On 1 June the colonel took Gaunt House near Oxford. It was at the storming of Bridgwater, and then suffered severely at the siege of Sherborne, a number of officers being picked off with birding pieces by two 'keepers of parkes', who sniped them from the towers.

At Bristol, as Cromwell tells us, the Regiment had 'the hardest task of all': the storming of Prior's Hill Fort. Resolute though the men were the Royalist garrison held them for two hours at push of pike.

Rainborow next took Berkeley Castle. He then besieged Corfe Castle for a time, before being sent to blockade Oxford (December). He took Woodstock (26 April 1646). After the fall of Oxford Rainborow took over the siege of Worcester, which held out until July 1646.

In 1647 the Regiment mutinied, left its quarters in Hampshire, and marched to Abingdon, meaning to join Ingoldsby's Regiment at Oxford and seize the train of artillery. Major John Edwards was almost killed by his own men. Rainborow, then in London, was sent down to restore discipline.

Rainborow was made Vice-Admiral of the Fleet (26 September), but his squadron declared for the King on 27 May 1648, and Rainborow was recalled to the army. He was surprised at Doncaster by Cavaliers from the garrison of Pontefract Castle and, as he refused to surrender, was killed.

The Regiment now passed to Richard Deane, the Controller of the Ordnance. In the Second Civil War it took part in the siege of Pembroke Castle and the battle of Preston.

On 23 February 1649 Deane was appointed one of the three 'generals at sea'. Thereafter until the Restoration the Regiment served in Ireland.

Succession of Colonels:

Robert Hammond (1621-1654). – 31 August 1647.
Isaac Ewer (-1650/1651), w.e.f. 31 August 1647.
Richard Lawrence (-1684).

As an ensign Hammond had distinguished himself storming the Castle of Carrickmain (March 1642). When his colonel, Sir Simon Harcourt, fell, Hammond was the first officer that led the men up the breach. 'Thou hast naturally a valiant spirit,' Cromwell wrote to him in 1648 – words which anyone might prize.

Hammond was a major of horse in 1644. When the New Model formed he was given a regiment six of whose company commanders came from Manchester's Army.

The Regiment was at the sieges of Bridgwater, Sherborne Castle, Nunney Castle and Bristol, where it took part in the assault of Prior's Hill Fort, the key of the City. Under Cromwell the Regiment took part in the sieges of Devizes Castle, Lacock House, Winchester and Basing House, where Hammond fell into the hands of the Cavaliers, who, it seems, helped themselves to practically everything he had about him. Parliament gave him £200 to make up for what they took from him!

The Regiment served at the siege of Exeter, the storming of Dartmouth, the battle of Torrington and the capture of St. Michael's Mount.

Hammond's Regiment, as a whole, supported the Army in its quarrel with Parliament, but behaved in an orderly fashion. The Colonel himself, who had no taste for military politics, applied, successfully, for the Governorship of the Isle of Wight, and was succeeded by Lt. Colonel Ewer. Ironically enough this posting, so far from giving Hammond the quiet retirement he had sought, brought him little but trouble, for on 13 November King Charles, who had escaped from Hampton Court, sought sanctuary in the Isle of Wight. For a year Hammond found himself an unwilling gaoler. Now under Ewer the Regiment served in South Wales with Cromwell. He besieged Chepstow Castle, which he stormed on 25 May. Afterwards, with six companies, he took part in the siege of Colchester.

Selected by lot to serve in Ireland, the Regiment went over without making any difficulties, It suffered heavily at the storming of Drogheda. Thereafter it was at the siege of Kilkenny; the abortive attempt to storm Clonmel (9 May 1650); the capture of Carlow; the siege of Waterford; and Ireton's unsuccessful attempt on Limerick.

Ewer died in the winter 1650/1651, and was succeeded by Richard Lawrence, who had been Commissary of Provisions in Manchester's Army, and Provost-Marshal-General of Horse in the New Model. He was a fanatic and his second wife was Agnes, daughter of the regicide, Colonel Hewson. For some reason he enjoyed the protection of Ormonde and though his Regiment was disbanded at the Restoration, he himself was employed as a member of the Council of Trade.

The Regiment saw no further active service after 1650.

HARLEY

Succession of Colonels:

Edward Harley (1624-1700)	April 1645.
¹Thomas Pride (-1658)	Summer 1647.
Richard Moss	w.e.f. 23 October 1658.

'Let not the foot of Pride come against me, and let not the hand of the wicked remove me'.

(Psalms XXXVI, 11)

Harley, a Herefordshire gentleman, had commanded a troop at Lansdown, Roundway Down and Cheriton, had raised a regiment of foot to serve under Massey. Disabled by a wound in the shoulder on 1 August 1644, he was nonetheless given a regiment of the New Model. It was commanded throughout the 1645 campaign by Lt. Colonel Thomas Pride. Four of its company commanders came from Henry Barclay's Regiment, which had belonged to Essex' Army.

The Regiment served at Bridgwater, Bristol, Berkeley Castle, Dartmouth; Exeter and Oxford.

In November 1646 Harley was elected M.P. for Herefordshire, and was one of those who opposed the demands of the soldiers, and pressed for their disbandment.

Pride, needless to say, took a contrary view. When the Army triumphed Harley was one of eleven members of the Commons to be impeached (15 June 1647), but, though he thought it prudent to withdraw from the House, he did not flee the country. Fairfax gave the Regiment to Pride, who led it at Chepstow, Pembroke and Preston (1648).

On 6 December Colonel Pride made his name with his famous – or infamous – Purge. Two other Naseby colonels, Hewson and Sir Hardress Waller played prominent parts in the events of that fatal day, but unquestionably Pride played the lead. He seized William Prynne as he was going up the stairs, saying : "Mr Prynne, you must not go into the House, but must go along with me." When Prynne persisted Pride thrust him down before, while Waller and others pulled at him forcibly from behind. Prynne demanded to know by what authority and commission they acted, whereupon the two colonels 'showing him their arm'd soldiers standing round about him with swords, musquets, and matches lighted, told him that there was their commission.' Pride's former colonel, Harley, was among the members arrested.[11]

Pride was one of King Charles' judges, and signed the death warrant.

The Regiment was with Cromwell at Dunbar and Worcester. In 1654 it was sent to Scotland at the time of Glencairn's rising, but Pride did not go with it. He was doing well in business, and bought Nonsuch Park and house. He was knighted by Cromwell in 1656 and was made one of the commissioners for the peace in London. He distinguished himself by suppressing bear-baiting : he had all the bears killed. He died at Nonsuch on the sixteenth anniversary of Edgehill, and was succeeded by his lieutenant-colonel, Richard Moss, a person of little account. Monck did not trust the Regiment and in April 1660 it was disbanded on Kennington Common. According to the Publick Intelligencer (21 April) the soldiers 'willingly submitted, and received their full arrears for all their former service.'

1 Regicides.
2 LJ 18 March 1645.
3 Firth and Davies, 327.
4 CSPD, 1645, p. 460.
5 Firth and Davies, p. 405.
6 Firth and Davies, 407, quoting *Fairfax Correspondence*, iv, 32-3.
7 Letter of Samuel Pepys, 6 December 1659. (Macmillan's Magazine November, 1893, p. 35.)
8 *Mercurius Publicus.*
9 C. Dalton. English Army Lists And Commission Registers, Vol I, pp. 13 and 14.
10 Firth and Davies, 431.
11 Prynne's narrative. *Old Parliamentary History*, xviii, p 449

Chapter Ten

DRAGOONS AND THE ORDNANCE

COLONEL JOHN OKEY'S REGIMENT OF DRAGOONS

Succession of commanding officers :

John Okey (1606-1662)	Quartermaster, Lord Brooke, 6 Troop, H. 1642.
	Captain, Lord Brooke, F. 1643.
	Captain Hesilrige, H.
	Fought at Cropredy Bridge, 1644.
	Major, H, by 12 July 1644[1]
	Colonel, D., NM, 28 March 1645.
	Courtmartialled and dismissed, 1654.
Colonel Tobias Bridge	1654-1659
John Okey	30 June-15 Oct. 1659.
Major John Daborne (or Dawborne)	
John Okey	13 Jan. 1660
Edward Rossiter	

Company or Troop commanders :

Colonel John Okey (1606-1662)	
Major Nicholas Moore	Major, D, Eastern Association. To Ireland, 1647.
Captain John Farmer	To Ireland, 1647
Captain Charles Mercer	Captain, Lilburne, D. Eastern Association.
Captain Daniel Abbott	Captain, Lilburne, D. Eastern Association. Major *vice* Moore, 1647 Colonel, D. in Ireland.

Captain Ralph Farr	To Ireland, 1647
Captain Tobias Bridges (or Bridge)	Maor *vice* Abbott, 1649.
	Colonel *vice* Okey, 1654.
	Lost command in 1659.
	Major at Dunkirk, Lockhart, H., 1659-1662.
	Capt. Independent Troop, H. Dunkirk, 4 March 1642.
	Knighted, 1663.
	Served at Tangier 1663-1664
	Capt. Duke of Richmond, H. Select Militia, 5 July 1666.
	Colonel, The Barbados Regt. of Foot, 11 Feb. 1667
	Took Tobago from the Dutch, 1673.
	Member of Council in Barbados, 1674.[2]
Captain Edward Wogan (-1654)	Deserted with his troop and went to Scotland, 1648.
	Joined Ormonde in Ireland.
	Governor of Duncannon, 1649.
	Held it against Ireton.
	PW Cork. Escaped, 1650.
	Fought at Worcester, 1651.
	With Middleton, 1654. K in an obscure skirmish.[3]
Captain Harold Scrimshaw	To Ireland, 1647.
Captain Turpin	K. early in the campaign?[4]

Later captains :

Captain Neale	Captain *vice* Turpin.

Captains promoted 1647 :

Captain Francis Freeman	
Captain Francis Barrington	
Captain Francis Bolton	
Captain John Garland	Distinguished himself at St. Fagans, 1648.
Captain Henry Fulcher	

196

The best authority for Okey and his Regiment is his bio-graphy by H. G. Tibbutt.[5] Little is known of his life before 1642. The Royalist Anthony Wood wrote of him 'His parentage was as mean as his calling, having been originally as 'tis supposed a drayman, afterwards a stoaker in a brew house at Islington near London, and then a poor chandler near Lyonkey in Thames Street in London.'[6] But in fact the family was armigerous, and Okey was commissioned at the very outset of the war. Tibbutt writes of him as 'the fiery Colonel, as lusty, stout and brave a man as ever fought in England.' Beyond question he was a soldier of ability – and he was well aware of the fact. His eloquent letters, especially those describing the battles of Naseby and St. Fagans, give a good idea of his capacity.

Okey's Regiment came in part from the Army of the Eastern Association, in which Major Moore and captains Mercer and Abbott had served – the last two named had been under Lt. Colonel John Lilburne, who had declined to serve in the New Model, and had handed over his men to Okey near Abingdon on 30 April 1645. Okey's Regiment had an establishment of 1000 men and it is quite possible that the three old armies found sufficient dragoons to make it up to strength without further recruiting.

We have Captain Wogan's assurance that the dragoons 'were always counted the best of the army', and this would be perfectly credible if the Regiment was full of soldiers with two or three campaigns behind them. The Regiment distinguished it-self at Naseby, Bath and Torrington.

When in 1647 the quarrel broke out between Parliament and the Army, Okey's troops were dispersed in Shropshire and at Holdenby, in Northamptonshire. Remote from the capital, the Regiment gave no trouble; the majority supported Fairfax and Cromwell, the only exception being Captain Wogan who had espoused the parliamentary side. In 1648 he persuaded his troop to follow him to Scotland, where he threw in his lot with the Duke of Hamilton and the 'Engagers'.

In the Second Civil War Okey's Dragoons helped in sup-pressing the rising in South Wales. The Regiment played an important part at St. Fagans (8 May 1648), where Captain John

Garland and Captain-Lieutenant Richard Nicholetts particularly distinguished themselves. Okey's men did well at the siege of Pembroke, and two troops sent against the Scots were doubtless with Cromwell at Preston.

Okey, chosen as one of King Charles' judges, was diligent in attending the tribunal and signed the death warrant. He was with Cromwell, when he suppressed the Levellers at Burford (May 1649), and was rewarded with the degree of M.A. Oxon! (19 May).

About this time half the troops were sent to Ireland as the cadre of a new dragoon regiment, of which Major Abbott was to be colonel. He took with him his own troop and those of Captains Mercer, Bolton, Garland and Fulcher.

Meanwhile, Okey, who was an Anabaptist, and Francis Freeman who was an 'extravagant mystic' — though not above singing bawdy songs — were waging an acrimonious quarrel over their theological views. In October 1650 the captain, who considered himself 'above ordinances', published a pamphlet named *Light Vanquishing Darknesse,* in which he gave a most detailed narrative of their differences. Okey was determined to 'roote out' Freeman and Captain Neale, whose ideas were similar. His Regiment had been pretty much free of Levellers and he was not going to tolerate men of advanced religious views. Eventually in the summer of 1650 Cromwell himself settled the case, by an informal interview in the presence of other officers. Freeman was persuaded to resign. Tibbutt gives a full account of this quarrel, which though not much to the purpose here, is very entertaining. It casts some light too on Okey's character. 'I have seen him,' wrote Freeman, 'sometimes merry with his Officers : and sometimes again not an Officer durst scarce speake to him ; and this verifies an expression, that one used of him once in my hearing, that he is either all hony or all —'.

In 1650 the Regiment — or what remained of it after Abbott's contingent left — went up in the world. It was converted from dragoons into horse, which meant better pay.

In 1651 Okey's six troops were with Lambert at the battle of Inverkeithing (20 July). Thereafter they were with Monck at the sieges of Stirling and Dundee.

Okey, who strongly disapproved of Cromwell's written constitution, 'The Instrument of Government', joined with colonels Matthew Alured and Thomas Saunders in the 'Petition of the Three Colonels', which demanded the election of a free parliament to act as a constituent assembly (October 1654). All three lost their commissions. Major Tobias Bridge took over command of the Regiment and Okey retired to the estates, which he had acquired in Bedfordshire. He was now a wealthy and influential man. His retirement was not particularly peaceful, however. Suspected of being implicated in the plots of the Fifth Monarchy Men he was arrested in 1656 and 1658. In consequence there were those who thought him some sort of martyr, and so when Oliver Cromwell was dead and Richard had tumbled down, the Long Parliament gave him back his Regiment. He showed his gratitude by supporting the Parliament in its struggle with Lambert and Fleetwood. Okey was sent down to Gloucester, which was threatened by Major-General Edward Massey and Lord Herbert. In this mission he was very successful.

Monck trusted neither Okey nor his Regiment, and towards the end of March, Okey found himself deprived of his command, which was given to Colonel Edward Rossiter another Naseby veteran.

Strange though it may seem, Okey joined in Lambert's ill-starred revolt (April 1660). His old Regiment, which was then quartered at Northampton, Peterborough, Newport Pagnell and Woburn, made no move to help him. Rossiter or his major, James Dennis, managed to keep the men quiet. Rossiter was knighted by King Charles at Canterbury on 27 May, and the Regiment was disbanded on 22 November 1660.

Rossiter sat in the Convention Parliament, and was one of only four old Parliamentarian colonels commissioned to raise troops of horse when, in June 1667, there was fear of a Dutch landing.

Okey, the regicide, had made matters worse for himself by supporting Lambert. He fled abroad and lived for a time at Hanau in Germany. But in 1662 he, Colonel John Barkstead and Miles Corbet visited Holland. They were betrayed to Sir George Downing, who treacherously seized them at Delft. Okey was executed on 19 April 1662. Needless to say Pepys was amongst the spectators : 'This morning . . . I went to Aldgate ; and at the corner shop, a draper's, I stood, and did see Barkesstead, Okey, and Corbet, drawne towards the gallows at Tiburne ; and there they were hanged and quartered. They all looked very cheerful ;. . .'[7]

Two days later Secretary Nicholas sent this order to the Sheriff of London : 'It is the King's pleasure that as Colonel Okey died with a sense of his horrid crime, and exhorted others to submit quietly to his government, his head and quarters be committed to Christian burial ;'. . .[8]

Tobias Bridge, who though one of Cromwell's major generals had not made enemies, enjoyed Monck's good opinion, and had a distinguished career after the Restoration. When Lord Teviot was defeated and slain by the Moors before Tangier, with the loss of 400 of the garrison, the surviving officers chose Bridge to take command, and it was his 'unshakennesse of mind' that preserved the place in the months to come.[9]

That Okey's was a good regiment cannot be doubted. Had it not been Cromwell would never have converted it into a regiment of horse.

What a lot they were these Roundhead cavalrymen ! As valiant in action as the men who fought at Ramillies or Waterloo or Megiddo, yet riddled with politics as no British cavalry ever were before or since. It is hard indeed to unravel their internal feuds, to decide why it was that, when Noll was gone, one followed Monck and another Lambert. Harrison and Okey, Packer and Disbrowe, Whalley, Berry and Bethell : they were great men in their time, but their days were numbered for fanatics like these bear within them the seeds of their own destruction.

The field officers of the New Model were :

HORSE

Colonels	Majors
Sir Thomas Fairfax (1612-1671)	John Disbrowe (1608-1680)
John Butler	Thomas Horton (-1649)
Thomas Sheffeild	Richard Fincher
Charles Fleetwood (-1692)	Thomas Harrison (1606-1660)

Edward Rossiter (c.1617-)	Philip Twistleton
Vermuyden	Robert Huntington
Nathaniel Rich (-1701)	John Alford
Sir Robert Pye (-1701)	Matthew Thomlinson (1617-1681)
Edward Whalley (-c.1675)	Christopher Bethell (-1645)
Richard Graves	Adrian Scroope (1601-1660)
Henry Ireton (1611-1651)	George Sedascue

All these regiments, except Graves', were at Naseby. Sir Robert Pye, taken at Leicester, was not present, and nor was Vermuyden, who had just given up his regiment. His regiment passed, not to Major Huntington his second-in-command, but to Oliver Cromwell.

DRAGOONS

Colonel	Major
John Okey (1606-1662)	Daniel Moore.

This regiment was at Naseby.

FOOT

Colonel	Lt. Colonel	Major
Sir Thomas Fairfax (1612-1671)	Thomas Jackson	Cook (-1645)
Major-General Philip Skippon (c.1600-1660)	Jo. Francis (-1645)	Richard Ashfield
Sir Hardress Waller (c.1604-c.1666)	Ralph Coatsworth	Smith
Robert Hammond (1621-1654)	Isaac Ewre	Robert Saunders
Edward Harley (1624-1700)	Thomas Pride (-1658)	William Cowell (-1648)
Edward Montagu (1625-1672)	Mark Grimes	Thomas Kelsey
Walter Lloyd (-1645)	Gray	Thomas Reade (-1662)
John Pickering (-1645)	John Hewson	John Jubbs
Richard Fortescue (-1655)	Jeffrey Richbell (-1645)	Severinus Durfey (-1645)
Richard Ingoldsby (-1685)	Farringdon	Philip Cromwell (-1645)
Thomas Rainborow (-1648)	Henry Bowen	John Done (-1645)
Ralph Weldon	Nicholas Kempson	William Masters

Of these regiments four, Lloyd's, Ingoldsby's, Fortescue's and Weldon's, were not at Naseby, having been employed in the relief of Taunton.

HORSE

	Army
Sir Thomas Fairfax	Eastern Association
	Lifeguard from Earl of Essex
John Butler	Sir William Waller
Thomas Sheffeild	Earl of Essex
Charles Fleetwood	Eastern Association
Edward Rossiter	Lincolnshire Horse
B Vermuyden	Eastern Association
Nathaniel Rich	Eastern Association
Sir Robert Pye	Earl of Essex
Edward Whalley	Eastern Association
Richard Graves	Earl of Essex
Henry Ireton	Sir William Waller

DRAGOONS

John Okey	2 tps, Eastern Association

FOOT

Sir Thomas Fairfax	Earl of Essex and 4 coys.
	Eastern Association
Major-General Philip Skippon	Earl of Essex
	Eastern Association
Sir Hardress Waller	Sir William Waller
Robert Hammond	6 coys. Eastern Association
Edward Harley	4 coys. Earl of Essex
Edward Montagu	Eastern Association
Walter Lloyd	Earl of Essex
John Pickering	Eastern Association
Richard Fortescue	Earl of Essex
Richard Ingoldsby	Earl of Essex
Thomas Rainborow	Eastern Association
Ralph Weldon	Sir William Waller
	4 coys. Earl of Essex

[1] Dr. John Adair, *Cheriton 1644, the Campaign and the Battle*, 1973, p. 217.
[2] Bridgetown the capital of Barbados was called after him.
[3] 'By this time he had become a legendary figure and Sir Walter Scott in *Waverley* makes Flora Mac-Iver compose verses on his death.' (Tibbutt, p. 6).

4 Tibbutt, p. 6.

5 *Colonel John Okey, 1606-1662* by H. G. Tibbutt. Bedfordshire Historical Record Society, Volume XXXV, 1955.

6 Fasti Oxoniensis, II, p. 135.

7 Diary.

8 CSPD. 1661-2, p. 344. Okey's biographer comments: 'Apparently this was a spontaneous gesture on the part of the authorities: the relatives of the dead Colonel had not asked for it.' Tibbutt, p. 168.

9 Firth and Davies, p. 306.

PART FOUR

Chapter Eleven

THE ARMIES TAKE THE FIELD

SIR THOMAS FAIRFAX was commissioned General on 1 April 1645, and on 3 April he went to Windsor 'to see and personally to assist in the frameing of a new Army.' Worthy chaplain Sprigge adds approvingly: 'He went in a private manner, purposely avoiding that pomp, which usually accompanies a General into the field'. He found no light task. 'The difficulty whereof (to say nothing of the danger, through the discontents of them that were reduced under new Commanders, and of those that went off the imployment; which rendered it a business requiring much wisdome and tenderness, as well as resolution)...'[1] Besides 'fitting the Traine for the field, and the attendance of the Recruits from London, which with the old that continued, were to make up the designed number; an entire *new forme* was to be introduced into the whole Army, the Forces that remained of the old Army being not only to be recruited, but to be reduced into new Companies and Regiments, as if they had been new raised.'

In this great work Fairfax had an efficient and diligent assistant in 'that valiant and discreet Commander,' Major-General Philip Skippon, 'whose prudent carriage added much life and expedition to the business,' . . . Skippon knew Essex' old army intimately, and having served at Second Newbury had more than a nodding acquaintance with those of Manchester and Waller. Fairfax had seen Manchester's men in action at Marston Moor, but for the most part the New Model were strangers to him.

Skippon had great influence with the men who had served under Essex and in 'an excellent, pious, and pithy hortatory speech' he gave them his word that they would be well treated and regularly paid : "As I have been with you hitherto," he concluded, "so upon all occasion of service to God and my country I shall, by the help of God, be willing to live and die with you."[2] The staunch Skippon, who is said to have begun his military career as a pikeman in the Dutch service, was just the man to act as a kind of super R.S.M. at a time when everything was in the melting pot, and when, with the coming of spring, the King might take the field any day. But the King lay still at Oxford, whilst his general, Rupert, in a sour humour, was struggling to restore Royalist fortunes in the Severn Valley, where the surprise and loss of Shrewsbury (2 February) had shaken their hold. In his somewhat incoherent letters to his intimate friend Colonel William Legge, the Governor of Oxford, he was urging that his uncle should take the field. As early as 24 March he had written : 'Hasten the King with ordnance, horse, and foot, and doubt nothing. We are few, but shrewd fellows as ever you saw ;. . .' And on 31 March, the Prince, then at Hereford, clearly expects Charles to move soon. 'Desire the King to bring as few scullions and beefeaters with him (as possible), else this army and he cannot quarter in a place.'[3] One hopes that Legge was a good enough friend to rephrase this request !

Clearly it was greatly to Charles' advantage to take the field before the New Model was ready. But precisely why Rupert thought the King would do so is not clear. The spring days went by and still Charles lingered at Oxford. As Sprigge puts it : 'Whilst the New Model Army lay about Windsor, thus forming and fitting for the field ; Prince Rupert with the King's main force for the midland, lay about Worcester and the frontiers of Wales, preparing from thence to take the field ; But the King's person, with most part of the Train, and some of their Foot, intended for the field being then in Oxford, a Convoy of horse, reputed about 2000, was ordered from Worcester to fetch them off from Oxford ; upon advertisement whereof, the Committee of both Kingdomes wrote to the General, to send some horse to march beyond Oxford, and lie on the further side thereof towards Worcester, to intercept that Convoy, and keep the King and his train from passing out.'[4]

It was on 20 April that the CBK sent John Priestley to Lt. General Cromwell with his orders.

'. . . Being informed that the enemy have mounted their ordnance at Oxford, and that Prince Maurice is come thither with 1,000 horse to convey his Majesty and those ordnance to join with the forces of the two Princes in Hereford and Worcester shires, and considering of what advantage it would be to the public to prevent this design of the enemy, we have thought fit to employ in that service your two regiments, Col (John) Fiennes' and the rest of that party which went with you into the west. We therefore desire you to take those forces into your charge, and marching the nearest way for interposing between the party from Oxford and the forces about Hereford and Worcester, to hinder the passing of those ordnance and to take all advantages you can against the enemy for the public good. We desire you also to hold correspondence with Maj-Genl. (Richard) Browne and Col. Edward Massie, who will be ready to take all occasions to advance this service.'[5]

Letters were sent to Fairfax, Browne and Massey to explain the situation. The last is of particular interest.

'Prince Maurice has come to conduct the King and his cannon towards his forces in Worcestershire. We conceive it of importance to prevent that juncture, and therefore have appointed Col. Cromwell to march with a considerable body of horse between Oxford and Gloucester. We know you are best acquainted both with that county and with the present posture of the enemy, and therefore desire you to write immediately your opinion to Col. Cromwell to what place he were best to march, and likewise your opinion to him in any other thing which may conduce to his advantage in that service. Give him what assistance you can with your forces upon all occasions. Besides these forces under Col. Cromwell, we have ordered the three regiments of Cols. Behre, Dalbier, and Cooke, with horse out of several garrisons to come to stay under your command." This was sent by Thos. Pidcock next morning at 9 a.m., and a duplicate by Mr Potter.[6]

Thus Cromwell, who by the Self-Denying Ordinance, was

due to give up his command, was sent with a brigade of horse upon a mission, which resulted in his celebrated Islip raid. He had repaired to Windsor on 19 April in order to pay his respects to Fairfax, before retiring, and here, no doubt with delight as well as surprise, he received his orders.

On 23 April though he failed to surprise the Earl of Northampton at Islip he managed to ferry his brigade across the River Cherwell.[7] Next day Northampton made 'an infall' upon Cromwell, whose men quickly concentrated, and routed the Cavaliers near Islip Bridge. Northampton's Brigade lost some 40 killed, 200 prisoners, 4-500 horses, and a standard of the Queen's Regiment. Northampton, who had shown his worth at Cropredy Bridge had a good brigade,[8] so this was no mean feat.

Cromwell followed up his success with an attack upon Bletchingdon House, one of the circle of minor fortresses which protected the Royalist capital. Cromwell faced the house with horse and dragoons and summoned the governor, Lt. Colonel Francis Windebanke with 'a sharp Message, (our Souldiers casting out words for the Foot to fall on, as if there had been Foot in readiness). . .[9] Windebanke, whose judgment is said to have been affected by the presence of his young wife and other ladies, surrendered. He had 150 men, well-armed, and his conduct admits of no excuse that any soldier worth the name would accept. Poor man, he paid for his lapse with his life (3 May), despite the courage he had shown at Cheriton as attested by Colonel Sir Henry Bard.[10] King Charles with an inconsistency typical of his wayward character awarded Windebanke's widow a pension.

Cromwell wrote: 'I did much doubt the storming of the house, it being strong and well manned, and I having few dragoons, and this not being my business; and yet we got it.' The pious Sprigge tells us 'Thus God was with our New-Model, . . . and declared himself so to be, betimes. Which was by the Enemy esteemed of such evil consequence to their affairs, and so great an affront (in regard it was done by the New-Nodel, as they scornfully termed this Army) that they could not tell which way to redeem their honours, but by calling the Governor to a Councel of War, whom for delivering the house, they condemned to be shot to death.'[11]

207

Symonds[12] tells us that Bletchingdon was 'sans workes, and provision onely for two or three days.' Nonetheless he is scathing about the surrender. 'About two or three of the clock, Friday morning 25 April the colonel valiantly gave up the howse and all his armes, &c., besides 50 horse that came in for shelter ; and this without a shott.' He tells us that Windebanke's advisers 'were disabled for from every bearing armes any more.' They were Colonel Hutchinson ; Major Earnley[13] and a Mr Eedes.

Cromwell sent the captured arms and ammunition to Aylesbury, and, quitting the house, pushed on westwards and fell upon a party of 350 Royalist foot, under Colonel Sir Henry Vaughan, at Bampton-in-the-Bush, 18 miles west of Oxford. Cromwell wrote :

> . . .'The enemy presently barricadoed up the town ; got a pretty strong house. My body came up about eleven in the night, I sent a summons. They slighted it ; I put myself in a posture that they should not escape me, hoping to deal with them in the morning. My men charged them up to their barricadoes in the night, but truly they were of so good resolution that we could not force them from it, and indeed they killed some of my horse, and I was forced to wait until the morning.'

The Royalists surrendered to a second summons and Sprigge puts the prisoners at 200. Meanwhile Colonel John Fiennes had fallen upon a party of horse, taking 40 prisoners and three colours.

These successes tempted Cromwell to try his luck at Faringdon Castle, which he summoned on 29 April, writing : 'I will not spare a man of you, if you put me to a storm.' To this bluff Lt. Colonel Roger Burges[14] staunchly replied :

> "We would have you know you are not now at Bletchington. . . . We fear not your storming nor will have any more parleys."

Meanwhile Major-General Richard Browne had sent Cromwell 5-600 Foot from Abingdon, and in the early hours of 30 April the Roundheads attempted to take the castle by escalade. Captain Henry Cannon led his men up a ladder to be received by Burges himself, who thrust him into the ditch with a pike.[15] The assault failed. The Royalists, who lost six men claimed to have slain 200, a figure which Sprigge reduced to 14.

Cromwell wrote to Burges (30 April): 'There shall be no interruption of your viewing and gathering together the dead bodies, and I do acknowledge it as a favour, your willingness to let me dispose of them.' He thanked the Royalist commander for his civility to his prisoners, adding, 'If you accept of equal exchange, I shall perform my part.'

Faringdon Castle was, of course, a very much stronger place than Bletchingdon; nor is it given to generals, however skilled, to be victorious upon every occasion. The truth is the raid had been a brilliant success, and by carrying off great numbers of draught horses Cromwell had seriously reduced the mobility of the Royalist Train.

It was on Saturday 3 May that, as Symonds relates:

'Cromwell's forces removed from before Farringdon, els if they had stayd Prince Rupert and Generall Goring had falne upon them; they were twice repulsed by Farringdon men, with great losse to them.'[16]

On the 4th the two Palatine princes, Rupert and Maurice came to Oxford and, on the following day, Goring arrived. No doubt the next two days were fully occupied with councils of war and then, at last, on 7 May the King took the field, marching that day to Woodstock, attended by Prince Rupert, Prince Maurice, the Duke of Richmond, the Earl of Lindsey and the Earl of Northampton; with the two troops of his Lifeguard as his escort.

To return to Windsor: Fairfax and Skippon had done their work well and by the end of April were ready to move. The strategic question was, as Sprigge puts it: 'Whither should they first bend. . . . Oxford and the West are put into the scales of competition.' There was a third course: to contrive a strategy which should embrace both these objects. Fairfax was, of course, much influenced by the views of the C.B.K. who at their meeting on 25 April ordered: 7. *To acquaint* Sir Thos. Fairfax with the condition of Taunton, and advise that he should send a sufficient party for its relief, about 5,000 foot and 2,000 horse. Also that he certify this Committee to-morrow of the strength of his forces, and from time to time how his recruits go on and in what condition his army is. Messrs (Anthony) Nicholls (Nicoll) and (Thomas) Erle[17] will inform him of the condition of the west, and some members[18] of this Committee will come to him on Monday about this business.' Northumberland, Essex, Manchester, Saye' and Stapleton were all at this meeting.[19]

The threat to Taunton 'wherein . . . most of the best affected in those parts had drawn themselves for safety ;' . . . prevailed with Fairfax, and the decision was taken 'to decline the designe upon Oxford at that time, though otherwise needfull enough :'..[20] This decision though accepted cheerfully by Fairfax was not made by him or even by the C.B.K. It was, it seems resolved upon by Parliament itself. In consequence on 28 April C.B.K. wrote a rather muddled letter to their four members who had gone down to the Army.

> . . .'By the enclosed order you see the resolution of both Houses about the march of Sir Thos. Fairfax and Major-Genl. Skippon toward the west, and for the numbers that are to march with them. We leave this to your judgment, provided it exceed not 6,000 foot and 2,500 horse and dragoons, which we desire you with all expedition to despatch away. For the remainder of your forces we recommend it to your consideration whether it will not be fittest to send them to Bletchington and Woodstock, or those parts where they will lie in the fittest posture to oppose the march of the Princes (Rupert and Maurice) towards the (Eastern) Association and our own quarters. This will also be an encouragement for the recruits to come up when our forces shall be so near to Oxford, and so (our position) strengthened on that side. We have this day received a letter from Sir Thos. Fairfax, desiring 7,000 foot and 3,000 horse, yet, in respect the forces with you are the main strength left for the preservation of the (Eastern) Association against any attempts of the enemy in the absence of those forces, we conceive it not fit to exceed the number resolved on, but if you conceive a smaller number may effect that design, we desire you to send no more than may be sufficient for that service, leaving the rest for the protection of the Association and those parts. What you shall resolve on concerning the forces to be left for securing these parts signify to Lieut.-Genl. Cromwell.'. . .[21]

Thus at the very outset the New Model was divided in two.

The idea of placing the smaller division between Bletchingdon and Woodstock appears rash in the extreme.

Chaplain Sprigge, with the advantage of hindsight, points out that by this Western expedition 'the whole fruit of that Yeares service was in great hazard to have been thereby blasted in the bud; the King being then in a condition ready to take the field, having made severall Dispatches for that purpose to imbody all his Forces, and we having no balancing Force to attend his motion' . . . . The force with Cromwell was far too small to engage the King's field army, and the Scots were too far off. Brereton was fully occupied with besieging Beeston Castle and blockading Chester. Massey was hard put to it to hold Gloucester and its circle of satellite garrisons,[22] for his forces included only two regiments of foot, in all, not more than 1,800 strong.

Sprigge shrewdly points out the danger involved in 'the slight retrenching and garrisoning of many Townes of no great strength by nature and situation, though it may serve for the present securing of particular Counties, and particular men's Estates from plundering Parties, yet are they predjudicial to the Publicke, and to the main of the wars: And therefore,' he concludes, 'it hath been held great wisdome by ancient and well experienced Souldiers, to have but few Garisons, and those very Strong, which may hold out long without relief; which is the more necessary, if they shall be in the corners of a country, and remote from reliefe.'[23]

On 1 May the New Model began its march, though without Cromwell's detachment of horse and dragoons and four regiments of foot, which, when their recruits had joined, were to join him 'to busie the enemy about Oxford.' On 5 May a mile beyond Andover the General halted for two or three hours and ordered a Council of War, which tried several offenders for their lives. A 'Renegado' and a mutineer 'were executed upon a Tree, at Wallop in the way of the Armies march, *in terrorem.*' Next day it was proclaimed throughout the Army that 'it should be death for any man to plunder'[24]. The mutineers were men of Sir Michael Livesay's,[25] later Ireton's, Regiment of Horse. The horse of the New Model were generally speaking old soldiers, but the ranks of the foot were full of recruits, many of them pressed men. Without discipline such men could not stand against Lord Astley's old soldiers. Fairfax did well to begin by showing that he meant to be obeyed.

That night (5 May) the New Model reached Salisbury. The Cavaliers were as yet unaware of their approach, as was discovered from intercepted letters in which Lord Hopton asked the Governors of Winchester and of Basing House[26] to send him word when they thought Fairfax would be able to take the field.

When, on 7 May, the King left Oxford the New Model had reached Blandford, Dorset, a distance of 91 miles from Windsor. Already the Prince's appearance at Oxford (4 May) had caused a considerable stir at Derby House, and some second thoughts. On 3 May the C.B.K. sent Fairfax a copy of a letter from Major John Bridges, the Governor of Warwick Castle in which he reported 'the Prince's march toward Oxford.' They had desired the General to halt about Salisbury with his foot till he should receive 'further advertisement of the Prince's motions about Oxford.' The letter is endorsed 'Sent by Newman that night,'[27] which seems to argue a certain sense of urgency. The following day the C.B.K. again wrote to Fairfax and this time desired him to halt next day about Andover[28] with his horse and foot 'till you receive further advertisement from us, which will be very speedily.' This was endorsed 'Sent by Crips that night, and a duplicate by (Thomas) Bulmer —'[29] both of whom got through and were to carry many another letter.

The Prince's march towards Oxford worried the Committee for, as they wrote to the Committee of the Eastern Association at Cambridge (4 May): 'we know not as yet which way they may bend their course, and whether they may not have some design upon your Association.'

On 5 May the C.B.K. decided to report to both Houses 'to know their pleasure whether, as affairs now stand, Sir Thos. Fairfax and Major-Genl. Skippon shall go into the west.'[30] But without waiting for Parliament's views they wrote to Fairfax giving him 'intelligence we have now received of the juncture of the Princes' forces with those of Goring now at or about Oxford.' They did not consider the party left behind to be sufficient to 'oppose their motions and defend the Associations.' Fairfax was to detach four regiments of foot, two of horse, and 'such a train of artillery as you shall judge necessary' to march with all possible expedition to the relief of Taunton. He was 'to take order to put this party in such a way of command as may be best for the service.' Fairfax and Skippon 'with the rest of the forces, upon intelligence held with Lieut-Genl. Cromwell's were to join 'in such place as may be most for the advantage of the service.'[31]

Little did the Princes suspect the stir their march to Oxford had caused! In fact to the Royalists their own situation, after Cromwell's recent raid, seemed far from brilliant.

Fairfax put the senior colonel, Ralph Weldon in command of the brigade appointed for the relief of Taunton, which consisted of these units:

FOOT   4-5000

Colonel Ralph Weldon[32]
Colonel Richard Fortescue[32]
Colonel Walter Lloyd[32]
Colonel Richard Ingoldsby[32]
Six companies from the garrison of Chichester which joined near Dorchester.
Six companies from the garrison of Lyme.

HORSE 1800-2000

Colonel Richard Graves[32]
Colonel Edward Cooke
Colonel Edward Popham
Colonel John Fitz-James
The Plymouth Regiment.

The Western Royalists, whose intelligence left something to be desired, conceived that this force was Fairfax' whole army, and so, in great disorder they broke up their siege.

'And so Colonel Welden had a fair passage to the town, which he entered, May 14, to no lesse joy to the Besieged, than discomfort to the Enemy.'[33] Thus it proved that a strong brigade of the New Model, with some local forces, was sufficient to save Taunton. The Prince's arrival at Oxford, though it caused what in World War II would have been called 'a flap' amongst the Roundheads had the effect of drawing Fairfax back towards the Royalist capital, which should probably have been his objective in the first place.

King Charles for his part, instead of seeking a decisive battle with the New Model, set out on one of his meanderings round the Midlands. To be fair this course was probably forced on him by his lack of numbers. He needed a little time to concentrate his forces. Whether he went the best way about it is another matter.

At Woodstock on 8 May, an alarm at one o'clock in the morning heralded the day. At daybreak the King marched away, doubtless *via* Enstone and Chipping Norton making for Stow-on-the-Wold (18 miles according to Symonds, but really 21). The King quartered at Stow, and his troop at Maugersbury just to the south. Charles now had with him:

HORSE	Approx. Strength
The Lifeguard	130
Prince Rupert's Regiment (Sir Thomas Dallison)	400
Earl of Northampton's Regiment	250[34]

FOOT	
The Lifeguard	300 [35]

TRAIN

4 pieces of cannon
8 boats in carriages
All manner of ammunition[36]

The King pushed on next day to Evesham (16 miles), a Royalist garrison, where he joined with Lord Astley's Foot, 3,300 strong.

Charles had now concentrated 6,300 Horse and 5,300 Foot, a total of 11,600 men. This was a stronger army than the one he had commanded at Second Newbury. But, incredible though it may seem, he and his councillors now decided to send Goring back into the West with 3,000 horse, including most of the Old Horse of the 'Oxford Army'.

This blunder Clarendon attributes to Rupert. 'The prince found that Goring, as a man of a ready wit and an excellent speaker, was like to have most credit with the King in all debates, and was jealous that he would quickly get such an interest with his majesty that his own credit would be much eclipsed.'[37] Goring was no less pleased to be independent than Rupert was to be rid of him. But if the army assembled at Evesham 'had been kept together, it is very probable that the summer might have been crowned with better success.'[38]

According to Symonds this left the King with :

HORSE

Langdale's[39]	2,500
Lifeguards	800
	3,300

FOOT

King's Lifeguard	200
Colonel George Lisle's	500
Sir Henry Bard	300
Prince Rupert's Foot	1,000
Lord Astley's	3,300
	5,300

Symonds' figures for the horse are not very useful. Langdale's two brigades of Northern Horse, as we shall see, cannot have numbered much more than 1,500 ; while the Lifeguards of the King and the two Palatine Princes would have totalled 390. Symonds does not account for Prince Rupert's and the Earl of Northampton's Regiments, another 650 men, or Bard's 100 horse from Campden House. A total of 2,640 may be nearer the true figure for the horse now with the King.

As to the foot, Lisle had been replaced as Governor of Farringdon Castle, by the aged Sir Marmaduke Rawdon, whose arrival with his regiment from Basing House Symonds records under 8 May. Lisle's 500 men must have included his own regiment ; and the four companies of Sir John Owen's Regiment, under Lt. Colonel Roger Burges, whose repulse of Cromwell we have already recorded. In addition he probably had Colonel Theophilus Gilby's regiment, which fought in his Tertia at Naseby. These three, 790 strong in April 1644[40] must surely have been able to field 500 officers and men in May 1645.

Bard's Regiment, which had wintered in Campden House, looks suspiciously strong at 300, but it may have had another small regiment with it, perhaps the one formerly commanded by Lord Percy, and which was now probably under Colonel William Murrey. These two regiments which had very similar histories, had usually been associated together.

Prince Rupert's 1,000 foot consisted of his own regiment, 500 strong, and the Shrewsbury Foot, under Lt. Colonel Smith another 500. These last were the remnants of five of the regiments sent over from Ireland to Cheshire in the winter 1643/4.

Symond's total for Lord Astley's Foot, 3,300 men, may be on the high side. They probably included the eight regiments of:

> The Duke of York
> Richard Page
> Edward Hopton
> The Queen (Colonel Rhys Thomas)
> Lord Astley
> Sir Barnard Astley
> Matthew Appleyard
> Sir John Paulet

The first three of these may have been strong, perhaps as many as 500 apiece, but it is unlikely that any of the others amounted to more than 200 or 300.

On 10 May the King was at Inkberrow, 11 miles from Worcester. The next day he went to the rendezvous of his foot, and then, escorted only by his Lifeguard and his regiment of foot, marched to Droitwich where he stayed until 14 May. During the time he was there Prince Rupert sat down before Hawkesley House, the property of Mr Middlemore, where there was a small Roundhead garrison commanded by Captain Gough, the governor, with 60 foot, and Captain Whichcott, with 'above 40 horse.'[41] This minor garrison can hardly have been much of a thorn in the side of the Worcester cavaliers. By lingering in a county, which was largely in the hands of his own party, the King was letting his army eat up his own quarters. It would have been more sensible to move on into Staffordshire, or some part where the Parliamentarians held sway, and live on their country.

Hawkesley House surrendered on 14 May. 'In this howse was a month's provision and ammunition, but the soldiers would not fight when they perceived it was the King's army'. 'After

Lord Astley had the pillage of the howse and the soldjers prisoners, the howse was sett on fyre.'[42]

The C.B.K. had some difficulty in making out what the King was at. On 10 May they wrote to the Committee of the Eastern Association at Cambridge, thanking them for calling out the trained bands to secure that city, but going on to say : 'From the intelligence now received we learn that the King with his forces has marched toward Worcester, from thence intending to go northward, so that you need not apprehend any danger from them. You can dismiss your trained bands from any further attendance for the present.'[43] The same day they ordered Lt. General Cromwell to march toward Warwick, so as to cover and preserve the Eastern Association, and be in position to join the Scottish Army and the rest of the northern forces.[44]

They also wrote to Major-General Richard Browne at Abingdon, and to Colonel John Fiennes, making arrangements for a garrison to be put into Bletchington House so as to 'straiten' Oxford, now that the King's army had marched away.

To Ferdinando Lord Fairfax they wrote, warning him that they had received intelligence that the King 'with his joined forces intends to march toward the Northern parts, where, if we have not a joint force to oppose him, he may soon grow to such numbers as may easily destroy our divided parties, and become thereby very dangerous to the whole kingdom.' They outline the arrangements they have made for a rendezvous with the Earl of Leven : 'Whither we would have you send 1,000 of your best horse and best armed, besides those that are with Sir Wm. Brereton. We have also appointed 200 horse and 1,000 foot from Lancashire, 500 horse and 1,000 foot from Cheshire, besides the 1,000 horse of yours which are with them, 600 horse and dragoons from Derbyshire, and 100 horse and 400 foot from Staffordshire. If the King should draw out his garrison of Newark, then Notts will send 200 horse and 200 foot, and Lincolnshire 400 horse and 500 foot ; all which, together with the Scottish army, we expect will be of good strength to prevent the King's march that way, and to preserve those counties.'[45]

Similar letters were sent to all the counties, which were supposed to contribute contingents.[46] By 11 May the C.B.K. had got the impression that the King was marching 'toward Cheshire and those parts,' and desired Leven to assist Brereton and the Deputy Lieutenant of Lancashire in taking care of the passes into Lancashire, where, 'as former experience has taught us,' the King might 'much increase the number of his forces.'[47] They were referring, of course, to Prince Rupert's march through Lancashire the previous year, when he had been able to recruit great numbers of men to march with him to the relief of York. They return to this theme in a letter of 13 May to Leven and the Committee of both kingdoms (residing) at the Scot's army. They conceive the King's intention to be toward Cheshire, for raising of those sieges and relief of his garrisons there.' They 'apprehend the danger and disorder that may ensue' if he should march into Lancashire and Yorkshire, 'where in all probability the disaffection of many in those parts may furnish his army with very great numbers.' They have arranged for a party of 2,000 horse and 500 dragoons under Colonel Vermuyden to join Leven and Lord Fairfax to prevent such a move on the King's part.[48] From a letter of the same date to Vermuyden we learn that his force was to consist of the regiments of colonels:

> Algernon Sidney[49]
> B   Vermuyden
> Sir Robert Pye
> John Fiennes

'and if these do not make 2,000, that number to be made up with such troops as are now under Major Sadaskew.' George Sedascue had been major to Sir Michael Livesey's Kentish regiment, which was to contribute about three troops to Henry Ireton's New Model regiment. Of these regiments only Fiennes' did not belong to the New Model.

On 15 May the Royalist army met near Hawksley House and slighted the works. That night the governors of three Royalist garrisons waited upon the King, at Himley Hall, Staffordshire. They were

> Colonel Barnaby Scudamore   Hereford
> Colonel Thomas Leveson   Dudley Castle
> Colonel Sir Michael Woodhouse   Ludlow

Oddly enough neither Scudamore nor Woodhouse seem to have been asked to provide reinforcements for the marching army, but Leveson evidently had his regiment of horse with him, for Symonds describes his three cornets.[50]

Next day (16 May) the King's army paraded betimes – about 4 o'clock in the morning – and at the rendezvous a soldier, chosen by lot from among a number, was hanged for mutiny. This done the army marched off into Shropshire, reaching the Newport area on 17 May. Here Colonel Richard Bagot, the Governor of Lichfield, joined the army with 300 foot and 200 horse.

Symonds notes that Bagot's horse had three blue cornets, without any manner of badge, motto or distinction; and that his foot colours were Azure, a mullet or, on a canton a cross.[51]

The Royalists were now in an area where, though they held several garrisons, the more important places were in Parliament - arian hands. They were therefore living in the enemy's quarters .

GARRISONS IN SHROPSHIRE[52]

ROYALIST

	Governor	Garrison
Longford House	Colonel John Young	
Lilleshall Abbey	Captain Henry Bostock[53]	160
	then	
	Major Radcliffe Duckenfield	
High Ercall	Captain Nicholas Armourer[54]	200
Cawes Castle	Colonel John Davalier	
Bridgnorth Castle	Colonel Sir Lewis Kirke	300 F
Ludlow Castle	Colonel Sir Michael Woodhouse	
Stokesay Castle	Captain Gerard Dannet[55]	
Shrawardine Castle	Captain James Vaughan[54]	
Chirk Castle	Lt. Colonel John Watts	

PARLIAMENTARIAN

Wem.	King
Morton Corbett Castle	
Shrewsbury	

GARRISONS IN STAFFORDSHIRE

ROYALIST

Lichfield	Colonel Richard Bagot	300H c.600F
Dudley Castle	Colonel Thomas Leveson	200H? 250F?
Tutbury Castle	Colonel Sir Andrew Kniveton	

Eccleshall Castle		
Stafford	Lt. Colonel Lewis Chadwick	
Rushall Hall		
Alton Castle		40 or 50
Paynsley House		c.50
Caverswall House	Capt. John Ashenhurst	20H 20F
Leek		
Tamworth Castle	Capt. Waldine Willington	
Trentham		
Uttoxeter		
Wrottesley		

Staffordshire was a county full of petty garrisons, though there is evidence that the Parliamentarian county committee did their best to cut down their number by demolishing those which seemed least useful.[56]

Meanwhile at Derby House the C.B.K. had heard glad tidings from Taunton, and on 15 May they wrote congratulatory letters to Sir Thomas Fairfax, Colonels Greaves and Weldon. To the latter they wrote: 'Whilst we desire to give the praise for the relief of Taunton to Him from whom all good success comes, we return thanks to you and all your officers for your careful and expeditious performance of this so good and successful a service, which we shall upon all occasions be ready to remember and acknowledge.'[57]

The C.B.K. took good strategic advantage of this success. Writing to inform Leven of it (15 May) they told him that the Royalists had retreated towards Exeter and Bridgwater. 'Sir Thos. Fairfax is returned from the west, and was yesternight about Newbury. We intend the forces with him and those with Cromwell and Browne to effect a junction and put themselves in order for besieging Oxford, which we hope may divert the enemy's marching northward with so great a force as otherwise he might. We have sent you a copy of the last intelligence we had of the King's army. We have sent two gentlemen[58] to hasten the despatching away of the party consisting of 2,000 horse and 500 dragoons to your army, and have left it, to their commander, Col. Vermuyden, to march by such way as he shall think fittest for his speedy advance and junction with you. As your occasions shall require and ours permit, we will send more forces for your assistance, but if the strength of the enemy should return this way we expect the like assistance from you.'[59]

On the same day the C.B.K. told Sir Thomas Fairfax, that Cromwell with the forces left with him, was to garrison Bletchington House and dispose the rest of his forces 'in the best way that may be for straitening of Oxford, which we have designed to be blocked up forthwith in order to a siege by those forces at present with you and with Cromwell, besides all the recruits that are to come up, and such other forces, both of the garrisons and counties as we may be able to send thither. We have designed this as the main action, to be prosecuted with all such forces as are not already employed elsewhere, unless any especial exigency should require these forces to be otherwise employed. We desire you, therefore, so to dispose your marches as may be of most advantage to that design of blocking up and besieging Oxford. We desire you to consider what is necessary for such a work, and advise us thereof.'[60]

This was good strategy : 'check to the King.'

THE MOVEMENTS OF THE ARMIES

MOVEMENTS OF THE NEW MODEL ARMY, 1645

		MILES	
		AA	*Sprigge*
30 April	From Windsor to Reading	18	12
1 May	To Theale, Berks.	5	4
2 May	To Newbury, Berks.	12	11
3 May	Newbury	—	—
4 May	To Andover, Wilts.	17	12
5 May	To Salisbury, Wilts.	18	15
6 May	To Sixpenny Hanley, Dorset	..	10
7 May	To Blandford, Dorset	..	7
8 May	To Wichampton	..	7
9 May	To Ringwood, Hants.	..	10
10 May	To Romsey, Hants.	18	14
11 May	Romsey	—	—
12 May	To Alresford, Hants.	..	14

13 May	To Whitchurch, Hants.	..	10
14 May	To Newbury, Berks.	13	10
15 May	Newbury	—	—
16 May	Newbury	—	—
17 May	To Blewbury	..	10
18 May	Blewbury	—	—
19 May	To Newnam (sic), Oxon.	..	0
20 May	To Garsington	..	2
21 May	Garsington	—	—
22 May	To Marston and the Siege of Oxford	..	4
23 May	to 4 June — Siege of Oxford		
5 June	To Marsh Gibbon, Bucks.	..	9
6 June	To Great Brickhill	..	12
7 June	To Sherrington, Bucks.	..	8
8 June	Sherrington	—	—
9 June	To Stony Stratford, Bucks.	..	4
10 June	Stony Stratford	—	—
11 June	To Wotton, Northants.	..	8
12 June	To Kislingbury, Northants.	..	4
13 June	To Guilsborough, Northants.	..	6
14 June	To battle of Naseby		
	To Market Harborough, Leics.	..	6
15 June	To Kibworth, to Great Glen	..	7
16 June	To Knighton, and Leicester Siege	..	6
17 June	Leicester Siege	—	—
18 June	To Leicester	..	$1\frac{1}{2}$
19 June	Leicester	—	—
20 June	To Lutterworth, Leics.	13	10

THE KING'S MOVES

Wednesday	7 May	To Woodstock (JPRM) Lifeguard also (Symonds).
Thursday	8 May	To Stow-on-the-Wold (JPRM) 18m. (Symonds)
Friday	9 May	To Evesham (JPRM). Tp. at Child's Wickham, Glos. (Sym.)
Saturday	10 May	To Inkberrow, (Great Ingborow) (JPRM) Worcs. (Inckburrough Magna) (Sym.)
Sunday	11 May	To Droitwich (JPRM). Night. HQ. Bromsgrove (Sym.)
Monday	12 May	Droitwich
Tuesday	13 May	Droitwich
Wednesday	14 May	To Cottenhall (JPRM). To Hawkesley at the moment of the surrender. To Cofton-Hall (2 m) (Sym.)
Thursday	15 May	RV nr, Cofton-Hall. To Himley Hall, Staffs. (Sym.)

Friday	16 May	To Bishburye (JPRM).
Saturday	17 May	To Chatwin Hall (JPRM). /Via Tong, Salop.
Sunday	18 May	Chatwin Hall [Chetwynd] Salop.
Monday	19 May	Chatwin Hall.
Tuesday	20 May	To Bitten. /From Chatwyn via Drayton, Salop and lay a mile beyond. E. of Lichfield at Norton.
Wednesday	21 May	Bitten.
Thursday	22 May	To Parkehall. /Drayton to Stone, Staffs. Mr Crompton's House.
Friday	23 May	Parkehall /The Army rested (Sym.)
Saturday	24 May	To Eaton in the Claye (Derbyshire). We marched to Uttoxeter (Sym.) Lichfield at Marston, nr. Cubley, Derbyshire.
Sunday	25 May	HM at To Tidbury [Tutbury] Castle. Tp. Rolleston. HQ Burton-on-Trent. (Sym.)
Monday	26 May	Tutbury Castle. Army rested. An alarm by Derby H to Col. H. Carey's qrs.
Tuesday	27 May	To Ashby-de-la-Zouch, Leics. Lichfield to Packington.
Wednesday	28 May	To Cotes /HQ Loughborough, Leics (Sym.) HM at Sir Henry Skipwith's house, Cotes, in Prestwould psh, Leics. (Sym.)
Thursday	29 May	To Elston by Leicester.
Friday	30 May	Leicester summoned (Sym.) HM at Leicester Abbey. Countess of Devon's (Sym.)
Saturday	31 May	Leicester taken.
Sunday	1 June	Leicester
Monday	2 June	Leicester
Tuesday	3 June	Leicester
Wednesday	4 June	To Great Glen. RV at Newton Harcourt King to Wistow (Sir Richard Halford) Lifeguard. Kilby & Foston.
Thursday	5 June	To [Market] Harborough. RV nr MH (Northants). HQ that night.
Friday	6 June	To Daventry.
Saturday	7 June	Daventry. HM to Daventry (Sym.) H Gds. to Staverton, 1 m. distant.
Sunday	8 June	Daventry
Monday	9 June	Daventry
Tuesday	10 June	Daventry
Wednesday	11 June	Daventry
Thursday	12 June	To [Market] Harborough
Friday	13 June	[Market] Harborough /Troop at Theddingworth, Leics. (Sym.)

Saturday	14 June	The battle of Naseby. Retreats through Naseby, and by morning to Ashby-de-la-Zouch.
		Marched 2 a.m. (Sym.). RV 7 a.m. M.H. 12 noon battle.
Sunday	15 June	To Lichfield Close. H in L. & villages
Monday	16 June	To Wolverhampton
Tuesday	17 June	To Bewdley.
		Lichfield to Neather Arley.
Wednesday	18 June	Rested (at Bewdley)
Thursday	19 June	To Bromyard, Herefordshire.
		To Hereford that night.
		K's tp. to Brinsop. aftwds. Pembridge.

PRINCE RUPERT'S MARCHES[61]

"LEYCESTER MARCHE"

Wednesday	7 May	Oxford to Chipping Norton
Thursday	8 May	To Bradwell
Friday	9 May	To Mr [ ] Cannings of Bradfarton.
Saturday	10 May	To Alcester
Sunday	11 May	To Droitwich
Monday	12 May	Droitwich
Tuesday	13 May	Droitwich
Wednesday	14 May	To besiege Hawksly House. His family to Bromsgrove.
Thursday	15 May	Hawksly House taken.
Friday	16 May	To Wolverhampton
Saturday	17 May	To Newport, Shropshire
Sunday	18 May	Newport
Monday	19 May	Newport
Tuesday	20 May	To Drayton
Wednesday	21 May	Drayton
Thursday	22 May	To Stone
Friday	23 May	Stone
Saturday	24 May	To Uttoxeter
Sunday	25 May	Prince's family to Burton-on-Trent
Monday	26 May	Burton-on-Trent
Tuesday	27 May	To Ashby-de-la-Zouch
Wednesday	28 May	To Loughborough
Thursday	29 May	To Elston. The Prince lay in the works before Leicester.
Friday	30 May	Before Leicester
Saturday	31 May	The Prince took Leicester by assault
Sunday	1 June	Leicester

Monday	2 June	Leicester
Tuesday	3 June	Leicester
Wednesday	4 June	To Great Glen
Thursday	5 June	To [Market] Harborough
Friday	6 June	To Daventry
Saturday	7 June	Daventry
Sunday	8 June	Daventry. The relief of cattle sent towards Oxford
Monday	9 June	Daventry
Tuesday	10 June	Daventry
Wednesday	11 June	Daventry
Thursday	12 June	To [Market] Harborough
Friday	13 June	[Market] Harborough
Saturday	14 June	The battle of Naseby. All retreated through Leicester: and by morning to Ashby-de-la-Zouch.
Sunday	15 June	To Lichfield
Monday	16 June	To Wolverhampton
Tuesday	17 June	To Bewdley
Wednesday	18 June	Bewdley
Thursday	19 June	To Hereford

[1] p.9.

[2] D.N.B. quoting Vicars, *Burning Bush*, p. 133; Rushworth vi. 8. 17.

[3] See Appendix.

[4] Sprigge, 10.

[5] C.S.P.D. p. 419.

[6] C.S.P.D. pp. 419-420.

[7] According to Robert Graves *Goodbye to All That*, p. 398, this was thanks to one Beckley, to whose family Cromwell gave perpetual fishing rights from Islip to the stretch of river near the Cherwell Hotel When Graves lived at Islip, William, "Fisher" Beckley, still enjoyed these rights!

[8] The Queen's Regiment, The Earl of Northampton's Regiment, Lord Wilmot's Regiment, Colonel Richard Palmer's Regiment.

[9] Sprigge, 11.

[10] C.S.P.D. p. 438. Letter from Campden House, 28 April 1645.

[11] Sprigge, 12.

[12] p. 163.

[13] Robert Earnley of Colonel Richard Palmer's Horse.

[14] Of Colonel John Owen's Regiment of Foot. The governor, Colonel George Lisle, was apparently at Oxford.

[15] Cannon was obliged to surrender, and climb up a ladder into the fortress.

[16] Diary, p. 164.

[17] M.Ps. for Bodmin and Wareham respectively. Erle had been a captain of horse.

18 Lords Saye and Warriston, Sir Henry Vane, Sr., and William Crew were to go down on 28 April (C.S.P.D. p. 437).

19 In passing it is noteworthy that, with remarkable prescience, the Committee wrote that same day to the Committee at Leicester. 'We are informed by such as are competent to judge that your town in not in so secure a posture as a place of that consequence ought to be, and would be in apparent danger should it be resolutely attempted. We recommend to your especial vigilance both the works and guards.' (C.S.P.D. p. 434).

20 Sprigge, 14.

21 C.S.P.D. pp. 441 & 442.

22 Tewkesbury, Sudeley Castle, Beverstone, Slimbridge, Newnham and Monmouth C.S.P.D. p. 18. 6 October 1644.

23 Sprigge, p. 14.

24 Sprigge, 15.

25 26 April, C.B.K. to Fairfax. C.S.P.D. p. 437.

26 Lord Ogle and the Marquis of Winchester.

27 C.S.P.D. p. 454.

28 In fact he marched on that day to Salisbury.

29 C.S.P.D. p. 455.

30 C.S.P.D. p. 457.

31 C.S.P.D. p. 459.

32 New Model regiments.

33 Sprigge, p. 18.

34 Symonds, p.181

35 Walker

36 Symonds, p. 165.

37 Rebellion, p. 264.

38 *Ibid.*, p. 263.

39 . . . 'which wee mett at Stow' . . . (Symonds, 166).

40 Symonds. BM. MS. Harl. 986.

41 Symonds, p. 167.

42 Symonds, *ibid*.

43 C.S.P.D. p. 475.

44 C.S.P.D. p. 476.

45 C.S.P.D. p. 477.

46 C.S.P.D. p. 478.

47 C.S.P.D. p. 481.

48 C.S.P.D. p. 485.

49 He had commanded Manchester's regiment in 1644, and Sir Thomas Fairfax had actually signed his commission (2 April 1645) for a New Model regiment. However, he preferred to serve under his brother, the Earl of Leicester and went to Ireland. Nathaniel Rich succeeded to command of this regiment.

50 Sable, an ostrich or, holding in its mouth a sword proper, and standing on a scroll with the motto HOC NUTRIOR. Vert, with a charge somewhat like a

sun in splendour (sic) A scroll, with the letters SA-SA (Symonds p. 168). SA, SA, SA was the battle cry of the Imperialists in the Thirty years war. It meant Kill, Kill, Kill.

[51] Symonds. p. 172. This must have been first captain's colour. It was among those taken at Naseby, as was the captain, Anthony Dyott.

[52] c.f. Symonds p. 172.

[53] Symonds notes 'Bostock Governour obijt' but exactly when he died is uncertain. Duckenfield was major of Sr. Wm. Vaughans Regiment of Horse.

[54] Sir Wm. Vaughan H.

[55] Sir Michael Woodhouse F.

[56] The Committee at Stafford 1643-1645. The Order Book of the Staffordshire County Committee. Ed. D. H. Pennington and I. A. Roots.

[57] C.S.P.D. p. 491.

[58] Colonel Moseley and Major James Ennis.

[59] C.S.P.D. pp. 492-493 – Sent by Mr Hutchins.

[60] C.S.P.D. p. 493. Sent by Hanbury.

[61] Based on *The Journal of Prince Rupert's Marches*. English Historical Review, 1898.

Chapter Twelve

THE STORMING OF LEICESTER

*'. . . the cruel massacre at Leicester being so general,
both of men, women and some children that (if one may
compare a small thing with a great) not much unlike
the sack at Magdeburg.'*

Major Leonard Watson[1]

LEICESTER WAS NOT particularly strong, nor was it strongly garrisoned. Even so the last time 'the Oxford Army' had stormed a
town it had cost the Cavaliers dear, and there were regiments of
foot present that had borne the brunt at Bristol in July 1643.[2]

The weakness of the defences can have been little consolation to the forlorn hope, those officers and men who were
invited to be first up the breach. The line to be defended was
about three miles in extent, and several buildings had been left
outside the works, because their owners were citizens with
sufficient local influence to prevent their destruction. These
included Master Chapman's houses near Belgrave Gate; Green's
houses near Humberstone Gate; Widow Swan's houses and
many near to Saint Sunday's Bridge. All these were within 120
paces of the works and most of them within pistol shot. The
Committee would not permit the fortification of the Newarke,
because their clerk, Mr Wadland, had a piece of land there,
which he was unwilling to have cut up.[3]

The Royalists were well aware of the weakness of the town
and on 30 April Lieutenant Henry Purefoy, a Leicestershire
man, who was a prisoner at Bristol heard Lord Hawley, the

Deputy-Governor, speaking of a plan to seize Leicester, where it seems there was some sort of Seventeenth Century Fifth Column. Purefoy managed to get home and reported this information to the Earl of Kent, to whom he was distantly related, and to the Leicester Committee. The C.B.K. was asked for cannon and for permission to press 1,000 men if need should arise. By 26 May it was evident that the main Royalist Army was approaching, and messengers were sent far and wide appealing for reinforcements. But it proved that Colonels Vermuyden and Rossiter, and the Committees at Coventry, Derby, Nottingham and Northampton all had doubts and fears of their own. Few reinforcements appeared but among them was Sir Robert Pye, a colonel of horse in the New Model. He was on his way to join Vermuyden, but very courageously, determined to throw in his lot with the feeble garrison. The Committee bestowed 20 gold pieces upon him! In addition Major Christopher Innes with 200 dragoons belonging to the garrison of Newport Pagnell, falling back before the approach of Sir Richard Willys and a strong detachment from Newark, threw himself into Leicester.

The Governor, Colonel Theophilus Grey, a younger brother of the Earl of Kent, already had about 950 troops, including 150 raw and reluctant recruits, and 100 dragoons drawn in from the abandoned garrison of Kirby Bellars. In all it is unlikely that the Roundheads numbered more than about 1,270 men of rather varied quality. In addition there were perhaps 1,000 townsmen of military age. The second-in-command, Lt. Colonel [   ] Whitbrooke, had seen service against the Spaniards in the Netherlands; but there were few officers of experience in Leicester. It was not much of a fortress to oppose the King with a formed army of 10,000 men, and an adequate siege train. On 29 May the Royalists sat down before the place, the King and Prince Rupert setting up their Headquarters at the Manor House in Aylestone, which belonged to the Earl of Rutland.

Rupert decided to make his main attack upon the south wall of the Newarke, and on the evening of the 29th his men began to make a battery upon ancient Roman earthworks at the Rawdykes.

The Royalist Army now consisted of:

Horse	5,520
Foot	5,300

10,820

In addition the King had 12 guns and 2 mortars.

By daybreak on 30 May the Royalist guns were in position, and at noon the Prince summoned the town to surrender. He offered quarter for the inhabitants and a free pardon for the mayor, William Billers. Major Innes and his men might leave unmolested if they quit the town at once.

Without delay the Committee met in the Mayor's Parlour at the Guildhall. One of them set the resolute tone of the meeting with: "We are a party of those who have taken the Parliament's cause – a cause so high that I desire to die in no other." The only dissenting voices were those of Sir Robert Pye and Major Innes, neither of them Leicester men, but arguably the most experienced officers present. Not all the soldiers were for capitulation: Captain Francis Hacker and Captain Thomas Babington voted with the majority.

At two o'clock a trumpet was sent to the Prince with a message asking whether the decision might be deferred until next morning, and requesting that meanwhile no more Royalist batteries should be raised. The Prince, however, was not so simple that he could not see the defenders raising a breastwork inside the Newarke wall. He told the envoy he would lay him by the heels if he came again with such a message, and when the Mayor and the Committee sent him once more to renew their plea for delay, the Prince committed him to the Provost Marshal. Rupert now sent his own messenger demanding an answer within a quarter of an hour, failing which they must take the consequences. Now, by the Laws of War then prevailing the consequences were No Quarter. If a defender was so rash as to compel the besieger to storm a practicable breach, with all the losses that involved, he could expect no mercy. We have it on the authority of the first Duke of Wellington that 'the practice which refuses quarter to a garrison that stands an assault is not a *useless* effusion of blood.'

The Mayor does not appear to have appreciated the urgency

of the business. While the Aldermen were still giving their opinions, granadoes from the Royalist mortars began to burst around the Newarke Wall. The quarter hour was up and Rupert proved as good as his word.

The Royalists began to cannonade about 3 p.m. and by 6 the wall, which stood on the north side of Mill Lane,[4] was battered down, but, with the help of women and children the Roundhead soldiers had thrown up a breastwork of woolsacks within the breach.

The sun went down about 9 o'clock and about 12 the Prince gave the signal. On that four columns advanced shouting "God and the Prince". Sir Barnard Astley's tertia charged across Saint Sunday's Bridge towards the North Mills and assaulted Saint Margaret's Church. On the East side Sir Henry Bard, with scaling ladders, fell on the hornwork by Belgrave Gate and the flanker at Humberstone Gate. Colonel John Russell with Rupert's bluecoats, and his firelocks, attacked the battery on Horsefair-Leys. The main assault on the Newarke breach was entrusted to Colonel George Lisle, and it was there that the fiercest fighting was seen. Sir Robert Pye and Major Innes commanded the defence of this sector. Colonel William St. George met his death leading his men into the cannon's mouth, but at the second assault the Royalist foot got as far as the woolsacks. The King sent his Lifeguard of Foot to support Lisle.

Meanwhile Sir Barnard Astley had stormed the North Mills, and his men were pushing on into the town. Bard after an initial repulse, drove the Roundheads from the Belgrave hornwork with grenades, got over the wall near Church Street with scaling ladders and outflanked the defenders of the East Gate. At Gallowtree Gate grenades did the trick once more, and soon the Cavaliers were pouring into the Market Place. The Roundheads fell back from the East Gate, retreating up the High Street towards the High Cross. By this time Lisle's men had stormed the Newarke breach, taking Pye and Innes prisoner, and were hunting the Parliamentarians through St. Mary's churchyard, and up South Gate Street towards the High Cross. Seeing that the Gallowtree Gate had fallen the Roundheads abandoned their battery on the Horsefair-Leys to Rupert's Regiment. 'They sett the Prince's black colours on the great battery within.'[5]

> 'Earl of Northampton's horse about one of the clokc
> were lett in at the ports, and they scowred the lyne and
> towne. In the meane time the foot gott in and fell to plunder,
> so that ere day fully open scarse a cottage unplundered.
> There were many Scotts in this towne, and no quarter was
> given to any in the heat.'[5]

In this hopeless situation the townsmen fought on. Lt.
Colonel Whitbrooke was killed at Saint Margaret's, and Colonel
Theophilus Grey, wounded in the back, was captured. Hacker
and Babington with the surviving defenders of the East Gate,
were surrounded in Saint Martin's churchyard, whence Hacker
escaped, pretending to be a Cavalier. Some of those, who had
defended the Newarke breach, continued the struggle about the
High Cross. A handful of Scots dragoons held out in the *Horse
and Trumpet*, picking off some of the advancing Cavaliers. For
this they and the other occupants of the inn paid with their lives.

The prolonged resistance cost the town dear in terms of
pillage and rape. Shops, inns and houses were looted from garret
to cellar, and there was considerable slaughter. This is not to be
wondered at. Storming a breach in the dark is hot work. Once
inside the Cavaliers found yet more resistance and had to storm
house after house. As is the way in such cases there were those
who found their way to the cellars, celebrating their victory with
beer or wine – or both. Those who failed to find a fistful of gold
pieces at the first house, pushed on to storm and search another,
and woe betide the man or woman who dared resist.

It is said that the Royalists lost about 30 officers, but with
the exception of Colonel St. George and Major Bunnington,
their names have not been preserved.[6] Bunnington, a gentleman
pensioner, was major of Prince Rupert's firelocks. He was
'shott in the eye just as he was on the top of the ladder. . . .'

Symonds wrote: 'I believe 200 on both sides were not
killed.' But it seems that the fatal casualties actually numbered
more than 700, about 200 being Royalist. Something like 400
of the Roundhead dead were townspeople.

The spoils of war were considerable :-

232

9	cannon
50-100	barrels of powder
1000	muskets
140	cartloads of the best goods and wares taken to Newark.
400	horses.

In addition, on 1 June 1645, the King demanded £2000 of the Mayor and inhabitants. The prisoners were marched off to Belvoir, Newark and Lichfield. Sir Robert Pye was perhaps the first to regain his freedom. Colonel Henry Tillier, taken at Marston Moor, where he was Sergeant-Major-General of the Foot to Prince Rupert, was set at liberty in exchange for him.

The Roundhead grip on Leicestershire was seriously weakened, for besides Kirby Bellars, Bagworth House, Barton House near Tutbury, Burley House and Coleorton were abandoned. Even so it was a grave error on the King's part to garrison Leicester, for it weakened the Royalist Army by some 1500 men. It would have been better to slight the defences, and march on to Northampton or Newport Pagnell, either of which was ripe for the same treatment.

Clarendon, who was not well versed in the Laws of War, wrote scathingly 'the conquerors pursued their advantage with the utmost license, and miserably sacked the whole town without distinction of people or places to the exceeding regret of the King.' No doubt Charles' surviving soldiers, long unaccustomed to being regularly paid, were happy to find that for once their pockets were full of gold pieces. From a purely military point of view the storming of Leicester must be regarded as a considerable victory.

NOTE

S.R. Gardiner in his *History of the Great Civil War*, Volume II, p. 233 seems rather to underrate the horrors of that night.

'Shortly before midnight the storming parties rushed forward to the assault. Before two in the morning of the 31st all resistance was at an end. About a hundred of the defenders were slain either in fair fight or in the heat of victory, and some women and children were found amongst the dead. There was, however, no general massacre. As a matter of course, the town was given over to plunder. The shops were stripped of their wares, and the hovels of the poorest fared no better than the dwellings of the richer townsmen. In the course of the day a hundred and forty carts laden with the spoil of Leicester rolled off to Newark.'

PARLIAMENTARIAN CASUALTIES

Colonel Theophilus Grey	W & PW
Colonel Sir Robert Pye	PW
Lt. Colonel Whitbrooke	K
Major Christopher Innes	PW
Captain Thomas Babington, H.	PW?
Captain Farmer	K
Captain Francis Hacker, H. Taken near Humberstone	PW
Captain Hurst, a professional soldier from the Netherlands.	K
Mr. Brown, a dissenting minister	K

The fall of Leicester posed the usual administrative problems. Order had to be restored amongst the foot who had left scarce a cottage unplundered.[7] There were wounded to be cared for, and may be 700 dead of both sides to be buried. A more pleasant task was discharged when for their gallantry the King knighted Colonels Matthew Appleyard and Richard Page, and Major William Bridges (2 June); and Colonel Edward Hopton (4 June). Appleyard was in addition rewarded with the governorship of Leicester. The town required a garrison of at least 1,500 foot as well as a body of horse. The cavalry seem to have been the three troops of Lord Loughborough's Regiment, 100 strong, with blue colours.[8]

As for the foot the Council of War expected to raise a good number locally. Symonds tells us: 'The whole county was summoned in to Leicester to list themselves under the Lord Loughborough;. . .'[9] But, of course, these raw levies needed a solid cadre. This was probably provided by Sir Matthew Appleyard's own regiment and those of Sir John Paulet, Lord Astley and Sir Barnard Astley, for although all these lost prisoners at Naseby none of them figure upon de Gomme's plan, which seems to show that they were only represented by 'commanded men'. It is not unlikely that they provided the 400 musketeers, who supported the cavalry wings under Rupert and Langdale.

The Prince was a tireless and diligent young officer. No doubt he spent some time during the four days' rest at Leicester in reorganizing his uncle's army. He would naturally draw up an Order of Battle, so that the commanders of wings and brigades and regiments would know precisely how they were to deploy when the time should come to offer battle. In this he had the assistance of the Walloon engineer, Bernard de Gomme (1620-1685). His plan in the British Museum[10] is a fair copy, but the original was almost certainly drawn *before* 4 June, when Sir Richard Willys, who is shown upon it, returned to Newark. In the ten or so days which intervened before the battle minor changes must have taken place, which would account in part for certain discrepancies between the plan and the regiments named in the list of prisoners.[11]

JOHN BUNYAN AT THE SIEGE OF LEICESTER

John Bunyan (1628-1688) appears to have been a soldier in the garrison of Newport Pagnell, from about November 1644-1646.

'When I was a soldier,' he wrote, I, with others, was drawn out to go to such a place to besiege it. But when I was just ready to go, one of the company desired to go in my room; to which when I consented, he took my place, and coming to the siege, as he stood sentinel he was shot in the head with a musket bullet and died.' It has been suggested that the siege was Leicester, and that Bunyan was present, but as he does not mention the locality of the siege in question, besides positively asserting that he was *not* present, we may dismiss the idea with some confidence.

[1] Tibbutt's Luke, p. 555.
[2] Colonels:
    Ratcliffe Gerard, formerly Sir Gilbert Gerard.
    Sir John Owen.
    Sir Jacob, now Lord, Astley.
    George Lisle, formerly Richard Bolle.
    Theophilus Gilby, formerly John Belasyse.
    Prince Rupert, formerly Henry Lunsford.
    Sir Barnard Astley, formerly Marquis of Hertford.
[3] Scaysbrook, pp. 82-83.

4 Where the Polytechnic Textiles Block stands today.

5 Symonds, p. 180.

6 It is said that two colonels, four majors, three other officers and many Royalist soldiers were buried at St. Martin's; 10 officers at St. Margaret's. (Scaysbrook, 93)

7 Symonds, 180.

8 Noted by Symonds as 'before Leicester' in May, and not shown in de Gomme's plan of Naseby. (Diary, p. 181).

9 *Ibid.*, p. 184.

10 D.N.B. Article by Gordon Goodwin on Sir Bernard de Gomme.

11 Peacock, pp. 94-100.

Chapter Thirteen

THE ROYALIST ORDER OF BATTLE

ON THE DAY of battle the Royalist Army was organized into four main groups. On the right wing were 1,610 or 1,710 Horse and 200 musketeers under Prince Rupert. On the left were 1,700 Horse and 200 musketeers under Langdale. In the centre were some 3,500 Foot and 880 Horse under Lord Astley and Colonel Thomas Howard. King Charles himself was at the head of the Reserve, 800 Horse and 700 Foot, which was some distance to the rear of Astley's Foot.

The Royalists began with the rather obvious disadvantage that they had too few men. Had they retained the 400 Horse which Willys had taken home to Newark on 4 June they would have had a formidable reserve. And as we have seen the King could very easily have kept at least half of Goring's 3,000 Horse, which had left on 9 May.

The lack of Foot could also have been redressed to some extent had the various garrisons been ruthlessly pruned. Newark could have spared Foot as well as Horse. Leicester could have been slighted rather than garrisoned. The defeat of the New Model would solve practically every problem at a stroke. It was worth hazarding even such an important garrison as Newark to meet Sir Thomas Fairfax on even terms. Beyond question that meant concentrating something like 6,000 horse and 6,000 foot. Though they would still have been outnumbered 12,000 Cavaliers might have destroyed the New Model. This is, of course, mere speculation, but one may at least assert that the King and his Council would have done well to make more ruthless demands on their various garrison commanders. No doubt they were handicapped by the difficulties of supply, but one suspects also that they underrated their opponents — an error which in War usually brings swift chastisement.

Nor were the resources, which the King did deploy, marshalled to the best advantage. The Left wing, the Northern Horse, was led by Langdale, who also commanded one of the brigades. On the Right there was no such arrangement for the two brigades of Southern Horse were divided : Howard's Brigade was deployed to support Lord Astley, an attempt no doubt to offset his lack of "battalions." The Right Wing consisted of Northampton's Brigade and three unbrigaded units. These were Prince Rupert's Regiment, and the Lifeguards of the two Palatine princes. Rupert, who it must be remembered was not the General of the Horse, but, under Charles, of the whole army, should have been with the reserve, as he had been at the beginning of the battle of Marston Moor. Prince Maurice was a soldier of experience, and it would have been reasonable to entrust command of the Right Wing to him. Northampton, who had done brilliantly at Cropredy Bridge, might have proved a match for Ireton, and so for that matter would that heavy-handed professional soldier, Sir William Vaughan. Rupert was in the wrong place.

Lord Astley's Foot were sensibly deployed. They simply needed another 1,000 men to bring the tertias of Lisle and Bard up to the same strength as Barnard Astley's.

As for the Reserve, not only was it very thin on the ground, it lacked an overall commander. King Charles' courage was beyond question, but he was small and inclined to stutter, and if Prince Rupert expected his uncle to launch the reserve at the right moment, he was being more obtuse than so talented a soldier should have been. No doubt the unfortunate prince felt that it cramped his style to operate under the eye of the King and his attendant lords. Still, he should have denied himself the luxury of hazarding his person in the first onset.

ROYALIST HORSE

PRINCE RUPERT AND PRINCE MAURICE

FRONT LINE

		Squadrons	
Prince Rupert's Lifeguard	Sir Richard Crane	1	140
Prince Maurice's Lifeguard	Lord Molyneux	1	120
Prince Rupert's Regiment	{ Sir Thomas Dallison	2	400
	{ Lord Grandison		
The Queen's Regiment	Sir John Campsfield	1	150
Prince Maurice's Regiment	Lt. Colonel Guy Molesworth	1	150

SECOND LINE

Earl of Northampton	{ Lt. Colonel Charles Compton	2	250
	{ Major Philip Honeywood		
Sir William Vaughan	{ Colonel Sir William Vaughan	2	400
	{ Lt. Colonel Henry Slaughter		
Sir George Boncle?	Colonel Sir George Boncle	1	 100

1,610 or 1,710 Horse supported by 200 commanded musketeers.

THE ROYALIST FOOT

SERGEANT-MAJOR-GENERAL LORD ASTLEY

Officers from no less than 26 regiments were among the Naseby casualties. Some of the regiments present were very small, and some were only represented by detachments. One cannot be certain to which body we should assign all these little bodies.

CENTRE
SIR BARNARD ASTLEY 3 'Divisions'

Regiment/Colonel		
Duke of York	Lt. Colonel Theodore Kirton	500
Sir Edward Hopton		500
Sir Richard Page		500

SIR HENRY BARD 2 'Divisions'

{ Sir Henry Bard		300
{ Rhys Thomas	The Queen's Regiment	
{ Ratcliffe Gerard	Lt. Colonel Richard Bishop	
{ Sir William Russell	Lt. Colonel Davies	
{ Sir John Owen	Lt. Colonel Roger Burges	100
{ Richard Bagot	Lt. Colonel Harvey Bagot 4 Companies	300
{ Thomas Leveson	Major Simon Heveningham	

{ George Lisle	Lt. Colonel Edward Littleton*	150?
{ Theophilus Gilby	Lt. Colonel Francis Godfrey	250?
Late William St. George	Major Thomas Whitmore	100?

LT. COLONEL SMITH   THE SHREWSBURY FOOT

⎧ Robert Broughton		⎫
⎪ Henry Tillyer		⎪
⎨ Sir Fulk Hunks		⎬ 500
⎪ Henry Warren	Major Daniel Moore	⎪
⎩ Richard Gibson	Major Nicholas (?) Deane or Denn?	⎭

RESERVE

The Lifeguard of Foot:	Lt. Colonel William Leighton	300
Prince Rupert's Regiment:	Lt. Colonel John Russell	500

400 COMMANDED MUSKETEERS

These were probably drawn from the following regiments :

> Lord Astley
> Sir Barnard Astley
> Sir Matthew Appleyard   Governor of Leicester
> Sir John Paulet

TRAIN OF ARTILLERY

Will. Murrey

The commanders of the nine bodies of Royalist Foot were probably :

> Sir Barnard Astley's Tertia
>> Lt. Colonel Theodore Kirton
>> Colonel Sir Edward Hopton
>> Colonel Sir Richard Page
> Sir Henry Bard's Tertia
>> Colonel Rhys Thomas
>> Colonel Ratcliffe Gerard
> Colonel George Lisle's Tertia
>> Colonel Theophilus Gilby
>> Lt. Colonel George Smith

*Littleton was Lisle's Brigade Major. Major Fowler may, therefore, have commanded the regiment.

ROYALIST HORSE

COLONEL THOMAS HOWARD

Three 'Divisions'

Colonels

Thomas Howard (1619-1706)		80
Richard Bagot (1618-1645)		200
Thomas Leveson (-1652)	Lt. Colonel Walter Gifford (?)	150
Samuel Sandys		150
Sir Robert Byron absent, PW	Lt. Colonel William Walton	100
Sir Henry Bard (1604?-1660?)	Lt. Colonel George Barker	100
Robert Werden (1622-1690), PW	Lt. Colonel Geoffrey Shakerley	100
		———
		880

Sandys was probably at his garrison, at Worcester. Byron had been captured at Liverpool (November, 1644) and Werden, taken at Christleton near Chester (January 1645), was still a prisoner at Stafford. Barker's rank is uncertain, but he was presumably a field officer. Howard, Bagot and Leveson probably commanded Howard's three divisions.

It is likely that the 'divisions' were organized:

HOWARD			
	Thomas Howard	80	
	Sir Robert Byron	100	
	Robert Werden	100	
		———	
			280
BAGOT			
	Richard Bagot	200	
	Sir Henry Bard	100	
		———	
			300
LEVESON			
	Thomas Leveson	150	
	Samuel Sandys	150	
		———	
			300
			880

RESERVE

Newark Horse	Sergeant-Major-General Anthony Eyre
Lifeguard	Earl of Lichfield
Newark Horse	Colonel Edward Villiers?

ROYALIST HORSE

LEFT WING

FRONT LINE

	Divisions	Squadrons
Northern Horse	3	6

SECOND LINE

	Divisions	Squadrons
Sir Horatio Carey's Regiment (200)	1	2
Northern Horse	1	2

1,700 Horse supported by 200 musketeers.

*   *   *

The command set-up on this wing presents certain problems. Langdale was the overall commander. Maybe he commanded the front line and Blackiston the second, but Horatio Carey had commanded a brigade as early as 10 April 1644.

The senior officers of the Northern Horse included:

Sir Gamaliel Dudley	
Francis Carnaby	Commanding a brigade in February 1645
Sir Philip Monckton	Commanded Langdale's Brigade at Rowton Heath
Sir Robert Hildiard	C.O. of Langdale's Regiment
Sir William Mason	
George Wray	
John Errington	
John Smyth	
Francis Malham	
Sir Francis Anderson	
(Sir) Henry ffetherstonhaugh	Colonel w.e.f. 3 July 1644
Francis Hungate	Colonel w.e.f. May 1644
Lt. Colonel John Thornton	O.C. Blackiston's Regiment
Major Thomas Craithorne	O.C. John Forcer's Regiment
Edward Grey	

Which of these officers commanded the four 'divisions' cannot be asserted with absolute certainty. It seems likely that Dudley, Carnaby and Monckton were among them. Wray was probably the next in seniority.

Some regiments were still strong enough to make up a

squadron on their own. The strongest were probably those of Forcer, Langdale, Carnaby, Wray, Blackiston, Monckton (ex-Savile), Anderson, and Hungate. Judging by the conventions of the day one would expect to find Langdale's own regiment in the left-hand 'division' of the front line and Blackiston's in the right-hand one. Blackiston's Brigade was probably split between the two lines. Monckton was to command Langdale's Brigade at Rowton Heath, and may safely be assigned to his formation. It seems not unlikely that Blackiston commanded the units from Northumberland and Durham, and that those from Yorkshire, Lancashire and Derbyshire served under Langdale.

If that were so the brigading may have been on these lines :

LANGDALE

Sir Marmaduke Langdale
Sir Philip Monckton. Late Sir William Savile
Francis Hungate
Sir William Mason
Francis Malham
Sir Francis Middleton
Rowland Eyre
Lord General King's
Sir John Preston
Francis Trafford
Late Sir John Gerlington
Thomas Howard
John Shallcross

BLACKISTON

John Forcer's
Francis Carnaby
George Wray
Sir William Blackiston
Sir Francis Anderson
(Sir) Henry ffetherstonhaugh
John Smyth
Sir Richard Tempest
Edward Grey

OTHERS (under Langdale?)

Anthony Bulmer	Dragoons
Sir Gamaliel Dudley	HD
John Errington	

A dozen of these regiments were doubtless represented by a mere handful. The late Colonel Cuthbert Conyers' Regiment of *Foot* provided a small group of mounted officers under Lt. Colonel Michael Pemberton.

Chapter Fourteen

THE PARLIAMENTARIAN ORDER OF BATTLE

THE NEW MODEL was drawn up in plain order with the foot in the centre and the horse on the wings. There was no brigading, whether of horse or foot. There were 11 guns with the foot and, if Sprigge's plan is to be believed, three more in the waggon-lager: siege guns perhaps. There was one touch of tactical subtlety. The single dragoon regiment was concealed in Sulby Hedge, so as to fire into the flank of the Royalist cavalry advancing against Ireton's wing.

		Regiments		*Approx. Strength*
Right	Cromwell	6½	H	3,900
Centre	Skippon	8	F	6,400
		11 guns		
Left	Ireton	5½	H	3,300
		1	D	1,000

Cromwell with some 3,900 men was opposed by Langdale with 1,700 horse and 200 musketeers.

Skippon, with 6,400 foot and 11 guns, had to resist Lord Astley, with 3,500 foot, 880 horse and 10 guns.

Ireton with 3,300 horse and perhaps 1,000 dragoons had to deal with 1,700 horse and 200 musketeers. At every point the Cavaliers were outmatched, but they did have, in addition, a reserve of perhaps 1,300 horse, 800 foot and 2 guns, at whose head rode the King himself.

The Parliamentarians kept no reserve beyond some 400 men of Harley's Regiment, which Skippon left in third line.

Cromwell had so many men that he scarcely had room to manoeuvre. In his front line were 5 squadrons, each about 300 strong. Opposite them were 6 squadrons of Northern Horse, amounting in all to about 1,100, with 100 unfortunate musketeers in support.

SQUADRONS

1 }	Fairfax' Regiment	Colonel (?) Charles Doyley (c.1611-c.1694)
2 }	and Lifeguard	Major John Disbrowe (1608-1680)
3	Sir Robert Pye's Regiment	Major Mathew Tomlinson (1617-1681)
4 }	Edward	{ Colonel Edward Whalley (-c.1675)
5 }	Whalley's	{ Major Christopher Bethel (-1645)

Pye had been taken at Leicester and there can be no doubt that Whalley led this line. It consisted of the best horse in the New Model for 1, 2, 4 and 5 squadrons all came from Cromwell's double regiment of Ironsides, from the Eastern Association, the men who had broken Rupert's iron wall at Marston Moor.

Squeezed in to the right rear of the right hand squadron (1) was half Colonel Edward Rossiter's Lincolnshire Regiment. Langdale's men had seen their backs at Melton Mowbray (25 February 1645).

6. Colonel Edward Rossiter

Then came the second line proper, four squadrons covering the intervals in Whalley's line.

7. Colonel John Fiennes
8. Sir Robert Pye's   Captain Ralph Margery
9. } Colonel Thomas Sheffeild   (Colonel Thomas Sheffeild
                                (Major Richard Fincher? or
10. }   Captain Robert Robotham

Cromwell himself commanded this line. Fincher, being Quartermaster General of the Horse, may not, perhaps, have commanded a squadron.

In the absence of Pye it is likely that Margery, the old Ironside whom Cromwell described, in September 1643, as a 'plain russet-coated captain' led half this regiment. Due to losses at Leicester Pye's Regiment was probably somewhat below its full strength of 600.

Cromwell had three squadrons in reserve:

11.	Colonel Edward Rossiter's Regiment	Major Philip Twistleton
12.	Colonel John Fiennes' Regiment	Major
13.	The Associated Horse	

The Associated Horse and Fiennes' Regiment were not New Model units.

It will be seen that Cromwell had ample supports and reserves to oppose the Newark Horse, or to assail Astley's flank, should Whalley succeed in disposing of Langdale. Still, considering how little room they had in which to manoeuvre, it seems odd that the Lt. General did not keep two regiments in reserve, behind Skippon's foot.

Skippon had five regiments in his front line.

	Colonel	
I	Sir Thomas Fairfax (1612-1671)	Lt. Colonel Thomas Jackson, C.O
II	Edward Montagu (1625-1672)	
III	John Pickering (-1645)	
IV	Sir Hardress Waller	Lt. Colonel Ralph Coatsworth,
	(c.1604-1666) absent	C.O.
V	Philip Skippon W.	Lt. Colonel John (?) Frances.
	(c.1600-1660)	K. C.O. (-1645)

There were eight guns, probably sakers, planted in pairs between the regiments. In front of the interval between IV and V was a forlorn hope of musketeers, perhaps 300 strong. No doubt these were commanded men, drawn out of several, if not all, of the foot regiments. We are not told who commanded them.

In the second line were two and a half regiments.

VI	Thomas Rainborow (-1648)	
VII	Robert Hammond (1621-1654)	
VIII	Edward Harley (1624-1700)	Lt. Colonel Thomas Pride

There were two guns between VI and VII and another on the left of VII.

Rainborow's Regiment of Redcoats, about 500 strong, had been at Abingdon in the Spring, according to an unknown Royalist at Oxford, who wrote an appreciation of that fortress and its garrison for Prince Rupert. No doubt some recruits had joined since April, but it is not likely that it had anything like its full establishment of 1,200. It is more probably that it was about 800 strong. and that it included some 300 rather raw recruits.

There is no evidence that Rainborow or Hammond commanded the second line, and Skippon does not seem to have had any second-in-command. His only staff officer seems to have been Lt. Colonel James Gray, the Adjutant-General of the Foot. Harley was absent due to a severe wound in the shoulder, received on 1 August 1644. Half of his regiment formed the third line.

IX   Edward Harley   Major William Cowell (-1648)

Ireton had plenty of room for his deployment, He had six squadrons in his front line, and five in support, covering the intervals.

1.	Commissary-General Henry Ireton		Henry Ireton (1611-1651)
2.			Major George Sedascue
3.	B. Vermuyden		Major Robert Huntington
4.			Captain John (?) Jenkins
5.	John Butler		Colonel John Butler. W.
6.			Major Thomas Horton. W.

Ireton, who had no previous experience of high command, rode with his first line, apparently leading the right squadron of his own regiment. It is odd that Cromwell should not have told him to lead the supports, as he himself did on the right wing.

Fleetwood probably commanded the second line. Vermuyden had retired a few days before the battle.

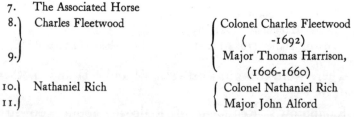

7.	The Associated Horse		
8.	Charles Fleetwood		Colonel Charles Fleetwood (-1692)
9.			Major Thomas Harrison, (1606-1660)
10.	Nathaniel Rich		Colonel Nathaniel Rich
11.			Major John Alford

Colonel John Okey (1606-1662) and his dragoons, lurking in ambush in Sulby Hedge do not appear to have been discovered before Rupert charged. At Edgehill the Royalist Army had three regiments of dragoons to clear its flanks before the onslaught of the horse. By 1645 no dragoon unit figured in their Order of Battle, though there were probably a few troops of them amongst the Northern or the Newark Horse – indeed one of the trophies of the battle was to be a guidon.

The New Model arranged its waggons in a lager, reminiscent of the Old West in the days of General Custer! It was guarded by firelocks. No such order seems to have reigned in the Royalist waggon train though Sprigge's picture-map shows several colours and numerous pikes amongst the carriages on the horizon, partially concealed by Dust Hill. No doubt these represent Colonel William Murrey and his Whitecoats.

THE PARLIAMENTARIAN ARTILLERY

'Being come within cannon shot, the ordnance began to play, but that being found at Marston Moor and other places but a loss of time, we resolved not to want daylight as usual, but to charge with the first.'[1]

Thus disparagingly the author of *A True Relation* dismisses the work of the artillery, but it must be said that the guns, though indispensable for sieges played but a modest part in the battles of the Civil Wars. This was due to their immobility, and the slow rate of fire of the cannon. The allotment of ammunition was usually 50 rounds per gun, from which it will be evident that a train of a dozen slow-firing guns was not going to make much difference to the outcome of the normal pitched battle of the period, even though the occasional lucky shot might wipe out a whole file.

On 19 April 1645 a list of the guns assigned to Fairfax was read in the Commons. They included two brass demi-culverins and eight brass sakers, all of which had previously belonged to the navy.[2]

Sprigge's map shows 14 cannon on the battlefield of Naseby, eleven with the infantry and three, siege guns perhaps, in the waggon-lager of the train. The eight guns in Skippon's front line were doubtless brass sakers, while those in the second line may have included the two brass demi-culverins.

As Sir Charles Firth has pointed out[3] some of Fairfax' guns probably came from Essex' army. But four guns, a long saker and three drakes, were sent from Cambridge to the Tower and thence to Fairfax at Windsor.[4]

The True Informer (29 April. 1645) throws a little light on the doings of the train:

> 'Tuesday in the evening these carriages following sent out of London towards Sir Thomas Fairfax, *viz.* 10 brasse peeces of ordnance, one mortar peece, 12 waggons and carriages, 5 load of match, 2 load of bullets, 6 carriages for ordnance.'[5]

Perfect Passages (1 May 1645) describes the order of march:

> 'Between every regiment is drawne foure pieces of ordnances, and 4 th next, and so all through the army: the horse march some before and·som behind, some on the one hande and some on the other, as there is occasion o as is most convenient: the carriages and traine is drawne in the middle of the army between the regiments and the pioneers, who march before the train, and make way as occasion serves, some of the pioneers also going in every place with the ordnance.'

On 6 March 1645 1,038 horses were voted by the Commons for the service of the train.[6]

The Establishment of the New Model Train has not survived, but that for 4 October 1647 is printed as an Appendix to this chapter. Sprigge gives the names of some of the chief officers.

The Parliamentarian Artillery was commanded by Thomas Hammond, Lieutenant-General of the Ordnance, who had served in the same capacity under Manchester.

The Staff of the Train of Artillery included:

Captain Richard Deane (1610-1653), Comptroller.
Master Hugh Peters (1598-1660), Chaplain.
Peter Manteau van Dalem, Engineer-General.
Captain John Hooper (-1647), Engineer Extraordinary.
Eval Tercene, Chief Engineer.
Joachim Hane, Fireworker.[7]
Master John Lyon }
Mr   Tomlindon } Engineers
Master Francis Frewin, Master-Gunner of the Field.
Master Matthew Martin, Paymaster.
Master John Phipps, Commissary of Ammunition.
Mr Thomas Robinson, Commissary of Draught Horses.

Eliazer Branch
} Quartermasters of Draught Horses.

     Porter

Capt. Lieut.   Desborough   } Firelocks.
Capt. Lieut.   Brent
Captain William (?) Cheese, Pioneer.
Thomas Trapham, Surgeon.

Lyon and Phipps had served in Essex' Army of 1642'
while Deane had commanded his artillery in Cornwall (1644)·
His accounts begin as early as 18 November 1642. No doubt
some of the other officers came from the armies of Manchester
or of Waller. Hooper had been engineer in the garrison of Nottingham, and Desborough had been in the army of the Eastern
Association.

Miles White, Gentleman of the Ordnance was killed at
Naseby.[8] At the storming of Bridgwater (23 July 1645) . . .
'Mr Martin, an officer in the train, had his leg shot, and afterwards cut off, whereof he died.'[9] At Sherborne Castle the Royalist
snipers picked off a chief gunner and gunner Jenkins (13 August
1645) and another gunner next day.[10]

During the campaign the New Model captured a quantity
of guns : twelve at Naseby ; two whole culverin and a mortar at
Langport. When on 17 June Fairfax laid siege to Leicester he
was glad to make use of his trophies . . . 'a battery was raised,
upon which two Demy-Cannon and a whole Culverine taken at
Naseby were planted, which played upon an old work called the
Newark ; being the very same Guns which the King not many
dayes before had used against the same place : . . .'[11] Fourteen
guns were taken when Leicester fell next day, and 44 when
Bridgwater was stormed on 23 July. Some of these were probably
taken into the New Model and employed in the numerous sieges
that followed.

In 1647 when the train of artillery was moved from Oxford
to St. Albans it comprised :

      16 demi-culverins,
      10 sakers,
      15 drakes,
      15 small field pieces,
      great store of ammunition.[12]

Richard Deane's signed accounts for payments received for the officers of the train have survived.[13] On 14 June 1645 he paid £56 to several soldiers for the 100 colours taken at Naseby. During the campaign he paid the artillerymen about £330 per week.

Between April 1645 and April 1646 no less than 4,739 horses were bought for the New Model at a cost of £32,500. A good horse cost £9 ; a dragoon's nag £4.[14]

If the cannon wrought no great havoc at Naseby, they did good service in the next battle : Langport (10 July 1645). Goring, intending to retreat, had sent off all but two of his guns towards Bridgwater. Fairfax' artillery soon silenced these two pieces. . . .'doing great execution upon the body of the enemy's army, both horse and foot, who stood in good order on the hill about musket shot from the pass, forcing them to draw off their ordnance, and their horse to remove their ground.'[15] Thus the guns paved the way for the successful assault of horse and foot, which routed Goring's army.

APPENDIX

A List of the Daily Pay of the Officers, Attendants and Artificers, belonging to the Train of Artillery; their several Entertainments to begin the Third Day of November, 1647.

		Per Diem		
		£.	s.	d.
Officers, Artificers, and Attendants, belonging to the Train of Artillery; (videlicet).	The Chief Engineer at Six Shillings, One Clerk Two Shillings, both		8.	o.
	Commissary of Ammunition Five Shillings, Two Clerks at Two Shillings each,		9.	o.
	One Master Fire Worker, Four Shillings, One Petarder Four Shillings, both		8.	o.
	One Assistant, at		2.	6.
	Three Conductors of Ammunition at Two Shillings each,		6.	o.
	Fourteen Gentlemen of the Ordnance at Three Shillings,		42.	o.
	One Master Gunner Four Shillings, Four Gunners Mates each at Two Shillings, Forty other Gunners each at Two Shillings,	4.	12.	o.
	One Hundred and Twenty Matrosses at Twelve pence each,	6.	o.	o.
	One Master Pioneer, at		4.	o.
	One Master Cooper,		2.	6.
	A Tent-maker,		2.	6.
	One Quarter-master with Sixty Horses,		38.	9.
	Twenty Waggoners at Eighteen Pence each,		30.	o.
	One Farrier,		3.	o.
	Sum	18.	8.	3.
Two Companies of Firelocks, consisting of Two Hundred, besides Officers; videlicet	Two Captains each at Eight Shillings,		16.	o.
	Two Lieutenants each at Four Shillings,		8.	o.
	Two Ensigns each at Three Shillings,		6.	o.
	Four Serjeants each at Eighteen Pence,		6.	o.
	Six Corporals at Twelve Pence each,		6.	o.
	Two Hundred Firelocks each at Eight Pence,	6.	13.	4.
	Sum	8.	15.	4.

Sum Total of the Pays and Entertainments belonging to the Train of Artillery abovementioned, 27. 3. 7.

(Lords Journals, Vol. 10, p.71)

Certain modifications to the November, 1647 Establishment for the Standing Army put forward in a paper from Sir Thomas Fairfax, the Commander in Chief, and his Council of War, were agreed by the Commons on 8th February, 1648. These modifications included the following additions to the Train of Artillery:

	£	s.	d.
One Paymaster per diem 4s. One Clerk 1s. 6d.	oo	o5	o6
Allowance for One Hundred Draught-Horses, each at 8d. per diem	o3	o6	o8
Eight Waggonmasters to be kept up in the Train, to be put to those Regiments which shall be appointed, from time to time, to keep the Field, each 3s.	o1	o4	oo
Four-and-twenty Waggoners more, each 2s. 6d.	o1	16	oo
One Waggonmaster for the General his Train	oo	o3	o4
To be added to the Master-Gunner's Pay; and he is to take the charge of Fireworker and Petardier, 4s. per diem	oo	o4	oo
	——	——	——
	o6	19	o6

(*Commons Journals*, Vol. 4 p.460)

[1] Firth, *Cromwell's Army*, p. 159.
[2] Firth, *Cromwell's Army*, p. 158.
[3] *Cromwell's Army*, p. 158.
[4] SP.28.140. Payments for the Train.
[5] *Cromwell's Army*, p. 158, fn.3.
[6] Commons Journals, Vol. 4, p. 71.
[7] Deane's Accounts.
[8] Commons Journals, Vol. 4, p. 464.
[9] Sprigge, p. 81.
[10] Sprigge, p. 94.
[11] Sprigge, p. 48.
[12] *The Last Newes from the Armie*, 20 *June 1647*.
[13] SP.28.146.
[14] Accounts in SP.28.148.
[15] Sprigge, p. 72.

Chapter Fifteen

NASEBY FIGHT

Sir John Falstaff: *I would it were bed-time, Hal, and all well.*

King Henry IV, Pt. I, Act V, Scene 1.

WITH LEICESTER IN their hands the Royalist Council of War fell to planning their next move. Fairfax, so far as they knew, was still before Oxford. Cromwell and Vermuyden were between them and the Eastern Association.

Oxford was well fortified; pretty well garrisoned, but not particularly well provisioned for a siege. Most of the Royalist hierarchy in general, and the Council of War in particular, had left their families and their property in their lodgings there. All but the most reckless of them would be much happier were the siege to be raised. However, to bring this about it was obviously not necessary to return to Oxford and endeavour to bring Fairfax to battle there. In the Midlands there were not a few Roundhead garrisons no stronger than Leicester. A threat to one of these, Northampton or Newport Pagnell for example, might well lure Fairfax away from the Royalist capital. The storming of Northampton would fill the soldiers pockets with gold. There would have been no lack of officers willing to vote for such an operation. But they would not include the commanders of the Northern Horse, who, even at the risk of seeming mutinous, were loud in their demands for a march into their own homeland. This would, they asserted, result in the relief of the Royalist fortresses there, notably Pontefract and Scarborough castles. Moreover this strategy might ultimately lead to a junction with Montrose, who lacked nothing but 500 horse to make a marching army capable of tipping the balance in England. If Langdale and Blackiston, Carnaby, Wray and the rest could get back into their northern recruiting areas there would be a year's harvest of young royalist recruits to swell their ranks. Rupert on the whole seems to have supported Langdale and his officers. At the distance of 336 years a march northward, and a junction with Montrose certainly seems the most attractive strategy for the King to have adopted, for it alone could redress the balance of forces upset at Marston Moor, nearly a year earlier.

Of course, there were those, Digby at their head, who pressed for a decisive battle with the New Model itself, and this was not altogether a bad idea, so long as the armies were more or less equal in numbers. The defeat of Fairfax could open the way to London, and that might bring decisive victory in its train. The trouble was that there was no guarantee that Fairfax could be induced to fight at a disadvantage. But, remembering their victories of 1644, Cropredy and Lostwithiel, the Cavaliers of the Oxford Army, outnumbered though they were, seem to have looked forward with astonishing confidence to forcing the hand of the New Model. It is hard to avoid the conclusion that they underrated the enemy and in War there is no more fatal error. Another simple and fundamental error is to accept battle without first concentrating every available man. To concentrate 15,000 men should not have been beyond the organizational powers of the King and his generals. Given equal numbers the story of Naseby might have been very different; but this is mere speculation.

For a few minutes the two armies stood deployed, more or less as we have shown them in the map.[1] One may imagine that the officers and men of either army peered about trying to make out what they were up against that bright summer day. The more sensitive may have been wondering what condition their carcases might be in when night fell.

Cromwell, whose rather heavy features concealed a temperament which owed something to his Welsh ancestry, rode about

256

setting his horse in order. With no brigade commanders he had plenty to do, and for such a man that was a relief.

> . . .'when I saw the enemy draw up and march in gallant order towards us, and we a company of poor ignorant men, to seek how to order our battle . . . I could not (riding about my business) but smile out to God in praises, in assurance of victory, because God would, by things that are not, bring to naught things that are . . . and God did it. O that men would therefore praise the Lord, and declare the wonders that He doth for the children of men !'

Ireton, made Commissary-General on the eve of the battle, he put in charge of his left wing, a doubtful choice as we shall see. Then after a few words with Colonel Okey he rode over to the right to give his orders to Whalley and the rest, before, very sensibly, taking up his own position at the head of his second line. Thus he had his supports and reserves ready under his hand to support the front line under Whalley when the moment came. Surveying his opponents, the Northern Horse under Langdale, he must have been well aware that he had a marked numerical advantage. It would be strange if it did not occur to him that he might be able to employ part of his numerous cavalry to support Skippon.

We cannot tell what orders Cromwell had given to Ireton. If he advised him to lead the second line, as he meant to do himself, the advice fell on deaf ears. Ireton, who had not previously commanded so large a body as the left wing of the New Model, evidently believing that leadership is done from in front, placed himself at the head of his regiment in the first line. Most other English generals of his day would have done the same thing. But Ireton might have done better to stay near the centre of his command rather than ride with the right-hand squadron. Perhaps as he surveyed the Royalists ranked against him he wondered who commanded on that wing. He must, of course, have known that Rupert was no longer general of the horse, and can hardly have been expecting to find himself opposed by the Prince in person.

Since Ireton himself meant to lead the first line we may imagine that he told Colonel Charles Fleetwood – a future lieutenant-general of the horse – to command his supports.

257

Okey tells us that he was in a meadow half a mile behind the Army, giving his men ammunition, when Cromwell came, and caused him to mount his men with all speed and 'flank our left Wing.'

In the centre old Skippon had work enough to deploy his eight new-modelled regiments of foot, for, as we have seen, the New Model had no brigade organization, whether of horse or foot. This clumsy arrangement meant that Skippon must give his orders to eight commanding officers, instead of two brigadiers.[2] Still, he managed somehow, and having a full complement of officers, and, indeed many reformadoes to leaven the mass, he had his men arrayed in rank and file a little before the Cavaliers began to move. He had time to gaze upon them through the perspective glass which, no doubt, old soldier that he was, he kept in one of his holsters.

Astley's well-drilled veterans must have made a pretty sight: redcoats, whitecoats, bluecoats and greencoats, all set out checker-wise, with scores of taffeta colours flaunting in the breeze. What Vanity it must have seemed to the souls of the Puritans, who made up no small proportion of the New Model. There were those, especially amongst Cromwell's horse, who felt confident that they could do the Lord's work: whatever the odds they would smite the Amalekites. There were others, who must have been relieved to perceive that the Amalekites were too few in numbers 'to set to partners' properly. Sir Thomas Fairfax' Regiment of Foot had no Royalist infantry over against it.

From the ridge the Cavaliers, who if George Digby is to be believed, were in a mood of almost overweening confidence looked for the first time upon the New Model, and, despite a disparity of numbers which must have been apparent, determined to attack. Why exactly they thought they would win is something of a mystery. They cannot have had much more than 9,000 men at the most. To put the New Model at less than 13,000 would be absurd: 14,000 is perhaps nearer the mark. The King and his entourage were evidently unimpressed. Did they think that their Cavaliers were so much the better that the balance would be redressed simply by quality? It may be, yet few indeed of the Royalist cavalry regiments had not suffered at Cromwell's hands at Marston Moor or, more recently, in the Islip Raid. Astley's Foot, it is true, had a pretty fair record of unbroken success, but the 1,000 belonging to Rupert's contingent had suffered severely at Marston Moor. The few survivors of Warren's, Gibson's and Hunk's Regiments had Nantwich and Montgomery Castle to add to these disagreeable memories. Still, to survive so many adventures argues a certain hardiness!

A soldier must expect disasters as well as triumphs, and in fact King Charles' Army had not been doing too badly of late. For the Northern Horse, and some of the Newarkers, their astonishing exploit at Pontefract was a recent memory. For the rest the sack of Leicester must have seemed a rewarding start to the campaigning season. A good bout with the New Model and maybe the next pillage would be London itself. Perhaps the men reasoned after this fashion, but it does not explain why the High Command should have expected victory. Was it that they had devised such a subtle Order of Battle? Certainly it was an improvement on the way they had deployed their rather larger army at Edgehill. This time they kept a proper reserve of horse and foot – which is more than Sir Thomas Fairfax did. And they had rather cleverly made up for Lord Astley's lack of numbers by giving him the close support of Thomas Howard's Brigade of cavalry.

On the wings the cavalry had the support of little bodies of "commanded" musketeers, each some 50 strong. This device, which Maurice had used at Lansdown, was popular with the Palatine princes – and doubtless highly unpopular with the musketeers. Presumably, being few in numbers, they were expected to approach unseen in rear of the squadrons of horse, and with a sudden close range volley, cause casualties and confusion, paving the way for the charge of their mounted comrades. That, no doubt, was the theory of it.

At Edgehill the three regiments of Royalist dragoons had done sterling service by clearing the Roundhead dragoons and musketeers from the flanks of Essex' Army. By the time of Naseby dragoons seem to have died out in Charles' Army. One guidon was among the trophies, but that is the only vestige of evidence that the King had any dragoons in the battle. Perhaps, as is the way of dragoons, they had promoted themselves to be horse!

Given the relatively small size of his uncle's army one can say that Rupert devised a fairly sensible way of deploying it. He seems to have thought it out well in advance, probably before the King marched from Leicester, and no doubt de Gomme's plan is a fair copy of the original draft.[3]

It was Rupert's plan and it was for Rupert to carry it out. But this did not come to pass. For some reason, probably sinister, Rupert was permitted to lead the right wing of horse, thus abdicating his rôle of Lord General. At Marston Moor he had stayed with the reserve, and attempted to influence the outcome by launching a fresh wave of horse at Cromwell, after the first onset. Now he left the reserve to be spent by the King and those about him as they should think fit. Was the Prince in a black mood, which could only be dispelled by one of those furious charges for which he is justly famous? Who can tell? Perhaps Digby and Ashburnham or some other of his enemies had been carping away, so that he could no longer endure to sit his charger at his uncle's right hand. This seems to be the explanation. Charles himself, so infirm of purpose, so little capable of being made great, however brilliant his ministers or his commanders, may not yet have recovered from the self-esteem which his victories at Cropredy Bridge and Lostwithiel had nourished. Perhaps he felt happier without the rather overwhelming presence of his fierce, dark nephew. And after all he had great lords about him: Lindsey, Belasyse, Digby and Carnwath[4] – not that anyone in the English court took much notice of the profane scion of the house of Dalzell.

Lindsey and Belasyse were men of honour and soldiers of repute, but whether they could get a word in with Digby at hand may be questioned. Rupert had the knack of giving out clear orders, and before he rode off, there can be little doubt he reminded the various commanders of his intentions. They knew how he meant the battle should be fought. But there were three officers with the right wing of horse, any one of whom was more than a match for Ireton. These were Prince Maurice, the Earl of Northampton and Sir William Vaughan. There was no obvious reason why Rupert should now take charge there in person. Perhaps he thought Cromwell would, as at Marston Moor, lead the enemy left. Maybe he could not resist the temptation to try another fall with Ironsides. But seeing that by custom the General of the Horse led the *right* wing, this is no more than speculation.

According to Clarendon the battle began at about ten of the clock. Others say the first charge was made at 11. In those days when control of an army was so difficult the signal for the advance was probably the simultaneous firing of the six biggest Royalist guns.[5] Hearing this Lord Astley one supposes rode out, shouting "March on, boys!" and signalling to his brigadiers. The drums began to beat, and the silken colours advanced. Slowly the foot, carefully dressing their ranks moved down the slope at a speed of about 70 paces to the minute, their pikes advanced.

Now, too, the cavalry of Rupert and Langdale began to march forward at a controlled walk. Almost at once Ireton's wing began to move out to meet Rupert. In the nature of things cavalry walk faster than infantry. The eight unlucky platoons of musketeers drawn up behind the cavalry squadrons could only keep up by running. The Prince soon saw, too, that he was drawing ahead of Astley's well-ordered ranks. With voice, and trumpet he and his colonels gave the command to halt. His commanders busied themselves with dressing the ranks of their veterans. Half a mile ahead Ireton, watching Rupert's every move, reacted by halting his own squadrons.

The Prince, satisfied that his musketeers had caught up, and that Astley's orderly tertias were progressing relentlessly across the valley, gave the signal to continue the advance. Almost at once the opposing regiments were in motion, and in an incredibly short space of time were within range. The panting musketeers doubled into the gaps between the squadrons and loosed off their vollies at the Roundhead horse. This was the moment for the charge, and almost before the smoke had blown away the Lifeguards of the two princes set about the regiment of Colonel John Butler. He and his major, Thomas Horton, were both wounded, whether by musketry or with the sword cannot be said, and in the mêlée that followed their 500 men were worsted by half their numbers.

Their neighbour, Colonel John Okey, ensconced in Sulby Hedge, was to opine that, had it not been for his dragoons, but few of Butler's men would have lived to tell the tale, and his dragoons certainly emptied a few saddles. But neither Butler nor Okey succeeded in holding the fierce onslaught of the two troops of the princes' Lifeguards. The victorious Cavaliers swept forward bent upon execution. History does not relate what became of the supporting musketeers, but given the sudden discovery of Okey's ambush it would be strange indeed if they did not now engage in a fire-fight with the Roundhead dragoons. This would have given valuable flank protection to the second line as it advanced to try conclusions with Fleetwood's squadrons.

At the other end of Rupert's front line things had gone badly for the Cavaliers. Ireton's right squadron routed Prince Maurice's Regiment, whose commanding officer, Lt. Colonel Guy Molesworth, was among the wounded. The right hand squadron of Vermuyden's routed the left squadron of Prince Rupert's Regiment. For some reason Ireton's left squadron did not charge home, but even so its opponent, the Queen's Regiment, was carried away by its broken neighbours. Ireton must have been well-pleased. Seeing the backs of three Royalist squadrons he evidently thought his work was done. Looking about him he was appalled to see Barnard Astley's tertia pressing sorely upon Skippon's line. Leaving the main body of his wing to look after itself, gallantly but ill-advisedly, he led his victorious squadron in a desperate charge upon the Duke of York's Regiment of Foot. How he fared we shall see later.

In fact things were not quite so bad with Rupert's men as Ireton seems to have supposed. Dallison still had two-thirds of Rupert's Regiment intact, and it was perhaps in leading them against the left squadron of Vermuyden's Regiment that he received his death-wound. The second line, the two good regiments of Northampton and Sir William Vaughan, though heavily out-numbered, proved more than a match for Fleetwood's squadrons which quit the field, though some at least managed to rally after a space. The rout was nothing like the panic that had seized Ramsay's troops at Edgehill. Even so Vaughan broke right through the Roundhead line, whilst Rupert himself did not turn his rein until he had almost reached Naseby. He would have been better employed in watching Astley's progress, and urging his officers to rally their men, so that he might go to the support of the foot.

Meanwhile Lord Astley was playing his part manfully, as he always did, and his men, many of whom had been with him since Edgehill, knew very well what was required of them. He had taught them well and now the steel-tipped hedgehogs came stamping in, sweeping aside the forlorn hope, and locking relentlessly in vigorous push of pike. Flanking each body the musketeers volleyed away, salvo after salvo, till the air was grey with powder smoke – and blue with profanities. Whether by luck or judgment, for musketry was in its infancy, someone put a bullet into Lt. Colonel Francis, the commander of Skippon's Regiment. The Duke of York's redcoats, well-drilled 'regulars', were driving their opponents before them in disorder, and when stout Skippon himself appeared upon the scene, hoping by his presence and example to restore order, he received a shot which carried a piece of his coat into his stomach, and was to keep him out of action for a year. With admirable resolution he did not quit the field till the battle was done.

All along the line the Royalist foot were making progress, and Sir Edward Walker amidst the King's entourage could see the Roundheads' colours falling. No wonder Ireton was dismayed by what he saw. It was in this crisis that he led his second charge, which proved a forlorn hope indeed. Lt. Colonel Theodore Kirton commanded the Duke of York's Regiment, and he evidently had his eyes open and his wits about him. Ireton charged home as a good cavalryman should, only to have his horse shot under him and to find himself impaled upon a pike which pierced his thigh. A sergeant laid into him with his halbert, wounding him in the face, and the bleeding hero was compelled to surrender. The Royalist hedgehog had weathered the storm. We are not told whether Thomas Howard sent his right-hand squadron to clear away the remnants of Ireton's men, but it seems the obvious move. Certainly the brigade had some fighting for Colonel Richard Bagot was wounded, and Lt. Colonel Walton was among the slain.

If Astley's men were doing all and more than could be expected of them, the same cannot be said of the Northern Horse. What happened is clear enough in broad outline. The Yorkshire colonel, Sir Henry Slingsby, who may have been with Langdale, but was possibly with the King's Lifeguard, gives us a brief glimpse of what took place. According to his account the Northern Horse and the Newark Horse, detailed as their reserve, being 'out fronted' and overpowered by their assailants stood 'a pritty while' after they were 'close joyn'd', until more Roundhead cavalry came up to their flanks and put them to rout.

Sprigge's account seems to confirm this:

. . .'It is hard to say, whether Wing of our Horse charged first. But the Lieutenant-General [Cromwell] not thinking it fit to stand and receive the Enemies charge, advanced forward with the Right wing of the Horse, in the same order wherein it was placed. Our Word that day was, *God our strength*; Their Word was, *Queen Mary*. Colonel Whaley being the left hand on the right wing, charged first two Divisions of Langdales Horse, who made a very gallant resistance, and firing at a very close charge, they came to the sword: wherein Col. Whaley's Divisions routed those two Divisions of Langdale's driving them back to Prince Rupert's Regiment, being the Reserve of the enemies Foot. whither indeed they fled for shelter, and rallied: the Reserves to Colonel Whaley were ordered[6] to second him, which they performed with a great deal of resolution.'

The Royalist divisions which Whalley had put into disorder probably belonged, one each, to the brigades of Blackiston and Langdale. It was probably in this encounter that Lt. Colonel Thornton and others were taken and that Sir Philip Monckton lost the first of the three horses killed under him that day.

It is evident that, with or without orders from the King, half of the Newark Horse intervened in an attempt to relieve Langdale's men. We cannot be sure who led them, but it was probably Colonel Edward Villiers.[7] It was probably in this charge that Colonel Maurice Baud fell. The Newarkers were outflanked and defeated in turn as Sprigge describes it:

'In the mean time, the rest of the Divisions of the Right wing, being straightened by Furzes on the right hand, advanced with great difficulty, as also by reason of the

264

uneavennesse of the ground, and a Cony-warren over which they were to march, which put them somewhat out of their order, in their advance. Notwithstanding which difficulty, they came up to the engaging [of] the residue of the Enemies horse on the left wing, whom they routed, and put into great confusion, not one body of the enemies horse which they charged, but they routed, and forced to flie beyond all their Foot, except some that were for a time sheltred by the Brigade of Foot before mentioned.'

In all these charges the Northern Horse seem to have lost at least three more field officers : Majors Ralph Hudson, Gilbert Markham and William Reveley.

Cromwell's front line and its supports had beaten Langdale's men, and half the Newarkers, from their foot, and made them retreat a quarter of a mile beyond the place where the battle was fought. Still the two right hand 'divisions' of Langdale's original front had rallied in rear of Prince Rupert's Bluecoats. Cromwell left only four of his thirteen squadrons to watch the broken Royalist horse. But, as Sprigge candidly admits 'The successe of our Main battail was not answerably ;'. . .

Sir Thomas Fairfax' Regiment of Foot 'stood, not being much pressed upon : Almost all the rest of the main Battail being overpressed, gave ground and went off in some disorder, falling behind the Reserves.' Their officers did their best to rally them but 'finding their attempt fruitless therein, fell into the Reserves with their Colours, choosing rather there to fight and die, then to quit the ground they stood on.' This is as much as to say that Astley's front line though outnumbered had driven back their opponents, at push of pike.

A glance at the map will indicate that the bodies 'set to partners' after this fashion :

Royalist commanders	New Model colonels
. . . . . .	Sir Thomas Fairfax
Theophilus Gilby	Edward Montague
Rhys Thomas	John Pickering
Sir Edward Hopton	Sir Hardress Waller
Lt. Colonel Theodore Kirton	Philip Skippon

Lt. Colonel Thomas Jackson, the commanding officer of Fairfax' Regiment had no foot over against him, but doubtless could see approaching the division of Howard's cavalry in support of Gilby's body. The thought that at any moment he might have to receive cavalry may have prevented him falling on Gilby's flank.

The Duke of York's redcoats, who had captured Ireton and driven back Skippon's Regiment, had done particularly well. It was too/good to last. The Parliamentarian reserves counter-attacked, launched no doubt by Fairfax himself. The regiments of Rainborow, Hammond and Harley (Lt. Colonel Pride) advanced and as Sprigge tells us 'repelled the Enemy, forcing them to a disorderly retreat.' He has probably somewhat over-simplified the story, for Astley also had reserves. The disorderly retreat was probably the result of pressure from Cromwell's third line, rather than the New Model's rather indifferent infantry.

The time had come for a Royalist counter-stroke. Indeed it was Now or Never. The King still had 'the rabble of gentility', which had joined his Lifeguard for the nonce, swelling its normal 120 to 500. He had the 300 men of his Lifeguard of Foot, and 400 of the Newark Horse, probably under Major-General Anthony Eyre. Had Charles led this body against Cromwell's wing he would have been able to pick up Rupert's Bluecoats and at least part of Langdale's cavalry. With something like 1,500 horse and 800 foot one would think he might have struck a resounding stroke. It was 'not to be. Clarendon,[8] though not an eyewitness, has left us a remarkable account of what now took place.

> . . .'The King's reserve of horse – which was his own guards, with himself in the head of them – were even ready to charge the enemy horse who followed those of the left wing, when, on a sudden, such a panic fear seized upon them that they all ran near a quarter of a mile without stopping. This happened upon an extraordinary accident, which hath seldom fallen out, and might well disturb and disorder very resolute troops, as these were the best horse in the army. The King, . . ., was even upon the point of charging the enemy, in the head of his guards, when the Earl of Carnwath, who rode next to him – a man never suspected for infidelity, nor one from whom the King would have received counsel in such a case – on a sudden laid his hand on the bridle of the King's horse, and swearing two or three full-

mouthed Scots' oaths (for of that nation he was) said, 'Will you go upon your death in an instant?' and, before his majesty understood what he would have, turned his horse round. Upon this a word ran through the troops that they should march to the right hand; which was away both from charging the enemy, or assisting their own men. Upon this they all turned their horses and rode upon the spur, as if they were every man to shift for himself.'

'It is very true that, upon the more soldierly word *Stand*, which was sent to run after them, many of them returned to the king; though the former unlucky word carried more from him.'

This extraordinary and fatal incident demands comment. It is absurd to assert as Clarendon does, that the Lifeguard were 'the best horse in the army.' They were not to be mentioned in the same breath as the units which made up the right wing of horse. The majority were gentlemen, courtiers and their attendants who never paraded save on the day of battle, and so knew little of drill or discipline.

It was, of course, all too common for noblemen, without any military command, to adorn a Monarch's staff when he went into action. To be fair to them they rarely exceeded their powers in the way that Carnwath did.[9] But what are we to think of a Commander-in-Chief, who is so slow-witted or confused as to let his horse be dragged about by a foul-mouthed Scots peer? A sharp blow on the wrist with the royal sword would have been as good a reply as another! If evidence were needed that King Charles was too often infirm of purpose this incident may be cited. In combat opportunities fleet away as swiftly as they appear. King Charles' chance had gone – and with it his crown, for surely this was the crisis of his decisive battle.

How long, one wonders, had the battle been going? We cannot tell, for if a few of the combatants possessed watches, they did not synchronize them and we can only speculate. It may be that it was about noon, before Rupert returned to the ground where the King was rallying the broken horse of his left wing. Rupert had prosecuted his success almost as far as Naseby. On his way back he had summoned the Train, offering them quarter, but the firelocks and a rearguard left to guard it 'fired with admirable courage on the Princes horse, refusing to hearken to his offer,'[10] . . . It seems extraordinary that a man of his intelligence, with the lessons of Edgehill engraved on his heart, should have wasted time in this fashion. If he won the battle the train would be his for the taking. His summons rejected, Rupert 'retreated in great haste to the rescue of the Kings Army' and found it in 'a general distresse'. He was being 'close followed in the Rear' by some of the survivors of Ireton's command, and instead of making any attempt to rescue Astley he rode on and joined the King and made a stand.[11] His own victorious horsemen were by this time in some confusion. In Clarendon's opinion they thought they had 'acted their parts and could never be brought to rally themselves again in order, or to charge the enemy.'[12] Even so there is no obvious reason why their commanders could not have induced them to support an advance led by the Newark Horse and the Lifeguard.

Prince Rupert returned from the chase to find the King endeavouring to rally his horse. The situation had deteriorated rapidly. Astley's men had fallen back some way and his tertias now found themselves assailed by horse as well as foot for Cromwell had launched his reserves. The remnants of Ireton's wing, now probably under Charles Fleetwood had ventured onto the field once more, and their commanders were putting them in order on the ground which Cromwell's wing had originally occupied.

Thus, though he had spent his reserve Cromwell still had some troops at hand, who, though not exactly fresh, might be capable of a further effort. It was more than the King and Rupert could bring their horse to do. They sat on the ridge and watched their foot being destroyed. According to Sprigge one tertia stood 'with incredible courage and resolution, although we attempted them in the Flanks, Front and Reare. . .'. At length Fairfax called up his own Regiment of Foot and they fell on with the butts of their muskets. Cromwell charging at the same time with the horse broke them. This gallant Royalist brigade was probably George Lisle's for he was more or less opposite Fairfax' Regiment in the Order of Battle. It was no doubt this struggle which Bulstrode Whitelock has described for us :-

'The general had his helmet beat off, and riding in the field bareheaded up and down from one part of his army to another, to see how they stood, and what advantage might be gained, and coming up to his own lifeguard commanded by Colonel Charles D'Oyley, he was told by him that he exposed himself to too much danger, and the whole army there by, riding bareheaded in the fields, and so many bullets flying about him, and D'Oyley offered his general his helmet, but he refused it, saying, 'It is well enough, Charles'; and seeing a body of the King's foot stand, and not all broken, he asked D'Oyley if he had charged that body, who answered, that he had twice charged them, but could not break them.

'With that, Fairfax bid him to charge them once again in the front, and that he would take a commanded party, and charge them in the rear at the same time, and they might meet together in the middle; and bade him, when Fairfax gave the sign, to begin the charge.

'D'Oyley pursued his general's orders; and both together charging that body put them into a confusion, and broke them; and Fairfax and D'Oyley met again in the middle of them, where Fairfax killed the ensign, and one of D'Oyley's troopers took the colours, bragging of the service he had done in killing the ensign and taking the chief colours.

'D'Oyley chid the trooper for his boasting and lying, telling him how many witnesses there were who saw the general do it with his own hand; but the general himself bade D'Oyley to let the trooper alone, and said to him, 'I have honour enough, let him take that to himself.'[13]

Meanwhile Colonel Okey and his dragoons had beaten off both horse and foot — the commanded musketeers no doubt — and held their ground. According to his brief account of his adventures it looks as if he was attacked by the King's Lifeguard, or at least part of it, though who led them down to Sulby Hedge does not appear. It certainly looks as if some of the King's Reserve made a forward movement in this part of the field:

. . .'When as the King's Horse had driven our men a mile before them on the left Wing at their first coming on; then wee discovered many of the King's Regiment, by reason that they came somewhat neare unto us; before they ever discharged a Pistoll at any Horse; and had not wee by

God's providence been there, there had been but a few of Colonell Butler's Regiment left. After this wee gave up our selves for lost men, but wee resolved every man to stand to the last, and presently upon it, God of his providence order-ed it so, that our right Wing, which was Colonel Cromwell his Regiment drave the Enemy before them; which I perceiving (after one houre's battail) caused all my men to mount and to charge into their Foot, which accordingly they did; and took all their Colours, and 500 Prisoners, besides what wee killed and all their Armes.'. . .[14]

The Royalists now had nothing left in the field but cavalry, but these 'they had put again into as good order as the shortnesse of their time, and our near pressing upon them would permit'.[15]

Sir Thomas Fairfax, seeing this, 'and our whole Army (saving some Bodies of horse which faced the enemy) being busied in the execution upon the foot, and taking, and securing prisoners,' now lost no time in putting his men in order again : 'our foot were somewhat more then a quarter of a mile behinde the horse, and although there wanted no courage nor resolution in the horse themselves alone to have charged the enemy, yet forasmuch as it was not judged fit to put anything to hazard,' the General prudently ordered that the horse should not charge until the foot were come up. These last, disordered in the first charge, rallied again 'in shorter time then is well imaginable'. . . . They came up 'upon a fast march' and joined the horse, 'who were again put into two wings, within Carbine shot of the enemy, leaving a wide space for the battail of foot to fall in, whereby there was framed, as it were in a trice, a second good Batalia at the latter end of the day.'[15]

Okey's dragoons began to fire upon the Cavaliers, who as Walker puts it 'were fain to quit the Field, and to leave Fairfax Master of all our Foot, Cannon, Baggage and Plunder taken at Leicester.'

The triumphant Roundheads gave quarter to the Royalist infantry. It was otherwise with the camp followers, for in the pursuit the Ironsides killed above 100 women and soldiers' wives, 'and some of them of Quality,. . . .' It has been suggested, as if to excuse it, that this massacre was due to the women being Irish or Welsh, whose outlandish talk incensed the godly troopers. A simpler explanation is that their blood was up – 'accursèd' be he that doth the Lord's work negligently.' The pursuit swept on for some 14 miles, and in the chase many prisoners were taken. The New Model horse 'had the execution of them all that way.'

There are indications that the King himself was in danger of being taken. One William Wimberley is said to have given him his own horse, and to have been killed in consequence. Two saddles are still preserved at the house where the King and Rupert got fresh horses, but there was no time to change their tack.

Sir Henry Slingsby tells us that, after the foot laid down their arms, the enemy did not pursue, which 'gave time to us to stop, & rally our men.' The Prince on the one hand, and Langdale on the other, 'ye King yet being upon yᵉ place,' having got together as many as they could, made an offer of a second charge, 'but could not abide it ; they being horse & foot in good order, & we but a few horse only, & those mightily discourag'd ;. . .' He tells us that though the waggons were left at a good distance they could not be carried off. Some were overthrown and 'monys shaked out, wᶜʰ made our soulgiers to venture their lives once more, wᶜʰ was but to stay & take it up.'

Slingsby took his own line and got safe to Leicester, with Lt. Colonel Atkinson[16] and three others, some time after the main body.

Symonds has very little to say about the battle. 'No question they had certayne intelligence where he [King Charles] was, for one that came in to the King's troope ran over to them, and they left all others to charge up to his body.' The horse escaped to Leicester that afternoon 'and were persued by a body of the enemyes horse and loose scowters, to Great Glyn [Glen] and there the Earle of Lichfield charged their loose men with half a score horse and beate them back.'

Belasyse, or rather his secretary, Joshua Moone, is scathing about the Royalist Horse. Langdale's, he asserts were 'first routed without any handsome dispute,' which, as we have seen, was not the opinion of their opponents. At the end of the battle : 'The horse knew well how to save themselves, tho' not their honours, by a hasty and shameful flight to Leicester, without staying to bring off His Majesty, who at last (with the best of his officers and his own guards) retired and found all those shattered horse under the walls of Leicester.' The old infantry, 'fought it out gallantly'.

Symonds ends the chronicle of the day's events:

'Towards night this dismall Satterday, his Majestie, after the wounded were taken care for in Leicester, and that the two Princes were come safe to him, and had taken order with that garrison, and left two regiments of horse there, *viz.* the Queenes and Colonel Caryes, he marched that night (for now wee had left running), to Ashby-de-la-Zouch.'[17]

The battle done, and the Horse gone off in pursuit, the New Model marched to Harborough, 5 miles, where Fairfax established his Headquarters. The prisoners were put that night into the Church, except for the wounded who were sent to Northampton. Then the generals sat down to write their despatches.

The second-in-command, Cromwell, took upon himself to give his general 'a mention':

. . .'The General served you with all faithfulness and honour; and the best commendation I can give him is, that I dare say he attributes all to God, and would rather perish than assume to himself. . . . Honest men served you faithfully in this action. Sir, they are trusty; I beseech you in the name of God, not to discourage them. . . . He that ventures his life for the liberty of his country, I wish he trust God for the liberty of his conscience, and you for the liberty he fights for.'

This is the letter of a Member of Parliament, rather than a general's despatch. Fairfax, the most modest of men, desired only 'That the honour of this great, never to be forgotten mercy, may be given to GOD, in an extraordinary day of Thanksgiving, and that it may be improved to the good of his Church.'

And so the battle was lost and won. Perhaps, from first to last, it took three hours, and of some 23,000 participants nearly a third, mostly Royalist, were casualties of one sort and another. Scarcely a man — or woman — was present who had not encountered sudden and unexpected adventure of the most hair-raising sort.

Of the New Model Fairfax had had his helmet dashed from his head, Skippon had received a dreadful wound, the battered Ireton had regained his freedom at the end of the day by promising his captor his liberty.

The left wing, roughly handled by Rupert, had quit the field, whilst Okey's Dragoons had given themselves up for lost. At least four of Skippon's foot regiments had been driven back by Astley's resolute onslaught, and owed their survival to the timely intervention of Cromwell, rather than any great skill or valour on their own part or that of the reserves.

For the Royalists things had, of course, been still more desperate. Many senior officers were taken or slain. Others escaped, though wounded, to Leicester, while Langdale turns up next at Newark. That doughty warrior, Sir Philip Monckton, who Clarendon thought was 'mad and not fit for any employment',[18] managed to get three horses killed under him, which gives an inkling that some of the Northern Horse, outnumbered and outflanked though they were, did not lightly abandon the struggle.

The little King himself had a pretty desperate time. First there was the Carnwath incident : then the Roundheads charging up to the body where he was in the hope of taking him. The fate of William Wimberley and the leaving of the saddles seem to show that the gallop back to Leicester was not exactly devoid of excitement.

There are many things about seventeenth century battles which are decidedly puzzling to a soldier of today. We have spoken already of the deficiencies of organization, which sometimes made the chain of command so unsatisfactory. But there are also tactical aspects which call for comment. For one thing there was very little effort to provide covering fire for an advance, what we now call 'fire and movement', very little effort to find the enemy's flank — except when as happened on the Roundhead right one side greatly outnumbered its opponents. Nor was there any idea of taking cover. And yet it must have been singularly unpleasant to be in a stand of pikes when a couple of sakers were firing roundshot into it at 800 yards range. We know now that there were only about 50 rounds per gun, and that the rate of fire was slow, but once a hit had been scored, there was no reason why another should not follow two minutes later. The cannon balls would plough through the ranks, six or eight deep, killing and maiming. Perhaps the best thing then was to advance a few paces leaving the stricken survivors to fend for themselves; those who could walk seeking for a surgeon, and those who could not praying for a victory, which might at least mean that they would be tended before the vanquished.

It seems quite probable that there were a fair number of casualties some time before Astley's men locked with Skippon's at push of pike. One may imagine wounded men stumbling to the rear, whilst riderless horses galloped about the field – or simply grazed.

The push of pike was a crude, late mediaeval tactic, which went back to the deadly Swiss phalanx of the days of Grandson (1476). Within 60 years it would be quite obsolete when with the introduction of the ring bayonet every musketeer became his own pikeman. But at Naseby the musketeers, having nothing better than a clumsy and slow-firing matchlock, still needed the support of pikemen, to whom they were considered inferior. The idea of ploughing steadily into a mêlée with a hedgehog of steel-tipped ash-poles is not one which will instantly recommend itself to the aspiring tactician. Nor can an infantry regiment, drawn up six or eight deep, pikes in the centre and muskets on the flanks have been an easy unit to control. It was all very well whilst it was engaging an enemy to its front, but an attack from flank or rear was another matter. If enemy cavalry threatened it was a question of forming square, with the musketeers taking cover as best they could amongst the pikes. In Wellington's time a well-drilled battalion could form square from line in under a minute. Such precision in drill was not to be expected in the days before the bayonet simplified the armament of the infantry. In the Peninsula a battalion could make a retrograde movement in the face of hostile cavalry without falling to pieces. This seems to have been beyond the capacity of a Civil War Foot Regiment. The fate of Waller's infantry at Roundway Down is a clear example.

Turning to the Cavalry there are certain factors which seem to be worthy of comment. We may take it that the majority of the mounted men at Naseby were capable horsemen, but there must have been many who were relatively unused to the movements of big units in a pitched battle. The Newark Horse, Bagot's men from Lichfield and Leveson's from Dudley Castle were experienced raiders, used to operations where a few troops were engaged, but they had not, like Rupert's men and Cromwell's Ironsides, been in several big battles. One wonders whether it was not difficult for the senior officers to preserve good order amongst these garrison troops. When it comes to a cavalry charge even the best regiments have their troubles. The horses, some of them hard-mouthed pullers in the first place, will race each other dashing forward, crashing into the enemy, and galloping on more or less out of control, troopers going down, horse and men, fallen leaders getting stamped into the turf. One can imagine the confusion of the mêlée, troopers slashing at each other with sword or pole axe, the cunning ones trying to get on the opponent's bridle-hand. With some resorting to their pistols the noise and confusion soon became such that the officers' voices could not be heard, and the trumpet went unheeded. It was in conquering these difficulties that Cromwell excelled. He seems in fact to have overcome them simply enough at Naseby. His trained eye showed him quickly and surely that he had the advantage of numbers, and he won the battle simply by spending his reserves wisely as the phases of the battle unrolled. It may be too that the horse on his wing were the pick of the New Model, troops from the Eastern Association, with a better record than those from the armies of Essex and Waller. But this is arguable.

The fight with enemy cavalry, violent and dangerous as it was, was as nothing to the horrid task of persuading the reluctant horses to hurl themselves against a hedgehog of pikes. Good foot have nothing to fear from horse as Wellington's redcoats showed at Waterloo, and we have seen what a struggle it was for Fairfax, Cromwell and D'Oyley to break up the last of the Royalist tertias.

The charge of Okey's Dragoons at the end of the day calls for comment. In those days dragoons were supposed to act simply as mounted infantry. They were not encouraged to regard themselves as the equal of horse. It may be that Okey's was the first mounted charge made by a dragoon regiment. Certainly no earlier episode of the sort occurs in the annals of our Civil War. The later history of the British Army is full of examples of dragoons getting ideas above their station, and gradually becoming converted into regular cavalry.

Several of the battles of the Civil War ended with a long pursuit. It cannot be said that Charles and Rupert conducted their troops from the field of Naseby with any skill. It was simply a case of *sauve qui peut*. One wonders, however, whether they might not have attempted to withdraw by alternate squadrons as Cromwell had done at Gainsborough, or under the cover of a rearguard as Hopton had done at Cheriton. One suspects that having attempted in vain to organize their men for a last desperate charge, the King and his nephew had abandoned hope. Be that as it may, they had lost their best Army and to suppose that they could ever assemble such another was a mere delusion.

The day of the New Model dawned on the field of Naseby.

NOTE ON THE CAPTURED COLOURS

Sprigge[19] tells us that nearly 100 standards or colours, of which perhaps 85 will have been foot colours, were taken at Naseby,and that they included :

The King's colours,
The Duke of York's standard, Horse
Six of the Duke of York's colours,
Four of the Queen's white colours,' with double crosses on each of them.[20]

Only 33 standards or colours, some much torn, are illustrated by Jonathan Turmile in the contemporary record preserved in Dr. Williams' Library.[21] No doubt some of the Roundhead soldiery kept captured colours as souvenirs or, as at Marston Moor, tore up their trophies for handkerchiefs (Silly fellows !)

Of the colours painted by Turmile some at least can be indentified :

FOOT

The King's Lifeguard	6
Prince Rupert's Regiment	5
Richard Bagot's Regiment	4
Sir Henry Bard's	4

Another colour bears the cinquefoil of Astley, but as there is no St. George's Cross in the upper canton, this is probably not that of the 1st Captain's company. It may have been a personal standard to mark Lord Astley's HQ or Command Post. Others taken were:

		Possible identification
Green	A Colonel's colour	Sir Richard Page
White	A Lt. Colonel's colour	Edward Littleton of Lisle's
Green	A Lt. Colonel's colour	Lt. Colonel of Broughton or Page or Tillier?

		Unidentified
Argent with bars	2	Of an old-fashioned type. St. George
Red and white		Much torn

HORSE

The Queen's Regiment	1
Unidentified	5

DRAGOON

White	Lt. Colonel's guidon	Northern or Newark H?

---

1 Page

2 As you may imagine it is a mystery to the present writer that any army should have ventured to take the field without such valuable officers. . . .

3 It mentions Sir Richard Willys as if he were present, but he left for Newark with 400 horse on 4 June.

4 d.1654.

5 This had been the signal for the assault at Leicester.

6 By Cromwell presumably.

7 Major-General Anthony Eyre, as the senior officer of the Newark Horse would command on the right.

8 History.

9 Though D.N.B. finds the story lacks support the story seems to ring true.

10 Sprigge, 38.

11 Sprigge, 38.

12 History, 270.

13 Memorials of the English Affairs, 1853, I, pp. 448-9.

14 Colonel John Okey, 1606-1662, by H. G. Tibbutt, p. 11.

15 Sprigge, p. 39.

16 Probably Richard Atkinson of Whixley, Yorkshire. An Ensign Richard Atkinson, who had been in Slingsby's Foot, was probably his son. *A List of [Indigent] Officers*, 1663, f.120.

17 p.194.

18 D.N.B.

19 p.40.

20 Crosses engrailed?

21 MS Modern, f.7.

Chapter Sixteen

THE AFTERMATH

. . ."God will not suffer rebels to prosper. . . ."
King Charles I

A FULL YEAR was to pass between the New Model's great victory at Naseby, and the surrender of Oxford, the Royalist capital (24 June 1646). During that period there were several battles or actions; Langport (10 July); Rowton Heath (24 September); Sherburn-in-Elmet (15 October); Torrington (16 February 1646) and Stow-on-the-Wold (21 March), all of which were more or less disastrous to the Cavaliers.

Sir Thomas Fairfax made no attempt to seek out the King in person. After retaking Leicester – a straightforward task – on 18 June, his strategy was to destroy the King's sole remaining army, that under Goring in the West.

Charles for his part went to Hereford, hoping to build up a new army upon the 2,000 horse and foot commanded by Lord Gerard, the General of South Wales. Clarendon, who, though he disliked soldiers, had occasional flashes of strategic insight wrote: 'Nothing can be here more wondered at, than that the king should amuse himself about forming a new army in counties which had been vexed and worn out with the oppressions of his own troops and the license of those governors whom he had put over them, and not have immediately repaired into the west, where he had an army already formed, and a people generally well devoted to his service, and whither General Gerard, and all his broken troops, might have transported themselves before Fairfax could have given them any interruption. . . .'[1] This is on the whole a most judicious observation. Even *after* Langport this was the best course the King could have adopted. Instead he made his way to Raglan Castle where from 3 to 16 July he basked in the hospitality of the Marquis of Worcester, and the optimistic imaginings of George Digby. His dour nephew, who could no longer stomach the atmosphere of intrigue in which his uncle chose to live, resigned – practically if not formally – his appointment as Lord General and put on his other hat: that of Governor of Bristol. There were not a few about the King, who were relieved to see the back of the German prince. Digby's dream world was not for Rupert. He was first and last a soldier and a practical one. By 28 July 1645 his logical mind had concluded that the war was lost. In bitter mood he wrote on that day to his confidant, Will Legge, complaining that the King, who had resolved to come to Bristol, had since 'altered his resolution, without my knowledge. He did send me no commands; and, to say truth, my humour is to do no man service against his will. They say he is gone northward. I have had no answer to ten letters I wrote; but from the Duke of Richmond, to whom I wrote plainly, and bid him be plain with the King, and desire him to consider of some way which might lead to a treaty, rather than undo his posterity. How this pleases I know not; but, rather than not do my duty, and speak my mind freely, I will take his unjust displeasure.'[2] It did not please at all. Next day in another letter from Bristol the Prince told Legge: 'You do well to wonder why Prince Rupert is not with the King, but when you know the Lord Digby's intentions to ruin him, you will then not find it strange. But all this shall not hinder me from doing my duty where I am. . . .'

Rupert's appreciation of the situation had in fact been clearly expressed in his letter to the Duke of Richmond of 28 July: 'If I were desired to deliver my opinion what other ways the King should take, this should be my opinion, which your Lordship may declare to the King. His Majesty hath now no way left to preserve his posterity, kingdom, and nobility, but by a treaty. I believe it a more prudent way to retain something, than to lose all.'[3] The Prince was straying out of the fields of Strategy into those of Statecraft.

After two such disasters as Marston Moor and Naseby it

was not, on the face of it, an unreasonable military opinion. But Rupert would have been troubled, one suspects, to explain what sort of terms he hoped the King might get from a treaty.

Richmond, as requested, showed this letter to the King, who wrote to Rupert on 3 August, 'that, speaking either as to mere soldier or statesman, I must say there is no probability but of my ruin ; but as a christian, I must tell you that God will not suffer rebels to prosper, or his cause to be overthrown, and whatsoever personal punishment it shall please them to inflict upon me must not make me repine, much less to give over this quarrel, which, by the grace of God, I am resolved against, whatsoever it cost me ; for I know my obligations to be both in conscience and honour neither to abandon God's cause, injure my successors, nor forsake my friends.'

Rupert had at least compelled the King to give us a clear, unstammered statement of his position. Charles might be beaten in the field, he might go to the block, but he was not prepared to admit the least erosion of his privileges and powers. And though Rupert may have been quite right in thinking that the War was, technically, lost, it was the King's determination to uphold his Divine Right that led him to the scaffold, and, since in political affairs the pendulum swings, eventually brought about the Restoration of his son, and so the Triumph of the Royalist cause. Rupert, who, in later life, became more English than the English, was still too much of a foreigner to see that the fight must be continued, whatever the odds, year after year and that the diehards, who were to come out again in 1648 and 1651, though beaten every time, were the men who would win in the end. The beheading of the King, brought on by Charles' determination to carry on the struggle, by force or cunning, come what might, was to pave the way for the Restoration, simply because the great majority of Englishmen felt that the victors had gone too far. They lose the battle who think they are beaten. Rupert was a far better soldier than his Uncle, but, at this point, the King, whilst making every kind of mistake in matters of detail, and in personnel selection, had struck upon the course which – long after his own cruel death – was to bring his son to the throne of his ancestors.

The battle of Naseby was decisive for it destroyed the Oxford Army, the backbone of the Royalist cause. It is true that the cavalry for the most part got away, but the train of artillery was lost and, far more important, so was the good, solid body of foot which with great care and honest pains old Lord Astley had built up over the last three years. Such foot could not be replaced. Another year was to pass before the fall of the Royalist capital, Oxford, but none of the schemes concocted by the King and his advisers during that period ever looked like reversing the verdict of Naseby.

Try as we may it is difficult to look back dispassionately at the events of those days. It gives the present writer no satisfaction to contemplate the defeat of a Royalist army. And yet, had it been the Cavaliers and not the New Model that won an overwhelming victory on that day, one may be permitted to wonder whther King Charles was the man to give a stable government to his war-torn realm. The very faults which lost them the battle made it highly improbable that Charles and Rupert and Digby could have exploited their triumph in such a way as to produce a settlement and a lasting peace.

An all-out victory at Edgehill, or even First Newbury, might have been a different matter, but too much had happened since. Too many of the moderate Royalists had withdrawn from the struggle. The direction of affairs was no longer in the hands of local magnates. To a great extent the territorial grandees, thanks to their military inefficiency, had been replaced by professional soldiers, appointed for the most part by Rupert, and sharing his narrow views on the political aspects of the struggle. Who can doubt that a decisive Royalist victory at Naseby would have been a triumph for despotic sovereignty, and a disaster for representative institutions? A King who looked upon his kingdom and its people as his by inheritance, might not have abolished the Parliament he had defeated, but he would have taken care to build up a strong, centralized monarchy, in which Parliament would have been impotent, preserving no right to criticize, far less control, the Royal policies. It would in effect have been reduced to registering his laws and voting him money.

But there is another side to the coin. Charles may not have

been a man to seek a balanced compromise between royal prerogative and parliamentary government, but nor was John Pym or any of his crew. Those who abhor the Puritan attitude to religion, and to life in general, should respect a King who provoked hostility by opposing it. Naseby led eventually to the Interregnum, and one can make a reasonable case for the view that that was a disaster – far more so than Charles' eleven years of personal rule. The King would never have lent himself to its drastic 'purges', its Irish atrocities – from which we suffer to this day – and the jack-boot methods of the Major-Generals.

Believing in the justice of his cause the King carried on the struggle long after his general, Rupert, had told him (28 July 1645) through the mouth of the Duke of Richmond, that the war was lost. This was not Charles' view. 'If I cannot live as a King, I will die as a gentleman', he wrote to Digby in March 1646. One can only admire such constancy. Even when in the hands of his enemies, he continued to snatch at any chance to fight back, and engineered the second civil war from his prison at Hampton Court. It was now evident to the rebels that, however well their arms might prosper, they would never be able to come to terms with their King.

Brought before an illegal tribunal Charles refused to plead. He was sentenced to death, but since his legally-minded subjects knew that the court which condemned him had no lawful authority, it could only be a matter of time until the monarchy was restored.

For all his faults, Charles made a good end. He was only 48 when he went to the scaffold and it was found that he was very fit: 'no man had ever all his vital parts so perfect and unhurt, and that he seemed to be of so admirable a composition and constitution that he would probably have lived as long as nature could subsist.'[4] He would not have attained his three score and ten until 1670 – 10 years after the Restoration of his far more subtle son, a man who could play a bad hand well, dividing the opposition, and playing off one enemy against another. One cannot imagine Charles II succeeding, as his father did in 1640, in compelling his English and Scottish subjects to make common cause against him! But even those who consider Charles obtuse and politically inept must concede that in his last weeks he saved the monarchy.

And so it came to pass that in 1660 the verdict which the New Model won on the field of Naseby was reversed. And yet not quite, for the restored Monarchy of the Clarendon Settlement was nothing like the absolute, if benevolent, despotism, which the first King Charles believed to be his by Divine Right.

THE FALL OF ROYALIST GARRISONS AFTER NASEBY

		Governor	Garrison
1645			
*18 June	Leicester	Lord Loughborough	
		Colonel Sir Matthew Appleyard	
23 June	Caus Castle, Shröpshire	Colonel John Davalier	300
*27 June	Highworth Garrison, Wilts.	Major Henry Hen.	74
29 June	Shrawardine Castle, Shropshire	Captain James Vaughan[5]	300
30 June	Stokesay Castle	Captain Gerard Dannet[6]	
2 July	Carlisle	Colonel-General Sir Thomas Glemham	
		Sir Philip Musgrave, Bart.	
* 8 July	Ilchester Garrison, Somerset	Colonel Robert Phelips	
8 July	Cholmondeley Hall, Cheshire	Captain Edmond Horton	36
*13 July	Burrough Hill Fort, Somerset		159
16 July	Shocklach House, Cheshire		13
21 July	Pontefract Castle	Colonel Sir John Redman	
22 July	Scarborough Castle	Colonel Sir Hugh Cholmley (16 -1657)	
*23 July	Bridgwater	Colonel Edmond Windham	1630
28 July	Raby Castle		
*30 July	Bath	Colonel Sir Thomas Bridges	140
Aug.	Benthall House, Shropshire		

284

		Governor	Garrison
*15 Aug.	Sherborne Castle, Dorset	*Colonel Sir Lewis Dyve*	340
*20 Aug.	Nunney Castle, Somerset	*Captain Turbervile*	5 K.
22 Aug.	Lilleshall House, Shropshire	*Captain Henry Bostock*[7]	
23 Aug.	Dawley House, Shropshire	*Major Radcliffe Duckenfield*[8]	
*28 Aug.	Portishead Point, Somerset		3 K.
*10 Sept.	Bristol	*Prince Rupert*	200 PW
*23 Sept.	Devizes Castle, Wiltshire	*Colonel Sir Charles Lloyd*	5 K.
*25 Sept.	Berkeley Castle, Gloucestershire	*Sir Charles Lucas*	5 K.
2 Oct.	Sandal Castle	*Captain George Bonivant*[9]	
* 8 Oct.	Winchester Castle Welbeck?	*Colonel Lord Ogle*	4 K.
*14 Oct.	Basing House, Hampshire	*Colonel Marquis of Winchester*	340
*18 Oct.	Langford House, Wiltshire	*Lt. Colonel Sir Bartholomew Pell*	
*20 Oct.	Tiverton Castle, Devon	*Colonel Sir Gilbert Talbot*	204
Nov.	Bolton Castle	*Colonel John Scrope*	
Nov.	Welbeck,[10] Nottinghamshire		
Before			
6 Nov.	Wiverton House, Nottinghamshire	*Colonel Rowland Hacker*	
Nov.	Shelford House, Nottinghamshire	*Colonel Philip Stanhope*	
15 Nov.	Beeston Castle, Cheshire	*Captain William Vallet*	56 or 90[11]
2 Dec.	Lathom House, Lancashire	*Colonel Edward Rosthorne*	200
18 Dec.	Hereford	*Colonel Sir Barnabas Scudamore*	500?
21 Dec.	Skipton Castle, Yorkshire	*Colonel Sir John Mallory*	
1646			
*19 Jan.	Dartmouth, Devon	*Colonel Sir Hugh Pollard*	820
*25 Jan.	Powderham Castle, Devon	*Sir Ames (?) Meredith*	

		Governor	Garrison
31 Jan.	Belvoir Castle	Colonel Gervase Lucas	
3 Feb.	Chester	Lord Byron	2000
*28 Feb.	Saltash Garrison, Cornwall		
28 Feb.	Chirk Castle, Shropshire	Lt. Colonel Sir John Watts	140+
* 3 Mar.	Mount Edgecumbe, Cornwall	Colonel Piers Edgecumbe, MP	
*13 Mar.	St. Mawes Castle, Cornwall	Colonel Sir Richard Vyvyan?	
*16 Mar.	Exmouth Fort, Devon	Colonel Arundell	
*16 Mar.	Dennis Fort, Cornwall		
16 Mar.	Hawarden Castle, Flintshire	Sir William Neale	120?
28 Mar.	High Ercall, Shropshire	Captain Nicholas Armorer	212
30 Mar.	Donnington Castle, Berkshire	Colonel Sir John Boys	
31 Mar.	Bridgnorth Town, Shropshire	Colonel Francis Billingsley, K.	
* Apr.	Corfe Castle, Dorset	Major Laurence	11 K.
12 Apr.	Ruthin Castle	Deputy-Governor John Reynolds[12] (Raignolds)	
*13 Apr.	Exeter	Colonel-General Sir John Berkeley	
14 Apr.	Aberystwyth Castle, Cardiganshire	Colonel Roger Whiteley	100+
*15 Apr.	St. Michael's Mount, Cornwall	Colonel Sir Arthur Basset	100 K.
*20 Apr.	Barnstaple, Devon	Colonel Sir Allen Apsley	20 K.
*20 Apr.	Dunster Castle, Somerset	Colonel Francis Windham	20 K.
28 Apr.	Bridgnorth Castle, Shropshire	Governor: Colonel Sir Lewis Kirke (c. 1588-1663) Commander: Colonel Sir Robert Howard	400
* Apr.	Woodstock Oxfordshire	Captain Samuel (?) Fawcett	40 K.
* May	Salcombe Fort, Devon	Colonel Fortescue	
8 May	Newark, Nottinghamshire	Colonel Lord Belasyse	

			Governor	Garrison
*	8 May	Banbury Castle, Oxfordshire	*Colonel Sir William Compton*	
*	24 May	Radcot Fort, Berkshire	*Colonel Richard Palmer*	6 K.
	29 May	Ludlow, Shropshire Town and Castle.	*Colonel Sir Michael Woodhouse*	380
	4 June	Caernarvon Castle	{*Lord Byron* {*Colonel John Bodvel*	
*	10 June	Boarstall House, Buckinghamshire	*Colonel Sir William Campion*	
	14 June	Beaumaris Castle Anglesey	*Viscount Bulkeley* *Colonel Richard Bulkeley*	
*	24 June	Oxford	*Colonel-General Sir Thomas Glemham*	60 K.
*	24 June	Faringdon Castle, Berkshire	*Colonel Sir William Courtney*	40 K.
*	22 July	Worcester	*Colonel Henry Washington*	
*	27 July	Wallingford Castle, Berkshire	*Colonel Thomas Blagge*	5 K.
	31 July	Goodrich Castle Herefordshire	*Colonel Sir Henry Lingen*	
	End of July	Rhuddlan Castle, Flintshire	[*Lt.?*] *Colonel Gilbert Byron*	c.230
	9 Aug.	Conway Town, Caernarvonshire		
*	17 Aug.	Pendennis Castle, Cornwall	*Colonel John Arundell*	17 K.
*	19 Aug.	Raglan Castle, Monmouthshire		
	24 Aug.	Flint Castle	*Colonel Roger Mostyn*	
	26 or 27 Oct.	Denbigh Castle	*Colonel William Salusbury*	200
	18 Nov.	Conway Castle, Caernarvonshire	*Major-General Sir John Owen*	500
1647				
	13 Jan.	Holt Castle, Denbighshire	*Colonel Sir Richard Lloyd*	
	16 Mar.	Harlech Castle, Merionethshire	*Lt. Colonel William Owen*	34

It cannot be asserted that this list is complete.

*   Taken by the New Model Army.

1 History of the Great Rebellion, pp. 272/3.
2 Warburton, III, 151.
3 Warburton, III, 149.
4 Clarendon, Book XI, 244 (Macray's edition.)
5 Ex-Sir William Vaughan's Regiment, H.
6 I.O. Salop. Colonel Sir Michael Woodhouse, F. [Prince Charles' Regiment.]
7 Sir Richard Leveson, H.
8 Sir William Vaughan, H.
9 Sometimes described as colonel.
10 Retaken 16 July 1645 by Major Jammot. Disgarrisoned and slighted in November.
11 Malbon gives 56; Brereton says 90.
12 Colonel Marcus Trevor, the Governor, was not present.

Chapter Seventeen

OF VETERANS

THE FIRST CIVIL WAR was fought between King Charles and his Parliament. In 1642 there had been at least 16 members in Essex' Army. At Naseby only one, Oliver Cromwell, fought in the New Model. He sat for the borough of Cambridge.

ROYALIST MEMBERS OF THE LONG PARLIAMENT OF 1640 PRESENT
AT NASEBY

		Member for
	John Ashburnham (1603-1671)	Hastings
	John Belasyse (1615-1689). Now Lord Belasyse.	Thirsk
	Sir Richard Cave (c.1598-1645). K.	Lichfield
	James Lord Compton (1622-1681). Now Earl of Northampton.	Warwickshire
?	Sir Frederick Cornwallis, Bart. (1610-1662)	Eye
	George Lord Digby (c.1611-c.1676). Called to the Lords, 10 June 1641.	Dorset
?	Ralph Goodwin (c.1592-1658)	Ludlow
	Thomas Howard (1619-1706)	Wallingford
	Sir William Portman, Bart.[1] (1608-1645). PW	Taunton
	John Russell (c.1620-1687)	Tavistock
?	Samuel Sandys (1615-1685). His regiment of Horse present.	Droitwich
	Sir Henry Slingsby, Bart. (1602-1658)	Knaresborough
	Henry Vaughan (c.1587-c.1660). PW	Carmarthenshire
?	Sir Philip Warwick (1609-1683).	Radnor

Thanks to the provisions of the Self-Denying Ordinance the Roundhead members of the Long Parliament no longer hazarded their persons for the Good Old Cause. It is true that Sir William Brereton, Bart. (1604-1661), M.P. for Cheshire was still in the field in the county which he represented, but in the New Model Army there was but a single M.P.

Perhaps a dozen of the Royalist members were present. One, Sir Richard Cave, lost his life. Two, Portman and Vaughan, were taken, the former dying in the Tower in the following September.[2]

Belasyse, who held important commands during the war, was present on this occasion as a volunteer. Compton, North-ampton as he now was, and Howard were commanding cavalry brigades and Russell was commanding Prince Rupert's Regiment of Foot.

Sandys was probably not present in person, but his regiment of horse was at Naseby in Howard's Brigade. It has been calculated that of the 547 members, elected in 1640, 182 were Royalists, and another 44 were reformers, who adhered to the King's party when war came.[3] The Parliament was far from being unanimous in its opposition to the King.

Colonel Thomas Howard (1619-1706), who succeeded his brother, Charles, as third Earl of Berkshire, outlived all but one of his fellow members of the Parliament of 1640. He was not, however, the longest lived of that body, a distinction enjoyed by the Parliamentarian member for Reading, old Sir Francis Knolles, (c.1550-1648), who was 99 years old when he died. He was born into this world a dozen years earlier than any other of the 547 members. He was not, of course, in arms during the war.[4] It is odd to think that a man born in the reign of King Edward VI sat in the same Parliament as a few who died in that of Queen Anne. The last to go was another Royalist, Francis Newport (1620-1708), but though his home was one of Sir William Vaughan's garrisons, High Ercall, there is no evidence that he was at Naseby, or even that he was 'in arms'. Clarendon, who described him as 'a young gentleman of great expectation and of excellent parts',[5] proved a fair prophet.

A number of Cavaliers who took part in the Naseby campaign were knighted before the King gave himself up to the Scots in 1646.

Name	Place	Date	Remarks
Colonel William Mason	Oxford	28 March 1645	Northern Horse. For the relief of Pontefract Castle.
Bartholomew La Roche	Oxford	5 May 1645	A Frenchman, Principal fireworker.
Colonel Richard Page	Leicester	2 June 1645	PW Naseby
Major William Bridges	Leicester	2 June 1645	PW Naseby
Colonel Matthew Appleyard	Leicester	2 June 1645	Governor of Leicester. Not at Naseby
Colonel Edward Hopton	Leicester	4 June 1645	W Naseby
Commissary-General Dudley Wyatt	Hereford	25 June 1645	
Cornet John Walpole	Cardiff Castle	31 July 1645	Lifeguard. H.
Lt. Colonel William Leighton	Hereford	5 Sept. 1645	Lifeguard. F.
Henry Wroth	Hereford	6 Sept. 1645	Gentleman Pensioner, Lifeguard H.
Colonel Theophilus Gilby	Newark	27 Oct. 1645	PW Naseby
Edward Cooper	Oxford	20 Dec. 1645	Gentleman Pensioner; probably at Naseby.
Colonel George Lisle	Oxford	21 Dec. 1645	W Naseby. Master of the King's Household.
Francis Rouse	Oxford	4 April 1646	Scoutmaster General

Naseby was the decisive battle of the First Civil War, for it ruined the King's main army. But it did not bring a swift end to the fighting. Many of those who survived the battle were to meet their death on other fields including-:

ROYALIST

KILLED IN ACTION OR DIED OF WOUNDS

1645

Captain Sir Richard Crane	Bristol	23 August	Rupert's Lifeguard
Colonel Sir Barnard Astley	Bristol	26 August	

ROWTON HEATH, 24 SEPTEMBER

Earl of Lichfield	King's Lifeguard
Colonel Francis Hungate	Northern Horse
Lt. Colonel Michael Constable	Langdale H.
Lt. Colonel Philip Howard	
Captain Abraham Lance ⎫	⎧Northern Horse?
Captain Robert Lance ⎭	⎨Brothers
William Lawes	King's Lifeguard H?

SHERBURN-IN-ELMET, 15 OCTOBER

Colonel Francis Carnaby	Northern Horse
Colonel Sir Richard Hutton	F. Volunteer with Northern Horse

SHELFORD, NOVEMBER

Major Lawrence Clifton		The Queen's Regiment
Captain Charles Charbo		The Queen's Regiment
George Carey	Gentleman Volunteer	of Horse
Capt. Lieut. Sir Troilus Turbervile	Near Newark	Nov. King's Lifeguard, H.
Colonel Charles Leake[6]	Newark	Buried 21 Dec. H.

1646

Major Thomas Whitmore[6]	Newark	March

1649

Colonel Ralph Pudsey	Drogheda	10 Sept.

1651

WIGAN LANE, 25 AUGUST

Lt. Colonel Jo. Gallard. In Sir William Mason. H. at Naseby.
Lt. Colonel Michael Trollope. Major to Sir George Boncle. H. at Naseby.

In addition some were sent to their death by some Parliamentarian tribunal, of more or less dubious legal standing.

	1648		
Colonel George Lisle	Colchester	28 Aug.	Shot

	1649		
King Charles I	Whitehall	30 Jan.	Beheaded

	1650		
Captain Robert Levinz DCL (1615-1650)	Cornhill	18 July	Hanged Lifeguard, F

	1658		
Colonel Sir Henry Slingsby (1602-1658)	Tower Hill	8 June	Beheaded

At least three of the Parliamentarian field officers perished on the scaffold. They were:

> Major-General Thomas Harrison (1606-1660)
> Colonel John Okey (1606-1662)
> Lt. Colonel Daniel Axtel (-1660)

Harrison and Okey were regicides. Axtel, who had commanded the guard at Charles I's trial, was accused of 'compassing and imagining the death of the King. . . .' Harrison and Okey both met their death with admirable fortitude. The latter exhorted the spectators to submit quietly to the new government, and in consequence King Charles II ordered that 'his head and quarters be committed to Christian burial; . . .'

The heroes of the New Model paid a price for their later triumphs.

SHERBORNE CASTLE, AUGUST

Major John Done	Rainborow, F.
Captain Thomas Crosse	
Captain Horsey	
Capt. Lieut. Fleming	

BRISTOL, 10 SEPTEMBER

Captain Edward Sterne	Rainborow, F. ?
Major Cooke	Fairfax, F.
Capt. Hill	Sir Hardress Waller, F.
Capt. Gayle	Pickering, F.
Lt. Colonel Severinus Durfey	Fortescue, F. Not at Naseby.

Major Philip Cromwell	Ingoldsby, F.
Capt. Ward	
Maj. Christopher Bethell	Whalley, H.
Capt. William Gwilliam	Ireton, H.

BASING HOUSE, 14 OCTOBER 1645

| Captain William Wilks | Montagu, F. |

OXFORD, 1646

| Lt. Colonel Ralph Coatsworth | Sir Hardress Waller, F. |

1648

Colonel Christopher Flemming.		Nr. Carmarthen, April
Captain Thomas Price.	Pickering	
	later	Maidstone, 1 June
	Hewson, F.	
Captain Adam Lawrence,	Fairfax H. Colchester,	13 August
Lt. Colonel William Cowell	Major Pride	MW Preston,
	then Lt. Col.	17 August
	Cromwell, F.	
Colonel Thomas Rainborow,	Doncaster,	29 October.

It is worth remarking that although Rupert was disgraced for the surrender of Bristol, his garrison seems to have inflicted more fatal casualties on the officers of the New Model, than Charles' Army did at Naseby.

Not very many of those who were company commanders in May 1643 appear amongst the Naseby prisoners :

	Regiment, 1643		Regiment, 1645
Lt. Colonel Theophilus Gilby	John Belasyse	Colonel	Theophilus Gilby
Captain Francis Godfrey		Lt. Colonel	
Captain Will Booth		Captain ?	?
Captain Edward ? Jackson	Richard Feild-ing	Captain	Lord Astley
Captain Isaac Walley		Captain	
Capt.-Lieut Raphe Wright		Captain	
Major George Boncle	Sir Thomas Salusbury	Colonel	Sir George Boncle H [7]
Lt. Colonel Edward Littleton	Richard Bolle	Lt. Colonel	George Lisle
Captain Edward Fowler		Major	
Captain Robert Skerrow		Captain	

Lt. Colonel Ratcliffe Gerard	Sir Gilbert Gerard	Colonel	Ratcliffe Gerard
Major Richard Bishop		Lt. Colonel	
Captain William Booth		Captain	
Major Roger Burges	John Owen	Lt. Colonel	Sir John Owen
Captain Hugh Hookes		Major	

Of these only George Boncle had transferred from one regiment to another. All the infantry regiments concerned, with the exception of Owen's, had changed hands since May 1643. It is evident that many of the company commanders had also become casualties.

This is certainly true of the King's Lifeguard also. Of the Naseby company commanders only the three field officers already had companies in May 1643.

The Earl of Lindsey, formerly Lord Willoughby d'Eresby, had been colonel since the beginning of the war. The senior of the officers who fought at Naseby had probably been advanced on or about 14 June 1643, when the original lieutenant-colonel, Sir William Vavasour was given a new command.[8] These were Lt. Colonel William Leighton, Major Robert Markham and, probably, Captain Charles Fox.

Symonds has left us a list of the eleven company commanders of Sir James Pennyman's Regiment as they were in November 1644. All the field officers left about that time and Richard Page, the senior captain, rapidly rose to colonel. Only one of the captains named by Symonds was not among the Naseby casualties. This was the oldest regiment in the army, raised by Sir William Pennyman in Yorkshire in 1642. He had died at Oxford in August 1643, and the regiment had passed to Sir James Pennyman, and later to (Sir) Richard Page.

Many of Charles I's officers lived to serve in the small standing army maintained after the Restoration. Veterans of Naseby included :-

THE ROYALL REGIMENT OF HORSE [GUARDS][9]

Colonel's Troop	*Former rank and unit*
QM William Montgomery	P. Rupert's Lifeguard, I.O. L & W

Sir Charles Compton's Troop

Capt. Sir Charles Compton (-1661)   Lt. Colonel. Earl of North-
                                     ampton, H.

QM Flamock Colborne   Major. Earl of Northampton, H.

Sir Edward Brett's Troop

Capt. Sir Edward Brett   Major. Queen's Lifeguard and
                                     commander of the Queen's Troop

Col. Sir Henry Wroth's Troop

Captain Sir Henry Wroth   Gentleman Volunteer. King's
                                     Lifeguard.

Col. John Frescheville's Troop

Lieutenant Thomas Carnaby   Major Francis Carnaby, H.

His Majesty's Own Regt. of Foot [Guards].

2 Coy. John Russell, Col. & Capt.   Lt. Colonel. Prince Rupert, F.

9 Coy. Phillip Honywood (-c.1682)   Major. Earl of Northampton, H.

11 Coy. William Rolleston ? (-1672)   Lt. Colonel. Ralph Eure, H.
                                     Deputy Governor of Newark.

GARRISONS

Tower of London

?Lt. Valentine Pine   Captain. Lunsford/Rupert, F.

Hull and the Block-Houses

John, Lord Belasyse. (-1689)   Colonel. F. Tertia commander.
    Governor and Captain   Governor of Newark.

Sir Robert Hildiard (-1685) Capt.   C.O. Langdale, H.

Tynmouth Castle

Col. Edwd. Villiers (1620-1689)   Lt. Colonel. Charles Gerard, F
    Gov. & Capt.   1642-1643.
                                     2 i/c Newark Horse at Naseby.

UNREGIMENTED HORSE
Commissioned 13 June 1667

Prince Rupert. Colonel.

Captains

    Earl of Lindsey   Lifeguard, F.
    Earl of Northampton   Brigadier, H.
    ?Sir Charles Wheeler   Newark Horse

| Sir Wm. Blackiston | Brigadier |
| Sir Ph. Monckton | Colonel |

| John Thornton | Lt. Colonel. Blackiston, H. |

No doubt many other Naseby veterans were commissioned again in Charles II's reign, but their records of service have not come down to us.

In 1642 after Edgehill there was a Creation in all faculties of Oxford University of such that had done the King service in the battle, 'or had retired to him at Oxon for shelter to avoid the barbarities of the Presbyterians then very frequent throughout the Nation. Some called this Creation the Caroline Creation'.[10]

Seven years later, in 1649, there followed what was called the Fairfaxian Creation, which comprised :-

Doctors of Law, 19 May
> Thomas Lord Fairfax, Baron of Cameron in Scotland, Generalissimo of all the Parliament Forces in England and Constable of the Tower of London.
>
> Oliver Cromwell, Lieutenant General of the Parliament Army. Chancellor of the University of Oxford.

Batchelors of Arts, 19 May.
> Robert Scrope, Fellow of Lincoln College, son of the regicide, Colonel Adrian Scrope.
> Aubrey Thompson of the Queens College, 31 May.
> Captain Francis Blackwall. Deputy-Treasurer at Warres.[11] Treasurer of the Army in 1657.

Batchelor of Law, 5 June.
> Captain Unton Croke. Later Colonel, H.

Master of Arts, 19 May
> Colonel Sir Hardress Waller, F.
> Colonel Thomas Harrison, H.
> Colonel Richard Ingoldsbie, F. Governor of the Garrison of Oxford.
> Colonel John Hewson, F.
> Colonel John Okey, D.
> George Sedascue, Adjutant General of the Parliament Army.
> Colonel Edward Grosvenor, Quartermaster General of the Parliament Army.
> Owen Roe, Scoutmaster General.

Colonel William Gough or Goffe, F.
Major John Blackmore, Cromwell H.
Major John Browne, Cromwell, H.
John Rushworth of Queen's College. Secretary to Lord Fairfax. 21 May.
Captain Edward Thelwall, F.
    Hugh Courtney 'an officer of note'.
Cornet[12] George Joyce, Whalley, H.
Lt. Colonel Ralph Cobbet, Fortescue, F.

Batchelor of Physic,
    Thomas Trapham, Chirurgeon to the General of the Parliament Army.

Of these a dozen had fought at Naseby, and ten were regicides. Trapham (d.1683) was the man who embalmed the body of King Charles I, and prepared it for burial. Afterwards he remarked to the company then present that *he had sewed on the Head of a Goose*.[13]

The list is remarkable for its omissions as for those it includes. Whalley, Pride, Horton, Alured, and Robert Lilburne are only a few of those who do not appear.

In 1660 Robert Chamberlen (1619-   ), formerly ensign in the Lifeguard of Foot, petitioned for the place of one of the four messengers to the Exchequer. He had, he said, served in the late wars till Naseby.[14] Chamberlain was a fellow of Pembroke College, Oxford, and signed the Protestation Return (22 February 1641).[15] He probably joined the Lifeguard when the King's Army occupied Oxford a week after the battle of Edgehill. It rather looks as if his petition was unsuccessful for Ens. Rob. Chamberlain appears as an indigent officer under 'Earl Lyndsy'.[16]

Francis Metcalf, who had been sworn as apothecary in ordinary to the Royal Household at York on 17 June 1642, lost his waggon of medicines at Naseby. In addition to this his office at Whitehall was plundered, and not £10 left to him in the world. At the Restoration he petitioned for continuance in the place to which he had been appointed 18 years earlier.[17]

Another supplicant was Bridget Rumney, who petitioned for restoration to the office of provider general of flowers and sweet herbs for the court. This had been granted by King Charles I to herself and her late mother, Elizabeth Burges, who with her own two sons was slain at Naseby.[18]

In memory of their great victory the Commonwealth named a Man-o'-War by the name of *Naseby*. It was in this vessel that Samuel Pepys accompanied his master and patron, Edward Mountagu, who commanded the Fleet that brought King Charles II home to England in 1660. Pepys, writing on 7 May records that 'Collonell Phill: Honiwood' was one of the company. This was the officer, who had been major to the Earl of Northampton's Regiment of Horse at Naseby,[19] where his host had led a regiment of foot on the other side.

On 24 May Pepys wrote a pass for Lord Mandeville to take up horses to London 'Which I wrote in the King's name and carried it to him to sign, which was the first and only one that ever he signed in the ship *Charles*.'[20]

After dinner on the 23rd the King and the Duke of York altered the names of the ships, and so the *Nazeby* (sic) became the *Royal Charles*; the *Dunbar* the *Menery*; the *Winsby*[21] the *Happy returne*; *Wakefield* – *Richmond*; *Lamport* – *Henrietta*; *Cheriton* – *Speedwell*; *Bradford* – *Successe*.[21]

The *Royal Charles* was taken by the Dutch when in 1667 they came up the Medway and burnt five of her companions.

1 Father of Sir William Portman, Bart. (c.1641-1690), the captor of the Duke of Monmouth after the battle of Sedgemoor.
2 Keeler, p. 311.
3 Keeler, p. 12.
4 Mary Frear Keeler, *The Long Parliament*, p. 243.
5 Rebellion, 2: 339.
6 Probably at Naseby.
7 Colonel *vice* Sir Arthur Aston, c.31 Jan. 1645.
8 Commander-in-Chief in the counties of Hereford, Monmouth, Glamorgan, Brecon and Radnor.
9 Later The Blues.
10 Wood's *Fasti Oxonienses*, p. 7.
11 Sprigge, p. 325.
12 '. . . an Officer of note, a Captain as it seems' . . . (Wood Fasti, 80).
13 Wood, Fasti, f.85.
14 C.S.P.D. 1660.
15 Oxford Protestation Returns, 1641-2, p. 109. Oxfordshire Record Society. Transcribed and edited by Christopher S. A. Dobson.
16 *A List of [Indigent] Officers, 1663*, f.90.
17 C.S.P.D. 1660.

[18] C.S.P.D. 1660. According to a certificate signed by Peter Newton Bridget Rumney was sworn in to the place of garnisher and trimmer of the chapel presence, and privy lodgings, in room of her mother, Elizabeth Burges, on 11 September 1647.

[19] p. 30. The Diary of Samuel Pepys, I. 1660. Edited by Robert Latham and William Matthews.

[20] p. 157.

[21] p. 154.

Appendix I

ROYALIST ACCOUNTS

THE RELIEF OF PONTEFRACT CASTLE

FROM *Mercurius Aulicus* COMMUNICATING THE INTELLIGENCE AND AFFAIRES OF THE COURT, TO THE REST OF THE KINGDOME. FROM MARCH 2 TO MARCH 9 1644.

But if this be not a sufficient Argument against this Rebellion, we have another which for present will make it selfe better understood, 'tis an Expresse sent from Sr *Marmaduke Langdale* to His Highnesse Prince *Rupert* by Colonel *William Mason*, of the severall Victories which it pleased God to grant him since he began his March Northwards, which is *verbatim* this that followes ;
May it please your Highnesse,
The zeale of our duties at once unto His Majesties Service, and the reliefe of our distressed Friends in *Pontefract*, being, by the blessing of God, seconded with successes of happinesse beyond our greatest hopes, I was commanded by Sir *Marmaduke Langdale*, to give unto your Highnesse at present a particular Accompt of each occurring circumstance in this our Expedition.
On Sunday the 23rd of *February*, we began our march from *Banbury* towards *Daventry*, where we had Intelligence of an uncertain number of Horse and Foot that attended thereabouts with designe to affront Us in our march, but Sir *William Compton* marching before Us with his Horse, was onely looked on by them at a good distance, and after the encounter of a little skirmishing, they perceiving the rest of our Horse advancing towards them, wheeled off in great disorder, and Sir *William Compton* had the execution of them in their flight very neare *Northampton*

Towne. Their particular losse in this defeat, I presume your Highnesse has already received account of at full from *Banbury*.

On Monday the 24 we continued our March to *Harborough* without any opposition or sight of Enemy, but here we were certainly advertized of a conjunction made that night of all the Horse of *Leicester, Darby, Nottingham, Grantham, Stanford, Burleigh, Kirby, & Rockingham*, associated under the conduct of Collonel *Rossiter*, (and then in present motion) drawn out, but upon what design, severally reported, until the next day being *Tuesday* the 25 marching from *Harborough* towards *Melton-Mowbray*, we were at full assured, for approaching neare the Towne, we discovered some Horse and Dragooners in it, and upon another passe of the same water in a faire Meade, about halfe a mile from the Towne, their main strength (as we judged them) being neare 2000 in all, were drawn up to oppose us (as Sir *Marm. Langdale* did conceive) at the passage, being a place of very great advantage, for which purpose he was instantly putting himselfe into a posture to endeavour to force the passe, but their eagernesse to fight saved us that labour ; for by that time that we were well in order drawn up, and had gained the brow of the Hill on the South side of *Melton*, the Enemy was advanced through the Towne to meet us, and in a gallant fury gave us a bold charge upon the very ground chosen by ourselves to fight upon ; the encounter continued hot and sharp a good while, with severall various appearances of successe on both sides ; but at length they were wholly routed, many of their Commanders slaine, many hurt, and all the body scattered unto their severall Garrisons, the fatigue of our long March, and the night intervening, prevented our very farre pursuit of them in a strange Country, but we slew upon the place neere 100, and took almost so many Prisoners and foure Colours of Horse. The losse we sustained was small, only Sir *John Girlington* and Captain *Gascoign*, two gallant Gentlemen, both slaine in the first charge, and some few wounded. One Captain *Hasker* held a Garrison for the Rebels at Sir *Erasmus de la Fountains* house in *Kirby*, within a mile of the place we fought upon, who being with his Horse and Drogooners totally routed in this battaile, went back in despaire to his Garrison and burnt it, and then fled with such as would follow him, being but two in all, in the night to *Leicester*, a common Parliament practice, to set a

House on fire, and then to runne away by the light of it. The pursuit of the Enemy being done, and the pillage of the field gathered by our men, wherein was good store both of Horse-mens Armes and Muskets.

Sir *Marm. Langdale* rallying all his Troops together again in order, continued his March that night beyond *Belvoir Castle*, and the next day, being *Wednesday* the 26, we advanced foure miles beyond *Newark*, at which time the Enemy with some Foot from *Lincoln*, *Welbeck*, and some other adjacent Garrisons, and with eight Regiments of Horse, and one of Dragooners, had besiedged Norwell House a Garrison holden by *Newark* Forces some miles from the Town. But having gained intelligence of our advance and successe had against *Rossiter*, (their admired Champion) they instantly deserted the attempt, and retreated in great disorder unto *Retford*, from whence the night following they fled in as much feare and distraction unto *Doncaster*.

Thursday 27, Sir *Rich. Willys* the Governour of *Newark* assisted us with 400 Foot and 400 Horse under the Conduct of his Lieutenant-Governour,* which joyned to us, we marched that night beyond *Tuxford*, not disturbed either in march or Quarters by any Enemy and the next day being Friday the 28th, we advanced towards *Doncaster;* about *Rossinton*-Bridge some three miles from the Towne, our Forlorne Parties discover'd some appearance of an Enemy, but still as we approached with our body they retreated, this night we expected they would have disputed our passage over the River *Dun*, but they onely made a *bon-mine* there, and left us the Towne of *Doncaster* to Quarter in that night.

The next morning, being Saturday the first of *March*, we drew early into the field, where immediately Sir *Marmaduke Langdale* put the Army into the posture of Battaile he did intend to fight in, and prepared the Souldiers with a knowledge of such difficulties as they should expect this day to encounter with, and therefore to goe armed with the constancy of undaunted resolutions, it being a businesse that was at First no lesse dangerous to undertake, then it was now desperate to decline ; The newes was entertained by a welcome from the Souldiers that eccho'd out aloud their joyfull acclamations. This prophetick Omen presaging clearly the happy consequence of their ensuing Victory.

*Lt. Colonel William Rolleston (d.1672)

We marched without sight of Enemy, till we came neare *Wentbrigge,* above three miles short of *Pontefract,* where about 1000 Horse, and 500 Dragooners of the Enemies, attended that place, as much as possibly they could, to impede the speed of our course that way; but without much danger in the dispute, we forc'd the Passe, but yet they so retarded our march, as the besiegers had gain'd time to be all drawne together both Horse and Foot in order, being in number about 2500 Foot, and neare 4000 Horse and Dragoones, all the strength of *English* that possibly the Lord *Fairfax* could draw together in the *North,* excepting the Forces that *Meldrom* lay withall before *Scarborough* & *St John Savile* before *Sandal,* with which he (the Lord *Fairfax)* himselfe in Person came this morning unto them, with two Regiments of Horse, and 500 Commanded Musqueteers.

Betwixt foure and five in the afternoone, we gained the Top of the Hill over against the Castle, their Army standing all drawne up in the bottome, and now me thought we view'd them with the fancy of that great Captaine when he first encountred Elephants, *Tandem par animu periculu video.* A good advantage was it to us, that our Forlorne Parties, seconded with severall Divisions of our Horse, had beaten in that great Body of their Van-curriers in such disorder into their Main Battaile, as taking that opportunity with a cotinued charge, they had not time to recover themselves into any setled order, and though the suddaïnesse of the Action gave not leave for each Division of our Horse to observe its proper time and place of their severall orders to Charge in, yet in the whole it was so fully done, as that there was not one Body of them all, but did foure or five severall times that day act their parts with very gallant Execution.

The Fight continued without a cleare Victory, at the least three houres, untill there was not left on our Party, standing in order to Charge withall, more than three final Bodies, consisting of above 120 in each Body, which with some Officers and Gentlemen together rally'd, gave a seasonable Charge to the last of the Enemies strength, the Castle at the same instant making a gallant Sally of 200 Musqueteers, who fell in the Reare of the Enemies Foot, our owne Foot firing upon them at the same time in their Flanck, and this totally cleared the Field. We followed the Execution six or seven miles, three severall wayes, as the

Enemy fled; A short time (with a Reserve of Foot, and *Morgans* Dragooners, and one peece of Cannon) they endeavoured to defend the Passe at *Ferrybrigge*, but were soon beaten off, lost their Cannon, and in the Pursuit their Carriages, with 34 double Barrels of Powder, and a proportionable quantity of Match and Bullet, and much other spoyle. There were slaine 300 upon the place, and many drowned in the River, which water they took as nimbly as if it had been their naturall Element, as yet we have not had time to fish for them : betwixt 7 and 800 Prisoners, of which 44 Officers of quality, 22 Colours of Foot, being all they had there, and not one escaped with their Armes, and 26 Standards of Horse, many of their chiefe Officers both of Horse and Foot slain, as Colonel *Armyn*, Colonel *Thornton*, Colonel *Malevery*, and many more, whose names I have not; all the Foot Armes we took, to the number of 2500 at the least, and many Horse Armes. We lost not one Officer (God be thanked) and but very few common Souldiers. *Te Deum Laudamus. Non nobis Domine, non nobis, &c.*

One remarkable circumstance I cannot omit to acquaint your Highnesse with ; They had some few dayes before given out, that they would take the Castle with a Stratagem, which should be thus : They would make, as if reliefe were comming to it, and so they would seem to draw all off, as to fight the Reliefe, (leaving onely an Ambuscada in the Towne) and then they would skirmish together, and seem defeated by the Releevers, and so retreat disorderly as beaten, in expectation the Castle should make a Sally, and then their Ambuscada should surprise it ; But I hope they were now taught the danger of jesting with edg'd Tooles, and will hereafter leave such mocking. At our first advance into the Country, it was generally reported, that your Highnesse was come in Person, which struck a great terrour into the Enemy, and Courage into our Souldiers, as had your Highnesse transmitted some of your Royall Spirit into their hearts, and your active strength into their Armes, scorning to be guilty of any Act that they should have had cause to have blusht, had your Highnesse looked on.

About two of the clock in the morning, all parties that had been in pursuit of the Enemy being returned, we drew into Quarters to refresh, and about eight of the clock in the morning, on Sunday : the second of *March*, Sir *Marm. Langdale* sent parties out into the Country, which brought in plenty of all sorts of provisions for the Castle, and then appoynted a Rendezvous the next morning. In the interim he was advertised that *Rossiter* with all his broken Troops rallyed, and others joyned to them, and 300 Dragooners, was come to *Doncaster* with intentions to joyne with *Fairfax*, whereupon we immediately Marched towards them, but they having secured the Bridge, Sir *Marm. Langdale* diverted his course over a ford at *Oldwark* neare *Rotheram*, and thence we continued our March (only halting some few howers by the way to refresh) without any losse at all, to *Newark*, whereabouts we are at present Quarter'd. I can assure Your Highnesse that the present effects of this Expedition are these,

Besides that our comming was highly seasonable, it being almost the very Criticall minute of the Castles necessity, *Scarborough*, *Bolton*, *Sandall*, and *Skipton* were all besiedged, and they were forced to draw off upon this occasion, and are now so shaken, as that they cannot suddenly be in any probable condition to begin new siedges hastily : besides the Country is so discouraged from their party, that whereas the L. *Fairfax* had undertaken to have raised an Army of 20000 Horse and Foot for his Sonne to move into the South withall, and had prepared his businesse in great forwardnesse, he will by this businesse doubtlesse receive a good diversion, the Countreys generally declining him, and whensoever your Highnesse shall be pleased to take this Countrey into your particular care, he hath chalked out unto Your Highness a ready track for to raise the same leavy in their own way, which that Your Highnesse may have a speedy opportunity to undertake, next the continuance of your Highnesse happinesse and honour, shall be the daily Praier of

May it please your Highnesse,
Newark this 4.   Your Most humbly and most faithfully
of March, 1644 devoted of all that serve your Highnesse
GAM. DUDLEY

SIR HENRY SLINGSBY'S ACCOUNT
FROM THE DIARY OF SIR HENRY SLINGSBY OF SCRIVEN, BART.

On ye back side of Maudlin Colledg, in a close where his artilliry stood, he makes choice of wt Guns should march out wth him, & out of ym chuseth 14 of bigger & less size : He caus'd 14 boats to be made for transporting his artilliry over any river, & one day makes tryall upon ye river by Oxford how these boats would carry these Guns, causing two of ye biggest to be drawn over by ym.

And now having all things in readiness, the prince of Wales being gone to Bristol & Generall Ruthen attending him, & my Ld Capell & Ld Collpepper, wth others whom ye King had appoint'd for his train, He gives orders for his march out of Oxford, upon ye 7 of May 1645, wth only his lifeguard of Horse and his lifeguard of foot command'd by my Ld of Linsey, as yt of horse, was command'd by my Ld of Litchfeild; he march'd ye first night to Woodstock, here he had my Ld Gorings horse to meet him, to keep a pass & prevent Cromwells horse from troubling our rear: & accordingly they did attempt, but were beaten and put to retreat. Ye next day my Ld of Northampton presents his Regiment to ye King; & so march we to Bradford Downs, where we had a randevuus of our whole army, upon ye two princes coming & Sr. Marmaduke Langdale wth his northern horse. Our army consist'd of about 3000 foot & 4000 horse, taking supplies from severall garisons as we march'd by, from hence we go to take our Quarters; the King to Evesham, wch at yt time was a garison held for ye King; ye rest of ye horse & foot Quarter'd in towns thereabouts; but before we part'd at ye randevous, ye prince had given command to Coll. Bard governour of Cambden to march along wth his Regiment; & least ye enemy should make use of yt house for a garison, wn we had left it, being so near Evesham, ye prince likewise command'd it to be burnt; wch I set on a light fire before we march'd off. A house as my Ld Cambden says yt had 30,000*l.* in building & furniture.

In our march coming by Hauckly [Hawksly] house in Worcestershire, a Garison held for ye parliament, The King sends to give it a summons & upon refusal commands ye army to sit down before it, & presently they fall to work, & in a short time they carry their Line close by ye Moat Side (for it was moat'd about) & by trenches draws away ye Water; wch ye beseig'd perceiving after we had made a shot or two, they call for a parley; & at last were fain to yeild ye house, their arms, & ymselves prisoners, wth out any loss great either of men, or time; only a Gentleman of prince Ruperts, standing by ye prince in ye Trench receiv'd a shott in ye shoulder. After ye governour & soulgiers were made prisoners, our soulgiers were let in to plunder, & having taken out wt they would, they set fire on ye rest.

From hence we march'd Northwards till we came to Burton on ye Trent, a town yt formerly had been kept a Garison for ye parliament. But ye Queen in her march Southward, wth those forces she had gotten in ye North & one Regiment of ye Yorkshire Trainbands command'd by Coll. Darcy, took it by storm, wth no great difficulty.

Here we quarter'd & being once come into ye Northside of Trent, our Northern horse chiefly were made glad wth hope yt we should still have march'd Northward, yet they were not much inquisitive, & hitherto shew'd a mind indifferent wt way they went so they follow'd their General; & such an army had Cæsar, of whom they write, yt he would be so severe & precise in exacting discipline, as he would not give ym warning of ye time either of Journey or of battle, but kept ym ready, intentive, & prest to be led forth upon a sudden every minute of an hour whither soever he would. Exactor gravissimus disciplinæ, ut neque itineris neque prœlii tempus denunciaret, sed paratum et intentum omnibus momentis, quo vellet subito educeret. & as Julius Cæsar was severe in requiring an exact observance of strict discipline, so he would teach ym to endure hardships, by his own example, lighting from his horse & leading ym on foot many times wth his head bare, whether ye sun did shine, or ye clouds did pour down rain ; & in this ye King did show ye like, for no weather how foul soever did ever fource him to take his coach, but would show ye like patience in enduring as any of yo rest.

At this Town of Burton we were at a stand, on whether side of Trent we should march, & yn command was given to march to Askby delazouch, & coming thither, orders were sent to Sr. Marmaduke Langdale to go wth ye Northorn horse of wch he had ye command, consisting of 1400 horse or therabout, to ly between Coventry & Leister, to hinder provisions, or any of ye Country people, for coming into Leister.

We march'd immediately away, till we came wth in 4 miles of Leister, & had drawn our horse into a Fair Meadow where we fed ym. Our Scouts gives us notice of some horse yt were within half a Mile of us where we lay, & Greyhounds wth ym a coursing ; Sr. Marmaduke sends some horse towards ym, & as they advanc'd we perceiv'd more horse coming from beyond ye Hill, & still as we drew out more horse towards ym, so did they, till they at last appear before us, in 3 bodys : We advance to charge ym,

& still as we advance they orderly draw off in ye rear, keeping still one body facing us; thus, sometimes retreating, & sometimes making a stand, we fourc'd ym under ye works [of] Leister, & our horse takes ye Hill, wch lyeth above ye town; from hence we sent to ye King to give him notice where we were, & where we lay yt night.

The next night the King comes wth ye rest of ye army & begirts ye town. The place of battery was upon yt part of ye town wch they call Newark, where he had mount'd 6 peices of Ordinance for battery, & in one afternoone had made a breach in yt part of ye Wall; for this was of stone, ye rest of ye Works were Ramparts of earth; nothing more was done yt day, for ye night was resolv'd upon to begin ye storm, only we did play ym wth shott to hinder ym from making up ye breach; yet for all this they had made a traverse & flanck'd it to defend yt part.

The warning to be giv'n to fall on on every side was, upon ye shooting of six guns, & ye time to be about 12 o'Clock; every one had their places set, how one should second another, both horse & foot, & Sr. Marmaduke had ye reserve; & there also was ye King ye 2 princes & my Ld Ashley, wth Coll. Lile who had ye charge to storm ye breech, & some men dismount'd wth Sword & pistol did second him; he entr'd ye breach 3 several times, but yet was repuls'd leaving many dead bodys, both wthin & upon it; where amongst ye rest lay Coll. William St. George. Yn at ye lower end of ye town, where Coll. Bard & Coll. Page had their post, this attempt was carry'd wth better success as it prov'd, some wth Ladders gets over their works, others break ye chain & letts down ye Drawbridge & fells down ye works in 2 or 3 several places yt our horse may enter, so yt by ye time it was light, ye town was ours & ye King [was] carry'd on ye outside of ye town by their works to a house of ————— to Quarter; as he went along by ye works, ye Committee, who were taken prisoners, puts up their heads & put off their hats, shewing some obeysance; & ye soulgiers would call unto ye King to shew him where such & such an officer lay dead upon ye ground, giving some testymony of his worth & gallantry.

The King stay'd here on Sunday, & had divine service & a Sermon preach'd before him, in ye Mayors Church: but ye Mayor of ye town had a foul disaster happen'd him; for wn he should have given his attendance upon ye King to ye Church, his mace was plunder'd from him. While his Majesty stay'd here, my Ld of Loubrough sends out his warrants to call in ye country to assist ye King wth their Arms, & in a short time I saw an appearance of near a 1000 men, & all taken out of one division. Hert came also ye news to ye King of taking Evesham & ye Sr. Tho. Fairfax had beseig'd Oxford, & likewise some intimation from thence, yt ye town was not so well provid'd for a seige; wch stopt ye King in his march & turn'd his thoughts how to releive it. It was no little trouble to our Northern men to think upon marching up Southward again, & began to hang backward, & discover their discontent. At ye next Randevous ye King talk'd wth ym, but still they shew'd an unwillengness. Sr. Marmaduke was sent to use his power & perswasions among ym but yet nothing would move ym. They doubt'd not in some of their opinions, but yt they should be able to march to ye warr of Mount-Ross, or they would keep together in ye North & make ye Country pay ym contributions; thus were they wavering & parts yt night, not knowing wt resolution they would take, but ye next morning we meet again & so marcheth to Dantry.

Sr. Tho. Fairfax had left ye seige at Oxford, & was come wth his army about Stony Stafford [Stony Stratford]: ye King at Dantry had sent a Convoy to Oxford, & stays their return.

In this Interim Sr. Tho Fairfax was come about wth his army to Northampton, & some of his horse in our Quarters, before we were aware of ym. This made ye King draw his whole army together & take ye Hills yt were about Dantry, yt wch is called ye Daws [Danes] Hills: where yet one may see ye intrenchments of an army, & so high as it overlooks a good part of ye Country between it & Northampton; & there upon yt Hill ye whole army of horse & foot stood in arms yt same night. The next Morning [we] were comand'd to march back again to Harborrow, & in our march we understood yt General Fairfax follow'd wth his army upon ye side of us 6 miles distant. Wn we took our Quarters, we made ye head Quarters at Harborrow; our horse lay Quarter'd in Villages between us & ye enemy, who gave ym an Alaram, but presently were encountr'd wth a party of our horse, & chas'd untill they came to see where they had made their fire, in an open feild. Upon ye charge Liet. Coll. Sair, receiving a Shott near ye shouldier, was brought off to Harborrow, to Sr. Marmaduke Langdales Quarter.

This alarm'd ye King who lay at a place a little beyond Harborrow; thereupon command was given to draw fourth; wch was ye 14th of June 1645, upon a Saturday; & by ye time it was light ye King himself was come into ye Town, & all in readiness to march; we had not march'd a Mile out of Town, having taken a Hill whereupon a Chappell stood, but we could diserne ye enemy's horse upon another Hill about a Mile or two before us, wch was ye same on wch Naseby stood: here we made a Hault, but after prayers being said, prince Ruport draws forth a good body of horse, & advanceth towards ye enemy, where he sees their horse marching up on ye side of ye Hill to yt place where after they imbattl'd their whole army: but being hindred of any nearer approach, by reason ye place between us & ym, was full of burts & Water, we wheel'd about, & by our guides were brought upon a fair peice of ground, partly corn & partly heath, under Nasby, about Half a mile distant from ye place.

The prince having taken his ground began to put in order [his] horse in sight of ye enemy, who were now come to ye top of ye Hill, & begin to draw down their Regiments upon ye side of ye hill: where they took their ground to imbattle their forces: immediately he sends to ye King, to hasten away ye foot, & Cannon, wch were not yet come off ye Hill where they first made ye randevous; & he perceiv'd yt General Fairfax intend'd not to quitt ye advantage of ye Hill, where he had drawn up his men: so advantageous was it, yt they could easily observe in wt body we drew up our men, & ye utmost yt we were, wn as they lay wthout our sight, having ye Hill to cover ym, & appear'd no more to us yn wt they had drawn out in Battalio upon ye side of Nasby Hill; besides, they had possess'd an Hedge upon our right wing wch they had lin'd wth Musqueteers to Gall our horse, (as indeed they did) before we could come up to charge theirs. It fell upon prince Ruport to charge at yt disadvantage, & many of ye Regiment [were] wound'd by shot from ye hedge before we could joyne wth theirs on yt wing: but [he] so behav'd himself in ye charge, yt he beat ym up upon yt wing beyond ye Hills, & had our success been ye like upon our left wing, in probability we might have had ye day.

But our Northern horse who stood upon yt wing, & ye Newark horse who was appoint'd their receive [relief] being out front'd & overpour'd by their assailants, after they were close joyn'd, they stood a pritty while, & neither seem'd to yeild, till more came up to their flanks & put ym to rout, & wheeling to our right took ym in disorder, & so presently made our whole horse run : & our foot thus left nak'd were fourc'd to lay down their arms. Ye enemy did not pursue, wch gave time to us to stop, & really our men, & ye prince on ye one hand, & Sr. Marmaduke Langdale on ye other, (ye King yet being upon ye place) having got together as many as they could, made an offer of a 2 charge, but could not abide it ; they being horse & foot in good order, & we but a few horse only, & those mightily discourag'd ; yt so we were immediately made to run, & ye enemy in pursuit of us gain'd bag & baggage all we had, wch they found to be a very rich pillage : & tho' our Waggons were left at a good distance yet could they not be carry'd off, but some were taken, & some over-thrown & monys shaken out, wch made our soulgiers to venture their lives once more, wch was but to stay & take it up.

The way I took was upon my right hand, leaving Harborrow on my left, only Leif. Coll. Atkinson & 3 more following me, wn all ours besides took Harborrow on ye right & were come to Leister long before we got thither. Ye King made no stay at Leister but march'd presently to Ashby Delazuch ; at Leister I met wth my Ld Bellasyse, & in ye night we went together wth my Ld Beamond, & ye next day, being Sunday, we came to ye King at Ashby, a Garison well stor'd wth good victuals & a good Cellar.

BRIEF MEMORIALS OF THE UNFORTUNATE SUCCESS OF HIS MAJESTY'S ARMY AND AFFAIRS IN THE YEAR 1645

His Majesty in the Year 1645, having altered the State of His Army, and consequently of His Affairs, by placing the sole Power on His Nephew Prince Rupert, under the Title of Lieutenant General unto His Son the Prince of Wales, (whom about that time He likewise sent into the West) and having thereby deprived Himself of the Advice of those who had formerly very much governed His Military and Civil Affairs, both by placing them Councillors and Officers about His Son ; upon the matter, He was then solely left to the Council and Will of His Nephew. With whom He took the Field the seventh of May 1645, marching from Oxford to Woodstock; near which place a party of General Goring's Horse gave that Evening a Defeat to some of Fairfax's Horse that attempted a Passage over Isis. This was a good Presage, but the Resolutions of the next Day were such as laid the Foundation of our future Ruin. For although the whole Design of the Winter past was to march Northward for the Relief of those Parts, and particularly Pomfret Castle; yet this March was the more hastned under the Pretence of relieving Chester, then besieged, and in danger to be lost; though the true cause was, the earnest Desire of Prince Rupert to be revenged of the Scots for the Defeat he had received the Year before; and had he not made too great haste, he had come time enough to have done it; for at this Instant an Opportunity was offered him in all probability both of restoring the King, and making himself most considerable. For that Day the Army being drawn to a Rendezvous near Stow on the Would consisting of 5000 Foot, and, with those Horse General Goring had then with him, at least 6000 Horse, Affairs were then stated, that Taunton was then besieged by us and brought to Extremity; that Fairfax with his new Army was then about Newbery, designing to relieve it; which, if he could effect, it would give him a Reputation and enforce the keeping of an Army in the West: Whereas on the contrary, if the King's Army bent that way, it would either keep Fairfax from relieving Taunton, or fight him before those of his Party in the West and Cromwel were jointed, and then in all probability would gain the Victory, and so make the King Master of all. As for Chester and Pomfret Castle, they might expect the Issue of this Enterprise, which could not have been the Work of above fourteen Days. But Prince Rupert, positive in his Design, would not admit to these Reasons, the rather being spurred on by the Northern Horse, who violently pursued their Desires of being at Home and preserving their Country. Besides in probability he was jealous of having a Rival in Command, and so feared Goring who had the Master Wit, and had by his late Actions gotten much Reputation, and therefore was the more willing that General Goring should return for the West, and take with him the Horse under his Command, which were the best Horse of the Army; and with them and the Forces then about Taunton, hinder the Relief of that place. This was concluded on the place, and presently put in execution, contrary to the Sence of all about the King, except Prince

Rupert and the Northern Officers. The King's Army (thus divided) marched to Evesham; by the way the Garrison in Campden House was drawn out, and the House (which cost above 30000l. the building) most unnecessarily burnt by Prince Rupert's Command. The Souldiers under the Gouvernour Sir Henry Bard were joined to the Army at Evesham; Major Robert Leg Brother of William Leg then Governour of Oxford, Prince Rupert's chief Favorite, was confirmed Governour of that place contrary to the Opinions of a Council of War of Officers assembled for that purpose, who adjuged the Government to Collonel Washington by Priority of Commission; but Prince Rupert's Pleasure was not to be contradicted, though Major Leg enjoyed his Command there not above fourteen Days longer, the Garrison being then for want of Men to defend it, stormed and taken by Massey and the Forces of Gloucester, and the Governour with all his Officers and Souldiers made Prisoners. The Loss of this Place was of great Disadvantage, stopping the Entercourse between Worcester and Oxford. As the Army marched through Worcestershire to better the Government of those Counties to Prince Maurice, and to satisfie the Gentlemen of the Country, it was employed to besiege Hawkesley House near Bromsgrove, possessed and fortified by the Rebels; which after two Days Siege and the draining of the Moat about it, was rendred, and all made Prisoners that were in it, being about 120 Persons. This Action gave some Reputation to the Army, which by easie Marches made towards Chester. By the way at Stone in Staffordshire, the Lord Byron Governour of Chester came to the King, and acquainted him, that the Rebels upon Notice of the Advance of the Army were drawn off, that he was not so pressed but that he could well enough defend the place (if they drew not a greater Strength about him) for many Months; but since His Majesty and the Army was so far advanced, if He would stay but few Days in Cheshire, He might make Himself Master of that Country by taking Nampwich, and so march Northward through Lancashire. But this Council as having more of particular than general Interest was not followed. The Fear of the Loss of Chester, which had lost us so fair an Opportunity in the West being taken away, the Design of the North was then pursued, and the Army advanced as far as Tutbury Castle; where intelligence was brought that Fairfax had sent a Party to relieve Taunton, and that himself with his

Army was sate down before Oxford. This staggered our
Design, yet not so as instantly to return thither, or solely
to abandon it; but only so retarded it, as to put the Army
in a Capacity to come to the timely Relief of that place if
there should be occasion; and also to act somewhat to divert
Fairfax's Designs, by attempting the taking of Leicester,
which was set on Foot as feasible. Prince Rupert, whose
Mastery and Chiefest Delight is in Attempts of this kind,
was easily induced to undertake it; to which end, Sir
Marmaduke Langdale was sent to surround it with the
Horse and about the last of May 1645, a Recruit of 800
Horse under the Command of Sir Richard Willys Governour of Newark being come up, the Army was drawn about
the Town. The next Day by the admirable Diligence and
Command of Prince Rupert, a Battery was raised against
a Stone Wall on the South side of the Town; which finished,
the Prince sent a Summons; but a Satisfactory Answer not
being returned in the time prefixed, he caused the Battery
to play, and within four Hours time made a Breach. That
Night the Army according to Orders, made a General
Assault, and principally at the Breach; where they were
repulsed twice, and had drawn off had not the Town been
entred on the other side by Sir Henry Bard, Collonel
Richard Page and the Newark Horse, on Foot with their
Swords and Pistols. By the Break of Day all ours were
entred the Line, and presently Sir Robert Pye the Governour, and all the Officers, Souldiers and Townsmen in Arms,
being about 1200, were made Prisoners, and the Town
miserably sackt without regard to Church or Hospital. It
cannot be said whether for the time ours better attempted
it, or they defended themselves: but I am confident we lost
three for one in the Assault; the number slain on both
sides being about 300, amongst whom of ours Collonel
St. George and some Officers lay dead in the Breach. After
the taking this Place, the Army rested four or five Days.
The Lord Loughborough was made Governour, Collonel
Matthew Appleyard Lieutenant Governour; who with
Collonel Page, and Major William Bridges were made
Knights for their Valour and Conduct in this Action.
During our stay the Breaches were repaired, and in regard
of the largeness of the Line, a Design was laid only to
fortifie the South part of the Town, the Country shewing
great cheerfulness in assisting; and it was verily thought
if in this Conjunction Darby had been but summoned, Sir

John Gel would have rendred it; but Prince Rupert would not do it, out of this Punctilio of Honour, that if he had sent a Summons he was obliged (if the other had repulsed) to besiege it. As the gaining of this place made the King and His Army terrible, so the use that was made of it, and the Consequence thereof, conduced to our Destruction; for now instead of either retiring towards Worcester to join with General Charles Gerrard, which was in few Days after by order to come to us with 3000 Horse and Foot, whereby we might have secured our new Conquests; or else of marching Northward with the Terror of being Victorious; we turned Faces towards Oxford, which I must needs say was much against the Will of Prince Rupert. But as he prevailed before against marching Westward, so now he yielded to the Importunity of those who possibly covered their private Designs under the Care of preserving the Duke of York, the Council, Magazine, and all the fair Ladies at Oxford; who likewise had too violent Apprehensions of their Dangers, and earnestly by Letters (as 'tis said) solicited Prince Rupert to their Rescue.

It was now about the fifth of June when we marched out of Leicester, and at our first Rendezvouz we found the Loss we had by the taking that Place; for what with those that were slain and wounded when we took the Town, those were left there in Garrison, and those that ran away afterwards with their Plunder, we were not 3500 Foot; besides the Northern Horse were all discontented, and could hardly be kept from disbanding or returning Home in Disorder. But with much ado they being appeased we continued our March, and the Next Day at Harborow had News that Fairfax was drawn off from Oxford, without having made any Attempt or Approach, and without doing or suffering much; and that after he had likewise attempted Bostal House, where he was notably repulsed by Sir William Campion the Governour, with some Loss, that he was marched towards Buckingham. This was not welcome News, yet such as obliged us rather to make towards him and hazard a Battel, than to march Northwards and be met in the Face with the Scots, and have him in our Rear. From Harborow the Army marched to Daventry, and there stayed five Days, both to mark the Motion of Fairfax and to receive some Provision from Oxford. Much about this time a Force of near 2000 Horse and Foot drawn together out of the Garrisons of Hereford, Worcester, Monmouth and

Ludlow, under the Command of Sir Thomas Lunsford,* Sir Michael Woodhouse, and others, were by a far less number of the Rebels defeated near Ludlow, Sir William Croft slain. This Defeat was ascribed to the ill Conduct and Strife of these Collonels about Superiority and Command. And although when we had the first Intelligence we could not see the sad Effects of this Loss, yet after the Battel at Naseby, when we retreated into those Parts and had occasion to use them, we too soon felt it.

Upon the 13 of June Intelligence being given of the Advance of Fairfax to Northampton, our Army retired back to Harborow with resolution to march the next Day to Melton Mowbray and so to Newark there to strengthen our Foot by Additions out of that and other adjacent Garrisons. But that Night an Allarum was given, that Fairfax with his Army was quartered within six Miles of us. This altered our design, and a Council being presently called, resolutions were taken to fight; and rather to march back and seek him out, than to be sought or pursued, contrary (as 'tis said) to Prince Rupert's Opinion; it being our unhappiness, that the Faction of the Court, whereof the most powerful were the Lord Digby and Mr John Ashburnham, and that of the Army ever opposed and were jealous of others. In the Morning early being Saturday the 14 of June, all the Army was drawn up upon a rising Ground of very great Advantage about a Mile from Harborow, which we left on our Back, and there put in order and disposed to give or receive the Charge. The main Battel of Foot was led by the Lord Asteley Serjeant Major General, consisting of 2500: The right Wing of the Horse being about 2000 by Prince Rupert, and the left Wing by Sir Marmaduke Langdale, with the Northern and Newark Horse; in the Reserve were the King's Lifeguard commanded by the Earl of Lindsey, and Prince Rupert's Regiment of Foot being 800, with the King's Horse Guards commanded by the Earl of Lichfield, which were that Day about 500 Horse. The Army thus disposed made a stand on that Ground, and about eight of the Clock in the Morning, it was a question whether the Intelligence were true; whereupon one Francis Ruce the Scoutmaster was sent to discover; who in short time returned with a Lye in his Mouth, that he had been two or three Miles forward, and could neither discover or hear of the Rebels. This and a Report

*Lunsford was certainly senior to Woodhouse, and probably to Croft.

they were retreated, made Prince Rupert impatient; and thereupon he drew out a Party of Horse and Musquetiers both to discover and engage them, leaving the Army in that Place and Posture.

But he had not marched above a Mile before he had certain Intelligence of their Advance, and saw their Van. Whereupon he drew nearer with his Horse, and sent back to have the Army to march up to him; and either supposing by their Motion, or being flatered into an Opinion they were upon a Retreat, he desired they should make haste. This made us quit our Ground of Advantage and in reasonable order to advance. Having marched about a Mile and half, we could perceive their Horse in the high Ground about Naseby, but could not judge of their Number or Intentions. To be short, the manner of our March being in full Campania, gave them the means of disposing themselves to the best Advantage; and the Heat of Prince Rupert, and his Opinion they durst not stand him, engaged us before we had either turned our Cannon or chosen fit Ground to fight on. About ten of the Clock the Battel began, the first Charge being given by Prince Rupert with his own and Prince Maurice's Troops; who did so well, and were so well seconded, as that they bore all down before them, and were (as 'tis said) Masters of six Pieces of the Rebels Cannon. Presently our Forces advanced up the Hill, the Rebels only discharging five Pieces at them, but over shot them, and so did their Musquetiers. The Foot on either side hardly saw each other until they were within Carabine Shot, and so only made one Volley; ours falling in with Sword and butt end of the Musquet did notable Execution; so much as I saw their Colours fall, and their Foot in great Disorder. And had our left Wing but at this time done half so well as either the Foot or right Wing, we had got in few Minutes a glorious Victory. Our Foot and Right Wing being thus engaged, our left Wing advanced, consisting of five Bodies of the Northern and Newark Horse; who were opposed by seven great Bodies drawn to their right Wing by Cromwell who commanded there, and who besides the Advantage of Number had that of the Ground, ours marching up the Hill to encounter them. Yet I must needs say ours did as well as the Place and their Number would admit; but being flanked and pressed back, they at last gave Ground and fled: Four of the Rebels Bodies close and in good Order followed them, the rest charged our Foot. At this instant the King's Horse-guards and the King at the Head of them were ready to charge those who followed ours, when a Person of Quality, 'tis said the Earl of Carnwath, took the King's Horse by the Bridle, turned him about, swearing at Him and saying, Will you go upon your Death? and at the same time the Word being given, March to the right Hand, (which was both from assisting ours or assailing them, and (as most concluded) was a civil Command for every one to shift for himself) we turned about and ran on the Spur almost a quarter of a Mile, and then the Word being given to make a Stand, we did so; though the Body could never be rallyed. Those that came back made a Charge, wherein some of them fell. By this time Prince Rupert was come with a good Body of Horse from the right Wing; but they having done their part, and not being in Order, could never be brought t' charge again, nor to rally any of the broken Troops; and so after all the endeavours of the King and Prince Rupert, to the hazard of their Persons, they were fain to quit the Field, and to leave Fairfax Master of all our Foot, Cannon, Baggage and Plunder taken at Leicester. Our Foot had Quarter given them, but were all Prisoners, except some few Officers who escaped, and our Horse made haste, never staying until they came under the Works of Leicester, and some not thinking themselves secure there rode that Night to Newark, the first sixteen, the other at least thirty Miles from the Place of Battel. The Number slain that Day is uncertain, those of Quality slain of the King's Army were Sir Thomas Dalizon, Sir Richard Cave, Sir Peter Browne, Collonel Thomas, Lieutenant Collonel Davies, and above 100 Officers and Gentlemen out of the Northern and New-ark Horse and Prince Rupert's Troops. In the Pursuit of the Rebels, cruelly killed above 100 Women and Souldiers Wives, and some of them of Quality; and with a Party followed us within two Miles of Leicester; whence in the Evening the King and Prince Rupert with the broken Troops marched to Ashby de la Zouch, and from thence the next Day to Lichfield, and in two Days more to Bewdley in Worcestershire, where He rested one Day. And upon Advice His Majesty resolved for Hereford, and so for Wales, concluding with the Forces of General Gerrard and some new Levies designed in those Counties, to form a new Army. This Opinion I fear excluded a better design, which had been to have made for the West and to have jointed with General Goring, and with that Army so reinforced and encreased by some of General Gerrard's Foot that might have easily been transported over Severne, have tried the Fortune of a second Day; the Issue of which, had it been lost, could not have proved worse than our being afterwards both in the West and in other Places destroyed by pieces, without either Conduct or Honour.

LORD JOHN BELASYSE'S ACCOUNT

FROM A BRIEFE RELATION OF THE LIFE AND MEMOIRES OF JOHN LORD BELASYSE

Written and Collected by his Secretary, Joshua Moone.

. . . after ten months' imprisonment in the Tower, he was conducted from thence with guards through the City (not being permitted to confer with any) to his coach without the line; and so the second night he arrived at Oxford, where immediately he presented himself to His Majesty, who the next day was pleased to call him into his bed-chamber alone, and told him that having no other way to recompense his services at present, he had not only ordered the prisoners aforesaid to be released for his exchange (he being then upon his parole to return within 20 days if they were not), but gave him a warrant to create him a baron of England, for which he kissed his hand, and in the Patent his services were expressed in the several battles and sieges and wounds that he had received. In recompense whereof he then told him also that he intended him to be general of the horse to my Lord Gorens [Goring's] army in the West; that army being designed to counterpoise the other, which Prince Rupert commanded (who from that time begun to decline in His Majesty's favour); but afterwards conceiving it might better suit with his service to employ him northwards, where he had more interest, and till the way was open by the success of that campaignia which followed, he commanded my Lord to attend his person, who took the field soon after and besieged Leicester and by storm took it, after two days' battery upon the works, whereby it was exposed to the sack of soldiers, tho' the commanders endeavoured the contrary all they could. This success alarmed Sir Thomas Fairfax's army who had then surrounded Oxford to divert the said siege; wherefore after three or four days' stay at Leicester they raised the siege from Oxford, our army being advanced as far as Daventry, and supplies of provisions put into Oxford. The King would not longer attend their motion, but rather invite them to follow him by a seeming retreat back to Leicester, the consequence of which proved to the sad ruin of his army, being the last great battle which was fought, for since the battle of Knaisby [Naseby] (which now immediately followed) no army for the King kept the field, except my Lord Gorens [Goring's] in the West, which soon received so many foils by the same army that had beaten the King's at Knaisby, as without any considerable resistance (more through the disorders of the officers then the soldiers) it was destroyed: the infantry being cut off at Torrington and other places, the cavalry surrendering themselves and horses upon dishonourable terms, tho' they were no fewer the 4,500 horse, which might timely have broken through the enemy and saved themselves.

But to return to Knaisby, at which battle my Lord waited on his Majesty as a volunteer, yet he was ever pleased to call him to that Council of War where himself was in person. Now the enemy followed our rear within four miles of Harborough, being our head-quarters the night before we fought. The next day, being the [14th] day of [June] 1646 [1645] early in the morning we turned towards them into a large army drawn up in a battalia (which as we conceived consisted of about 15,000 ours not exceeding 12,000 Horse and Foot). They suffered us to advance and give them the charge, which to our disadvantage we did, for they being possessed of the higher ground our horse upon the left wing (commanded by Sir Marmaduke Langdale) was first routed without any handsome dispute: those under Prince Rupert upon the right beat the enemy off their ground, and pursued them beyond their train and baggage, but could not retreat in order to our other bodies, being broken in the retreat, and after charged by the same body of their horse which had before beaten our left wing; so as in effect our whole horse being routed, and the King's Guards where himself in person stood last, with the Duke of Richmond, Lord Lichfield, Digby, my Lord and some few others that kept with him, tho' he laboured to make the horse stand and offered to lead them on (after rallied to a charge), yet neither His Majesty nor the endeavours of those that waited on him could ever prevail with those shattered and frightened troops either to give or stand one charge more. All this time our old infantry fought it out gallantly (amongst which my Lord's old regiment which he had given to Sir Theophilus Gilby was) and beat those of the enemy's, making themselves masters of their cannon, till such times as finding no relief from our horse and being surrounded by the enemy's whole army overpowering them, they were at last forced to yield themselves prisoners upon quarter. Not 200 lost their lives in this battle, so ill it was disputed. All the foot (officers and soldiers) remained prisoners. The horse knew well how to save themselves, tho' not their honours, by a hasty and shameful flight to Leicester, without staying to bring off His Majesty, who at last (with the best of his officers and his own guards) retired and found all those shattered horse under the walls of Leicester. Here the King made to stay, but marched directly to Ashby and then to Hereford and Ragland Castle to recruit himself with a new foot army in South Wales, but those which were raised there were otherwise disposed of being sent over the Severn, some to supply the garrisons in the West, others to Prince Rupert at Bristol, who was gone thither to his Government to defend that place during His Majesty's residence in South Wales.

THE
Kings Cabinet opened:
OR
CERTAIN PACKETS
OF SECRET
LETTERS & PAPERS,
Written with the Kings own Hand,
and taken in his Cabinet at *Nasby-Field*,
June 14. 1645.
By Victorious Sr. *Thomas Fairfax;*
Wherein many mysteries of State, tending to the
Justification of that Cause, for which
Sir *Thomas Fairfax* joyned battell that
memorable day are clearly laid open;
Together, with some Annotations thereupon.

Published by Special Order of the *Parliament.*

LONDON
Printed for *Robert Bostock*, dwelling in *Pauls* Churchyard, at the Signe of the Kings-head, 1645.

It were a great sin against the mercies of God, to
conceale those evidences of truth, which hee so graciously
(and almost miraculously) by surprizall of these Papers,
hath put into our hands; nor dare we smother this light
under a Bushell, but freely hold it out to our seduced
brethren, (for so in the spirit of meeknesse labouring to
reclaim them, we still speak) that they may see their errors,
and return into the right way: For those that wilfully
deviate, and make it their profession to oppose the truth,
we think it below us, to revile them with opprobrious
language, remembring the Apostle St. *Jude*, and that
example which he gives us in his Epistle. They may see
here in his privat Letters what affection the King beares to
his people, what language and titles he bestowes upon his
great Councell; which we return not again, but consider
with sorrow, that it comes from a Prince seduced out of his
proper sphear; one that has left that seat in which he ought,
and hath bound himselfe to sit, to sit (as the Psalmist
speaks) in the *Chair of the scornfull;* & to the ruine (almost)
of three Kingdoms, hath *walked in the counsels of the ungodly;*
and though in our tenents we annex no infallibility to the
seat of a King in Parliament, as the *Romanists* do to the

Papall Chaire, (since all men are subject to errour) yet we dare boldly say, that no *English* King did ever from that place, speak destruction to his people, but safety and honour; nor any that abhorred that Seat and Councell, but did the contrary. Therefore, Reader, to come now to the present businesse of these Letters, thou art either a friend or enemy to our cause: If thou art well affected to that Cause of Liberty & Religion, which the two Parliaments of *England* and *Scotland* now maintain against a combination of all the Papists in *Europe* almost, especially the bloody Tygers of *Ireland*, and some of the Prelaticall and Court Faction in *England*: thou wilt be abundantly satisfied with these Letters here printed, and take notice there from, how the Court has been *Caiolde*, (thats the new authentick word now amongst our Cabalisticall adversaries) by the Papists, and we the more beleeving sort of Protestants, by the Court. If thou art an enemy to Parliaments and Reformation, and made willfull in thy enmity beyond the help of miracles, or such revelations as these are, then *tis* to be expected, that thou wilt either deny these papers to have been written by the Kings own hand, or else that we make just constructions and inferences out of them: Or lastly, thou wilt deny, though they be the Kings own, and beare such a sense as we understand them in, yet that they are blameable, or unjustifiable against such rebels as we are. As to the first, know that the Parliament was never yet guilty of such forgery, the King yet in all the Letters of his, which have been hitherto intercepted, never objected any such thing, and we dare appeale to 'his own conscience now, knowing that he cannot disavow either his own hand writing, or the matters themselves here written. All the Ciphers, Letters, all circumstances of time, and fact, and the very hand by which they are signed (so generally known and now exposed to the view of all) will averre for us, that no such forgery could be possible. As to our Comments and Annotations, if there be not perspicuity and modesty in them, there is no common justice nor place for credit left amongst mankind: but indeed most of the main circumstances want no illustration at all to the most vulgar capacities: and therefore we affirm nothing necessary to be beleeved, but what the printed papers will themselves utter in their own language: and yet for that which is not so clearly warranted here, we have other Papers for their warrant, were they not too numerous, and vast, and too much intermixed with other matter of no pertinence for publication at this time. Touching the last objection, if thou art a perfect malignant, and dost not stick to deny, that there is any thing in these letters unbeseeming a Prince, who professes himself Defender of the true Faith, a tender Father of his Country, and has been so sanctimoniously ingaged with frequent, speciall vowes of affection, candour, sincerity, and constancie to his particular protestant subjects of *England* and *Scotland:* Then know, that thou art scarce worthy of any reply, or satisfaction in this point. Our cause is now the same as it was when the King first took up Armes, and as it was when the King made most of these oathes and professions. Our three propositions concerning the abolition of Episcopacy, the setling the Militia of the three Kingdomes in good hands, by advice of Parliament, the vindication of the *Irish* rebels, being all our main demands as the Treaty in February last, and no other than the Propositions sent in June 1642. before any stroke struck, will beare us witnesse that we have rather straitned then enlarged our complaints. But were our cause altered, as it is not ; or were we worse rebels then formerly, as none can affirm which takes notice of our late sufferings, and our strange patience even now after the discovery of these Papers, and our late extraordinary success in the Field, yet still this clandestine proceeding against us here, and condemning all that are in any degree Protestants at *Oxford;* as also granting a toleration of Idolatry to Papists, indemnity to the murtherous Irish, in a close trading way for meer particular advantage, cannot be defended by any, but by the falsest of men, Papists ; or the falsest of Papists, Jesuits. Hitherto the *English* have had commission to chastise the *Irish*, the *Irish* have had the like to chastise the *English*, both have spilt each others blood by the Kings warrant ; yet as both have been in part owned, so both have been in part disowned, and the King himselfe has not appeared with an open face in the busines, but now by Gods good providence the traverse Curtain is drawn, and the King writing to *Ormond*, and the Queen, what they must not disclose, is presented upon the stage. God grant that the drawing of this Curtain may bee as fatall to Popery, and all Antichristian heresie here now, as the rending of the vaile was to the Jewish Ceremonies in *Iudea*, at the expiration of our Saviour.

Oxford

I

Deare heart,

Since my last, which was by *Talbot*, the Scots Commissioners have sent to desire me to send a Commission to the generall Assembly in *Edinburgh*, which I am resolved not to do; but to the end of making some use of this occasion, by sending an honest man to *London*, and that I may have the more time for the making a handsome negative, I have demanded a passeport for *Philip Warwick*, by whom to return my answer. I forgot in my former to tell thee, that *Lentall* the speaker brags, that Cardinall *Mazarin* keeps a strict intelligence with him; though I will not sweare that *Lentall* sayes true, I am sure it is fit for thee to know. As for *Sabrian*, I am confident that either he or his Instructions are not right for him who is eternally thine.

Even now I am advertised from *London*, that there are three or four Lords, and eight Commons (besides four Scotch Commissioners) appointed to treat, and they have named *Uxbridge* for the place, though not yet the particular persons I am likewise newly advertised that General *Goring* prospers wel where he is, and since *Munday* last hath taken 80 of the Rebels Horse: and upon his advance they have quitted *Peterfield* and *Condry*.

POSTSCRIPT

The setling of Religion, and the Militia, are the first to be treated on: and bee confident, that I will neither quit Episcopacy, nor that sword which God hath given into my hands.

$$\begin{array}{cc} 29 & 15. \end{array}$$
Copie to my wife 9 Jan. 1644.
By P. A.

This is a true Copie, examined by *Edm. Prideaux.*

Oxford

B

II

Oxford, Sunday 30 *March*. Deare heart, since my last (which was but 3 dayes ago) there are no alterations hapned of moment, preparations rather then actions being yet our chiefest bussinesse, in which we hope that we proceed faster then the Rebels, whose levies both of men and money (for certain) goes on very slowly; and I beleeve, they are much weaker then is thought, even here at *Oxford*. For instance, A very honest servant of mine, and no fool, shewed me a proposition from one of the most considerable *London* Rebels, who will not let his name be known untill he have hope that his proposition will take effect; it is this, That since the Treaty is so broken off, that neither the rebels nor I can resume it without at least a seeming totall yeelding to the other. The Treaty should be renewed upon thy motion, with a pre-assurance that the rebels will submit to reason. The answer that I permitted my servant to give, was, That thou art the much fittest person to be the means of so happy & glorious a work as is the peace of this Kingdom ; *but that upon no terms thy name was to be prophaned,* therefore he was to be *satisfied of the rebels willingnesse to yeeld to reason, before he would consent that any such intimation should be made to thee, and particularly concerning Religion and the Militia, that nothing must be insisted upon but according to my former offers.* This I beleeve will come to nothing, yet I cannot but advertise thee of any thing that comes to my knowledge of this consequence.

I must again tell thee, That most assuredly France will bee the best way for transportation of the D. of Lorraines Army there being divers fit and safe places of landing for them upon the western coasts, besides the Ports under my obedience, as Shelsey neer Chichester and others, of which I will advertise thee when the time comes.

By my next I think to tell thee when I shall march into the Field, for which money is now his greatest want (I need say no more) who is eternally thine,

18   31.

To my Wife 30 March. 1645. by *Petit.*
This is a true Copie examined by *Edmond Prideaux.*

Oxford

III

Oxford Thursday 27. March

Dear heart, I wrote to thee yesterday by *Sakefield*, the subject of it was onely kindnesse to thee ; which, I assure thee shall ever be visible in all my actions : And now I come to *Jermins* account, given me by thy command, which is very cleare, hopefull in most particulars, and absolutely satisfactory as concerning thy care & industry. As for the main impediment in the D. of *Lorrains* businesse (which is his passage) why may thou not procure him passage through *France?* (if that of *Holland* be stuck at) it will much secure

327

and facilitate the Sea transportation in respect of landing on the Western Coast, which I beleeve will be found the best, there being not so many places to chuse on, any where else. But this an opinion, not a direction.

The generall face of my affairs me thinks begins to mend, the dissensions at *London* rather increasing then ceasing, *Montrosse* daily prospering, my Western businesse mending apace, and hopefull in all the rest. So that if I had reasonable supplies of money and powder (not to exclude any other,) I am confident to be in a better condition this yeare, then I have been since this rebellion began and possibly I may put faire for the whole, and so enjoy thy company again, without which nothing can be a contentment unto me. And so farewell dear heart.

I intend (if thou like it) to bestow Percies *place on the M. of Newcastle, to whom yet I am no wayes ingaged, nor will be before I have thy answer. As for* Jack Barclay, *I do not remember that I gave thee any hope of making of him Master of the Wards: For* Cottington *had it long ago before thou went hence, and I intended it to Secr.* Nich. *if he then would have received it: and I am deceived if I did not tell thee of it.*

I desire thee to command Lo. Jer. to read to thee the Ds Letter, which goes herwith, and in it to mark well that part concerning the transportation of the D. Lorrains Army.

23.   30.
To my Wife 27. Mar. 1645. by P.A.
This is a true Copy examined by *Miles Corbet.*

IIII

Oxford, Sunday 4. *May.* Dear Heart, the Rebels new brutish Generall hath refused to meddle with forrain Passes, so as yet I cannot dispatch *Adrian May* to thee, by the way of London which if I cannot very shortly, I will send him by the West, and now, if I could be assured of thy recovery, I would have but few melancholy thoughts, for I thank God my Affairs begins to smile upon me again, Wales being well swept of the Rebels. Farrington having relieved it self; and now being secured by *Gorings* coming, my Nephues likewise having brought me a strong party of Horse and Foot, these Quarters are so free that I hope to be marching within three or foure dayes, and am still confident to have the start of the Rebels this year: I am likewise very hopeful that my

Son will shortly be in the head of a good Army, for this I have the cheerfull assurance of *Culpeper* and *Hyde:* Of late I have been much pressed to make *Southampton* Master of my Horse, not more for good will to him, as out of fear that *Hamilton* might return to a capacity of recosening me ; wherein if I had done nothing, both jealousie and discontents were like to arise, wherefore I thought fit to put my Nephew *Rupert* in that place, which will both save me charge, and stop other mens grumblings : I have now no more to say, but praying for and impatiently expecting of good news from thee; I rest eternally thine.

39
To my wife 4 *May 1645*. By *Malin St. Ravy*.
This is a true Copie examined by *Edm. Prideaux*

V

13
Oxford. 2. Jan.

Dear Heart,

Having decyphered thine which I received yesterday I was much surprised to find thee, blame me for neglecting to write to thee, for indeed I have often complained for want, never mist any occasion of sending to thee ; and I assure thee never any dispatch went from either of my Secretaries without one from me when I knew of it.

As for my calling those at London a Parliament, I shall refer thee to *Digby* for particular satisfaction, this in generall ; If there had been but two (besides my Self) of my opinion, I had not done it, and the Argument that prevailed with me, was, that the calling did no wayes acknowledge them, to be a Parliament, upon which condition and construction I did it and no otherwayes, and accordingly it is registred in the Councell books, with the Councels unanimous approbation ; but thou will find, that it was by misfortune, not neglect that thou hast been no sooner advertised of it.

As for the conclusion of thy Letter, it would much trouble me, if thou didst not know, thy desire granted before it was asked ; yet I wonder not at it, since that which may bear a bad construction, hath been presented to thee in the ugliest form, not having received the true reason and meaning of it, the fear of some such mischance made me the more carefull, to give thee a full account by *Tom Eliot*, of the reasons of the D. of R. and E. of S. journey to London, which if it come soon enough I am confident will free thee from much trouble, but if thou hast not the patience to forbear judging harshly of my actions, before thou hearest the reasons of them, from me, thou may be often subject to be doubly vext, first with slanders, then with having given too much eare unto them. To conclude, esteeme me as thou findest me constant to those grounds thou lefts me withall, & so farewell Dear heart.

21.   13.

Copie to my wife 2 *Jan.* 1645 : by *P.A.*

This is a true Copie examined by *Edm. Prideaux.*

VI

21

Oxford, 19. Feb. old stile. Dear heart, I cannot yet send thee any certain word concerning the issue of our Treaty, onely, the unreasonable stubbornnesse of the Rebels, gives daily lesse and lesse hopes, of any accommodation this way ; wherefore I hope no rumors shall hinder thee from hastening all thou may, all possible assistance to me, and particularly that of the D. of Lorraines ; concerning which I received yesterday, good news from Dr. *Goffe,* that the P. of Orange will furnish Shipping for his transportation, and that the rest of his Negotiation goes hopefully on, by which, and many other wayes, I find thy affection so accompanied with dexterity, as I know not whether (in their severall kinds) to ésteeme most ; but I will say no more of this, lest thou may think that I pretend to do this way, what is but possible to be done by the continued actions of my life ; though I leave news to others, yet I cannot but tell thee, that even now I have received certain intelligence of a great defeat given to *Argyle* by *Muntrose;* who upon surprise, totally routed those Rebels, killed 1500. upon the place. Yesterday I received thine of 27. Jan. by the Portugal Agent, the onely way (but expresses) I am confident on, either to receive Letters from thee, or to send them to thee ; indeed *Sabran* sent me word yesterday, besides *some complements of the Imbargo of the rebels ships in France (which I likewise put upon thy score of kindnesse)* but is well enough content that the Portugall should be charged with thy dispatches. As for trusting the rebels either by going to

330

London, or dis-banding my Army before a peace, do no wayes feare my hazarding so cheaply or foolishly : for I esteem the interest thou hast in me at a farre dearer rate, and pretend to have a little more wit (at least by the sympathy that is betwixt us) then to put my selfe into the reverence of perfidious rebels. So impatiently expecting the expresse thou hast promised me, I rest eternally thine.

I can now assure thee, that Hertogen *the Irish Agent, is an arrant knave, which shall be made manifest to thee by the first opportunity of sending Pacquets.*

11.   21.

To my Wife 19. Feb. 1645. by P.A.

4

This is a true Copy examined by *Edmond Prideaux.*

VII

20

Dear heart, the expectation of an expresse from thee (as I find by thine of the 4. *Febr.*) is very good newes to me, as likewise that thou art now well satisfied with my diligence in writing. As for our treaty, there is every day lesse hopes then other, that it will produce a peace. But I will absolutely promise thee, that if we have one, it shall be such as shall invite thy return. For I avow that without thy company I can neither have peace nor comfort within my self. The limited dayes for treating, are now almost expired without the least agreement upon any one Article. Wherefore I have sent for enlargement of dayes, that the whole treaty may be laid open to the world. And I assure thee, that thou *needst not doubt the issue of this treaty; for my Commissioners are so well chosen (though I say it) that they will neither be threatned nor disputed from the grounds I have given them; which (upon my word) is according to the little Note thou so well remembers.* And in this not onely their obedience, but *their* judgements concur. I confesse in some respects thou hast reason to bid me beware of going too soon to *London:* for indeed some amongst us had a greater mind that way then was fit ; of which perswasion *Percy* is one of the chief, who is shortly like to see thee, of whom having said this, is enough to shew thee how he is to be trusted, or beleeved by thee concerning our proceedings here. *In short, there is little or no appearance but that this Summer will be the hottest for war of any that hath been yet: and be confident, that in making peace,*

I shall ever shew my constancy in adhering to Bishops, and all our friends, and not forget to put a short period to this perpetual Parliament. But as thou loves me, let none perswade thee to slaken thine assistance for him who is eternally thine, C.R.

1 5   4

Oxford 25. Feb. 1645.

3.   20.

To my Wife 15. Feb. 1645, by *P.A.*

This is a true Copie examined by *Edmond Prideaux*

VIII

22

Dear heart, now is come to passe what I fore-saw, the fruitlesse end (as to a present peace) of this treaty; but I am still confident, that I shall find very good effects of it: for besides that my Commissioners have offered, to say no more, full measured reason, and the rebels have stucken rigidly to their demands, which I dare say had been too much, though they had taken me prisoner, so that assuredly the breach will light soully upon them. We have likewise at this time discovered, and shall make it evidently appeare to the world, that the *English* Rebels, (whether basely or ignorantly, will be no very great difference) have as much as in them lies, transmitted the command of *Ireland* from the Crown of *England* to the Scots, which (besides the reflections it will have upon these rebels) will clearly shew, that reformation of the Church is not the chief, much lesse the onely end of the Scotch Rebellion; but it being presumption, & no pietie: so to trust to a good cause, as not to use *all lawfull means to maintain it, I have thought of one means more to furnish thee with for my assistance, then hitherto thou hast had: It is that I give thee power to promise in my name (to whom thou thinkest most fit) that I will take away all the penall laws against the Roman Catholicks in England as soon as God shall inable me to do it; so as by their means, or in their favours, I may have so powerfull assistance as may deserve so great a favour, and enable me to do it.* But if thou ask what I call that assistance, I answer, that when thou knowest what may be, done for it, it will be easily seen, if it deserve to be so esteemed I need not tell thee what secrecy this busines requires; yet this I will say, that this is the greatest point of confidence I can express to thee; for it is no thanks to me to trust thee in anything else but in

332

this which is the only thing of difference in opinion betwix us : *And yet I know thou wilt make as good a bargain for me, even in this.* I trusting thee, (though it concern religion) as if thou wert a protestant, the visible good of my affairs so much depending on it, I have so fully intrusted this bearer *Pooly*, that I will not say more to thee now, but that herewith I. send thee a new Cypher (assuring thee, that none hath or shal have any copy of it but my selfe, to the end thou mayst use it, when thou shalt find fit to write any thing which thou wilt judge worthy of thy pains to put in cypher, and to be decyphered by none but me ; and so likewise from him to thee, who is eternally thine.

20   23

To my wife the 5. March. *by Pooly.*

This is a true Copie examined by Edm. Prideaux.

IX

The little that is here in Cypher is   '33.
in that which I sent to thee by *Pooly*

Oxford, Wednesday 9 *April.* 1645

Dear Heart:

Though it be an uncomfortable thing to write by a slow Messenger, yet all occasions, of this (which is now the onely) way of conversing with thee, is so welcome to me as I shall be loath to loose any ; but expect neither news or publick busines, from me, by this way of conveyance : yet judging thee by myself even these nothings will not be unwelcom to thee, though I should chide thee, which if I could I would do, for thy too sudden taking Alarms ; I pray thee consider, since I love thee above all earthly things, & that my contentment is unseperably conjoyned with thine, must not all my Actions tend to serve and please thee? *If thou knew what a life I lead, (I speak not in respect of the common distractions) even in point of conversation, which in my mind, is the chief joy or vexation of ones life, I dare say thou would pity me; for some are too wise, others too foolish, some too busie, others too reserved, many fantastick. In a word, when I know none better (I speak not now in relation to businesse) then* 359.8. 270.55: 5: 7 :67 :18. 294: 35: 69: 16: 54: 6: 38: 1: 67 :68: 9 :66: *thou may easily judge how my conversation pleaseth me.* I confesse thy company hath perhaps made me in this, hard to be pleased, but not lesse to be pitied by thee, who art the only cure for this disease. The end of all is this, to desire thee to comfort me as often as thou can with thy letters, & dost not thou think, that to know particulars of thy health, & how thou spendest the time, are pleasing subjects unto me, though thou hast no other businesse to write of? Beleeve me, sweet heart, thy kindnesse is as necessary to comfort my heart, as thy assistance is for my affairs.

To my Wife 9 April 1645. by *Binion*.

This is a true Copy examined by Miles Corbet.

Oxford

Appendix II

PARLIAMENTARIAN ACCOUNTS

SIR THOMAS FAIRFAX' ACCOUNT

For the Hon. William Lenthall Esq : speaker of the House of Commons.

"Mr. Speaker,

"Besides the general account I have alreadie given by one of my servants whom I sent up to London yesterday, I thought fit to send the bearer, Mr Boles,* who may more particularlye inform you concerninge the abundant goodness of God to this army and the whole kingdome in the late victorie at Naseby field. The whole body of their foot taken or slaine ; such a list of prisoners as could be made up in this short time I have sent, the horse all quitted the fielde and were pursued within three miles of Leicester : theire ammunition, ordnance, and carriages all taken ; among which there were two demy-canons, a whole culverin, and a mortar piece, besides lesser peeces. We intend to move to Leicester, as soon as we have taken orders, with our prisoners and wounded men. All that I desire is, that the honor of this great and never to be forgotten mercie may be given to God in an extraordinary day of thanksgiving, and that it may be improved to the good of his churche and his kingdome, which shall be faithfully endeavoured by Sir

Your most humble servant,

THO. FAIRFAX

"Some Irish are among the prisoners as I am informed, I have not time to make enquiry into it, I desire they may be proceeded against according to ordnance of parliament. Major Gen. Skippon was shot thro' his side, but notwithstanding he continued in the ffielde with great resolution, and when I desired him to goe off the ffielde, he answered

*Chaplain to the Army.

335

he would not goe so long as a man would stand, still doing his office as a valiant and wise commander. Also Colonel Butler and Colonel Ireton upon their first charge were both dangerouslie wounded, behaving themselves very gallantlie. If I could enter into particulars, much might be spoken of the resolution and courage of many commanders both horse and ffoot in this days service."

LIEUTENANT-GENERAL OLIVER CROMWELL'S ACCOUNT

For the Honourable William Lenthall, speaker of the Commons House of Parliament : these

Sir,

Being commanded by you to this service, I think myself bound to acquaint you with the good hand of God towards you and us.

We marched yesterday after the King, who went before us from Daventry to Harborough ; and quartered about six miles from him. This day we marched towards him. He drew out to meet us ; both armies engaged. We, after three hours fight very doubtful, at last routed his army ; killed and took about 5,000, very many officers, but of what quality we yet know not. We took also about 200 carriages, all he had ; and all his guns, being 12 in number, whereof two were demi-cannon, two demiculverins, and (I think) the rest sackers. We pursued the enemy from three miles short of Harborough to nine beyond, even to sight of Leicester, whither the King fled.

Sir, this is none other but the hand of God ; and to Him alone belongs the glory, wherein none are to share with Him. The General served you with all faithfulness and honour ; and the best commendations I can give him is, that I dare say he attributes all to God, and would rather perish than assume to himself. Which is an honest and a thriving way, and yet as much for bravery may be given to him, in this action, as to a man. Honest men served you faithfully in this action. Sir, they are trusty ; I beseech you in the name of God, not to discourage them. I wish this action may beget thankfulness and humility in all that are concerned in it. He that ventures his life for the liberty of his country, I wish he trust God for the liberty of his conscience, and you for the liberty he fights for. In this he rests, who is

Haverbrowe,   Your most humble servant,
14 June 1645.   OLIVER CROMWELL

To the Hon. Wm. Lenthall, Esq., Speaker to the House
of Commons – Haste.

"Honorable Sir,

"This morning, by day brake, wee marcht out Guils-
boro, after the enemy. After an hours march wee discovered
their horse drawne up at Sibbertoff three miles this side
Harborough; an hour after their foot appeared; this was
about 8 in the morning: by 10 we were disposed into a
battalia on both sides; both sides with mighty shouts,
exprest a hearty desire of fighting, having for our parts
recommended our cause to God's protection, and received
the word, which was, God our strength; theirs Queen
Mary; our forlorne hopes begun the pla[y?] while both
sides laboured for the hill and wynd, which in conclusyon
w[as] as it were equally divided. Our forlorne hope gave
back, and their right wing of horse fell upon our left, with
such gallantry, that ours were immediately routed; about
1000 ran along with them, but such was the courage and
diligence of the right wing, backt with the foot, that they
not only beat back the enemy, from the traine; but fell in
with their ffoot, and after 2 hours dispute won all their
field peeces (of which some are cannon) most of their
baggage, mortar-peeces, boats, 3000 arms, much powder,
match, &c. and nigh 4000 prisoners; some 600 slayne,
many commanders of note: of ours not above 200. Our
horse are still in pursuit, and have taken many officers;
their standard is ours, the King's waggon, and many
ladyes. God Almighty give us thankful hearts for this great
victory, the most absolute as yet obtayned. The General,
Lieut. Gen. Cromwell, and Major Gen. Skippon did
beyond expression gallantly; so did all the other commanders and soldiers: wee have lost but 2 Captains. Tho
this come late be pleased to accept it from your Honors

most Humble Servants,

HAR. LEIGHTON.

THO. HERBERT

Naseby where this fight was
this Saturday 14 June 1645.

"Capt. Potter is dangerously wounded but hopes of
his recovery, so is Capt. Cook."

337

Noble Sir,

Having little opportunity and good newes through God's goodnesse to send unto you, I thought good to neglect no opportunity, but the first convenient messenger to send to you, that so you might receive true intelligence, and might with the rest of God's people joyne together in praises to the Lord for his infinite Mercy to us in particular, and to all the whole Land in generall. I am not Ignorant that news will come to you of this great Victory before my Letter comes to your hands; but it is my desire so neere as I can to relate to you the certainty of it. After many tedious houers night and day since I saw you, and Watching every night with my Regiment upon there quarters, having the forelorn guard every night, it pleased God that upon Saturday the 14 of this instant month between 7 & 8 of the clock in the morning, wee drew neere to a place called Nasby, unto Clypsome [Clipston] field a mile and a halfe from our quarters, where we had the guard the night before; and so soone as wee came into the field, the Enemy was drawn up into a Battalia ready to give us battell; and so ready that, had it not pleased the Lord of his infinite Mercy to shew himselfe, wee had beene all cut off, for they were ready to advance upon us, before wee were drawn up into a Battalia for to incounter with them; But our Noble Generall and Lieutenant Generall, Cromwell, and major Generall Skippon were so carefull of the great worke in hand; as that they soone drew us up into a body, in such a manner, as that wee were presently ready to encounter with the Enemy, as the Enemy was to fall upon us. For although they had marched in a very stately way in a whole Body towards us, thinking thereby to daunt us, or at least to take us before wee were ready to give them entertainment; for they had a very large Body both of Foot and Horse, but especially of Horse.

I was half a mile behinde in a Medow giving my men Ammunition, and had not the Lieutenant Gen. come presently, & caused me with all speed to mount my men, & flank our left Wing, which was the King's right Wing of horse; where was Prince Maurice, who charged at the head of his Regiment, and the King himself in the next reserve charged at the head of his men; but by that time I could get my men to light, and deliver up their Horses, in a little close, the Enemy drew towards us: which my men perceiving, they with shooting and rejoycing received them, although they were incompassed on the one side with the King's Horse, and on the other side with Foot and Horse to get the Close ; but it pleased God that wee beat off both the Horse and the Foot on the left, and the right Wing, and cleared the Field, and kept our ground : When as the King's Horse had driven our men a mile before them on the left Wing at their first comming on ; then wee discovered many of the King's Regiment, by reason that they came somewhat neare unto us ; before ever they discharged a Pistoll at any Horse ; and had not wee by God's providence been there, there had been but few of Colonell Butler's Regiment left. After this wee gave up our selves for lost men, but wee resolved every man to stand to the last, and presently upon it, God of his providence ordered it so, that our right Wing, which was Colonel Cromwell his Regiment drave the Enemy before them ; which I perceiving (after one houre's battail) caused all my men to mount and to charge into their Foot, which accordingly they did ; and took all their Colours, and 500 Prisoners, besides what wee killed, and all their Armes. After this the King his Horse drew up into a body againe : and then I drew up my Dragoons, and charged the King's Regiment of Horse, and they faced about and run away and never made any stay till they came to Leicester, which was about 15 miles from the place where we fought : Wee took, as neare as we can guesse, between 4 and 5000 men, with many Horse, all their Ordinance, Bag and Baggage ; and there was as we were informed, but two Footmen went into Leicester ; the King himselfe very hardly escaped.

Now what remaines, but that you and wee should magnifie the name of our God, that did remember a poore handfull of dispised men, whom they had thought to have swallowed up before them. And I desire you, that you would in our behalfe blesse God that hath made us any instruments for our Kingdomes good, and that wee may walke worthy of so great a Mercy and Deliverance. And I humbly desire that Thanks may be given to Almighty God that did so miraculously deliver us. I lost not one man, and had but three men wounded in all my Regiment. Thus in hast I rest, desiring the Lord to keepe you and all yours. And remaine

Your Friend to Command

John Okey.

COLONEL JOHN OKEY, 1606-1662, BY H. G. TIBBUTT.
Bedfordshire Historical Record Society, Vol. XXXV, p. 10-11.

* *A more particular and exact relation* (E.288 38). For a recent study of Naseby see
Lieut.-Col. A. H. Burne, *The Battlefields of England*, pp. 239-56. See also R. W.
Ramsey, *Henry Ireton*, pp. 35-7.

ENGLAND'S
RECOVERY

The Army commanded to rise from before Oxford;
Their severall Marches till the Battel at Naseby,
with all the particulars thereof, fully related.

Upon the sad news of the losse of Leicester, and the danger thereupon of the Kings
breaking into the Associated Counties; Lieutenant-General Cromwel was ordered by the
Committee of both Kingdomes, to march only
with three Troops of horse to secure the Isle of
Ely; which commands, he, in greater tender-
nesse of the publique service, then his own
honour, in such a time of extremity as that was,
disputed not, but fulfilled. And his Excellency
Sir Thomas Fairfax was commanded to rise
from before Oxford, and to march to defend
the Association, accordingly. Orders were immediately given for the Forces on the other
side the river to march to Islip, and Major-
General Brown was desired to put a garison
into Gaunt-house, being a place that was conceived would much conduce to the straitning
of Oxford; which accordingly was done, and
the bridge lately made, pulled up: and the next
day, being June 5 the Army rose from before
Oxford, and marched that day to Marsh-
Gibeon, ten miles. The General in his march
turned out of the way, to see the siege before
Bostol-house, where Major-General Skippon,
according to order, had that morning made
some attempt, but the successe was not according to our desires (the Moat being much deeper
than we expected.) This night, at the Head-
quarter, intelligence came that the King was

Though Granadoes
(after the attempt)
did great execution,
yet the Govern. held
it out very resolutely

marching from Leicester towards Daventry, with intention to raise the siege at Oxford, as was conceived ; which was by order before done to his hand.

Friday, June 6. the Army marched to great Brickhil, twelve miles, where the head-quarter was that night, which was once intended to be at Stony-Stratford, but that the intelligence which came that night to us of the Kings horse facing Northampton that day, rendred it not safe so to adventure : whilest the greatest body of our Horse, sent into Derbyshire, were not as yet returned.

Anno 1645.
June

This night a great fire happened at the Generals quarters at Brickhil, which was so sudden and violent for the time, that a man and a boy, and three or four horses were burnt in the Barn where the fire began, before the Guard could get to preserve them. It happened most remarkably, in the house of one who expressed no good affection to this Army, and denyed to furnish those conveniences for quarter, (affirming that he had them not,) which afterwards by occasion of the fire, he was enforced to bring out. The next day, June 7, the Army marched to Sherrington, a mile East of Newport-Pagnel, to the end the Forces with Colonel Vermuden (who upon the Scots retreat to Westmerland were recalled, and upon their march back) might more conveniently joyn, but especially to be on that side of the River, the better to secure the Association, in case the King, who the day before had faced North-ampton, and seemed to intend that way, should attempt to break into it ; wherein it appeared they did not consult their safety and quarter on the back of a garison, as without incurring any great censure they might have done ; but rather consulted their honour and the publick service. Expresses were sent to Lieutenant-General Cromwel into the Association, to inform him whereabout our Army was, that in case the Association were in danger, he might know how to joyn with us. Lords day, June 8.

The King sent horse
to face Northampton

341

the Army resting in their quarters, severall parties of horse were sent out as far as Tocester, to gain intelligence of the motions of the Kings Army, who brought in some prisoners of Sir Marmaduke Langdales Brigade, from whom information was gathered that the Kings Army continued still about Daventry: Whereupon the General called a Councel of War, to consider of the best ways to engage the Enemy. Where taking into consideration of what use Lieutenant-General Cromwel would be to them in a time of so great action: The General propounded to the Councel of War, and it was by them unanimously consented unto, that a Letter should be writ to the Parliament, to desire that they would please for a time to dispence with L.Gen. Cromwels absence from the House; and to give way he might command their Horse, there being like to be very speedily an engagement. Which Letter was sent by Colonel Hammond, who went Post the same day to the Parliament, and was instantly returned with an answer according as we desired, to the great content of the General, and the whole Army.

Anno 1645
June

This day, Colonel Vermuden, who the day before was with his party of Horse returned, and come near to the quarters of the army, himself came to the General, desiring (in regard of some speciall occasions which he said he had to draw him beyond seas) that he might have leave to lay down his Commission, which was yielded unto, and accordingly he received his discharge. At this dayes debate, Major-General Skippon was desired to draw the form of a battell: and at the same time the Army was divided into severall Brigades of Horse and Foot, in order to their being better disposed for an engagement. The General, though not depending upon multitudes, yet serving Providence in the use of all good means; sent one Post after another to Sir John Gel, Colonel Rossiter, to the Governours of Coventry, Warwick, Northampton, and Nottingham, To march with all speed with their Forces to the

342

Army, for that there was likely to be speedily an engagement with the Enemy. In the mean, the Army neglected no time, but on Wednesday, June 11, though a rainy day, marched from Stony-Stratford to Wootton, within three miles of Northampton, where intelligence still confirmed the Kings continuance at Daventry, quartering all his Foot and Carriages upon Burrough-hill; a place of great advantage (having formerly been an ancient fortification) and making show, as if he had chosen that place to fight upon, in case we durst advance to him.

But afterwards it appeared, that his stay there, was only till a part of 1200 horse were returned, which he had sent from his Army to Oxford, as a convoy with the plundered cattel & sheep of Leicestershire, Northamptonshire, &c. the better to enable Oxford to endure a siege, in case it should be attempted again in his absence, himself being intent upon a march for the relief of Pomfract and Scarborough; which he then apprehended to have smal difficulty in it, understanding the removal of the Scotish army.

The Army being come to Wootton, they found there none of the best accommodation for quarter; only, what was wanting that way, was kindly and respectively endeavoured to be supplied by the Major and Magistrates of Northampton, who the same night came to the General at the head quarter, upon the errand of a congratulatry visit and present. The next day, the Army marched to Gilsborough, (four miles on the west of Northampton, and within five miles of Burrough-hill, where the Enemy still continued). Marching in very good order; for that they did advance directly upon the place where the enemy had pitcht himself. A commanded party of horse gave the Enemy an alarm, and took some prisoners, by whom they understood the King was a hunting, the Souldiers in no order, and their horses all at grasse, having not the least knowledge of our advance, and being in the greatest security that could be; but the alarm was so quickly taken thorow all their quarters, that our Foot being somewhat behinde, and night approaching, it was not thought wisdome to make any further attempt. About twelve that night, the General took horse, and rode about both the Horse and Foot guards, till four in the morning (expecting the Enemy would have shewn some gallantry that night, and fallen upon some of his quarters, as he had hindred them in their sport at hunting the day before). In the very entrance whereof this hard condition befell the General himself; That having forgot the Word, he was stopped at the first Guard; and requiring the Souldier that stood Sentinel, to give it him, he refused to do it, telling him he was to demand the Word from all that past him, but to give it to none, and so made the General stand in the wet, till he sent for the Captain of the guard to receive his commission to give the General the word, (In such subjection are the Highest, to those lawes that erst derived their sanction and authority in great part from themselves) and in the end the Souldier was rewarded for his duty and carefulnesse, (as it was interpreted). As the General was riding in the morning about three of the clock, within a mile and half of Flowre, where the Enemy kept an horse-guard; He could discern the Enemy riding fast over Burrough-hill, to make fires in abundance, as if they were firing their Huts; which gave some cause to believe they were about to march, as indeed it proved afterwards. For,

About five in the morning, June 13. the General being returned to the head-quarter, the Scoutmaster gen. Watson (whose continued diligence in getting timely intelligence of the Enemies motion, then, and alwayes, redounded not a little to the enablement of the Army) brought him certain notice, that the Enemy was drawing off from Burrough-hill; had stood in arms all night, and were all amazed that our Army was so neer, it being spread abroad in their army we were gone for security into the Association; And four or five more of the Spies came one after another, confirming the same intelligence, adding further, that most of their carriages were drawn from Burrough-hill towards Harborough. And indeed, the Convoy of Horse being returned from Oxford the night before, and this unexpected march of the Army close up to them, being in a manner a surprise of them; caused them speedily to resolve upon their forementioned march towards Pomfract; either judging, the Army would not follow them, or if they did, they should be able to fight us at more advantage, after they had drawn us further Northward.

About six of the clock in the morning, a Councel of War was called, to consider what attempt to make upon the Enemy. In the middest of the debate, came in Lieutenant-General Cromwel, out of the Association, with 600 Horse and Dragoons, who was with the greatest joy received by the General and the whole army. Instantly orders were given for Drums to beat, Trumpets to sound to horse, and all our army to draw to a rendezvous; from whence a good party of Horse were sent towards Daventry, under the command of Major Harrison, (of whose continued fidelity the Publique hath had sufficient testimony) to bring further intelligence of the Enemies motion: and another strong party of Horse was sent under the command of Colonel Ireton, to fall upon the flank of the Enemy, if he saw cause: and the main body of our Army marched to flank the Enemy in the way to Harborough, and came that night to Gilling; the Countrey much rejoycing at our comming, having been miserably plundered by the Enemy, and some having had their children taken from them, and sold before their faces to the Irish of that Army, whom the parents were enforced to redeem with the price of money. That evening we understood that the Van of the Enemies army was at Harborough, the Rear within two miles of Naseby: and no sooner was the General got to his quarters, but tidings was brought him of the good service done by

Colonel Ireton, in falling into the Enemies quarters, which they had newly taken up in Naseby Town; where he took many prisoners, some of the Princes Life-guard, and Langdales Brigade, and gave a sound alarm throughout the Enemies army (the confidence of the Enemy in possessing these quarters, grounded upon their slight esteem of this Army, and want of intelligence, was very remarkable.) Upon this alarm, the King (not having notice of it till eleven at night, as he had little imagined the nearnesse of our Army, or that they durst bear up to him) much amazed, left his own quarters at that unseasonable time; and for security went to Harborough, where Prince Rupert quartered, and so soon as he came thither, sent to call up his Nephew, (resting himself in a chair, in a low-room, in the mean time) who presently arose; a Councel of War was called: the question was put, What was best to be done seeing our Army was so neer, and as they then perceived fully intended to ingage them. It was considered by them, that should they march on to Leicester, if the Rear were engaged, the whole Army might be put in hazard; and there was no marching with the Van unlesse they could bring the Rear clear off, which they discerned to be very difficult. Whereupon it was resolved to give battell, taking themselves (as indeed they were) for a more considerable force then we, especially in Horse, on which they chiefly depended; being also as confident, they might relye upon their Infantry for valiant resolute men; & they resolved (as appeared) not to abide in that place till we marched up to them, but in a gallant bravery to seek us out. Herein the Kings Counsel prevailed against the minde of the most of his great Officers, who were of opinion, that it was best to avoid fighting.

Anno 1645
June

Saturday June 14. The General with the Army advanced by three of the clock in the morning, from Gilling towards Naseby, with an intention to follow close upon the Enemy, and (if possible) retard their march with our

Horse, till our foot could draw up to them, in case they should have marched on to Leicester (the intelligence being that they had drawn some of their Carriages in the night through Harborough) that way. By five in the morning, the Army was at a Rendezvouz near Naseby, where his Excellency received intelligence by our Spies, that the Enemy was at Harborough; with this further, that it was still doubtfull, whther he meant to march away, or to stand us. But immediately the doubt was resolved : great Bodies of the Enemies horse were discerned on the top of the hill on this side Harborough, which increasing more and more in our view, begat a confidence in the General, and the residue of the Officers that he meant not to draw away, as some imagined, but that he was putting his Army in order, either there to receive us, or to come to us, to engage us upon the ground we stood : whilst the General was thus observing the countenance of the Enemy, directions were given to put the Army into such a posture, as that if the Enemy came on, we might take the advantage of our ground, and be in readinesse to receive him ; or if not, that we might advance towards him. And whilest these things were in consultation and action, the Enemies Army, which before was the greatest part of it out of our view, by reason of the Hill that interposed, we saw plainly advancing in order towards us : and the winde blowing somewhat Westwardly, by the Enemies advance so much on their right hand, it was evident, that he designed to get the winde of us : which occasioned the General to draw down into a large fallow field on the Northwest side of Naseby, flanked on the left hand with a hedge, which was a convenient place for us to fight the Enemy in. And indeed seeing his resolution to advance upon us, we took the best advantage we could of the ground, possessing the ledge of a Hill, running from East to West ; upon which our Army being drawn up, fronted towards the Enemy. But considering it might

347

be of advantage to us to draw up our Army out
of sight of the Enemy; who marched upon a
plain ground towards us: we retreated about an
1000 paces from the ledge of the Hill, that so
the Enemy might not perceive in what form
our battell was drawn, nor see any confusion
therein, and yet we to see the form of their
battell; to which we could conform ourselves
for advantages, and recover the advantage of
the Hill when we pleased, which accordingly
we did. The enemy perceiving this retreat,
thought (as since they had confessed) we were
drawing off to avoid fighting (and just then it
was brought to the King, that our Army was
flying to Northampton) which did occasion
them the more to precipitate; for they made so
much haste, that they left many of their Ordnance behinde them.

The General, together with the Major-
General, put the severall Brigades of Foot into

order: having committed the Ordering of the
Horse to Lieutenant-General Cromwel, who
did obtain from the General, That seeing the
Horse were neere 6000 and were to bee fought
in two wings; His Excellency would please to
make Col. Ireton Commissary gen. of horse,
and appoint him to command the Left Wing,
that day, the command of the Right wing being
as much as the Lieutenant-General could apply
himself unto. Which being granted by the
General the Lieutenant-General assigned him
five Regiments of Horse, a Division of 200
Horse of the Association, for that Wing; and
the Dragoons to line the forementioned hedge,
to prevent the enemy from annoying the Left
flank of the Army. In the mean time the Lieutenant-General having sixe Regiments of Horse
with him for the Right wing, disposed them
according as the place gave leave. And the form
of the whole Battail you have here inserted.

Upon the Enemies approach, the Parliaments army marcht up to the brow of the hill,
having placed a Forlorn of Foot (musquetiers)
consisting of about 300 down the steep of the

hill towards the enemy, somewhere more than Carbine shot from the Main battail, who were ordered to retreat to the battail, whensoever they should be hard pressed upon by the Enemy. The Enemy this while marched up in good order, a swift march, with a great deal of gallantry and resolution, according to the form here inserted. It is hard to say, whether Wing of our Horse charged first : But the Lieutenant-General not thinking it fit to stand and receive the Enemies charge, advanced forward with the Right wing of the Horse, in the same order wherein it was placed. Our Word that day was, God our strength; Their Word was, Queen Mary. Colonel Whaley being the left hand on the right wing, charged first two Divisions of Langdales Horse, who made a very gallant resistance, and firing at a very close charge, they came to the sword : wherein Col. Whaley's Divisions routed those two Divisions of Lang-dales, driving them back to Prince Ruperts Regiment, being the Reserve of the enemies Foot, whither indeed they fled for shelter, and rallied: the Reserves to Colonel Whaley, were ordered to second him, which they performed with a great deal of resolution. In the mean time, the rest of the Divisions of the Right wing, being straightned by Furzes on the right hand, advanced with great difficulty, as also by reason of the uneavennesse of the ground, and a Cony-warren over which they were to march, which put them somewhat out of their order, in their advance. Notwithstanding which difficulty, they came up to the engaging the residue of the Enemies horse on the left wing, whom they routed, and put into great confusion, not one body of the enemies horse which they charged, but they routed, and forced to flie beyond all their Foot, except some that were for a time shel-tred by the Brigade of Foot before mentioned.

Colonel Rossiter, who with his Regiment was just come into the field as the Armies were ready to close ; was edged in upon the right flank of the right wing of horse, time not permitting a more fitting and equal disposal of him : whose timely comming (according to his Orders) gave him opportunity of such gallant performance in the battel, as deserves an honourable mentioning.

The Horse of the enemies Left wing being thus beaten from their Foot, retreated back about a quarter of a mile beyond the place where the battail was fought. The success of our Main battail was not answerably ; The right hand of the Foot, being the Generals Regiment, stood, not being much pressed upon : Almost all the rest of the main Battail being overpressed, gave ground and went off in some disorder, falling behinde the Reserves ; But the Colonels and Officers, doing the duty of very gallant Men, in endeavouring to keep their men from disorder, and finding their attempt fruitless therein, fell into the Reserves with their Colours, choosing rather there to fight and die, then to quit the ground they stood on. The Reserves advancing, commanded by Col. Rainsborough, Col. Hammond, and Lieut. col. Pride, repelled the Enemy, forcing them to a disorderly retreat. Thus much being said of the Right wing and the main battail, it comes next in order, that an account be given of the Left wing of our Horse.

Upon the approach of the Enemies Right wing of Horse, our Left wing drawing down the brow of the hill to meet them, the Enemy comming on fast, suddenly made a stand, as if they had not expected us in so ready a posture : Ours seeing them stand, made a little stand also, partly by reason of some disadvantage of the ground, and untill the rest of the Divisions of Horse might recover their stations. Upon that the Enemy advanced again, whereupon our Left wing sounded a Charge, and fell upon them : The three right hand Divisions of our Left wing made the first onset, and those Divisions of the Enemy opposite them, received the Charge : the two left hand Divisions of the Left wing did not advance equally, but being more backward, the opposite Divisions of the Enemy advanced upon them. Of the three right hand Divisions (before mentioned) which advanced, the middlemost charged not home, the other two comming to a close Charge, routed the two opposite Divisions of the Enemy, (And the Commissary Generall seeing one of the enemies Brigades of Foot on his right hand, pressing sore upon our Foot, commanded the Division that was with him, to charge that Body of Foot, and for their better encouragement, he himself with great resolution fell in amongst the Musquetiers, where his horse being shot under him, and himself run through the thigh with a Pike, and into the face with an Halbert, was taken prisoner by the enemy, untill afterwards, when the battell turning, and the enemy in great distraction, he had an happy opportunity to offer his Keeper his liberty, if he would carry him off, which was performed on both parts accordingly). That Division of the enemies which was between, which the other Division of ours should have charged, was carried away in the disorder of the other two, the one of those right hand Divisions of our Left wing that did rout the front of the enemy, charged the Reserve too, and broke them, the other Reserves of the enemy came on, and broke those Divisions of ours that charged them ; the Divisions of the left hand of the right wing were likewise overborn, having much disadvantage, by reason of pits of water, and other pieces of ditches that they expected not, which hindred them in their order to Charge.

The Enemy thus having worsted our left wing, pursued their advantage, and Prince Rupert himself having prosecuted his successe upon the left wing, almost to Naseby town, in his return summoned the Train, offering them quarter, which being well defended with the Fire-locks, and a Rear-guard left for that purpose, who fired with admirable courage on the Princes horse, refusing to hearken to his offer, and the Prince probably perceiving by that time the successe of our Right wing of Horse, he retreated in great haste to the rescue of the Kings Army, which he found in such a general distresse, that instead of attempting anything in the rescue of them (being close followed in the Rear by some of Commissary Generals, Col. Riches, Col. Fleetwoods, Major Huntingtons, and Col. Butlers horse) he made up further untill he came to the ground where the King was rallying the broken horse of his Left wing, and there joyned with them, and made a stand.

To return again to our right wing, which prosecuting their success, by this time had beaten all the enemies horse quite behinde their foot, which when they had accomplished the remaining business was with part to keep the enemies horse from coming to the rescue of their foot, which were now all at mercy, except one Tertia, which with the other part of the horse we endeavoured to break, but could not, they standing with incredible courage & resolution, although we attempted them in the Flanks, Front and Rear, untill such time as the General called up his own Regiment of foot (the Lieut. General being likewise hastening of them) which immediately fell in with them, with But-end of Muskets (the General charging them at the same time with horse) and so broke them. The enemy had now nothing left in the Field, but his horse, (with whom was the King himself) which they had put again into as good order as the shortnesse of their time, and our near pressing upon them would permit.

The Generall (whom God preserved in many hazardous ingagements of his person that day) seeing them in that order, and our whole Army (saving some Bodies of horse which faced the enemy) being busied in the execution upon the foot, and taking, and securing prisoners, endeavouring to put the Army again into as good order as they could receive, to the perfecting of the work that remained: Our foot were somewhat more then a quarter of a mile

behinde the horse, and although there wanted
no courage nor resolution in the horse themselves alone to have charged the enemy, yet forasmuch as it was not judged fit to put anything
to hazard, the businesse being brought
(through the goodnesse of God) to so hopefull
an issue It was ordered our horse should not
charge the enemy untill the foot were come up ;
for by this time our foot that were disordered
upon the first Charge, being in shorter time
then is well imaginable, rallyed again, were
comming up upon a fast march to joyn with our
horse, who were again put in to two wings,
within Carbine shot of the enemy, leaving a
wide space for the battail of foot to fall in,
whereby there was framed, as it were in a trice,
a second good Batalia at the latter end of the
day ; which the enemy perceiving, and that if
they stood, they must expect a second Charge
from our Horse, Foot, and Artillery (they having lost all their Foot and Guns before) and our
Dragoons having already begun to fire upon
their horse, they not willing to abide a second
shock upon so great disadvantage as this was
like to be, immediately ran away, both Fronts
and Reserves, without standing one stroke
more : Our horse had the Chase of them from
that place, within two miles of Leicester (being
the space of fourteen miles) took many prisoners, and had the execution of them all that
way : The number of the slain we had not a
certain account of by reason of the prosecution
of our Victory, and speedy advance to the reducing of Leicester : the prisoners taken in the
field were about five thousand, whereof were
six Colonels, eight Lieut. Colonels, eighteen
Majors, seventy Captains, eighty Lieutenants,
eighty Ensignes, two hundred other inferiour
Officers, besides the Kings Footmen, and
houshold servants, the rest common Souldiers,
four thousand five hundred. The enemy lost
very gallant men, and indeed their foot, commanded by the Lord Astley, were not wanting
in courage ; the whole booty of the Field fell to

the Souldier, which was very rich and considerable, there being amongst it, besides the riches of the Court, and Officers, the rich plunder of Leicester.

Their Train of Artillery was taken, all their Ordnance, (being brasse Guns) where of two were Demi-Canon, besides two Morterpieces, (the enemy got away not one Carriage) eight thousand Arms and more, forty Barrels of powder, two hundred horse, with their riders, the Kings Colours, the Duke of Yorks Standard, and six of his Colours, four of the Queens white Colours, with double Crosses on each of them, and near one hundred other Colours both of horse and foot, the Kings Cabinet the Kings Sumpter, many Coaches, with store of wealth in them: It was not the least mercy in this Victory that the Cabinet Letters, which discover so much to satisfie all honest men of the intention of the adverse party, fell likewise into our hands, and have been since published by the Authority of the Parliament, to the view of the whole Kingdome.

The Field was about a mile broad where the battail was fought, and from the outmost Flank of the right, to the left Wing, took up the whole ground.

Thus you have a true and exact relation of the work of this happy day.

1. The battail was fought much upon equall advantage, whether you respect the numbers on each side, there being in that not 500. odds, or the ground it was fought upon being on both sides Champaign, and in that respect equal, and the winde at length favouring neither side more then other. But in this the enemy had much the odds of us, that they had on their side not so few as fifteen hundred Officers, that were old souldiers, of great experience through long experience in forraign parts; when on the other hand, we had not ten Officers that could pretend to any such thing, as the experience of a souldier, save what this war had given them, being for the most part such whose Religion, Valour

354

and present Reason was their best Conduct; and herein God went beyond our Enemies in their pride, and seeming friends, in their contempt of this Army.

2. Of how great consequence this Victory was to the whole Kingdom : That it may the better appear, let us take a view of it. and suppose we beheld it through the counter-prospective of the contrary event, as if the Enemy had had the victory, and we been beaten, and then me thinks I see, not only this Army, the only guardion of the Kingdom, lying on a heap, furnishing the enemy with insulting Trophees, but also our party in the West ruined, and the enemy there like a violent Torrent, carrying all before him. Me thinks I see the King and Goring united, making a formidable Army, and marching up to the Walls of London, incouraging their souldiers, as formerly with the promise of the spoyle of that famous City. And if this successe had been indulged them, and London not denyed, (as who should such an Army have asked it of) what could have ensued worse or more ! When once that City by such a fate had restored an Embleme of undone Rome, when Caesar came against it, That

The Senate shooke, the affrighted Fathers leave
Their Seats, and flying, to the Consuls give
Directions for the War, where safe to live,
What place t' avoid they know not, whether ere
A blest-ripe wit could guide their steps, they bear,
Th' amazed people forth in Troops, whom
                                    nought
So long had stird.

(Ingenni nec modo vulgus
Perculfum terror pavet, fed curia, & ipfi
Sedibus exiliere Patros, invifaque Belli
Confulibus fugiens mandat decreta Senatus
Tunc quae tuta petant & quae metuenda
                                    relinquant
Incerti, quocunque fugae tulit impetus urgent
Praecipitem populim, ferieq ; haerentia. longa
Agmina prorumpunt.)

355

And who needs any interpretation of this to have been, a being cast in our Cause, and a lossing of our Charges. All this did God mercifully prevent by the successe of that battail, and turned over this condition to the enemy, and thereby laid the happy foundation of all the blessed successes we have had since.

He that shall not in this victory look beyond the instrument will injuriously withhold from God his due : he that doth not behold God in the instruments, will not know how to give him his due ; for when he doth actions by instruments, his glory is to be seen in instruments : now had I only to deale with actions, I might possibly by a competent expression give on account of them ; but who may undertake to represent the lively frame of an heightened soul, and the working of the affections in such Heroick actions. The General, a man subject to the like infirmities of body, as well as passions of mind with other men, especially to some infirmities (contracted by former wounds) which however at other times they may hinder that puissant and illustrious soul that dwels within, from giving a character of its selfe in his countenance, yet when he hath come upon action, or been near an engagement, it hath been observed, another spirit hath come upon him, another soul hath lookt out at his eyes ; I mean he hath been so raised, elevated, and transported, as that he hath been not only unlike himself at other times, but indeed more like an Angell, then a man. And this was observed of him at this time : now with what triumphs of faith with what exultation of spirit, and with what a joynt shout of all the affections God is received into that heart, whose eyes he uses as an Optick to look through, and trouble a proud enemy, it self only is privy to ? what high transactions, what deep and endearing ingagements passe mutually between God and such a soul ? (for certainly the most immediate worship gives not a greater advantage) is better felt experimentally, then described historically ; but such a discovery of these things was made in his outward man at this Battel as highly animated his Souldiers.

Lieutenant-General Cromwell useth these expressions concerning Him, in his Letter to the House of Commons:

The General served you with all faithfullnesse and honour, and the best commendations I can give of him, is, That I dare say he attributes all to God, and would rather perish, then assume any thing to himself, which is an honest and thriving way; and yet as much for bravery may be given him in this action as to a man.

I shall inlarge no further in this particular, but conclude it was none of the least pleadges, none of the lowest speaking Providences betokening good successe to this Army, and Promising much happinesse to this Nation; GOD's giving us such a General, and so giving out himself to our General.

The great share Lieutenant General Cromwell had in this action, who commanded the Right wing of Horse, (which did such service, carrying the field before them, as they did at Marston-moor) is so known and acknowledged, that envy itself can neither detract nor deny. One passage relating to his service in this Battel, which I have received from those that well knew it, I shall commend to this Historie: That he being come not above two days before out of the Association, and (that day the battel was) attending the General in the field, who was going to draw up for an ingagement; He had the charge and ordering of all the Horse cast upon him by the General unexpectedly, but a little before the Battel; which he had no sooner received, but it was high time to apply himself to the discharge of it: for before the Field-Officers could give a tolerable account of the drawing up of the Army, the Enemy came on a main in passing good order, while our Army was yet in disorder, or the order of it but an Embrio: which the Lieut. General perceiving, was so far from being dismayed at it, that it was

357

the rise and occasion of a most triumphant faith, and joy in him, expecting that GOD would do great things, by small means; and by the things that are not, bring to nought things that are. A happy time, when the Lord of Hosts shall make his Tabernacle in the hearts and countenance of our chief Commanders; from thence to laugh his enemies to destruction, and have them in derision to confusion!

Had not Major gen. Skippon done gallantly, he had not received such an early wound in his side, and had he not had a Spring of Resolution, he had not stayed in the field, as he did, till the battel was ended; (for being desired by his Excellencie to go off the Field, he answered, He would not stirre, so long as a man would stand). That I mention not all those Officers and Souldiers particularly, who behaved themselves so gallantly in this Action, is to avoyd emulation and partiality. I shall satisfie myself, to adde concerning them, and the whole business, the words of the General and Lieutenant-General, in their several Letters to the Speaker of the house of Commons, with which I shall conclude. "Honest men served

Lt. Gen. Cromwels close of his Letter to the Speaker of the House of Commons

you faithfully in this action; Sir, they are trusty; I beseech you in the name of God, not to discourage them:" (which they have not done, blessed be God, and I hope never will). He proceeds, and wisheth, "This action may beget thankfullnesse and humility in all that are concerned in it;" And concludes thus modestly himself, "He that ventures his life for the liberty of his Country, I wish he trust GOD for the liberty of his Conscience, and You for the Liberty he fights for, &c." All that I desire, sayes the General, is, "That the honour

The close of the Generals Letter to the Speaker

of this great, never to be forgotten mercy, may be given to GOD, in an extraordinary day of Thanksgiving, and that it may be improved to the good of his Church, which shall be faithfully endeavoured by, Sir,

Your most humble Servant,

Thomas Fairfax.

After the Battel was ended, and the Horse gone in pursuit; the Army marched (5 miles) that night, to Harborough, (the head quarter) Most of the Prisoners that were taken in the fight, were that night brought into Harborough church, except those that were wounded and sent to Northampton.

Among other Writings taken in the Battel, there was a Manuscript presented to the General, (written by one Sir Edward Walker Herald of Arms) of the Kings great Victories in this War; wherein there was one passage very observable: That whereas he, taking occasion to speak of the Irish, cals them Rebels; the King having perused the Book, among the alterations he had made therein in divers places with his own hand, in that place puts out Rebels, and writes over the head, Irish, with his own hand, 'so much care was there to correct and qualifie any Expression that might reflect on those blood-thirsty Rebels). There was also brought to the head-quarter, a wooden Image, in the shape of a man, and in such a form, as they blasphemously called it the God of the Roundheads; and this they carried in scorn and contempt of our Army, in a publike manner, a little before the Battel begun.

The next day, Colonel John Fiennes, with his Regiment, was sent up to London by the General, with the Prisoners and Colours taken in the Fight; Who had a great share in the performance of that Day, (being placed with his Regiment in the Right wing of Horse) carried himself gallantly, and was very happy in his successe.

His Regiment took 11 Colours in the Battel.

The Victory at Naseby improved, by pursuing the Enemy who fled into Wales. Leicester (not long before taken by the Enemy) summoned, and after preparations for Storm, surrendred upon Articles. Some clamours of the Enemy for breach of Articles, found to be unjust, and the charge retorted on them. An instance of the Enemies desperate Prophanenesse, joyned with barbarous and inhumane Cruelty.

The Enemy thus driven out of the field, his Excellencie gave Orders for the Army, Horse, Foot and Train, to march after them the next day, which was Lords day, without any more intermission; the pursuing of the Victory, being of parallel consequence with the getting it: In obeying of which Orders, the readinesse and chearfulnesse of the Souldiers was admirable, and worthy our observation and remembrance, That when in respect of their long and hard March for many dayes together before the Battel, and the vehement and sharp battel they had fought, they might well have pleaded for some time of refreshment; yet no sooner was the Generals order given for marching, but they repaired all to their Colours, and that very next day after the battel, marched to great Glyn, the head-quarter, four miles short of Leicester. The Horse marched within a mile of Leicester that night, and kept Guards, which so alarm'd the Nobles and Gentry that had fled thither for security, that they departed thence in much haste, leaving the Lord Hastings to defend that place.

This day his Excellencie received intelligence, that Sir John Gell, with about 2000 Horse, was on his march towards the Army, according to Orders formerly sent him; as also that the King, with one part of the Routed horse, not judging himself safe in Leicester, went thence that evening to Ashby-de-la-Zouch, where he reposed himself some few houres: but understanding that our Army advanced, and that our Horse pursued the chase; Mounted on horse-back in the night, and fled to Lichfield, and from thence into Wales, without any considerable stay, (so great was the affright), the other part of the Rout being the Northern horse, under Sir Marmaduke Langdale, fled the same night near Newark; both passing so, that it was the wonder of all men how they (being in such a tired and distracted condition) could escape Sir John Gels horse, who the same day were on their march from Nottingham towards Leicester.

This day furnished his Excellency with a full intelligence of the state both of our friends, and our enemies affaires in the West, by means of the contrivement of Scout-Master-generall, the manner thus: A Spie of his, formerly imployed by him to Secretary Nicholas in Oxford, was the day that the Army rose from before it, sent to him again, (yet as one comming of his own accord) to give him intelligence, that the Army would that morning march away (a thing they in Oxford knew well enough) it being conceived that either the Secretary would send him, or he might find some opportunity to go into the West, where Generall Goring then lay with his Army about Taunton, and bring us the intelligence we desired; accordingly it fell out: Into the West he was sent, first to Bath, where the Prince of Wales then was, to whom he brought the first news of the Parliaments Army rising from before Oxford, from thence (bearing the reward of ten pieces from the Prince) to General Goring about Taunton, who received him and the news very gladly, and looking upon him as a fit instrument to be imployed to the King, then about Leicester, and as they supposed, intending Northward; deal with him (as about a businesse of great concernment) to carry a Pacquet of Letters from him, the Prince, and his Councell, to the King; He with some seeming difficulty suffered himselfe to be perswaded, received the Pacquet brought them to his Excellency fair sealed up, discovering to him the true state of the Enemies Armies and affairs in the West: The Letters from the Lord Goring to the King signifying how that in Three weeks time (nine days whereof was then expired) he was confident to master our Forces at Taunton, and by consequence, to settle the West of England in an absolute posture for his

Majesties service, and march up with a considerable Army to his assistance; advising the King by all means in the mean time to stand upon a defensive posture, and not to engage till his forces were joyned with his Majesty; Had these Letters bin delivered to the King (as they might have bin but for this defeatment) in all probability he had declined fighting with us for the present, and staid for those additionals which would have been a far greater hazard: this intelligence, did withall much quicken us to make speed to relieve Taunton, yet being so neer Leicester, and Leicester in all probability being easily to be made ours, (considering the fear that they within were possesst withall by the losse of the day at Naseby, besides the want of men thereby (in all likelihood) to make good their Works, it was resolved first to assay that, accordingly, Monday June 16, about noon the whole Army came before the Town: The General sent a Summons to the Lord Hastings, to surrender the Garrison, with all the Ordnance Arms, and Ammunition therein, who returned a peremptory answer, as if he meant to defend it to the last man; whereupon a Councel of War being called, it was resolved to storm the place; warrants were sent to the hundreds to bring in ladders, carts, hay, straw, & other things fitting for a storm; wherein the country was very forward to give assistance.

Tuesday June 17. great store of ladders were brought in, a battery was raised, upon which two Demy-Cannon and a whole Culverine taken at Naseby were planted, which played upon an old work called the Newark; being the very same Guns which the King not many dayes before had used against the same place: The Lord Hastings now beginning to perceive his condition was like to be desperate, sent a Trumpeter with a Letter to the Generall, desiring a parly concerning the surrender of the towne, which his Excellency desirous to save blood, hearkened unto: Commissioners were appointed to treat (on our side Colonel Pickering and

Colonel Rainsborough). Hostages on both sides were given ; the Treaty begun that evening and held debate till twelve a clock that night, and was concluded upon these Articles :

1. That the Lord Loughborough shall have quarter granted him, and have protection for his person to be safely conveighed to the Garrison of Ashby-de-la-Zouch.

2. That all Field Officers, Colonels, Lieutenant Colonels, Serjeants, Majors and Captains, and Lieutenants of Horse, (but not of Foot) shall march away with their own particular single Horse and Arms, with protections for their own Persons.

3. That all the rest of the Officers shall be conveyed safely to the Garrison of Lichfield, with Staves only, and no other weapons in their hand.

4. That all common Souldiers have quarter only for their lives and be conveyed to Lichfield without any other weapon save only staves in their hands.

5. That before 10 of the clocke the said morning June the 18 the Governour of the Towne, and the Lord Loughborough and all the rest of the Officers, and Souldiers march out of the Garrison according to the agreement aforesaid.

6. That Sir Thomas Fairfax be permitted to enter in at 10 of the clock the said Wednesday morning aforesaid, with his Forces, and take possession of the Garrison.

7. That all the Pieces of Canon, great and small now in the Garrison of Leicester, be left to Sir Thomas Fairfax.

8. That all the Armes, and Ammunition now in Leicester be left to Sir Thomas Fairfax, save only what is agreed to for the Officers of Horse aforesaid.

9. That all the Provisions, Colours, Bag and Baggage be also left to Sir Thomas Fairfax.

10. That all the Horse (save onely those excepted for the Officers aforesaid) that are

in the Garrison of Leicester be delivered up to Sir Thomas Fairfax, for the service of the Parliament.

11. That all the officers and souldiers have quarter for their lives.

12. That all the Prisoners of War that are in Leicester at the same time be released and set free to serve the Parliament.

The Guards and Centinels of the gate-house prison in the Newark, hearing of the conclusion of the Articles, about four a clock on Wednesday morning went away from their duty, and left their Armes behind them, and the prison doors open, whereupon the prisoners went out, and finding the Enemy, a plundering, they fell a plundering too. About seven a clock all their guards were drawn off, the souldiers on the Line threw downe their Armes, quit their Posts, and the gates were opened, which gave invitation to divers of our stragling souldiers to get into the Town at the Ports, and over the works: Complaint hereof being made to his Excellency by some from the Lord Hastings (or Loughborow) of the violation of the Articles by our souldiers: His Excellency sent to the Lord Loughborow to keep all his men upon their guards, and if any offered violently to enter the Towne before the time, to fire upon them, and immediately issued out a Proclamation, commanding the punctuall observance of the Articles by his owne souldiers, under paine of death. But the Lord Hastings instead of standing upon his guard (according to the Articles, till ten of the clock that morning, which he ought to have done, whereby he might have prevented that inconveniency which fell out, and have performed his ·Articles in delivering the Towne to his Excellency with the Arms and Ammunition:) mounted on horse-back in the morning with divers Gentleman (officers and others) and left the Towne some houres before the time appointed for his marching forth, so that when our Commissioners came according to appointments to see the Articles punctually performed, they found the Lord Hastings was gone, and all the towne in a confusion; but the souldiers were commanded off, and things were presently settled in good order, and about eleven a clock that day, the Army entred the towne, where we found divers Commanders of note, viz. Serjeant-Major-Generall Anthony Eyres, Colonell George Lisle, Lieutenant Colonell Guy Mouldsworth, Lieutenant Colonell Michael Pemberton, Major Jo Naylor, Major Michael Trollop, besides divers persons of quality, all wounded in the battail.*

There were taken in the towne, fourteen peece of Ordnance, thirty Colours, two thousand Armes, five hundred horse, fifty barrels of Powder, and other Ammunition, in a good proportion: The poor inhabitants were overjoyed at their deliverance, though in a sad Condition, being so plundered by the Enemy at first taking the towne, that many had nothing left but the bare walls, who before had their shops and houses well furnished: the Mayors house only escaped at that time, which now suffered for it: There is one piece of eminent wickednesse, fit to be transmitted to the notice of the world, not only for its relation to this story, but to rectifie their consciences, who have been led with too good an opinion of the Enemy; and it is attested by persons of good credit and quality; It is concerning Colonell Thomas a Welch-man, a Papist, who was slaine at the battail of Naseby: There were two brothers of them; the other was a Lieutenant Colonell taken prisoner in the battail, the former was conceived to be the man, by the discription of some of the inhabitants of Leicester who have under their hands given this information. That the next day after the King had taken Leicester by storme, this Colonell Thomas came to the Gaole, where the prisoners they had taken at the entring the Town were put, and called for the prisoners, and commanded such as were willing to serve the King, to come to one side of the room, divers of them comming accordingly, he commands them one by one to kneel down, and swear by Jesus Ile serve the King, which some of them accordingly did : He not satisfied therewith, required them to swear God-dammee Ile serve the King, affirming publiquely he was not fit to serve the King, that refused that Oath, which they refusing, he drew his Sword, cut them in the Head, in the Arms, and other parts of the Body, wounding them in a most cruell manner ; some of the Town of Leicester (amongst others) were the persons on whom this cruelty was exercised, and remain still to this day maimed by these wounds.

Wednesday June 18. The Treasure being come down, the Army was mustered, and the Town was setled in some order, and an Expresse sent up unto the Parliament, with the Conditions upon which Leicester was surrendred. Intelligence came this day, that the King was gone towards Hereford ; it was taken into consideration to send horse after him, but the thoughts of the West occasioned the deferring the debate thereof for the present.

Thursday June 19. Complaint being made to his Excellency by some of the Kings party, that they had been pillaged by our souldiers, his Excellency declared, whosoever should be found guilty thereof, they should suffer the extremity of that punishment that belonged to the violators and betrayers of the justice and honour of the Army, and therefore willed they might be informed against to the Judge Advocate of the Army. But upon examination of divers witnesses, his Excellency saw cause to charge the breach of Articles on the Lord Loughborough, and the injuries he complained of to his own failour, and therefore to demand reparation of Him, and the carriage on the enemies part appearing so foule in many particulars, which were here too tedious to mention, the General thought fit to detain the

hostages ; offering notwithstanding an examination of the business by Commissioners, and
engaging himself to make good whatsoever
could be demanded of him in Justice and
Honour, as he should expect the like from
them. But they loath to trust to the issue,
answered not the meeting of our Commissioners ; his Excellency therefore for a time de-
tained the Hostages, till afterwards, upon noble
considerations, the indempnity of his own, and
the Armies honour being sufficiently cautioned,
he was pleased to release them.

Serjeant-Major-General Anthony Eyre, *Newark Horse*; Colonel George Lisle,
Foote; Lt. Colonel Guy Molesworth, *Prince Maurice's Horse*; Lt. Colonel Michael
Pemberton, *Ex-Cuthbert Conyers*, now *Northern Horse*; Major Joseph Naylor,
Northern Horse; Major Michael Trollope, *Boncle Horse*.

THE PROCEEDINGS OF THE NEW-MOULDED ARMY FROM THE TIME
THEY WERE BROUGHT TOGETHER IN 1645, TILL THE KING'S GOING
TO THE ISLE OF WIGHT IN 1647.
Written by Col. Edward Wogan, *till then an Officer of that Army.*

The first day of *April 1645*, we marched
from *Windsor* to *Reading*, where we received
four months pay, both horse and foot, with an
order on pain of death to take nothing from the
country, but what we paid for ; no, not so much
as grass for our horses. From thence we march-
to *Newberry*, from *Newberry* to *Salisbury*, from
Salisbury to *Dorchester*, with an intention to
relieve *Taunton-Dean*, which was closely besieged by my Lord *Goring*.

Being on our march, the General received
order from both Houses to march back with all
possible speed, and to attend the King's army
which was then about *Leicestershire*, and to send
part of his army to relieve *Taunton-Dean*, if they
could, which was accordingly done. The horse
that were commanded for that service, were
commanded by Col. *Graves*, and the foot were
commanded by Col. *Wielding*. The party consisted of 1400 horse and 2000 foot.

The General marched back again with the

rest of the army in all haste and came before *Oxford*, and lay before it 14 days, thinking to draw the King towards it, and to engage as he thought fit. But news was brought him that *Leicester* was taken. Forthwith we marched from thence towards *Northampton*. On our march Lieutenant-General *Cromwell* came to take his leave of the General and army, being not of the new model: and a number of the House of Commons could not stay any longer without leave of both Houses of Parliament. Upon which the General writ to both Houses to desire leave for Lieutenant-General *Cromwell* to stay in the army, and to command as Lieutenant-General, only for one action: which was accordingly granted.

Then we came on still towards *Naseby*, and lay in *Naseby* town. The King hearing of our advancing, marched back from *Harborough* to meet us. About 7 a-clock in the morning the vanguards of the armies appeared each to other, and skirmished till both armies were drawn up. The right wing of our horse was commanded by Lieutenant-General *Cromwell*; the left by Commissary-General *Ireton*: the body of foot was led by the General and Major-General *Skippon*. Col. *Okey's* regiment of Dragoons was on the left-hand of all our horse, and lined the hedges: which did mightily annoy the King's right wing of horse, as they advanced towards us.

The right wing of the King's horse charged our left wing, and routed us clear beyond our carriages. The King's horse fell a plundering our waggons and gave us time to rally: but a great many of our horse went clear away to *Northampton* and could never be stopt. The King's foot got ground apace, upon our foot being discouraged by our horse running away, and by Major-General *Skippon's* being desperately wounded; insomuch that all our foot gave ground and were in a manner running away. *Cromwell* feeling almost all lost, charged the King's left wing, and disordered them; but by no means would pursue his advantage. The King's right wing, seeing their left wing of horse beat in, marched back again the same way they came. Then our left wing advanced to *Cromwell's* former ground and stood, being much discouraged for the loss of our Commissary-General, and Col. *Bourcher* [Butler], which was wounded. Our foot got heart again and stood their ground. *Cromwell* with his wing joined with Col. *Rossiter's* horse that came to us at that present, and charged the King's right wing of horse in the flank as they went by, and utterly disordered them, and pursued them to the top of the hill towards *Harborough*. The King's both wings of horse went clear away and never rallied. We divided our left wing of horse, that stood in *Cromwell's* former ground, into several bodies, and charged the King's foot that fought most manfully all this while, and forced divers of our bodies to retire. But seeing all their horse beaten out of the field, and surrounded with our horse and foot, they laid down their arms with condition not to be plundered. Presently a noise was spread among our horse, that no man must light to plunder on pain of death, and forthwith to follow the King's horse; which accordingly we did, but very leisurely, being much discontented to leave all the plunder of the field to our foot. Certainly if there had but 1000 of the King's horse rallied, and charged us in our disorderly and discontented pursuit, they might without doubt have beaten back again, and routed our foot which was richly laden with plunder and could by no means be brought together in a long time.

We leisurely continued the pursuit till we came within 2 miles of *Leicester*, where we found part of the King's horse drawn up; but they never offered to charge us, not we them, but stood and looked on each other till night came on. They marched into *Leicester*, and we were called back again.

That day Sir *John Gell* was marching towards us with 1500 horse, and might easily have stopped all the King's party as they were going to *Leicester:* for which neglect he was by *Cromwell* soundly chid, and ever after suspected to be well-wisher to the King's party.

Within two days after the battle, we came before the town of *Leicester* with our whole army; hearing that the King was gone towards *Wales* with all his horse, we lay down before the town, with a resolution to take it before we went further. The town being pestered with abundance of unnecessary people that staid behind the King, and a great many that were wounded at *Naseby*, and the wanting of provisions both for man and horse caused the Governor to surrender the town upon honourable conditions.

After the town was surrendered, all our horse were sent to refresh for 2 or 3 days. Then a Council was called, and it was resolved that we should follow the King, and not suffer him to draw to an head again. That very night there came a member of the House of Commons to give thanks to the General and army for their good service, with a command from both Houses to march forthwith for the relief of *Taunton-Dean*, which could not possibly hold out three weeks longer, and to encourage us thereunto, brought with him a dispensation for Lieutenant-General *Cromwell* to stay 40 days longer in the army.

By this may be observed, that when the King took *Leicester*, if he had but marched Northwards, or for the Associated Counties, or for *Wales*, or had kept himself from fighting but for one month, we were all ruined: our new moulded soldiers were all suspected for the loss of their old officers; so that it was the only advantage we could have in the world, that of uniting our officers and soldiers together by engaging them in so seasonable a time as that was. And as I have said before,

If the King had but kept from engaging his army but one month, (which he might easily have done) we were certainly undone.

370

The army in the West would be lost, with *Taunton-Dean,* and all the West left clearly to the King. All the North would have done their endeavour for him; and so would the Associated Counties: and I believe the Scots would have declared for him, or at least stood neuters; but that the change of that unfortunate battle did harden their hearts. *Wales* was then in a gallant condition under my Lord *Gerrard's* command.*

*Carte: *Original Letters and Papers,* from pp. 126-130.

A TRUE
RELATION
Of A Victory obtained over the
King's Forces by the Army of SIR
THOMAS FAIRFAX:
Being Fought between *Harborough,*
AND
NASIBY
On *Saturday June 14. 1645.*
Published by Authority.
LONDON
Printed for *Robert White*

JUNE 14. 1645.
Honoured Sir,

I should bee much too blame if I should not acquaint so publique a spirit as your selfe with what God hath done for this Kingdome by our poore despised, and contemptible Army: I shall enlarge so much as time will permit: I pray let such as love us, know what a mercy we have had, and intreat them to be reall in praises.

Thursday the 12. we had some feares, grounded upon the advantage of ground, with intrenchments which his Majesties Army had at *Daventry,* as also because Lieutenant General *Cromwell* was not come to us, lest we should engage without him, our approaching giving the enemy opportunity of fighting us, to their great advantage, but for what reason we know not they did not, and so we were delivered

Royall Armies leaving their advantages, and marching toward *Southam,* and also by the arrival of *Cromwell,* though but   horse the next morning.

371

We being thus re-inforct by the comming of *Cromwell*, and the party he brought, resolved to follow the enemy, who left the way to *Warwicke*, which was Woodland, for what reason like *Corfe* we know not, and wheeled, to *Harborough*, which we having full knowledge of advanced that night had our quarters in, and about *Harborough*, and after Naseby, in which field the battle was : The enemy about six in the morning we saw (for there was Champion enough) advanced towards us in a full body, which was as much joy to us (who sought that above all) as it was to hear they had left *Daventry*.

As to the ordering of our Army for Battaile, the Generall appointed Lieut. Gen. *Cromwell* to the right wing of Horse, and Col. *Ireton* at that time made Commissary Generall of the Horse, to the left wing. Himselfe, and Major Generall *Skippon* to the Infantry, and body of the Army, and in this posture we marched to meet our resolute enemy, who with undaunted courage came on, as who would not, having a King with them, that was able to honour   and promise large revenues afterwards.

Being come within Canon-shot the Ordnance began to play, but that being found at *Marston* Moore and other places but a losse of time, we resolved not to want daylight, as is usuall, but to charge with the first : About eleven a clock the Trumpets began to sound, the Drums to beat, the horses to neigh and prance, and now thought both sides. An afternoon for a Kingdome : *Caesar or nothing* was we suppose the voice of one Army, *The Liberties of England* of the other : And thus they charged each other with all their might and equall courage, which continued somewhat lesse then half an houre, by which time they had shattered our left wing, who a little gave back, and were almost masters of our Artillery ; but in the same time our right wing had done more upon them and besides, our left recovered, and in half an hour and a little more, we had driven them quite out of the Field, and so broke their foot, that we do believe there went not off 100 in any one party.

After this they rallyed againe and put their Horse into a posture to Charge, which party wee are assured his Majesty led up, and charged with : what will he do when he shall go against God and his Countries enemies? But this body was also within lesse then half an houre dissipated, and then they fled, and we after at the breech of them, killing as fast as we could all we found in Armes. We had the pursute of

372

them 13 miles, even within sight of *Leicester*, the longest pursuite that was since this unhappy war began.

But not to hold you over long, we had a great and wonderfull Victory as since this War began; five thousand prisoners of Foot taken, more then twise so many Armes; two thousand Horse, and their Riders taken; also two hundred Carriages, all but two they had; all their Ordnance great and small, twelve in all; a great number of Officers, many of speciall quality, the prisoners as yet not sorted, and so not known; Prince *Ruperts* Sumpter Horse taken, and much treasure, besides what was in the Carts and Wagons; the number slaine was not known, being as great in the pursute, as upon the place, only we heare the number of whores that were killed, were about three or four hundred.

This Victory, as it is to be attributed to God alone as the chiefe cause, so as to instruments, in the first place Sir *Thomas Fairfax* hath merited exceedingly, shewing such courage and resolution as hath rarely been seen, which did so animate the Souldiers, as is hardly to be exprest. Sir, had you seen him, and how his spirit was raised, it would have made an impression in you never to be obliterated, God knowes I speake the truth, and do not hyperbolize: Major-Generall *Skippon* did as gallantly as man could do, he received a wound with a Musquet-bullet, not mortall; Lieutenant General *Cromwell* did admirable well, and not to speak Out of affection, but what I saw, which was, that our right wing carried all the field before them: see Sir, how God honours those who honour him, spite the mallice of Enemies; All our Officers and Souldiers did as bravely as could be: The former performed all poynts of Souldery as well, though Envy hath frequently bespattered them, as not able to Command, and therefore deserted by so many out of feare: Commissary Generall *Ireton* is sorely wounded, we feare mortally ,so is Colonel *Butler*, both of undaunted courage, and did admirable service: Our Foot are soberly marched towards *Leicester*, and we beleeve Colonel *Rossiters* Regiment or partee of Horse, and likewise the Regiment of *Hartfordshire* Horse, who were not in the fight, and some of ours, and after these our other Horse, who we hope will suddenly be able: Col. *John Fines* who fought with courage, and did notably in the action is to bring up the prisoners, and to set forwards on *Monday:* We heare not of any *Irish* among them its probable they turned Foot men to Prince *Rupert* and Prince *Maurice*, who are now in *Leicester*, more

373

faded now than loved when last there and well requited for their unkind dealing with that Town, and having left nothing but bare wales bare wales must content them. Hay there is not for one night for their horses so thinking must   running again suddenly : This shall is present, when I have more particulars I shall not faile to acquaint you in the intention

FROM SIR WILLIAM BRERETON'S SIEGE OF CHESTER AND THE CAMPAIGN OF NASEBY, 1645

"To Sir William Brereton.
Sir,
    The intelligence you had from the Committee of Coventry concerneing Major Generall Browne and myselfe and the forces under our command being in these parts was true. Wee lye here attending the Kings motions with commands to dispose of ourselves according to the directions which we have received from the Committee of both kingdomes with relation to the motions of the enemy, as they shall be either the one way or the other. Wee should be very Glad to hould the correspondancey of intelligence with you. Sir Thomas Farefax is not yet come up, but we have sent to him upon your letter to hasten to us. The force is great under our hands ; wee should be gladd to Improve it either to conjunction with our freinds or other Impeachment of the enemy. I thinke it were happy you were conjoyned with the Scotts and wee with Sir Tho. Fairfax and then I know not why wee might [not] be in as hopefull a posture as ever wee were, haveing the King's Army betweene us, with the blessing of God to bring him into great straights, but God has sett the way and tyme of putteing a period to the miseries of this distressed kingdome. It is good for us to waite upon God, and to seeke his face which I am persuaded you doe and herein Concurres with you
                    your most humble servant
May 18, 1645.   Oliver Cromwell"

[In margin] Lt. Generall Cromwel's letter to Sir Wm· Brereton touching his being at Coventry."

"Sir
    I hartily thanke you for your Intelligience ; Noe man is more troubled (that I cannot advance to the assistance of

frends) then myselfe; I must obey Comands and truely, Sir. I am just now by orders which I received this day to returne backe upon Important Service, How be it a very great body of horse and dragoons is to attend the motions of the king's Army: Of this I thought to give you notice, to the end you may hold Correspondance with it; the Party will lye not farr from Rugby and will be marching on Northwards towards the Scottish Army. Sir I much desire your better acquaintance subscribing myselfe

your servant

May 19, 1645.   Oliver Cromwell
Killingworth [Kenilworth] Castell".

"To the Committee of Both Kingdomes.
Though nothing can be more greiveous (except an absolute defeate) than the deserteing and the delivereing up of this Countrie which hath been so Reall [*sic*] and faithfull to the Cause and will therefore be exposed to more misery then it falls to their lott, to be subjected to the enemyes fury and revenge, and though the strength of horse now with us might have bin a great preservation to the Country by snatching up and restraineing straglers and small parties from plundering and driveing away Cattell and the like; notwithstanding in obedience to your commands which I will allwayes make the Rule of my actions and according to the intimation received from the Lord Leven and the Lord Fairefax I have withdrawne my horse and dragoones and am upon my march towards the Rendezvous at Barlow More tomorrow, which is the tyme by the Lord Fairefax appointed for the uniteing the Cheshire, Lancashire and Staffordshire fforces. The foote assigned for this service were drawne out of our Garrisons and almost ready to march when wee received intelligence of the enemyes approach and discovered both by letters intercepted and by the relation of Prisoners and by the course which the enemy seemes to hould, that their first designe was for Chester and then to Cleare this County and soe for Lancashire and the North. Whereupon, upon various debate it was resolved to be of absolute necessity to strengthen our Garrisons with more foote and the Gentlemen and Inhabitants were very Importunate that this might be done: Their first designe as the Prisoners say will be againest Tarvin and Hooton, which they apprehend must either be taken in or Chester remaines halfe besieged.

Thence it may come to passe I may not be able to bring so many forces [as] I desire, but I shall hope to bring some Choyce dragoones which are firelockes mounted which may doe good service. And the numbers of horse apointed, though I am Constrained to leave many Horse in and about our Garrisons to protect the Country soe longe as they are able and then to retreate to the Armyes.

The King's march is slow and with much ease as well knowing there is no army near to disturb and anoy them. Hee marched yesterday seven miles from Newport to Drayhton and the Adiacent partes; which way he may incline this day you shall heare speedyly. But I was this day advertised that there was another Army came last night to Newport, their number I heard not nor whence they came but I doe Imagine out of South Wales, which it is most probable they are Gerrard's forces, before which tyme their number (as I beleeve) was not above 8000 or 9000 at the utmost, the most whereof was horse : The forces of the Lord Byron and of North Wales are upon thir march to unite with the other, quartered last night at Malpas and Sir William Vaughan's (as it is said) at Whitchurch. I have nó more tyme to enlarge myselfe being now upon my march towards the Rendezvous at Barlow More, tomorrow being the tyme appointed by the Lord Fairfax, whence I purpose (by God's assistance) soe to order the forces under my command as may be moste for the advantage of this cause. But I doe beleeve it to be most impossible to keep the passes into Lancashire which I know to be very many and in the Iudgement of all those soldiers with whome I have conferred it is Conceived of most dangerous consequence, seeing there are many of them : as Halefoard, Ronchorne Foard below Warrington and Thelwall foard, Erlamefoard, Crosfoard Bridg, Ashton Bridg, Carington Bridg, Northerden boate and foard, Stockport Bridg, where Prince Rupert passed the last yeare and divers other indefensible passes wherewith I am well acquainted, besides I have heard of divers other foards and passes.

So as it being admitted that these passes are not to be made good I have and will hasten the Scotts Armey and in the meane tyme according to your Comand will observe my Lord Leven and Lord fairefax's orders, I resolve (by God's Assistance) to omitt noething that may possibly be efected by me to advance the Publique Service or give you assurance that I am

Sir

your most faithfull frend and servant

Knotsford, May 21, 1645.   Wm. Brereton

Post : Since I writt this letter I received one from my Lord Leven which intimates that he intends to march by Westmoreland into Lancashire which will be soe teadious that we cannot hope for their assistance in due tyme, and the Lancashire forces with the Cheshire and Staffordshire horse (I being forced to leave my foote to service our Garrisons) will be neither able to Defend the passes or make opposition to the enemy who now grow so Potent that if Sir Tho. fairfax or Lt. Generall Cromwell be not Speedily sent into these parts with a good Strength the north is in much dainger to be lost.

Take this into your searious thoughts and beleeve it ; if your forces be not otherwise disposed the north is in much dainger to be lost and your faithfullest servants oppressed, whilst your forces under Lt. Generall Cromwell are Called backe from the Pursuite of the enemy and the Scotch fforces remaine further from them, as the bearer can inform you."

Index

Skipton Castle 285
Skipwith, Lt. Colonel to Sir Charles Bolle 69
Slany, Captain Gyles 46
Slaughter, Lieutenant-Colonel Henry 50, 51, 52-3
Slater (or Slaughter), Lieutenant-Colonel (Henry) 55
Slingsby, Sir Henry 64, 264, 289, 293, 306
Slingsby, Colonel Walter 43
Smith, Lieut. 104
Smith, Major 201
Smith, Major Jeremiah 150
Smyth, Lieutenant-Colonel George ix, 95, 107, 240
Smyth, Colonel John 60, 73, 75, 242
Smyth, Colonel William 62
Somerset, Charles Lord 14
Sotheby, Lt. Colonel Henry 74
Sparrey, Lieutenant John 101
Speen village 183
Spencer, Quartermaster-General 129
Spencer, John 138
Spinage, Captain Anthony 137
Sprigge's map of Naseby 63
Staffordshire, Royalist and Parliamentarian garrisons 219-20
  Stafford 220
Standish, James 131
Stane, Commissary-General 131
Stanford, Ensign 88, 89
Stanley, Capt. William 84
Stapleton, Colonel Sir Philip 115, 154
Startin, Anne 89
Startin, Captain-Lieutenant Timothy 88, 89, 90
St. Colomb, Cornwall 174
Steley, Lieut. John 105
Sterne, Captain Edward 293
Stoakes, Sergeant William 100
Stockton, 70-2
Stokesay Castle 15, 219, 284
Stow, Lieutenant John 88
Stow-on-the-Wold 53
Stradling, Colonel Sir Edward 107
Stradling, Sir Henry 66
Stradling, Colonel John 103, 107
Stratton, battle of xviii
Strawhill, Doctor 131
Streeter, Colonel John 186, 187
Stuart, Captain-General Bernard, titular Earl of Lichfield see Lichfield
Sugar, Captain William 55
Sulby Hedge, concealment of Parliamentarian dragoon regiment 245, 248, 262
Sumpner, Cornet 175, 176
Survivors of Naseby killed on other fields 292-5
Swallow, Colonel Robert 143, 144, 147, 148, 150
Swansea 14

Swift, Capt. Lieut. Ralph 86, 87, 89
Sydenham, Colonel William 188
Symms, Lt. Colonel George 80
Symonds, Richard 66, 67
Tactical deficiencies at Naseby 273-6
Tailer, Cornet Richard 48
Talbot, Colonel Sir Gilbert 10
Taunton, 8-9, 11, 209-13, 220, 361-2
Taylor, George 49
Taylor, Captain Gilman 169
Tempest, Colonel Sir Richard 75
Tercene, Eval 130, 250
Teviot, Earl of (Andrew Rutherford) 200
Thacham, QM Rob 42
Thelwall, Colonel Anthony 107
Thelwall, Captain Edward 298
Theobald, Lieut. Thomas 105
Thomas, Ensign 87, 88
Thomas, Lt. Colonel 83, 106, 365
Thomas, Colonel Rhys 82-3, 106, 239, 365
Thomas, Captain Richard 85
Thomlinson, Major Matthew 201
Thompson, Aubrey 297
Thompson, Colonel George 116
Thompson, Corporal William 146-7
Thompson, Lt. Colonel William 74
Thomson, Lieut. James 102
Thornes, Ensign Fran 55
Thornhagh, Colonel Francis 123
Thornton, Cornet John 297
Thornton, Lt. Colonel John 60, 63, 73, 74, 242, 264, 305
Throckmorton, Sir Nicholas 13
Thurloe, John 188
Thwaytes, QM Thomas 42
Tilden, Capt. John 101
Tillier, Colonel Henry 70, 95, 141, 233, 240, 277
Tipton 14
Tirwhytt, Captain John 102
Tiverton Castle 10, 285
Tomlindon, Mr., Engineer 250
Tompkins, ?Lt.Colonel? William 73
Tomlinson, Mr. 130
Tomlinson, Colonel Matthew 133, 134, 139, 140, 141, 143
Tonge, Lt. Colonel George 60, 73, 74
Toomes, Capt. Lieut. John 175, 176
Transport, gunnery train 111
Trapham, Thomas, Surgeon 251, 298
Trevor, Colonel Mark 17
Trollop, Captain Michael 56, 292
Turbervile, Captain-Lieutenant Sir Troilus 10, 66, 291
Turner, Cornet John 45
Turnpenny, Captain Zachariah 88, 89, 90
Turpin, Ensign 91
Turpin, Captain 196
Tutbury Castle 14, 219

391

"A Description of His Majestie's Army of Horse & Foot, and of
Several Bodies at the BATTA...

THE ARMY OF THE KING		
1 THE KING'S MAJESTY	THE RIGHT WING: (P. Rupert)	
THE RESERVE	8 Pr. Rupert's Life Guard of Horse	
2 The Newark Horse	9 Pr. Maurice's Life Guard of Horse	
3 The King's Life Guard of Foot	10,11,12 Pr. Rupert's Regt. of Horse	
4 The King's Life Guard of Horse	13 The Queen's Regt.	
5 Pr. Rupert's Bluecoats	14 Pr. Maurice's Regt.	
6 The Newark Horse	15,16 The E. of Northampton's Regt.	
7 Commanded Musketeers	17,18,19 Sr William Vaughan's Regt.(?)	

THE CENTRE

Lord Astley ; Sr Bernard Astley ; FOOT
Sr Henry Bard ; Sr George Lisle.

20 | (D. of York's ; Sr Ed. Hopton's ;
21 Astley Sr Richard Page's.)
28 |

22 | (Bard's ; Thomas's ; Owen's ;
27 Bard Radcliff Gerard's.)

23	Lisle (Wm. Sr George's; The Shrew-
26	bury Foot: Tillier's, Broughton
24	
25	Howard Sr Thomas Howard's Reg
29	

THE LEFT WING
(Sr Marmaduke Langdale)
30-40 The Northern Horse